BATTLE OF
STONES
RIVER

BATTLE OF
STONES
RIVER

The Forgotten Conflict between
the Confederate Army of Tennessee and
the Union Army of the Cumberland

LARRY J. DANIEL

Louisiana State University Press  Baton Rouge

Published by Louisiana State University Press
Manufactured in the United States of America
First printing

Designer: Barbara Neely Bourgoyne
Typeface: MillerText
Printer: McNaughton & Gunn, Inc.
Binder: Acme Bookbinding, Inc.

All maps by Mary Lee Eggart

Library of Congress Cataloging-in-Publication Data
Daniel, Larry J., 1947–
  Battle of Stones River : the forgotten conflict between the Confederate Army of Tennessee
and the Union Army of the Cumberland / Larry J. Daniel.
    pages cm
  Includes bibliographical references and index.
  ISBN 978-0-8071-4516-6 (cloth : alk. paper) — ISBN 978-0-8071-4517-3 (pdf) — ISBN
978-0-8071-4518-0 (epub) — ISBN 978-0-8071-4519-7 (mobi) 1. Stones River, Battle of,
Murfreesboro, Tenn., 1862–1863. I. Title.
  E474.77.D36 2012
  973.7'3—dc23

                                                                              2012000886

For my children,
Lauren and Mark

CONTENTS

ILLUSTRATIONS

PREFACE

In the late 1960s, Thomas L. Connelly took a critical look at the Civil War by examining the great expanse between the Appalachians and the Mississippi River known as the Western Theater. He would become the father of western revisionism. Over three decades a series of talented writers emerged who reshaped the national debate—that is, that the war was not North versus South but East versus West. It was in the last, they argued, that our national trauma was determined, by a series of Federal victories between 1861 and 1863. In recent years, the pendulum has begun to swing back to Virginia, with some historians insisting that the war was won in the Eastern Theater.[1]

I wrote *Battle of Stones River: The Forgotten Conflict between the Confederate Army of Tennessee and the Union Army of the Cumberland* to give the battle its proper place in the war. The Battle of Fredericksburg in December 1862 gave stark evidence that the war in Virginia had ground to a stalemate. William T. Sherman's expedition against Vicksburg, Mississippi, had likewise been checked. The fall 1862 U.S. congressional races had proven damaging to the prowar effort. The nation now focused its attention upon what Connelly referred to as "the Heartland." The hope of both sides lay in Tennessee. Indeed, argues Donald Stoker, the Union effort in Mississippi proved a "most glaring mistake," since "the 'real' war was in Tennessee," or as he termed it, "a Confederate center of gravity."[2]

Fought on the cusp of 1862–63, the Army of the Cumberland under Major General William S. Rosecrans and the Army of Tennessee under General Braxton Bragg clashed in a death struggle at Murfreesboro, Tennessee. Nearly 100,000 men fought in the three-day battle, and the two armies between them sustained 23,500 casualties. The battle would prove to be a draw, although strategically it was a Northern victory. Yet the mention of Stones River frequently brings puzzled expressions to those beyond the region. Perhaps the burgeoning growth of modern-day Murfreesboro, with a current population of 102,000, has unwittingly added to the battle's obscurity, as developers have swallowed up land around the small national battlefield park. The ground over which the Confederates launched their assault, and which was so valiantly defended by the Federals, is now a huge mall and multi-story hotel.

Untapped primary material, including letters, diaries, and dozens of small-town newspapers, have added to previous works by James Lee Mc-Donough and Peter Cozzens. First-hand accounts frequently proved to be more candid than official reports by officers who had careers to protect. These accounts also relate the grim reality of fighting a winter campaign in wretched, often bitter weather, in which thousands of troops on both sides forded waist-deep Stones River. Additionally, more detail is given to the role of politics, so that the reader can understand not only what happened but why it happened and why it mattered so much. Contemporary Northern accounts refer to the Battle of Stone's River or Stone River. Because the National Park Service, the State of Tennessee, and most modern accounts refer to Stones River, I have accepted this usage. It should be noted that the Confederate press preferred the Battle of Murfreesboro. The town of La Vergne, Tennessee, was typically spelled Lavergne at the time. I have again chosen the modern spelling.

On the surface, it would appear that Stones River accomplished little more than an enormous body count. Bragg simply fell back twenty-six miles, and the war dragged wearily on. What was at stake, however, was how a protracted war, which clearly it had become by the winter of 1862–63, might come to conclusion. Could the South, as has been suggested, "win by not losing"? That is, could the Northern will to win be broken by an indefinitely extended war? This question was very much undecided in December 1862. For both sides to avoid the ramifications of such an issue, they had to accomplish the very thing they failed to accomplish—destruction of their opponent's army. The bloody butcher's list of casualties would bear mute testimony that it was not from a lack of trying. After the battle, a Rebel gave his evaluation: "I am sick and tired of this war, and, I can see no prospects for having peace for a long time to come[.] I don't think it will ever be stopped by fighting, the Yankees cant whip us and we can never whip them."[3]

With the war trending toward protraction, one side or the other had to gain the upper hand. A war of attrition for the South was not sustainable—"facing the arithmetic" as Stoker referred to it. A protracted war for the North meant a growing antiwar movement that could ultimately undermine the will to win. For both sides Stones River was therefore a must win. Bragg needed to counter the loss in Kentucky and permanently reclaim Middle Tennessee. As for Rosecrans, he had to undermine the growing antiwar movement, undercut a "Tennessee argument" for British intervention, and recoup Union morale after the stunning loss at the Battle of Fredericksburg.

ACKNOWLEDGMENTS

I am deeply indebted to the staff of the Stones River National Military Park, particularly Gib Backland, Jim Lewis, and John George. They offered their knowledge, assistance, patience, and encouraging support so that this project might be completed in time for the sesquicentennial of the battle in 2012. My appreciation is also extended to Lanny K. Smith. Although working on his own project on Stones River, he unselfishly shared all his material with me. Lanny, who probably knows more about the battle than any living person, enthusiastically received all my calls. He also gave his permission to base several of my maps upon those that appear in his two-volume work. I should also mention Dan Masters. His work on chronicling soldiers' letters of the battle from dozens of small-town newspapers from Ohio and Illinois proved breathtaking. He readily shared his labor of love, thus adding the voices of scores of soldiers that otherwise would have been silent.

BATTLE OF
STONES RIVER

1

A WAR OF EGOS

Richmond correspondent George Bagby, whose news and gossip column appeared in the *Charleston Mercury* under the pen name "Hermes," had done his research. Even before General Braxton Bragg, commanding the Confederate Army of the Mississippi, arrived in Richmond on Saturday, October 25, 1862, Bagby had uncovered a confidential source that positively debunked the story that had propelled the general to national prominence during the Mexican War. At the Battle of Buena Vista, on February 23, 1847, the American infantry collapsed at a critical moment, leaving Bragg's battery alone to face an enemy charge. As reported by the press at the time, the battery braced as General Zachary Taylor rode up and shouted, "A little more grape, Captain Bragg!" The story soon became a part of American lore. According to Bagby, the scene was a fraud. A reliable source had related to him that the battery was in fact withdrawing, not standing firm, as Taylor rode up and cried out, "What the —— are your guns worth if we lose the battle?" "How curiously reputations are made," Hermes concluded. Bagby later retracted the story and half-apologized by stating that Bragg's personal courage was never in doubt, although he could not resist a concluding jab—"his capacity is another thing." Given Bragg's failure in the recent Kentucky Campaign, the entire Richmond press corps (the "dogs of detraction," as Bragg referred to them) joined in the denunciation, openly predicting his removal from command.[1]

President Jefferson Davis, who had summoned Bragg, cordially received him and, according to Bagby, the general appeared "in high spirits." Following breakfast, Davis and Bragg engaged in a six-hour private session at the War Department, the old four-story Mechanics Institute on Franklin Street. On

Monday February 27, the general stole away for a few moments to meet with his brother Thomas Bragg. Thomas found him "well & in good spirits," and he believed the president to be "entirely satisfied" with the handing of the late campaign, despite its disappointing outcome. The next day John Jones, a perceptive clerk in the War Department, detecting that the tide had changed in Bragg's favor, jotted in his journal, "Gen. Bragg is here, but will not probably be deprived of his command."[2]

Jones was correct, much to the chagrin of Bragg's enemies—and they were many. The general's problems did in fact not start in the West, but only a few blocks away, in the halls of the Confederate Congress. Kentucky politicians, such as Senator Henry C. Burnette and Congressman George B. Hodge, angry over the abandonment of their state, expressed opposition, as did Tennessee Senator Gustavus A. Henry. Due to Bragg's perceived close ties to the president (the two had in fact not been cordial prior to the war), some politicians, such as Tennessee Congressman Henry S. Foote, a Davis antagonist long before the war, attacked the general as an extension of the administration. Alabama Senator William L. Yancey, who had a son in Bragg's army, joined the anti-administration/anti-Bragg bloc, as did South Carolina Senator Robert Barnwell Rhett, who denounced the Kentucky Campaign as an "egregious failure." South Carolina Senator James L. Orr likewise disparaged the army commander. How this easterner drifted into the anti-Bragg camp was a story in itself. Back in the summer of 1862, shortly after Bragg assumed command of the army, a rumor floated that he had had a soldier shot for stealing a chicken. The tale, totally baseless, made its way to Orr, who believed it and thereafter became a staunch critic. Texas Senator William C. Oldham had never even met the general and held no animus, but he had opposed the invasion of Kentucky. Texas Senator Louis T. Wigfall openly lobbied for Bragg's removal.[3]

The present hue and cry contrasted dramatically from the scene four months earlier, when Bragg received command of an army wasting away at Tupelo, Mississippi. A series of early defeats at Mill Springs, Pea Ridge, Fort Donelson, Island No. 10, and New Orleans had resulted in huge territorial losses—the state of Kentucky, the Tennessee Valley, the entire Mississippi River (with the exception of a gap between Port Hudson, Louisiana, and Vicksburg, Mississippi), and much of Arkansas. Fears mounted for Vicksburg, and the governor of Arkansas, Henry Rector, feeling that his state had been abandoned, threatened to pull out of the Confederacy. Bragg immediately shifted his army to Mobile, Alabama, and then northeast to Chattanooga, Tennessee, a 776-mile trek over six railroads, which left the pursuing Federal Army, under Don Carlos Buell, tediously tramping over-land through northern Mississippi and Alabama. This audacious strategy meant a reversal of momentum and renewed hope in the West.[4]

Along the journey to Kentucky, the general stopped at McIntyre's Studio in Montgomery, Alabama, for a photograph. His graying hair, making him appear much older than his forty-five years, and gaunt appearance were ev-ident, yet standing erect in full-dress uniform, and imparting a half-smile, he appeared almost dashing. What the photograph could not convey was a normally stooped posture, and a body racked with illnesses—boils, head-aches, chronic dysentery, rheumatism, and stomach ailments. Bragg had come from a moderately wealthy North Carolina family, which had none-theless been snubbed by the local aristocracy. This rejection served to mold his contentious, anti-social, and humorless personality. He entered West Point at age sixteen, graduating in the class of 1837. In the Regular Army, he soon acquired a reputation of being "the most cantankerous man in the army." As army commander, he proved a ferocious disciplinarian, yet he could never control his corps and division commanders, who frequently un-dercut him. His unfortunate personality traits led him to see disagreements as personal attacks. Lacking charisma, what the general needed was the very thing the army lacked and his suspicious temperament could not have accepted at any rate—a good second-in-command who befriended him.[5]

Before shifting his army east, Bragg had to secure Mississippi and pin down General Ulysses S. Grant's army group, comprised of the Army of the Tennessee and the Army of the Mississippi. He had available two Louisi-ana brigades from the former New Orleans garrison, two divisions from Earl Van Dorn's old Army of the West, transferred from Arkansas, and some scattered regiments from his own army. Fortunately, the passage of the Conscript Act in April 1862 resulted in thousands of new "volunteers," who hurriedly enlisted to avoid the onus of being drafted. A dozen of the newly organized Mississippi and Alabama regiments (labeled "conscript regiments" by the veterans, but technically not) were channeled to the Mis-sissippi army forming under Van Dorn and Sterling Price. In addition, the revolving door of prisoner exchange meant that 14,000 of the Fort Donel-son and Island No. 10 captives could re-enter the ranks, which they did in early September 1862. Although 4,000 had to be discharged due to ill-health, 2,000 went to Bragg's army (too late for the Kentucky Campaign), and 8,000 to the emerging Mississippi army. Not waiting for these men to be assimilated, Van Dorn, with 22,000 troops, launched an ill-advised attack upon a Federal army of similar size at Corinth on October 3, 1862. In the bloody repulse and retreat that followed, Van Dorn lost 5,000 men.[6]

Back at Chattanooga, Bragg, acting in consort with Major General Edmund Kirby Smith's Army of East Tennessee, went on the offensive, but with only vague strategic plans. He sidestepped the Federal garrison at Nashville and by September 14 had concentrated at Glasgow, Kentucky. Three days later his army captured the 4,000-man garrison at Munfordville. The issue came to a head in early October. On October 7, Bragg received information that a portion of the Federal Army approached Major General William J. Hardee's corps at Perryville. Believing that the great battle of the campaign would be fought at Harrodsburg, Bragg dispatched Major General Leonidas Polk with a division to Perryville, with orders for Polk and Hardee to attack the Yankee column (perhaps a division or two) on October 8 and then hurriedly concentrate at Harrodsburg.

Early morning came and went, but with no attack. Hardee and Polk, worried about increasing Federal strength, rationalized that Bragg had only *suggested* an attack, pleaded confusion, and in the end ignored his implicit instructions. When the commanding general arrived in mid-morning, he angrily ordered an immediate attack. Operating in an intelligence fog, Bragg did not realize that the entire Union Army had by now come up, placing his 16,000 against Buell's 58,000! Nonetheless, the 2:00 attack went well, driving the Union left wing a mile before darkness ended the fighting. In truth, Bragg had been saved only by Federal ineptness (a trait not limited to the southerners) and a natural phenomenon called an acoustic shadow, which muffled the sound of gunfire so that Buell did not know that a battle raged on his flank. Four days later, Bragg, wearied of Kentucky and mentally, if not tactically, defeated, ordered a retreat along the Old Wilderness Road back into Tennessee.[7]

If the Kentucky Campaign had been executed as a raid, the results might have been viewed differently. With the loss of 4,500 casualties, Bragg's and Smith's forces inflicted losses of 13,600 (including 10,500 prisoners), captured 13,000 arms and 27 guns, added 2,000 recruits (Kentucky cavalry) to the ranks, and redeemed North Alabama and Middle Tennessee south of Nashville. What the South expected, however, was the total defeat of

Buell and the restoration of Kentucky. For Bragg to accomplish this, he needed unified command over Smith and for Kentuckians to volunteer en masse—not just a brigade, but a division. On the other hand, the Northern Army, reflecting the sheer raw manpower reserves of the Midwest, raised 45,000 recruits within weeks, giving Buell a third corps.[8]

The simultaneous invasion of Maryland by General Robert E. Lee's Army of Northern Virginia had likewise ended in defeat, and with more far-reaching implications than Bragg's failure. British and French intervention had been dealt a death blow, and with it a possible northern armistice. Yet, few critics judged Lee harshly. Both foreign and southern writers applied a double standard to Bragg. After the Maryland Campaign, a Virginian, commenting on the loss in Kentucky, wrote, "Oh, that we had another Lee and [Thomas Jonathan] Jackson to send out there."[9]

Although privately confiding his "bitter disappointment" at the results of the campaign, Davis had reason to sustain Bragg. First, he understood what many did not: Bragg had done all he could under the circumstances and had wisely chosen retreat. Far better to lose reticent Kentucky than all or part of the army, such as Albert Sidney Johnston, the army's first commander, had done at Fort Donelson back in February 1862. Second, the general's detractors doubled as enemies of the administration. The president viewed their carping as nothing more than a not-so-veiled attempt to get at him. He thus formed an affinity with the beleaguered general. Third, decisions are not made in a vacuum. If not Bragg, who? Sidney Johnston had been killed on the front lines at Shiloh in April 1862. Lee could not be spared. General P. G. T. Beauregard, Davis's archenemy and the Army of the Mississippi's deposed second commander, proved unacceptable to the administration, despite strong congressional support. "If the whole world were to ask me to restore General Beauregard . . . I would refuse it," Davis emphatically declared. The highly popular General Joseph E. Johnston, barely more palatable to the president than Beauregard, still recovered from wounds sustained at the Battle of Seven Pines in Virginia. (As late as November 14, Jones saw him "standing idle in the street" in Richmond.) While conceding that a general other than Bragg might "excite more enthusiasm," Davis's short list proved very short.[10]

Bagby's private sleuthing enabled him to file a column on November 1: "The President has been invisible since last Saturday [October 25]. Up to yesterday he was closeted all the time with Bragg, who returns with his

command with the approving smiles of the Executive." South Carolina ag-
riculturist and fire-eater Edmund Ruffin, now living in Richmond, noted
in his journal on November 4: "Gen. Bragg was called from his command
to report himself to Richmond. This was understood as showing the displeasure of the government. But if so, he has removed that ill-opinion &
has been sent back to resume his command." Bragg had won, if not in
Kentucky, at least in Richmond.[11]

. . . .

Assurances to Bragg aside, Davis remained troubled. With expressions of
discontent leaking from the western army (Bagby noted that a number
of Bragg's officers strolled about the capital, criticizing their commander
"without mercy"), the president individually summoned the three major
generals now with the army in Knoxville, Tennessee—Edmund Kirby
Smith, Leonidas Polk, and William J. Hardee. Since Davis had already
determined to sustain Bragg, the meetings were an attempt to heal the discontent. In reality the conferences appeared to place the three malcontents
on the same level as Bragg, and offered a venue for their complaints; two of
the three jumped at the chance. Davis would bestow all three of them with
lieutenant generals' commissions, ostensibly for their performance in the
late campaign, but it smacked more at a pitiful bribe for their cooperation.[12]

The trouble with Edmund Kirby Smith (he began signing his name
"Kirby Smith" at the beginning of the war simply as a way of distinguishing
himself from other Smiths) was that he believed his own press. Although
he had been brevetted for gallantry in the Mexican War and taught at
West Point, his claim to fame was that he had opportunely arrived with his
brigade at the Battle of First Manassas in July 1861. The press thus hailed
him as a military genius, comparing him to Prussian General Gebhard von
Blucher, whose timely arrival at the Battle of Waterloo had saved the day
for the Allies. As for Smith, he compared himself to Napoleon. Yet more
recent scholarship dismisses earlier harsh portraits, claiming that he was
complex and at heart "a bright, sweet man." While he was recovering from
a wound received at Manassas, Miss Cassie Seldon, a Lynchburg socialite,
nurtured him back to health; they would marry within two months. Upon
his recovery in the fall of 1861, he received a major general's commission
and was assigned to the command of the Army of East Tennessee. His

spectacles (for nearsightedness) and receding hairline belied his thirty-eight years.[13]

On the retreat into Tennessee, Bragg had ordered Smith's corps to serve as rear guard, with the responsibility of guarding the army's extensive wagon train. Smith believed that Bragg virtually abandoned him on the retreat. Actually, Smith's lack of cooperation had in large part been responsible for the dismal results of the campaign. Davis wrote the East Tennessee commander that Bragg, while in Richmond, "uniformly spoke of you in the most complimentary terms, and does not seem to imagine your dissatisfaction." Smith arrived at the capital on November 2 or 3. He attempted to have the president replace Bragg with Joe Johnston, but to no avail. On his return to East Tennessee, Bragg and Smith accidentally met at the Knoxville train depot. Though Smith honestly related what he told the president, and everyone predicted "a stormy meeting," the army commander, in a rare moment of conciliation, "spoke kindly to me & in the highest terms of praise and admiration of my 'personal character and soldierly qualities'—I was astonished but believe he is honest & means well," Smith related to Cassie. Thereafter, neither he, nor his staff, ever again spoke publicly of the Kentucky Campaign.[14]

On November 4 it became Major General Leonidas Polk's turn to board the train for Richmond. Two upper-class roommates had befriended Jefferson Davis during his West Point years—Albert Sidney Johnston and Polk; he would forever idolize them both. When Polk graduated in 1827, he quit the army to study for the Episcopalian ministry. Fourteen years later, based primarily upon his name (he was cousin to President James K. Polk) and family wealth, he became a bishop. A friend admitted that he was neither a deep theologian nor well versed in church law. Despite his lack of army experience, Davis appointed him major general in the fall of 1861; the West had been saddled with him ever since. The Bishop upon his own authority moved into Kentucky, thus opening an entire new front. His troops hunkered down in the earthworks of Columbus, Kentucky, where, but for Beauregard's later insistence that the corps be withdrawn, it probably would have shared the same fate as Fort Donelson. During the Kentucky Campaign, Polk disobeyed Bragg's orders to come to his assistance (he had been a bishop too long to take orders), and he misarranged his troops on the battlefield of Perryville which, but for Bragg's timely arrival and redeployment, would have led to disaster. Bragg wanted him cashiered, but Davis revered Polk and was closer to him than the army commander. Everyone in the army loved the Bishop—he "won the hearts of the whole army," noted Dr. Charles Quintard. Bragg nonetheless saw through him and disdained him as "an encumbrance." When Bragg was baptized and joined the Episcopalian Church in the spring of 1863, he pointedly had a visiting bishop perform the sacrament rather than the general. Polk appeared lofty and pious and could well have served in the role of the army's healer; he instead became its primary conniver.[15]

Desiring to relocate some of his family to North Carolina, the Bishop delayed his departure to the capital until November 7 so that they could accompany him. On November 10, Hermes noted his presence in Richmond— "for what purpose we can only conjecture." His purpose was to undermine Bragg, which he promptly proceeded to do. He spoke contemptuously of the army commander, denounced the former campaign as a failure, and claimed he would have handled matters differently (by going directly through Middle Tennessee rather than taking the round-about through Chattanooga). He supported Johnston for army commander, but the thought of his own ascent to top command surely must have entered his mind. Bragg had organizational and administrative skills, he admitted, but he clearly could not command and inspire. Like Smith he proved adamant in his opinion; unlike Smith, he refused to keep quiet on his return to the army.[16]

Georgia-born, forty-seven-year-old Major General William J. "Old Reliable" Hardee, a better soldier than either Smith or Polk, graduated West Point in 1838. He served in both the Seminole and Mexican wars, but it was his authorship of a pamphlet on military drill, adopted in 1854 by the U.S. War Department, that gave him name recognition. His streamlined innovations, especially in loading and firing and the rate of advance during an attack, would become standard for both armies during the war. Like Polk, Hardee had a close prewar association with the president. In 1858, when Davis went blind in one eye, Hardee, while visiting Washington, would sit with him for hours, reading to him and writing correspondence. By 1862 Hardee had been a widower for nine years. He would remarry in 1864, but in between his "running with women" became a source of displeasure for some. Despite his mediocre performance in the Kentucky Campaign, the Georgian maintained Bragg's respect. Unfortunately, he had a proclivity for fault-finding, and he increasingly came under the influence of Polk. Not having the stomach to openly attack Bragg, Hardee begged off the trip to Richmond, but he did write a letter to William Preston Johnston, aide to the president with an office directly across the hallway, in which he essentially agreed with Polk. "Grave, unpardonable errors were committed," in the last campaign, although he admitted that finding a successor would not be easy.[17]

Bragg had taken the western Confederate army as far north as it would ever go during the war, but it had not been enough. Perhaps the tortured command structure ensured failure. Perhaps a Confederate Kentucky was too much to hope for. Perhaps the ability of the North to raise manpower meant that any southern victory would be short-lived. Perhaps. The only certainty was that Bragg's popularity had started a decline from which it would never rebound.

OLD ROSY

By the fall of 1862, support for the war had waned in the North. The peace wing of the Democratic Party, the so-called Copperheads, appeared to be gaining influence. With the approach of the bitterly contested congressional races in October and November, President Lincoln had cause for concern. While the North had not instituted a draft, as in the South, it had accomplished the same end with the congressional passage of the Militia Act—nothing more than a de facto draft of 300,000 men. A popular song attempted to spur enlistments: "We Are Coming, Father Abraham, 300,000 More." Due to draft dodging and interference by local governors, however, overall results proved disappointing.[18]

Lincoln's September 1862 announcement that he would emancipate all slaves alarmed Democrats, and even moderate Republicans. In the Army of the Ohio, resistance proved especially troublesome. "I did not come here to fight for negroes but I am afraid I am," D. K. Newhouse of the 101st Ohio wrote. "Nigger is all the cry here. Some of the old regiments say they never thought of such thing as laying down Arms before now. They say things has got to change soon[.] They won't fight for niggers and guard rebel property too." Hillory Shifflett of the 1st Ohio related his disgust: "The war wood a bin over if ould [old] Lincoln had let the negro question alone. If he was in hell and a negro tied to him I would be glad." The war dragged sluggishly onward, taking longer and costing more in blood than anyone ever anticipated.[19]

Congressmen and governors from Illinois, Ohio, and Indiana demanded the removal of Don Carlos Buell as commander of the Army of the Ohio. "The butchery of our troops at Perryville was terrible. Nothing but success, speedy and decided, will save our cause from utter destruction. In the Northwest distrust and despair are seizing upon the hearts of the people." Thus wrote Indiana Governor Oliver P. Morton to Lincoln on October 22. Ohio Senator John Sherman spoke of "dissatisfied and discouraged people." Although Kentucky had been saved, the entire Midwest had been shaken by the Confederate incursion. Buell had a tepid pursuit and, direct orders to the contrary, refused to enter East Tennessee (a pet project of Lincoln's), retiring the army instead to Nashville, Tennessee, by way of Bowling Green, Kentucky. Morton had journeyed to Washington earlier in the month, ostensibly to lobby for the early prisoner exchange of 7,000 Hoosiers captured at Munfordville and Richmond, Kentucky. Since no provision existed for absentee ballots, he desired that they be furloughed and sent home to vote. The governor also took the occasion to denounce Buell, whom he saw as "utterly unfit for command of the great army under him— is slow, opposed to Emancipation, and had [a] bad influence in every way." At the end of the month, the press leaked that Morton, Illinois Governor Richard Yates, and Ohio Governor David Tod, all Republicans, planned a Washington conference.[20]

Lincoln understood the problem. He wrote about General George B. McClellan, commander of the Army of the Potomac in Virginia, but his comments could well have extended to Buell: "They have got the idea in their heads that we are going to get out of this fix, somehow, by strategy! That's the word—strategy! General McClellan thinks he is going to whip the rebels by strategy; and the army has got the same notion." What Lincoln needed was a fighter, not a maneuverer. Buell's conservative war aims also muddied the water. Wishing to simply restore the antebellum South, he believed that the war should be waged against the southern army, not its people.[21]

On the heels of the Kentucky Campaign, rumors floated of Buell's imminent removal (it officially came on October 24). The obvious choice was George Thomas, who had been offered the command a month earlier, but had begged off due to an imminent battle. Forty-six-year-old Virginia-born Thomas graduated from West Point in 1840 and had fought in the Seminole and Mexican wars. Lincoln reportedly had doubts about Thomas's loyalty, but General William T. Sherman vouched: "Mr. President, Old Tom is as loyal as I am." Indeed, Thomas's sisters would never forgive him for choosing the North. A man of few personal friends, the rejection of his family injured him more deeply than has been suggested. He and his wife Frances had no children. Brevetted for gallantry at Buena Vista during the Mexican War, a West Point instructor during the 1850s and a major in the famed 2nd U.S. Cavalry, Thomas proved to be a man of integrity in an army where egos dominated.

Thomas wrote that he taught himself "not to feel," but on several occasions the normally reserved general revealed controlled anger. He quietly opposed Buell, although one unsubstantiated story claimed that the two quarreled and nearly came to blows. Charges that Thomas moved too slowly dogged him throughout the war. The *Chicago Tribune* attacked the Virginian as being "a slower man than Buell. It takes Thomas half an hour to say no." The men nonetheless loved "Old Pap," as he became known. In many respects the general was an enigma. Some viewed him as stern and unapproachable, having little patience with idle talk. Others testified that he loved small children and was generally more sociable and possessing of a sense of humor than credited. Thomas defeated the Confederates early at Mill Springs, Kentucky, but he had not participated in the Battles of Shiloh and Perryville.[22]

Another name had by now emerged, however, one outside the Army of the Ohio—Major General William S. Rosecrans, the victor of the Battle of Corinth. A war Democrat, he would also serve to strengthen Lincoln's war coalition base. General-in-Chief Henry Halleck supported him, although Secretary of War Edwin M. Stanton, who favored Thomas and had earlier clashed with Rosecrans, expressed opposition. Clearly the president considered Thomas's name, but the fact that he had previously refused the position now weighed heavily against him. Lincoln reportedly declared: "Let the Virginian wait; we will try Rosecrans."[23]

Rosecrans felt uncomfortable in relieving Buell of command at Bowling Green—more "like a constable bearing a writ for the ejection of a tenet than like a general on his way to relieve a brother officer." Little in his prewar background suggested that the Ohio-born general was prepared for such an assignment. Acquiring the sobriquet "Old Rosy" at West Point, he missed the Mexican War and spent the balance of his Regular Army career in routine engineering and teaching stints. He resigned the army in 1854 due to impaired health, in truth an infrequently mentioned nervous breakdown. In civilian pursuits, Rosecrans developed a kerosene refinery business in Cincinnati. The accidental explosion of a lamp in 1859 left him badly burned, with permanent and clearly visible scars on the corner of his mouth and forehead. He spent the next year-and-a-half recuperating. Early in the war he became colonel of the 23rd Ohio, but the next day a brigadier's commission arrived.

Upon McClellan's appointment to the Army of the Potomac, Rosecrans assumed command of the Department of the Ohio. In May 1862 he went west to command two divisions in John Pope's Army of the Mississippi. When Pope went east to command an army in Virginia, Old Rosy assumed command, under the supervision of Grant. It did not take long for the relationship between the two to deteriorate. In September Rosecrans held his own with a superior Confederate force at Iuka, Mississippi, and in October he defeated Van Dorn's army at Corinth. Even though the Rebels had escaped, the victory had been sufficient to catch Lincoln's attention. The president had his fighter.[24]

Unlike Buell, whom the troops rarely saw, Rosecrans had high visibility—the men loved him. "Old Rosy looks like he has not sympathy for the secesh and is greatly beloved by all the boys in the army," Winfield Scott Miller related to his parents. During division reviews, the army commander would walk up and down the ranks speaking a kind word to all. A Buckeye hoped that Rosecrans would "prove the right man in the right place. The boys are all very proud of him. . . . He is not above talking to a soldier." One officer described the general thus: "calm, self-possessed—a cigar in his mouth, not lighted, never is—never saw him without it; an old hat on, a common blue overcoat. His long, large hooked nose, sharp eyes, give him the appearance of a Jew peddler." Nonetheless, Colonel John Beatty predicated that within a year Rosecrans would be as unpopular as Buell.[25]

The new commander displayed promising traits—he was a skilled strategist, a quick learner, and possessed enormous endurance. He could nonetheless become rattled under pressure. Even in addressing soldiers at a review he would sometimes stammer. He could also be edgy, egotistical (an old acquaintance found him "completely turned by the greatness of his promotion"), lacking tact, and hot tempered. Rosecrans admitted that "some men I like to scold for I don't like them." Brigadier General John Palmer, who would grow to detest Rosecrans, wrote: "Another weakness of his is the facility with which he listens to flattery and sycophants. Anybody may acquire his favor by telling him he is a great man." An adult convert to Catholicism (his parents were strict Methodists), he became, according to an acquaintance, "a crank on the subject." Yet, he swore and drank freely.[26]

Thomas, who read of Rosecrans's appointment in the paper, clearly felt rebuffed at the turn of events, and he immediately fired off a letter to Halleck. The Virginian had known Rosecrans at the academy and, though the two had markedly different personalities (Thomas deliberate, Rosecrans impulsive), they had maintained a cordial friendship. The issue for Thomas (at least officially) related to seniority; his commission predated Rosecrans's. Upon meeting him, Rosecrans insisted that he had the senior commission. Taken aback, Thomas backed down. Rosecrans had told a half-truth. Thomas did have the senior commission, but to skirt the issue, Halleck had Rosecrans's commission backdated before coming to the Army of the Ohio. The truth ultimately came out, much to Thomas's chagrin. In a strongly worded protest to Halleck, the Virginian bordered on insubordination, hinting that he would act independently if the situation necessitated it.[27]

Rosecrans inherited two other corps commanders—Alexander McCook and Thomas Crittenden. Thirty-one-year-old Major General Alexander McDowell McCook, "Alex" to his friends, "McD" to his closer friends, came from a distinguished Ohio military family—the famed "Fighting McCooks." Upon graduation from West Point, he served five years fighting Apaches on the New Mexico frontier, and then returned to West Point in 1858 as an instructor. At the beginning of the war, he became colonel of the 1st Ohio and fought at First Bull Run. He assumed division command in the West in October 1861 and a year later rose to corps command. McCook fell in love with the lovely twenty-three-year-old Kate Phillips, a Dayton socialite; the two would marry in January 1863.

Yet, there were chinks in what appeared to be an otherwise promising career. Colonel Beatty denounced him as a "chucklehead" and "deficient in the upper story." The troops called him "Gut," a reference to his portly appearance, and one Illinois soldier observed that "he prides himself on *being* General McCook." A captain in the 93rd Ohio, noticing a certain lack of gravitas in the general, concluded that he "don't look to be equal to the position he holds; he seems to have drawn a lucky card." Another soldier derided the corps commander as part of a "drunken lot" who surrounded himself with "several drunken aides who are perfect court fools," who "merely make fun of their master, laugh at his jokes, mix his liquor for him, and play the flunkery in every conceivable way." At the Battle of Perryville, the Rebels routed his corps—"I was badly whipped," the general confessed.[28]

The birthplace of the Army of the Ohio had been Kentucky, resulting in a significant number of Kentucky generals in the high command. One of these, forty-three-year-old Major General Thomas L. Crittenden, could not exactly be branded as a political general—he had served as General Zachary Taylor's aide during the Mexican War and held a major general's commission in the state militia. His prominent father, Kentucky Senator John J. Crittenden, nonetheless helped him to land his present position. Thomas would marry his father's step-daughter. He remained untested on the battlefield; sickness kept him out of Shiloh and his corps remained idle at Perryville. A correspondent described him as five foot, nine inches, weatherbeaten face, resembled his father, mild-mannered, and very popular with the officers and men. Another officer expressed a different view—he "has just enough sense to keep still, say nothing, and do little." A hard curser and heavy drinker, he had little to recommend him beyond personal popularity.[29]

Rosecrans could do little about McCook and Crittenden, but he received an excellent chief of staff, Colonel Julius "Jules" Garasche, a forty-two-year-old Cuban-born (to French parents) officer who had served in the adjutant general's office. Nearly the same age as Rosecrans (they had known one another as West Point), Garesche also shared his pious Catholic faith. The commanding general welcomed him "with open arms." Garesche related to his wife: "I get along most smoothly with Rosecrans. He is at most but little in advance of me in his Abolitionist views."[30]

For his cavalry chief, Rosecrans requested Brigadier General David Stanley, who had commanded an infantry division in Rosecrans's former army, and who had cavalry experience in the Regular Army. He proved a mixed blessing. Stanley clearly had skills (he would eventually rise to corps command in the army), but he held antiquated quirks about cavalry use, maintained a low view of most other generals, and allegations of drunkenness would dog him. Additionally, he was a Catholic, which led to whisperings that the army commander held a religious bias.[31]

The victor of Corinth would have a brief honeymoon. Expectations in Washington were high and patience in short supply. What the War Department hoped to have in Rosecrans was the anti-Buell, someone who could stop the bleeding, both politically and on the battlefield, with a resounding victory. Officials would soon discover that he had a mind of his own.

2

THE DARK WINTER

A NECK AND NECK RACE FOR MURFREESBORO

Bragg's so-called offensive into Middle Tennessee, following his failed Kentucky Campaign, has long been misunderstood. Historians have concluded that the general, even while in Kentucky, contemplated an offensive as early as mid-September 1862, when he dispatched Nathan Bedford Forrest to Murfreesboro to secure the countryside from foraging expeditions. In truth, Bragg sent Forrest back accompanied only by his escort and four Alabama cavalry companies, with instructions to raise a new command. Exactly why he did this is not known—Forrest's supporters claim that the cavalry leader requested it, and Bragg's critics suggest that he wanted to rid himself of the rough-hewn, non-professional Tennessean.[1]

The genesis of the offensive came not with Bragg, but with Tennessee Governor Isham G. Harris, who became convinced that the Federals had nearly abandoned Nashville. On September 20, 1862, the governor claimed that the garrison had dwindled to between 5,000 and 8,000 troops, and he pleaded for Sterling Price's small "army" (two divisions) to advance from Mississippi and attack the city. Nine days later he placed garrison strength at 4,000, based upon what information he never stated, but presumably civilian reports. The Yankee garrison never dropped below 12,000, more than enough to handle Price's 16,800, even if they had succeeded in breaking out of Grant's western Tennessee–northern Mississippi defensive perimeter. The Confederate defeat at Corinth in early October settled the issue once and for all, and after that Price could not even put up the pretense of an offensive.[2]

Harris turned to the one remaining available command—Major General John C. Breckinridge's division. In the summer of 1862 the division had been detached from Bragg's army to contest the Federal advance up the

Mississippi River at Baton Rouge, Louisiana. The expedition failed, and the division, reduced to 3,000 men primarily due to sickness, was ordered to Knoxville to re-unite with the parent army in Kentucky. At Jackson, Mississippi, 2,000 exchanged prisoners joined. On September 29 Harris pleaded with the secretary of war to divert the division to attack Nashville. Though initially refusing, the War Department subsequently ordered a brigade from Breckinridge's division to Murfreesboro. Bragg did not order the division back to Middle Tennessee until October 14, after he had begun his Kentucky retreat.[3]

William Preston's brigade of Breckinridge's division arrived at Murfreesboro around October 20. A railroad town of 4,000, located thirty-five miles southeast of Nashville, Murfreesboro had been named after Colonel Hardy Murfree, a Revolutionary War hero and extensive land owner. The most substantial building in town, the all-brick Rutherford County Courthouse, had been completed in 1859. One observer noted that virtually no middle class existed in the town, only aristocrats or "white trash." One of Preston's men thought the citizens to be "the kindest I've met yet." The balance of the division arrived on October 27–28, and the men began preparing winter quarters. The Army of Middle Tennessee, as Breckinridge grandiosely labeled his force, comprised only his division, Forrest's newly organized brigade, and Major J. T. Montgomery's 14th Georgia Artillery Battalion of two batteries (one battery had previously linked up with Bragg's army), organized at Griffin and Calhoun the previous spring.[4]

Believing that the Federals would attempt a counter-move into middle Tennessee, Breckinridge wrote, "It is a neck and neck race for Murfreesboro and Nashville. I do not think Buell will follow Bragg across the desert [mountains]. They will push all their force into Tennessee by the other route. We must be ready to meet them." It was a fair assessment, although no evidence indicates that the Federals actually had designs south of Nashville. Bragg, who had to feed his army, get out of Smith's jurisdiction, and mitigate the damage of the late campaign, contemplated an offensive in Middle Tennessee. Pressure may also have come from the War Department. Colonel George Brent, the general's forty-one-year-old chief of staff and former Virginia politician, confidentially wrote on November 4: "The troops he [Bragg] directly command, do not exceed 30,000, and yet he is ordered to move." On the November 6 he added: "The Department orders and expects a great movement." Within two weeks of this entry, Bragg notified the War Department that Nashville remained heavily fortified. The move into Middle Tennessee would commence the first week in November, but thoughts of an offensive were abandoned.[5]

Bragg prepared his army for another arduous trek from Knoxville to Chattanooga via the rickety East Tennessee & Georgia Railroad. From there the troops would board the cars of the Nashville & Chattanooga into Middle Tennessee. The army remained in a fragile state, 42 percent being absent, mostly from sickness and desertion. The November 2 return revealed 27,520 men present for duty (including cavalry). Some regiments counted barely a hundred men. The Conscript Law had been in effect for seven months, yet not a single draftee had arrived in the army. The general quickly went about the task of placing detailed men back into the ranks. He also received permission to draft all Kentucky emigrants who had not volunteered, sent officers to various camps of instruction to bring back conscripts, and insisted that all absent soldiers not sick immediately return to the army. Soon "large accessions" of recruits and returning convalescents began arriving.[6]

Bragg took the opportunity to reorganize his command, now called the Army of Tennessee. Polk's corps counted the divisions of Benjamin F. Cheatham, Jones Withers, and Breckinridge. Forty-two-year-old Cheatham, an unsavory Tennessean widely known for his drinking, outbursts of profanity, and ownership of the Nashville Race Track, had fought in the Mexican War and held prominence in the Tennessee militia. Known as "Mars Franklin," the highly popular bachelor had fought at Shiloh and Perryville, and now commanded the Tennessee division. Bragg nonetheless detested him and minced no words in his desire to be rid of him. Withers, a West Pointer, lawyer, and former mayor of Mobile, had become a Bragg ally during his brief stint at Pensacola. Commanding arguably the best-disciplined division in the army, his problem related to health; he had been in and out of hospitals ever since May 1862. Withers's future with the army appeared problematic. At age thirty-five, Breckinridge became the youngest vice-president in United States history, although his 1860 bid for the presidency failed. Dashing in appearance, he nonetheless proved western in character—a hard-drinking tobacco chewer. Although vain and stubborn, he could be a passable general. Bragg unjustly placed much of his frustration about Kentucky's lack of response in the recent campaign upon him; the relationship between the two quickly deteriorated.[7]

Patrick R. "Old Pat" Cleburne and James Patton Anderson commanded Hardee's two divisions. Cleburne, an Irishman with experience in the British Army, had immigrated to the United States only fifteen years earlier. He settled in Helena, Arkansas, where he became a prominent attorney. Shot in the back in an 1856 street fight, Cleburne never fully recovered. He easily caught cold, his mouth would occasionally fill with blood, and, standing a little less than six feet, he never weighed more than 135 pounds during the war. At the Battle of Richmond, Kentucky, where his battle plan resulted in the capture of an entire Federal division, a bullet passed through his cheek, knocking out several teeth, and five weeks later, at Perryville, he received an ankle wound. Prior to Chickamauga, Bragg considered Cleburne an ally, although the major general would increasingly come under the influence of his mentor Hardee. Anderson, a brigadier, commanded Hardee's other division, but it was later broken up and the brigades divided between the two corps. Thereafter Polk had Cheatham and Withers, and Hardee claimed Cleburne and Breckinridge. Initially Smith brought with him two divisions (15,000 troops on paper, but reduced by sickness to 11,000), thus forming a third corps. Carter Stevenson's division would later depart (explained below), leaving only the division of Major General John P. McCown, which became attached to Hardee's corps. Bragg considered McCown, a Tennessee West Pointer, to be useless.[8]

Bragg also used the opportunity to restructure his oversized cavalry. At full strength, he had five brigades totaling nearly 11,500 troopers—Forrest (2,500), John Hunt Morgan (2,500), Joseph Wheeler (2,000), John A. Wharton (2,000), John Pegram of Smith's department (1,800), and Abraham Buford's demi-brigade of 631. Both Forrest and Morgan, though in and out of the army at various times, served essentially as independent raiders, thus whittling the cavalry down to about 6,500.[9]

Bragg's selection of Joseph "Fightin' Joe" Wheeler, an aloof twenty-six-year-old Georgian, as cavalry chief proved an interesting if not predictable selection. Two factors recommended him for the position. First, he had graduated West Point (Class of '59), taught at the Cavalry School of Practice at Carlisle Barracks, Pennsylvania, and had served in the Regular cavalry. Second, early in the war Wheeler became a part of the pro-Bragg Pensacola bloc. Although his performance during the Kentucky Campaign had been spotty, and Forrest held seniority, Bragg had no intention of appointing the Tennessean, whom he saw as merely a partisan. Standing only five feet, two inches, Wheeler, like so many of his fellow generals, was a bachelor. One trooper was surprised to see "what a boyish looking general he was." In the fall of 1863, he would meet a wealthy nineteen-year-old widow (she had inherited her elderly husband's estate) by the name of Daniella Sherrod. The two began to correspond and would marry at the end of the war.[10]

Bragg's troops debarked the cars at Bridgeport, Alabama, to cross the Tennessee River, the Federals having previously destroyed the Howe Turn Bridge. Once ferried across to the west bank, the railroad stock proved so limited that half of the men had to march the final leg into Tullahoma. On November 14 Bragg arrived at Tullahoma—"A miserable village. Our office a mere pig sty," Brent groused. Anxious to advance his line, Bragg relocated his headquarters to Murfreesboro on November 16. The general and his staff took residence at Oaklands, the exquisite plantation of Major Lewis Maney, grandson of Colonel Hardee Murfree. A general's conference was held on November 17, and the next day Polk's corps was ordered to Murfreesboro, Hardee's to Shelbyville, and Smith's to Manchester. Brent confided his discomfort in the triangular position, with Murfreesboro as the apex; it would take "two marches" for Smith to close in on the center. Advancing beyond the Duck River and the hills of southern Rutherford County would prove Bragg's first mistake. Even though the Duck River line presented its own unique problems, it was far better than Murfreesboro, which had too many approaches, allowing it to be outflanked.[11]

The War Department, under political pressure and in a quandary concerning the Mississippi conundrum, assigned Joseph E. Johnston as the Western Theater commander on November 12, with authority between the Appalachians and the Mississippi River, a massive 180,000 square miles. He would be given the role of shuffling forces back and forth between John C. Pemberton's Army of Mississippi, Bragg's Army of Tennessee, and Smith's East Tennessee Department. From the outset, Johnston expressed reservations with the structure, believing that the Mississippi Army should be linked with the trans-Mississippi. While he had the authority to personally command either the Mississippi or Tennessee Army when he was present (thus taking care of the Bragg issue), Johnston personally saw his role as only a visiting advisor and refused to exercise his authority. Moreover, he suspected that Davis had set him up as a scapegoat. The Virginian complained to the president about his assignment, but he received no response. On November 24, Johnston departed Richmond for Chattanooga.[12]

SOMETHING IS EXPECTED FROM YOU

While still at Bowling Green, Rosecrans made army reorganization his top priority, forestalling strategy for the time being. By order of the War Department, the area in Tennessee east of the Ohio River would now be known as the Department of the Cumberland. Rosecrans's army would oddly be styled the "Fourteenth Army Corps," although after the Battle of Stones River it would be named the Army of the Cumberland, for which it would forever be known. Rosecrans would no longer number the corps, as had Buell, but he would style them the "Right Wing," the "Center," and the "Left Wing," commanded respectively by McCook, Thomas, and Crittenden. Buell's notion of consecutively numbering all the divisions in the army was dispensed. Nonetheless, he continued the former commander's policy of mixing state regiments within brigades.[13]

McCook's Right Wing comprised the divisions of Brigadier Generals Jefferson C. Davis, Richard W. Johnson, and Philip Sheridan. No relation to the Rebel president, "Jef" Davis, as he signed his name, was an old Regular Army officer, although his application to West Point had been declined. Known for his fiery temper, he had murdered Major General William "Bull" Nelson in a personal dispute back during the Kentucky Campaign, although the issue strangely never came to a trial. A pro-slavery Democrat, his political views alienated him with many officers. Johnson, a Kentucky West Pointer, had only limited combat experience; he missed Shiloh due to sickness and, in an embarrassing episode, had been captured by John Hunt Morgan back in May 1862. Only recently returned to the army, the upcoming battle would test the mettle of this officer of dubious quality. At age thirty-one, the diminutive Philip "Little Phil" Sheridan, still a bachelor in 1862, became the youngest division commander in the army. Although his performance at Perryville had not been stellar, Rosecrans supported his fellow Ohioan and Catholic. He was fated to become the most aggressive division commander in the army, but first there must be Stones River.[14]

Thomas's Center had only Lovell H. Rousseau's and James S. Negley's divisions and a brigade from Speed Fry's division ready for the field, with Robert Paine's division being assigned to garrison duty in Nashville, and Fry's and Joseph Reynolds's divisions guarding the railroad tunnel at Gallatin, Tennessee. At six feet, two inches, the heavy set, rough-edged, bourbon-loving Rousseau was perhaps the most conspicuous of all the generals—

handsome, a commanding presence, but "a little too bulky" for the taste of Colonel Beatty. A Kentucky political general, he had supported Buell's strategy and politics, thus making him a liability, but he had proven that he could fight at Shiloh and Perryville, and, if not the best general, he was at least a popular one. Thirty-six-year-old Negley, a banker and wine-grower with a background in the Pennsylvania militia, was unpopular with the clique of professional officers, but he remained in Rosecrans's graces—some suspected due to his Catholicism. Never having been in combat, he was an unknown quantity.[15]

Leading the divisions of the Left Wing were Brigadier Generals Thomas Wood, John M. Palmer, and Horatio Van Cleve. A solid professional with eighteen years' experience in the Regular Army, the feisty, hard-cursing, self-promoting Wood ably led the First Division. Illinois political general John Palmer, who detested West Pointers nearly as much as the Rebels, commanded the Second Division. Described as "the most common" general in the army, it would not take him long to collide with Rosecrans. Horatio Van Cleve, unassuming, aging, and colorless, had been out of the Regular Army for twenty-five years by the beginning of the war. Distinguished by his long face and spectacles, he proved as good as most.[16]

Although Rosecrans's cavalry had not yet come of age, his long arm, both in numbers and armament, far exceeded that of the enemy. Colonel James Barnett, the forty-two-year-old army artillery chief, had a background in the Ohio militia, but prior to the war, he worked in a Cleveland hardware business. The army's three wings counted twenty-five batteries of 137 guns, comprised of one-half rifles (mostly 10-pounder Parrotts and James rifles), and one-half smoothbores (predominately 6-pounders and 12-pounder howitzers.) After the Battle of Stones River, the 12-pounder Napoleon gun would become the backbone of the western Federal artillery, but at this stage the army counted only ten.[17]

Rosecrans, himself a former engineer, made a significant contribution in expanding the army's limited engineer organization. The highly intelligent but rather eccentric thirty-three-year-old Captain James St. Clair Morton, a blond-headed, long-haired West Pointer, served as army chief engineer, but he and his assistant were stretched impossibly thin. "The Army of the Potomac cannot possibly be as much in need of engineers as I am," Rosecrans wrote Washington. His complaint marginally worked; he received two additional engineers. Meanwhile, he implemented a new topographical organization, ordering every division and brigade commander to detail a soldier for data gathering of roads, bridges, and fords, and to serve as geography advisors. Rosecrans also organized a Pioneer Brigade for traditional engineer work—the repairing of roads and construction of bridges. Each regiment contributed twenty men (two from each company), which included half laborers and half mechanics. Comprised of three battalions, the brigade could also serve as combat infantry in an emergency.[18]

The army commander would claim, and modern historians would accept without questioning, that he had a force of 43,400 on the battlefield—40,100 infantry and artillery, 1,700 pioneers, and 3,200 cavalry, minus 1,600 infantry for wagon guards, thus giving him virtual parity with Bragg's army. The number proved so inaccurate (after-battle strengths were used and Walker's brigade of Thomas's corps left out altogether) that it is difficult not to conclude that he manipulated the numbers. The correct present for duty strength should have been 55,127. Sickness and details thinned the ranks and, due to a Federal law that permitted conscripts to go into new regiments rather than fill depleted ones, veteran regiments remained undermanned. Just before the army marched out to Murfreesboro, a member of the 55th Ohio noted that only five months earlier his regiment counted 1,100, but the total had now dwindled to a fraction over 400.[19]

While Rosecrans sized up his generals, the War Department did the same to him. What Halleck desired was the rapid re-occupation of Middle Tennessee, and then a turning movement into East Tennessee. In early November, hysterical press and scout reports indicated that Nashville was threatened—in reality there was only roving Confederate cavalry. On November 4 Morgan attempted to destroy the Cumberland River Bridge, while Forest feinted from the south of Nashville. The big guns at Fort Negley boomed, the muffled sound being heard all the way to Bowling Green, sixty-five miles away. Becoming jittery, Rosecrans directed McCook's corps to relieve the city, which it did on the seventh. Rosecrans arrived on the thirteenth, establishing his headquarters at the George W. Cunningham home at 13 High Street. It soon became clear that the perceived threats had been exaggerated. The general thus took his time, desiring to have the Louisville & Nashville Railroad repaired as he advanced (the track would not be completed until November 26), and he hoped for a rise in the Cumberland River, thus allowing supplies to be accumulated from St. Louis. His dispatches to Washington might as well have been written by Buell.[20]

Rosecrans realized that Bragg would rush to fill the vacuum in Middle Tennessee ("he cannot live elsewhere"), but throughout November, Federal spies related that Bragg's target remained Tullahoma, not Murfreesboro. According to "Holloway," a Union spy, the town had been occupied merely as an outpost to "visit their friends and obtain clothing, and also to carry off all the provisions in middle Tennessee, and to fill up the old Tennessee regiments with conscripts." Polk's corps, with four divisions, remained at Tullahoma. No one knew precisely where Hardee's corps had gone, and rumors circulated that it had slipped away to Mississippi or Virginia. If confirmed, wired Rosecrans, "[I] will press them up solidly." On November 16, reports placed Hardee at Shelbyville, indicating that the Rebels might be moving farther west. Nonetheless, Rosecrans believed, "They will try to fight us on the table-lands near Tullahoma." Some reports indicated that Bragg might not give battle north of the Tennessee River. As for Murfreesboro, the Rebel force there could be easily brushed aside and the town occupied when the Federals desired. Rosecrans continued to badger for more carbines to give his cavalry an edge. Halleck dispatched thirty-six hundred carbines and Colt's revolving rifles, but they came with a warning: "No effort shall be spared to supply what you ask for, but something is expected from you."[21]

On November 17, Rosy related to Halleck his strategic plan to "lull them" into thinking that he "was not going to move soon." The trick appeared to be working on Halleck as well. "If you remain long in Nashville you will disappoint the wishes of the Government," he admonished. The general reassured Washington of his commitment to a timely offensive, but no schedule was forthcoming. Confiding to his wife on November 22, Rosecrans wrote: "The Administration expects much of me. I have a bad country to advance over, but my hopes are all in God. . . . I work 18 hours a day. . . . I am in the hopes of beginning to move very soon with the intention of moving rapidly and continuously. The next battle in this department is likely to decide the war. There must be no failure. I will not move until I am ready." A showdown brewed between the army command and Washington officials.[22]

The truth be known, Rosecrans hoped that Bragg *would* occupy Murfreesboro. On November 1 he had written to his brother Sylvester, "It would be a great thing if the rebels would come and fight us near our base. For the only remedy for this evil is *fighting*. We must crush their power. This must be done by battles. If we can make the enemy wear himself out by marches, and then fight him near our base and far from his own he runs the risk of annihilation." Again he wrote to his wife on November 24: "I am in hopes of beginning to move very soon with the intention of moving rapidly and continuously. . . . I pray we will have the opportunity [to fight] the rebels this side of the Tennessee River! It would save much marching and suffering. I will try what can be done to get them to stay."[23]

Oblivious to the workings at army headquarters, the soldiers could only appreciate the "quiet gentry" weather throughout early December. On December 5 it snowed rapidly, but most of it melted before it hit the ground. Two inches nonetheless accumulated and froze that night, but on the seventh a bright sun returned. "O how I wish the war was over so we could all be at home where we could be sure of a few moments repose," A. Stanley Camp of the 18th Ohio wrote his wife.[24]

VISITORS

Colonel Brent took a glance at the December 1 returns. The numbers came in at 43,500 (17,000 in Polk's corps, 13,000 in Hardee's corps, and 13,500 in Smith's corps). Wheeler's 6,000 or so cavalry swelled the total to 49,500, a near-parity with Rosecrans, although the Confederates estimated Union strength at 65,000. Bragg's widely spread position troubled the chief of staff. Two days earlier he had written, "Our position is not very secure. If enemy has a superior force we must fall back." On December 2 he added: "Our position critical. Supplies short. If enemy were to press us vigorously disaster would befall us."[25]

Joseph E. Johnston arrived in Murfreesboro on December 5; the reaction proved electric. The "wildest enthusiasm" prevailed, and "cheer after cheer rang out in the cold air." Exactly how Bragg felt about the general's arrival (he would in time grow suspicious) is not known, but the press openly reported that the new theater commander would probably replace Bragg, who would be sent elsewhere, Mississippi being the prevailing thought. Later that day the wings of the army were drawn in—Hardee to College Grove (leaving a brigade at Triune) and Smith to Readyville. The move had to be postponed until December 7 due to sleet and snow.[26]

Advised that an enemy brigade stood isolated on the Cumberland River at Hartsville, Tennessee, Bragg determined to unleash Morgan. As a diversion, he sent two of Cheatham's brigades from Murfreesboro to La Vergne on December 6. The march proved a miserable fifteen-mile trudge through four inches of snow. Meanwhile, Morgan pulled out of Murfreesboro on the sixth with 1,400 cavalry, two regiments of infantry from the Kentucky brigade, and two guns, a total of 2,140. The next day he swept down on the unsuspecting Hartsville garrison, bagging the 2,100 troops. News of the cavalier's exploits quickly got back to the army. "This is a joyous night in camp. Every mouth is full of Hosannas to the heroic Morgan," a Tennessean recorded.[27]

Prompted by concerns of infighting within the Army of Tennessee and the troubling military situation in Mississippi, Davis, despite his feeble health, determined to visit the west. He arrived in Murfreesboro on December 12. At sunrise the next morning, in a field a mile south of town, the president reviewed Polk's corps. He rode the full length of each division, finding the troops "in fine spirits." The corps then passed in review. Davis "passed within ten steps of me and I got a look at him," wrote Reuben Searcy. An Alabamian thought him to be "a good looking man," although James Hall candidly remarked that "you could not tell him from any other *old citizen*." Hall continued to his sister: "Some of them [troops] hardly believe yet that it was the real Simon pure Jeff. They have been deceived so often by reports that Jeff Davis was in camp that they would not really believe it when it did come!" The president joined the generals for dinner that evening; speeches followed by Bragg, Breckinridge, and Polk. Officers kept their personal comments to themselves, prompting Davis to believe that the bickering had ceased. Several promotions were handed out—Cleburne to major general and Lucius Polk, E. C. Walthall, Zacharias Deas, and Roger Hanson to brigadier. Brent thought that "Polk's and Hanson's should not have been made."[28]

The president's visit had proven far from social. Davis needed immediate reinforcements for Mississippi to check a threatened invasion, and the troops had to come from either Tennessee or Arkansas. Johnston had for weeks advocated uniting Lieutenant General Theophilus Holmes's army in Arkansas with Pemberton's Mississippi forces and sending them into Missouri, while Bragg and Kirby Smith marched to Ohio. To draw troops from Bragg, he argued, would lose Tennessee and free the Army of the Cumberland for operations in either Mississippi or Virginia. Johnston based his crystal ball upon faulty assumptions. First, he believed that Bragg remained heavily outnumbered (65,000 to 42,000), while Holmes's Arkansas army held numerical superiority with its opposing Federal forces. He also reasoned that reinforcements from Tennessee could not arrive in Mississippi in less than a month. Davis, who viewed Richmond and Mississippi as the prime Federal targets, determined otherwise. Besides, Rosecrans appeared content to remain passive. If the enemy did advance, Bragg could always fall behind the Tennessee River and trade land for time. Johnston thus ordered Carter Stevenson's division and an attached brigade from John McCown's division, 8,776 men, to Mississippi. The troops would traverse the same summer 1862 railroad itinerary (in reverse) through Mobile. The first two brigades departed on December 18 and arrived within ten days, although the last two required three weeks.[29]

For some time, rumors had circulated that the Federals would abandon Nashville. Federal picket posts had been drawn in, and smoke could be seen, which some surmised to be the burning of machinery at the state penitentiary. The press was all abuzz with the story, and Senator Clement C. Clay, who visited the Army of Tennessee on December 19, came to the same conclusion. Bragg believed the stories, although his own intelligence reports (from civilians and prisoners) gave a different conclusion. On the 18th, the very day Stevenson's division departed, Colonel Brent jotted in his diary: "Rumors afloat of the evacuation of Nashville. General Bragg feels confident of it. Thinks it certain because enemy cannot subsist there. I doubt it much." Two days later, still convinced of a withdrawal, Bragg ordered a reconnaissance. His scouts reported on December 21 that the Yankees had not withdrawn; indeed, evidence indicated an enemy buildup—actually the arrival of Thomas's corps. The die had been cast.[30]

Business could wait; the social event of the winter was about to occur. On December 14, Colonel John Hunt Morgan wed Miss Mattie Ready, a local socialite sixteen years his junior. Polk, wearing his robe over his uniform, performed the ceremony, with Bragg, Hardee, Cheatham, and Breckinridge present. Colonel George St. Leger Grenfell, a former British officer now serving as Morgan's adjutant, stood as groomsman, although he disapproved of the union, fearing that the attractive lass would curve the raider's fighting edge. Colonel Horace Ready, brother of the bride and a member of Hardee's staff, also served as a groomsman. Two bands provided background music for the dinner that followed. A group of officers gathered in the library and encouraged Dr. David Yandell to do his famous officer impersonations. He responded by doing Polk, then Hardee, and finishing with Bragg. On the last he paced back and forth, waved his arms, and in a raspy voice barked out curt sentences about the use of whiskey. Much to the doctor's embarrassment, he looked up to see that the army commander had walked in. In a rare light mood, Bragg said: "Go on, doctor; don't let me interrupt you. It is certainly entertaining and doubtless quite true."[31]

The next night, Morgan's staff honored the newlyweds with a dance at the courthouse. Talk centered on Morgan's upcoming raid. Indeed, some feared there had been too much talk. The northern press had published a correct list of Morgan's command and its potential destination. Although Bragg still thought the L&N Railroad non-operational (it had in fact been in use for two weeks), he decided upon a second strike. Four days earlier he had dispatched Forrest's brigade into western Tennessee against the Mobile & Ohio to disrupt Grant's supply line. Morgan's raid unfortunately came too late; large amounts of stores had already been stockpiled in Nashville. It would later be argued, correctly so, that the Hartsville Raid should have been directed against the L&N.[32]

Gala events notwithstanding, the grim realities of war could not be escaped. James A. Hall informed his father on December 22: "A man in our Brigade was condemned to be shot for desertion. The whole brigade was turning out to witness. It was horrible. Owing to some blunder, the squad fired three volleys into him before he was killed. It made a deep impression. I think any man who witnessed it would resolve never to die such a death." In Breckinridge's division three deserters were shot, Asa Lewis of the 6th Kentucky among them. Motivated by a pitiful letter from his mother, the young boy deserted; some said it was not his first time. The entire Kentucky brigade nonetheless took up his cause, and Breckinridge pleaded with Bragg to commute his sentence. The army commander proved unrelenting, and the crack of the firing squad sounded. A sickened Breckinridge leaned forward on his horse and had to be caught by his staff. The breach between the two generals widened. E. P. Norman of the 28th Alabama was one of those slated to be executed. He expressed his bitterness at the court's verdict. "I must now be put to death for going home to make some necessary preparations for my little family, while others that left at the same time are not even arrested."[33]

With the loss of Stevenson's division and some shrinkage in Wheeler's cavalry, the Army of Tennessee had dropped from 49,500 on December 1 to 38,844 by the end of the month. The breakdown would tally at: Polk's corps, 16,604, Hardee's corps, 12,909, McCown's division (attached to Hardee),

3,940, Jackson's brigade, 874 (attached to Polk), Wheeler's brigade, 1,169, Wharton's brigade, 1,960, Buford's brigade, 638, and Pegram's brigade, about 750, totaling 34,327 infantry and artillery and 4,517 cavalry.[34]

THERE MUST BE NO FAILURE

Throughout December, pressure intensified for an offensive. Halleck wrote Rosecrans in unmistakable terms on December 4: "The President is very impatient at your long stay in Nashville. The favorable season for your campaign will soon be over. . . . Twice have I been asked to designate some one else to command your army. If you remain one week more in Nashville, I cannot prevent your removal." At 10:45 that night, Rosecrans fired back an angry response: "If my superiors have lost confidence in me, they had better at once put someone in my place and let the future test the propriety of the change. . . . To threats of removal and the like I must be permitted to say that I am insensible." W. D. Bickham, a Cincinnati correspondent, overheard the general's outburst: "I will not budge till I am ready. I will not move for popular effect. . . . The next battle in this department is likely to be decisive of the war. There must be no failure."[35]

Halleck refused to blink, writing the next day: "My telegram was not a threat, but merely a statement of facts. The President is greatly dissatisfied with your delay, and has sent for me several times to account for it." Political and diplomatic considerations, he insisted, made an offensive imperative. "Tennessee is the only State which can be used as an argument in favor of intervention by England," he disclosed. Halleck concluded that an advance by December 15 had been expected, and then added insult by making some not-so-veiled comparisons to Buell. Salmon Chase, one of Rosecrans's supporters, followed up with his own warning. As for Rosecrans, he confided to his brother on the fifteenth that he still hoped the Rebels would come to him and fight near Nashville, "thus saving us the wear, tear, detachments and delays of pursuing them through the mountains and fighting them in force."[36]

Rosecrans continued to build up his stockpile, but with the low gauge of the Cumberland River he had to rely almost exclusively upon the L&N. By mid-December, seventy to eighty cars arrived daily, increasing his stockpile to twenty days by December 24. In order not to draw down on his supplies, the army commander sent out numerous foraging expeditions. The wagons scattered over such a wide area, however, that, even in guarded convoys of seventy to ninety wagons, they constantly came under attack. Adding to Rosecrans woes were the reports of Forrest's and Morgan's exploits.[37]

More bad news arrived—this time from the killing fields in Virginia. General Ambrose Burnside's Army of the Potomac had attacked Lee at Fredericksburg, losing 13,000 men in what amounted to a bloodbath. "The news from Fredericksburg has cast a shadow over the army," Colonel Beatty admitted. Robert H. Caldwell of the 21st Ohio noted to his father: "We have received the news of the repulse of Burnside at Fredericksburg, and I am now confident if Rosecrans don't move forward and gain a decisive victory at Murfreesboro the cry of Foreign intervention will again be the cry. Certainly Rosecrans has the material for giving the Rebels their dues and when he does[,] look for some big tracks."[38]

John Hunt Morgan, with 3,900 men, now threatened a sortie into Kentucky; he was everywhere, he was nowhere. Exaggerated reports placed the raider's strength at 6,000–12,000, with eighteen guns. The subsequent Stones River Campaign cannot be understood apart from Morgan's raid. The over-reaction by Federal authorities resulted in two moves. First, the siphoning off of two of Thomas's divisions—two brigades from Speed Fry's division (Thomas retained the third) and Joseph Reynolds's division of two brigades to guard Gallatin, Tennessee. Only four months earlier, Morgan had destroyed the Big South Tunnel of the L&N, shutting down rail traffic for weeks. Second, some 30,000 troops (Major General Horatio Wright's Department of the Ohio) were kept pinned down in western and central Kentucky, guarding bridges and points of dubious value. They proved utterly worthless in stopping Morgan's destructive path in Kentucky, much less capturing him.

After the Battle of Stones River, Halleck ordered Wright to concentrate his troops along the line of the L&N, and then ordered 15,000 of Wright's men (three divisions under Gordon Granger) into Tennessee, to act in conjunction with the Army of the Cumberland. If Halleck had done *before* the battle what he did *after* the battle, the results might have been very different. Even if only a single division from Wright's department had been ordered into Tennessee to assist Fry at Gallatin, John Reynolds's division could have been released back to Thomas. One must wonder what difference, if any, Reynolds's 4,500 infantry and two batteries would have made on the Stones River battlefield. Instead, they wasted away guarding a tunnel that Morgan simply bypassed for softer targets that produced the same result. The easy destruction of the Bacon Creek and Nolin bridges at Elizabethtown and Muldraugh's Hill shut down the railroad for a month. Rosecrans even naively hoped that Reynolds's division could help bag Morgan's men. So much for the idea that infantry could stop cavalry.[39]

The raid produced yet one more effect. As early as December 9, and continuing for many days, reports arrived that Kirby Smith's "army" was moving on Lebanon, Tennessee, twenty-six miles north of Murfreesboro, to support Morgan. Continued reports of what amounted to a phantom army clouded strategic thought at army headquarters. For the first time, Rosecrans began to write of an offensive on Murfreesboro—not to attack Bragg, but to cut off Smith's corps. As late as December 24, Rosecrans placed Smith near Gainesboro, Tennessee, on the Cumberland River. Not until 8:45 that night did confirmation arrive that one of Smith's divisions had in fact gone to Mississippi, not Kentucky.[40]

A DISMAL CHRISTMAS

On Christmas Eve, the 1st Louisiana and 2nd Kentucky sponsored an officer's ball at the Rutherford County Courthouse. Decorations included four *B*s made of evergreen—two for Bragg and Beauregard from Louisiana and two for Breckinridge and Simon Buckner from Kentucky. Upside-down U.S. flags hung conspicuously—trophies from Morgan's Hartsville Raid. Those in attendance included Bragg, Polk, Cheatham, Breckinridge, and Wheeler. At midnight, according to a correspondent, "the band struck up a grand march, and the company repaired to the supper room, where a magnificent 'spread' awaited them. There was no sparkling champagne, but the delicious egg nogg [*sic*] made up for it." A false report of a potential Federal advance abruptly ended the party.[41]

Christmas Day proved dismal in the Rebel camps; many imbibed to dull the senses. A member of the 13th Tennessee remarked that "Captains, Lieutenants, and Privates was drunk and very troublesome." Captain Tom Spence, in the camp of the 2nd Arkansas Mounted Rifles at Readyville, wrote with disgust of the drunken officers in his regiment: "I assure you we have a very poor set of Field Officers. To tell the truth, we have no commanders." Reuben Searcy, of the 34th Alabama, remarked to his mother, "The only thing that impressed me with the fact that it was Christmas was that we did not have to drill." Hardee spent the day with his visiting thirteen-year-old son, a student in a military academy in Marietta, Georgia. The boy would have only two more Christmases to enjoy; in 1865, in the waning days of the war, he would be killed.[42]

The misery extended to the Union camps. A Buckeye, G. Allen Vaughn of the 49th Ohio, took time to write his wife: "I almost forgot this was Christmas. It was the loneliest Christmas I ever seen. I wish I had something to send you for a Christmas gift, but I have nothing to send." A soldier of the 36th Illinois remarked: "This is Christmas Day and Santa Clause has not come, unless he visited the little ones at home. Would give a great deal to be at home today." To most the day provided nothing more than regular camp duties.[43]

Whether or not Rosecrans's heart was in a winter campaign will never be known. He remained under intense pressure from Washington, and he knew that time was growing short. Additionally, with adequate stockpiles and a reduced Confederate Army, he no longer had any reason *not* to move. The Rebels had gone into winter quarters and clearly did not anticipate an offensive. On the late afternoon of December 24, Rosecrans determined to advance the next day. The order had to be countermanded, however, due to McCook's corps, which could not march at noon as planned. The army commander moved the schedule back a day.

The conference that occurred on Christmas night, and made famous by Bickham's detailed description, was perhaps over-dramatized, as the decision to move had been made twenty-four hours earlier. According to the reporter, Rosecrans engaged in deep and animated conversation in a mumbled tone. Others in the room, including McCook, Crittenden, Stanley, Johnson, Negley, and Sheridan, chatted more openly. Garasche busily wrote orders, hampered by his nearsightedness. Staff officers tiptoed about. Stanley's saber rattled as he paced. Suddenly the army commander slammed his mug on Garesche's desk and boldly announced: "We move tomorrow, gentlemen! We shall begin to skirmish, probably as soon as we pass their outposts. Press them hard. Drive them out of their nests! Make them fight or run. Strike hard and fast! Give them no rest! Fight them! Fight, I say!" Thomas gave an approving grin.

The order of march belied the strategy. McCook's corps would proceed down the Nolensville Pike twenty-eight miles to Triune, where scouts had placed the majority of Hardee's corps. His movement would be screened by the reserve cavalry brigade, under the personal leadership of Stanley. Thomas's two divisions would march on McCook's right via the Franklin and Wilson pikes, threatening Hardee's left. Colonel Lewis Zahm's cavalry brigade would clear Franklin of any enemy and then protect McCook's right. At the intersection of the Wilson Pike and the Old Liberty Road, Thomas would veer east and continue to Nolensville. Crittenden's corps, screened by Minty's cavalry, would march directly down the Nashville Pike to La Vergne. If Bragg made a stand at Stewart's Creek, five miles south of La Vergne, Thomas would come in on his flank and McCook his rear. The 4th U.S. Cavalry would serve as scouts and escorts. Past midnight Thomas arose to excuse himself. As the others began to depart, Rosecrans gave them a parting admonition: "Fight them! Spread out your skirmishers far and wide! Keep pushing ahead! Expose their nests! Fight! Keep fighting! They will not stand it. Good night."[44]

In the camp of August Willich's brigade in Richard Johnson's division, the officers assembled to enjoy some Christmas libations. Someone spotted Willich approaching and said, "Oh, by all that's blessed, here comes the colonel. For the Lord's sake act decent, or he'll think he is in an institute for the reformation of the brainless." Came the reply: "Well, we are doing the best we can. The punch is nearly out; of the raw material we have plenty." The officers began to retire, but upon Willich's arrival he admonished them: "Sit still, gentlemen. I know what it is, and you shall know to. We march upon the enemy at daylight." The officers talked briefly, drank more punch, shook hands, and departed. The army would soon be on the march.[45]

3

ARMIES ON THE MOVE

Chilled winds and ominously dark clouds ushered in Friday, December 26. At 4:30 a.m. a dispatch clicked over the wire at Right Wing headquarters at St. John's Church on Mill Creek, five miles from Nashville. McCook was ordered to proceed with his corps to Nolensville, with Sheridan's and Johnson's divisions marching south down the main Nolensville highway. Davis's division would veer south down the Edmonson Pike, which ran about seven miles, where it connected with the Old Liberty Road at Prim's Blacksmith Shop. There Davis would march east for the final six miles into Nolensville. Despite the early hour, something had already gone wrong. Stanley's reserve cavalry brigade, ordered to screen the movement, trailed four hours in the rear. By the time the troopers arrived, the baggage wagons headed back to Nashville had already choked the road. Rather than delay the schedule, Davis used his mounted infantry escort, Company B, 36th Illinois, as his screen. Further complicating matters, Sheridan's division took up the line of march first, leaving Davis no choice but to wait until he cleared the road. The matter self-corrected when a black guide led Sheridan's division off the pike to go around a creek and got lost. By the time Sheridan's troops re-entered the road, Davis's division had taken its proper lead.[1]

A heavy mist appeared as the men began stirring, but by 6:00, as McCook's corps snaked south, the skies unleashed a torrent. "Fairly poured. Worst mud I ever walked in" as a sergeant in the 74th Illinois put it. Webb Baker, in Davis's division, wrote his mother that the troops had to carry their shelter tent, three day's rations, and a hundred rounds, "a pretty good load when the roads are good, & a big one when the rain is pouring down & the mud half knee deep." The corps nonetheless maintained a respectable two miles per hour. Some men, believing they would be back the next day, refused to carry their tents, but it did not take long before even the most skeptical could see that a general movement had commenced.[2]

It is not clear if the plan to send Davis's division on a different road was meant to keep congestion down, or to catch the Rebels napping by approaching Nolensville from the west while the main column made a stir from the north. If the latter, it didn't work. Not two miles outside camp, Davis's escort brushed with enemy pickets and sporadic skirmishing continued to within a mile of town. The rain broke at noon and at 2:00 Sidney Post's brigade, in the van, approached to within a mile of Nolensville. The brigade would have been there sooner but for the wretched, near-impassable condition of the Old Liberty Road. Intelligence from scouts and local citizens indicated that John Wharton's cavalry brigade and a battery held the town. On paper Wharton had 2,000 men, but a 400-man regiment and a battalion covered Franklin and, with pickets fanned out on various roads, he probably counted no more than a thousand. As for the town, founded in 1797 by William Nolen, a Federal described it as "a miserable poor village of perhaps 3 dozen one[-]storied frame Shanties, all unpainted and most of them in a tumble down condition; no gardens or fruit trees, or shrubbery around the buildings; a regular city for the 'poor white trash.'" Wharton had his headquarters at the Page Plantation, south of town.[3]

Davis deployed to the left of the road, with Oscar F. Pinney's 5th Wisconsin Battery to his right, on a hill commanding the village from the southwest. Wharton's artillery got off a few rounds, but fell silent when Pinney's six guns began shelling the town. As the 59th Illinois spread out on a skirmish line ("we had quite a little skirmish," Alexander L. Pippen admitted), enemy cavalry could be seen galloping southwest of the town and dismounting on Post's right, apparently with a view of attacking his rear. The 22nd Indiana and a section of Pinney's battery moved to the right to secure the flank. Davis brought up his Second Brigade, under Colonel William P. Carlin, placed it on Post's right, and then deployed the Third Brigade, under Colonel William E. Woodruff, on the extreme right to guard against a wide flanking swing. The Rebels slowly withdrew. The 59th Illinois swept the village, with the Confederate rear guard taking potshots from houses. The enemy attempted to unlimber their battery on a hill a half-mile from the village, but the rapid approach of the 101st Ohio, a raw outfit, caused them to have second thoughts.[4]

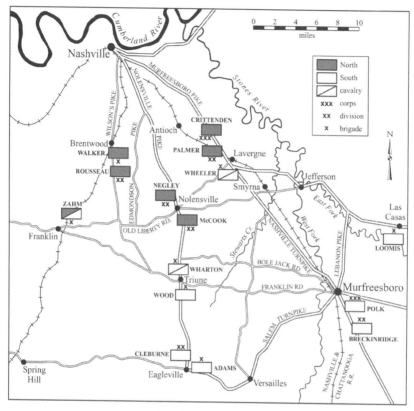

Situation, December 26

By 3:00 the town had been cleared. With Sheridan's division and a brigade from Negley's division of Thomas's corps moving up in support, Davis determined to push ahead. A range of hills stretched about two miles south of Nolensville, and there the southerners took up their next position. The Nolensville-Triune Road passed through Knob Creek Gap, a three-hundred-yard-wide defile, flanked on either side by a hill. Davis deployed at 4:00, Post's brigade on the left astride the road, Carlin in the center, and Woodruff on the right. Advancing independently of one another, the brigades soon came under artillery fire, Carlin incurring several casualties nearly a mile out. Pinney unlimbered on a hill to the left of the pike, Captain William A. Hotchkiss's 2nd Minnesota Battery in the road, where his guns opened a counter-fire.[5]

Post easily cleared the heights to the left, and Woodruff drove the enemy skirmishers on the right. In the center, however, Carlin advanced through an open field so muddy that "each man seemed to lift on his shoes a square foot of mud three inches deep at every step." As the troops scaled a fence, artillery projectiles sent splinters flying in every direction. Carlin ordered a charge but, according to a Buckeye, it was "not a beautiful one, the mud was too deep." The 15th Wisconsin, 21st Illinois, and 101st Ohio crested the ridge through the cedars, chasing off Wharton's men and capturing a 6-pounder marked "Shiloh," indicating that it had been previously captured from the Federals. Colonel John W. S. Alexander of the 21st Illinois and Colonel Hans Heg of the 15th Wisconsin gallantly rode to the summit of the ridge in advance of their regiments.[6]

Sheridan's division moved south of Mill Creek at 6:00 a.m., followed a half-hour later by Johnson's division. They brushed aside Wharton's pickets and advanced uneventfully along the main Nolensville highway, with Joshua Sill's brigade covering the left flank on a parallel road via Patterson's Mill. The column arrived at Nolensville about 4:00, just as Davis launched his attack to the south. With little daylight remaining, the corps bivouacked for the evening. The Right Wing sustained seventy-two killed and wounded throughout the day.[7]

Later that evening, accompanied by his staff and escort, Rosecrans arrived. The general had made a dangerous night ride over back roads, having to stop at several farmhouses to ask directions. Once at McCook's headquarters, the two generals met in a small covered road master's wagon, where they squatted on the floor, with a candle stuck in a bayonet offering light; there they discussed the next day's operations. Scouts placed Hardee's corps seven miles ahead at Triune. McCook was directed to advance at daylight and "push the enemy hard." Rosecrans departed at 11:00, the corps commander shaking his hand and saying: "Good night general. With the blessings of God, General, I will whip my friend Hardee tomorrow!" It soon began to rain; for the first time the men pitched their shelter tents. "We found them rain-proof and comfortable," noted a bluecoat.[8]

In what would prove an uneventful day, Thomas's corps marched down the Franklin Pike to Brentwood. His screen, Zahm's brigade, had gotten off to a late start and had to fall in the rear of the infantry-congested column. Thomas planned to camp on Wilson's Pike, but Negley's division, in response to Davis's request to move up in support, turned east at Owen's Store and hurried on the Nolensville. Negley would be taking the same wretched road over which Davis's men had previously passed, and the churned-up, muddy lane now had the "consistency of cream or a very thick paste." On more than one occasion, Negley dismounted and assisted in extraditing wagons. Battery G, 1st Ohio Light Artillery, used up every one of its spare wheels. By the time the division arrived, Nolensville had been secured. Rousseau's division camped at Owen's Store, and Moses B. Walker's unattached brigade pitched tents at Brentwood.[9]

Zahm's 950 troopers, traveling with only one wagon per regiment, got caught in the tangle of Thomas's wagons south of Brentwood. After a futile attempt to find the corps commander, the colonel continued southwest to Franklin, with orders to clean the town of an estimated 700 enemy cavalry. About two-and-a-half miles north of town, the 3rd Ohio Cavalry, spearheading the brigade, clashed with enemy skirmishers—the rear guard of the 4th Tennessee Cavalry and Davis's Tennessee Cavalry Battalion of Wharton's brigade. At 4:00 the Ohioans arrived at the Harpeth River. Zahm crossed over, ordered a charge, and within minutes had secured the town, along with ten prisoners. After chasing the enemy for two miles, the Bavarian re-crossed the river and galloped cross-country toward Nolensville, arriving at 10:00.[10]

Crittenden's Left Wing aroused early, and all excess wagons filed to the rear. The pared-down train included only a forage wagon, hospital wagon, and two ambulances per regiment. The column would move down the Nashville Pike to La Vergne ("a miserable little village" of thirty or so dwellings), with Robert Minty's cavalry brigade screening the movement, followed by Palmer's, Wood's, and Van Cleve's divisions. The men began giving articles of value to the remaining sick, if they "should happen not to get back." At the State Lunatic Asylum, not four miles from camp, a steady rain and strong west wind settled in, the same weather front that had mired the Right and Center wings. A problem developed when Palmer, interpreting his orders to begin the march at 8:00 a.m., promptly moved out, thus getting ahead of Wood, who read to same order to be "ready to move" at 8:00. It would be Saturday before Wood would regain his rightful place in line. Not an hour into the march, the men received orders to halt and simply squat in the mud; they could "only stand and take it," remembered a chagrinned Ohio corporal. The corps commander had previously estimated that he could arrive at the village in a few hours; today the Confederates would deny him altogether.[11]

Around noon, at the eleven-mile marker, Minty brushed with Wheeler's advanced outpost. A brief skirmish ensued, in which the Rebels withdrew with a loss of five prisoners. Minty continued to press hard, with the 3rd Kentucky Cavalry left of the pike, the 7th Pennsylvania Cavalry on the right, and the 4th Michigan Cavalry in reserve. About two miles from La Vergne, the two 3-inch rifles of Lieutenant Nathaniel M. Newell's Battery D, 1st Ohio Light Artillery, managed to scatter the graycoats after only four rounds. The blue troopers surged ahead to Hurricane Creek, where they uncovered the enemy's main force.[12]

• • • •

Wheeler dashed to the front and initially witnessed only Minty's cavalry. Uncertain of Federal intentions, he called up his brigade at Stewart's Creek, nearly an hour's ride from La Vergne. Trailing it would be the infantry support, Brigadier General George Maney's Tennessee brigade. It soon became apparent that the Yankees were on no mere foraging expedition. Wheeler dismounted his men and advanced as skirmishers, covering the pike and the crossings of Hurricane Creek, two miles northwest of La Vergne. The forces collided at a distance of 150 yards—"we had as hot a little brush as one would want on a December day," Captain Knox Miller of the 8th Confederate Cavalry described. The two sides traded blows for nearly an hour, "each man to his tree."[13]

In a spirited half-hour duel, Wiggins's Arkansas Battery exchanged fire with Newell's section. "We commenced shelling them, expecting to see them skeedaddle, but they astonished us not a little," explained a trooper in the 7th Pennsylvania Cavalry, when a shell suddenly came shrieking over their head, and "demolished the chimney of a house close by." During the exchange, Robert H. Crittenden, the civilian brother of the Left Wing commander, had a shell pass within a yard of him as he ventured too close for a better view. About 4:00 Brigadier General Charles Cruft's brigade of Palmer's division moved up in support, thus adding the six guns of Battery B, 1st Ohio Light Artillery. Under cover of the woods, the 1st Kentucky and 31st Indiana formed for an attack on the enemy right, while the 9th Indiana and 6th Kentucky demonstrated upstream on their left. Fixing bayonets, the Indiana and Kentucky troops "rushed forward with a shout," toward a small frame church, occupying the west bank of Hurricane Creek, with the loss of eight killed and wounded. Crittenden called off the advance at 4:30, a mile short of La Vergne. He counted eighteen killed and wounded in the day's fray, and had captured a dozen prisoners. To Palmer's disgust, Wood eyed an elevated space of land with a nice house on the left side of the pike and, ignoring that his sector was to the right of the road, claimed it as his headquarters. This forced Palmer's division down Stewart's Creek to some rocky lowland.[14]

That night Captain Miller gazed at the Union camps in the darkness to see "the whole horizon lit up with his innumerable campfires. It took no ghost to tell us that Rosecranz had begun his long expected advance from Nashville and what confirmed it, we could distinctly hear cannonading all day to our left on the Nolensville pike, showing that he was advancing with a heavy column on each road." Rain fell the greater portion of the night, dousing all camp fires.[15]

· · · ·

Back at army headquarters in Murfreesboro, Bragg received his first dispatch from Wheeler at 2:00. The cavalry leader had telegraph communication from Stewart's Creek to Murfreesboro, and an old dirt road from Nolensville directly to Stewart's Creek permitted courier dispatches from Wharton. Wheeler's 2:00 dispatch to the army chief of staff read:

Col.

The enemy are advancing in our front and we are engaging them. They are also advancing on the Nolensville Pike and we are engaging [them] very warmly. There is very heavy firing on the Nolensville Pike.

Very Respectfully,
Jos. Wheeler
Brig. Gen. & Chief of Cav.

Later that afternoon, "Allen," the Stewart's Creek operator, sent his own message. "I think enemy are in strong force and I think on this side of La Vergne as I can hear small arms here. The enemy attacked our pickets about eleven o'clock." He revealed that the telegraph line had been "cut by some of our soldiers at this place," but that he had made the appropriate repairs. Allen concluded: "Cannonading being heard. . . . Cannonading is heaviest on the left."

A belated 9:00 p.m. dispatch from Wheeler gave an update:

Col.

Since my last [dispatch] two prisoners have been brought in who state that Genl. Rosecrans entire army moved out today and it was understood among them to be a general movement. They have been sending up rockets and sounding their bugles. In our engagement today we had a few men killed and about twenty wounded.

In a postscript he added: "They [Federals] were ordered to have three days cooked rations in haversack & rations were put in the wagons." That evening Colonel Brent jotted in his diary: "Wheeler thinks a forward movement probable."[16]

Bragg would later write in his after-action report: "Before night on that day [26th] the object of the movement was developed." If by "the object of the movement" he meant a general advance by the enemy, his assertion was true. In terms of specific Federal intentions, however, Bragg could not have known whether both Federal columns were of equal strength, or whether the column on the Nashville Pike was a feint to distract and/or pin down Polk's corps, while the main enemy force approached from the west or made a wide flanking movement farther south toward Shelbyville.[17]

Bragg had dispersed his infantry over a thirty-six-mile front. McCown's division held the right at Readyville, twelve miles east of Murfreesboro on the McMinnville Road. Polk's corps and Breckinridge's division of Hardee's corps occupied the center at Murfreesboro, with Maney's brigade advanced to Stewart's Creek as Wheeler's support. The vulnerable left flank, along the Nashville-Shelbyville Pike, proved problematic. Pat Cleburne's reinforced division held that sector at College Grove, with S. A. M. Wood's brigade at Triune, four miles north of College Grove, in support of Wharton. An incursion down the Shelbyville Pike meant that the enemy could turn west either at Triune (sixteen miles from Murfreesboro), or Eagleville (twenty-four miles from Murfreesboro on the Salem Pike). The Federals could also take the fifteen-mile road from Eagleville to Christiana, which would place Rosecrans astride the Nashville & Chattanooga Railroad, Bragg's main line of communication. If the Yankees continued south down the Shelbyville Pike, they could cross the Duck River and swing east, leaving Bragg stranded on the north bank. The 39th North Carolina, the only regiment that Kirby Smith claimed he could spare, held the vital railroad bridge, but it would join the army on the night of the first day's battle, leaving the bridge dangerously unprotected. The army commander was discovering the inherent weakness of Murfreesboro as a point of defense—multiple approaches (at least five of them) making the enemy approach anybody's guess.[18]

That night Bragg held a council of war. Unable to develop the enemy's intentions, he hesitated to concentrate at Murfreesboro, yet *something* had to be done. At 9:00 he issued orders for Polk's corps to cook three day's rations and be prepared to move at a moment's notice. Since all reports indicated that the Federal threat remained west of Stones River, at midnight Bragg ordered McCown's division from Readyville to Murfreesboro. Aroused at 1:00 a.m., the troops trudged throughout the night in a cold rain. Bragg needed time and for that he turned to his cavalry commander. "How long can you hold them on the [Nashville] road?" he asked Wheeler. "About four days, general," came the reply (the Alabamian would later claim that he said "two or three days"), prompting Hardee to blurt out, "They will run right over you!" Regardless of the exact words, Wheeler (aided by the wretched weather) would deliver.[19]

Bragg remained worried about his vulnerable left flank. If he prematurely ordered Cleburne's division to Murfreesboro, he could face a turning movement to the south. If he closed up on the center too slowly, however, the Federals could get between Eagleville and Murfreesboro via the Bole Jack Road, isolating Cleburne. Bragg needed additional information. The task fell to Major W. D. Pickett of Hardee's staff. About 9:00, the major, accompanied by Colonel Tom Harrison of the 8th Texas Cavalry, detoured a mile to the left of the Federal pickets and emerged onto a wooded ridge overlooking the Triune Creek valley. Before them, not 150 yards distant, they glanced upon a sweeping panoramic view of the campfires of an entire division, with other fires beyond. Pickett sent Hardee a dispatch that the concentration on Murfreesboro "should not be long delayed."

Hardee could wait no longer. If he delayed till daylight, he might be struck in flank as he was strung out along the road. During the early morning hours of December 27 he ordered Cleburne's division to Murfreesboro, along the Salem Pike north of Versailles, a "town of four houses." "We left College Grove in the rain," an Alabama gunner recalled, but despite the wretched road and weather, the men "plodded on without a word." The division marched throughout the day, camping within a mile of Stones River. Yet Hardee remained uncertain. He rode to Triune and positioned himself with

Wood's most advanced outpost. At 4:00 a.m. he sent a message to Bragg: "I feel confident that the enemy is moving in this direction in heavy force with a view certainly of driving me from my position, perhaps of marching on Shelbyville." Even if the Federal objective was Shelbyville, Cleburne's division would have been insufficient to contest McCook's entire corps.[20]

• • • •

Hardee was mistaken; Rosecrans had his eye on Murfreesboro, not Shelbyville. Orders issued at 9:20 directed that the Right Wing push south at daylight. If Hardee gave battle and was defeated, the Confederates would retreat either by way of Shelbyville or Murfreesboro. If the first, McCook would pursue with one division, sending the other two divisions to Murfreesboro. If the last, he would follow with his entire corps. If Hardee retreated to Shelbyville without giving battle, McCook would trail him with two divisions, sending the third to Murfreesboro.[21]

Crittenden would continue to press Wheeler at La Vergne. If a battle engaged at Triune, Thomas would support McCook at Nolensville. Otherwise, he would turn Wheeler's position by marching Negley's division from Nolansville west to Stewartsboro, nearly six miles in the rear of La Vergne and attempt to save the Stewart's Creek Bridge. Rousseau's division would advance to Nolensville, and Walker's brigade to the Wilson's Pike. Rosecrans should have rested at McCook's headquarters that night, but characteristically he chose a brutal night ride (again getting lost) back to Hamilton's Church, arriving at 1:00 a.m.[22]

NOT MUCH PROGRESS TODAY

Awakening to a heavy fog on Saturday, December 27, Rosecrans mumbled: "Not much progress today, I fear." It had not yet begun to rain, so staff officers spread maps on a table in a grove. Bragg might possibly make a stand at Stewart's Creek, but Rosecrans suspected that the Confederates would not offer serious opposition north of Duck River, forcing him to stretch his line of communications.[23]

Rain and a thick fog restricted visibility on the Right Wing to 150 yards; by mid-morning it would be down to fifty yards. Stanley's brigade, comprised of the 15th Pennsylvania Cavalry (an outfit recently riddled with mutinies), the 1st Middle Tennessee Cavalry and 1st East Tennessee Cavalry (both under-strength and operating as a single unit), and the 3rd Battalion, 3rd Indiana Cavalry (assigned to Johnson's division but commandeered by the cavalry) took the lead. A mile north of the intersection of the Shelbyville Pike and the Bole Jack Road, the advance encountered Wharton's horsemen. Stanley rode up to Major Robert Klein, commanding the Indiana battalion, and commented that he "understood the Third knew how to take these rebels." Klein sent Company G ahead of the column, which soon collided with the enemy in a sharp firefight, until the balance of Stanley's brigade came up, driving the Rebels south.[24]

The fog lifted at 1:00 p.m., and the march resumed. Outside of Triune the Federals occupied a ridge overlooking the town. A Rebel battery, supported by dismounted cavalry, blasted away from a ridge three-fourths of a mile from the pike behind Nelson's Creek. Warren P. Edgarton's Battery E, 1st Ohio Light Artillery, unlimbered, two guns on the pike and the other four on a hill to the left. Under cover of Edgarton's guns, and in the midst of a driving rain, the 29th Indiana and 34th Illinois advanced so close to the enemy guns that only an ill-timed bugle call ordering a halt (due to sleet) prevented their capture. By 3:00 it was evident that the Confederates were simply fighting a delaying action, and McCook sent a dispatch to army headquarters to that effect. Prisoners indicated that Hardee had escaped under cover of the fog, but they told conflicting stories as whether to Murfreesboro or Shelbyville.[25]

Wharton's men retired south of Triune, destroying the bridge over Nelson's Creek. Johnson's infantry entered the village at 4:00, having made eight miles in nine hours. The troops proceeded to ransack the town and stuff their knapsacks. Several companies of Stanley's cavalry crossed Nelson's Creek to the west and got in the rear of the town, only to encounter more Confederates behind a stone wall near the Franklin Road—not cavalry but veteran infantry of the 16th Alabama of Wood's brigade, supported by Darden's Mississippi Battery. The Yankee troopers attempted an attack across an open field, but a few well-placed blasts of Darden's guns sent them "fleeing in confusion." That night Wood withdrew three miles north of Eagleville. During the night he received orders to rejoin the division at Murfreesboro the next day.[26]

McCook's corps camped for the night, Johnson's division a mile south of Triune, Sheridan's division in the town, and Davis's division at Bole Jack

Pass. For the men, the day had been "the most disagreeable march we have seen in the service of Uncle Sam," grumbled David Shotts in the 18th Ohio. Meanwhile, Zahm's brigade, at Nolensville, scouted south to Triune and west toward Petersburg. A battalion of the 3rd Ohio Cavalry went back to Franklin to see if it had been re-occupied. It had, and in strength, causing the Buckeyes to retire.[27]

Thomas, his wagon trains bogged down, made slow headway. Negley did not start his march to Stewartsboro until 10:00. In order to lighten the load, an order directed that all excess baggage be dumped—tents, clothing, mess chests. He would not arrive at the town until 6:00—so much for trapping Wheeler. Rousseau's division, which did not begin the march until 4:00, tramped wearily into Nolensville at 11:00. Walker's brigade remained on the Wilson's Pike.[28]

The same fog that delayed McCook held up Crittenden's advance until 10:00. "It rained very hard last night," Lieutenant Colonel Thomas C. Honnell of Van Cleve's division observed. "Poured down at times in torrents and the men were drenched with the rain. It is a very dreary, damp day." About an hour later, Brigadier General Milo Hascall advanced a line of skirmishers and formed his brigade of Wood's division in two lines, with a section of artillery in between. As his infantry swept over an open field toward La Vergne, they came under fire from snipers in the town. The troops laid down in the mud, while the artillery shelled the dwellings. When the barrage ceased, the infantry fixed bayonets and charged, easily driving the enemy. As the bluecoats continued their advance, a heavy rain set in, making the plowed fields "ankle deep in mud." Wheeler again employed his hit-and-run tactics of the day before. At 2:00 he confidently informed Bragg that he did not think that Rosecrans would arrive at Murfreesboro until late on the twenty-eighth or the morning of the twenty-ninth.[29]

Despite Rosecrans's instructions to Crittenden to "Tell Wood to drive the enemy vigorously and give them no time to breathe," Hascall's brigade did not arrive at Stewart's Creek until 5:00. Confederate dismounted cavalry held the north bank, with a battery firing from a hill behind the creek. A section of the 8th Indiana Battery responded. Even as their own men continued skirmishing on the north bank, the Confederates piled rails on the arched wooden bridge and attempted to set it ablaze. Some of the Rebels crossed at a ford a quarter-of-a-mile above the bridge, but twenty-four got separated and were captured. The 3rd Kentucky (U.S.) rushed the damaged Nashville Pike Bridge and saved it, Confederate reports to the contrary.[30]

Colonel Charles Harker's brigade, also of Wood's division, veered east onto the Jefferson Pike in an attempt to save the upriver bridge near Smyrna. Two of Van Cleve's brigades at the Nashville Pike–Jefferson Pike intersection offered support. Preceding William B. Hazen would be a battalion of the 4th Michigan Cavalry under Captain James Mix, who had orders to "put spurs to his troops, and not slack rein until the bridge was crossed." About two-and-a-half miles from Stewart's Creek, Mix's horsemen clashed with the 51st Alabama Cavalry. The gray troopers bolted to the rear, and the race was on. On the front porch of a house near the bridge, three Confederate officers gave a hurried farewell to a young lady before dashing off. Writing to his parents, Captain Henry Potter of the 4th Michigan Cavalry noted: "There was about 150 of us[.] we charged upon 200 of them, drove them about 2 miles[,] shot 5 of their men, a no. of horses and took 8 prisoners." Mix secured the bridge and held it till Hazen's infantry arrived. The enemy on the south bank "stayed for only a half dozen shells, when it also skedaddled," gloated an officer.[31]

By sunset, Thomas and Crittenden had a three-and-a-half mile line fronting Stewart's Creek, with Hazen's brigade on the left at the Jefferson Pike crossing, Wood's division and two brigades of Palmer's division in the center, on either side on the Nashville Pike crossing, and Negley's division on the right, where it finally arrived at Stewartsboro. Rousseau's division supported the line a couple of miles to the rear.[32]

· · · ·

That night, in the midst of a drenching rain, three of Cleburne's brigades slogged wearily along the miserable Salem Turnpike, southwest of Murfreesboro, the troops encamping a mile from Stones River. Wood's brigade, which served as the rear guard, did not arrive until the next morning, "with men and horses very much fatigued by the march and exposure." Colonel Brent scribbled in his diary that Saturday night: "The day dark & stormy. The enemy still pressing forward. Wheeler has fallen back to Stewart's Creek 10 miles from this place [Murfreesboro]. Casualties not yet reported. The enemy's intention not fully developed. If he [Rosecrans] advances Gen.

Bragg will give him battle a short distance from here. Everyone is anxious."
John Magee, a Mississippi artilleryman, understood matters only from the
limited vantage point of the ranks, but even he saw "the whole Army stirring. . . . Everything in a state of excitement; everybody expects a battle."[33]

IT WOULD MAKE FOR A PICTURE

At 7:30 a.m. on Sunday, December 28, Bragg met with his corps, division,
and brigade commanders at the Nashville Pike crossing of Stones River
to reconnoiter the ground. The dense fog obscured vision on this cold,
raw morning, with icicles hanging from the branches of trees, pools of
water coated with ice, and the roads frozen and slippery. Polk arrived a
half-hour late, delaying the meeting. As the officers waited, an occasional
shot reverberated in the distance, followed by some of Wheeler's wounded
troopers coming in. Interspersed with the wounded came a line of civilians, with carts piled to immense heights, and farmers and blacks driving
in horses, cows, and sheep. "I was much interested in all I saw during this
half-hour, and could not help thinking what a subject it would make for
a picture," Colonel Arthur M. Manigault remembered. "The variety of the
expressions of the different groups of men, women, and animals, and all
the other features of the scene, would indicate beyond the possibility of
doubt, 'A Battle Imminent.'"[34]

The river, or specifically the west branch of the river, represented the
chief terrain feature of the countryside. It flowed through low banks of
limestone north and then northwest about two miles west of Murfreesboro. Discovered by Uriah Stone in 1766, it would forever bear his name.
Though it was typically ankle deep and passable everywhere, recent rains
had swollen the water to waist deep at the fords. During a torrential rain,
the river could become an impassable torrent. About two miles northeast
of Murfreesboro, the Nashville Pike intersected with the Nashville & Chattanooga Railroad. The pike, macadamized during the 1830s, consisted of a
thirty-foot roadbed with ditches on either side. The railroad began service
from Nashville to Murfreesboro in 1851, but the final leg into Chattanooga
was not completed until 1854. Dense cedar brakes and limestone outcrop-
pings fringed the open fields beyond town.[35]

Bragg deployed Polk's corps west of the river, and Hardee's east of it.
Withers's division came on line between the Nashville and Franklin pikes,

a front of nearly one-and-three-fourths miles. Brigadier General James R. Chalmers's Mississippi brigade occupied Withers's right, his right resting on the Nashville Pike. The line crossed an open cornfield, its left extending up a slope. Given his exposed position, Chalmers put his men to work on temporary breastworks. Eighty yards separated Chalmers's left and Patton Anderson's right. The 27th Mississippi and Barret's Missouri Battery, the last on a hill north of the Wilkinson Pike between Chalmers and Patton Anderson, threw up temporary breastworks. The balance of the brigade extended 300 yards into a dense cedar thicket, where the men piled stones for protection. Next in line came Manigault's brigade, posted on the edge of a cedar wood and fronting a four-hundred-yard-wide cottonfield, which rose gently toward a wooded ridge at least twenty feet higher than the South Carolinian's position. Manigault's right formed a weak right angle salient toward the enemy. "I do not believe that either Generals Bragg, Polk, or Withers "knows to this day [1866] how excessively sharp an angle existed in the line of battle at this point," the colonel recalled, indicating that no inspection was made. Colonel J. Q. Loomis's Alabama brigade arrived from outpost duty and deployed on Manigault's right, extending the division line to the Franklin Pike, where Robertson's Alabama Battery unlimbered at the Widow Smith House. Polk's other division, Cheatham's, remained in Murfreesboro for the time being.[36]

Bragg feared that, if he aligned totally on the west bank of the river, Rosecrans could approach Murfreesboro from the north via the Lebanon Pike. He therefore deployed Hardee's corps east of Stones River, forming an obtuse angle with Polk's corps, stretching from the river to the Lebanon Pike. Bragg's seeming obsession with the Lebanon Pike has been misunderstood. A good, twenty-six-mile road connected Murfreesboro and Lebanon. Bragg knew that Rosecrans maintained a sizable force (two divisions of Thomas's corps) at Gallatin, fifteen miles northwest of Lebanon via the Cole's Ferry Road. Rosecrans could distract Bragg northeast of Murfreesboro while the Gallatin column marched due south from Lebanon, gaining the Confederate rear. John Pegram's brigade, whittled down to two regiments due to detachments, had been posted north of Fall Creek at Baird's Mill, seven miles south of Lebanon, patrolling the pike.[37]

By mid-morning Hardee's troops struck their tents and tramped through the mud to their positions. As a portion of Hardee's corps marched through the town with colors flying and music playing, the troops "displayed the most undaunting and cheering spirit," observed a Mobile correspondent. "There was evident alarm felt among many of the inhabitants, who prepared to leave the town in case of disaster, while others moved out to the country. No church bells tolled for morning services, the dread expectation of the hourly expected conflict having wholly engrossed other thoughts." Tents had been sent to the rear, and the abandoned camps, with only chimneys remaining, appeared to one soldier as though "a city had been destroyed on the spot."[38]

Breckinridge's division deployed a mile and a half from town facing north, between Stones River and the Lebanon Pike—not even the direction from which the enemy approached. Brigadier General Roger Hanson's Kentucky brigade, anchored on the river, held the division left. Colonel J. B. Palmer's brigade came on line to the right of Hanson, Brigadier General William Preston's brigade to the left of Palmer, and Daniel Adams's Louisiana brigade on the division right, its right on the Lebanon Pike. Upon its arrival from Bridgeport, Brigadier General John Jackson's under-strength independent brigade was assigned the high ground to the right of the pike near the toll gate, 400 yards in advance of Adams's line. Cleburne's division deployed parallel to Breckinridge, 600 yards in his rear.

Hardee personally inspected Breckinridge's position. Modern claims that the Kentuckian largely deployed in open fields is not true. The defensive line between the river and Skilling Creek followed an arching 1,400-yard wooded edge that ran east-west. The single exception was a 400-yard-wide open field on Preston's line, held only by Wright's Tennessee Battery and supported by the 20th Tennessee. More problematic was the 350-yard open-country gap between Preston's right and Adams's left, which remained unprotected. Other problems remained. In order to get the advantage of the wooded edge, Breckinridge drew his line 600 yards south of Wayne's Hill, the most prominent high ground on the east bank. Not until Monday did he marginally occupy it with a battery.[39]

Modern writers have too easily accepted the fact that Stones River forced Bragg to divide his army on both banks, yet other options existed. He could have deployed Breckinridge's division on the west bank, extending from Polk's right to McFadden's Hill. This deployment would also have given him possession of the highest elevation east of the river. Artillery posted on McFadden's Hill would have commanded the Nashville Pike and allowed Breckinridge to attack Crittenden's corps in flank as it as it advanced toward Murfreesboro.[40]

Since Cleburne, in support of Breckinridge, would subsequently be called to the left, such a hypothetical alignment would have left only Jackson's independent brigade, perhaps reinforced with one of Breckinridge's brigades, and Pegram's cavalry to guard the Lebanon Pike. Other troops were available, specifically Wheeler's brigade, but Bragg had bigger plans for the Alabamian—a raid behind the enemy lines. If the army commander genuinely believed that his 40,000 faced Rosecrans's 65,000, he should have retained Wheeler. With Jackson's brigade and one of Breckinridge's brigades, reinforced with Wheeler's and Pegram's cavalry, Bragg would have had about 2,000 infantry and 2,500 dismounted troopers watching the Lebanon Pike. Such a deployment would have freed Breckinridge's other three brigades to stretch the Confederate line on the west bank to McFadden's Ford and the all-important high ground.[41]

. . . .

Rosecrans began Sunday by attending mass. In deference to the Sabbath, he directed a day of rest. After the morning fog dissipated, the sun peaked through. Fraternization and exchange of newspapers even occurred with the enemy along Stewart's Creek. From the vantage point of the Confederates, Captain Miller recorded: "Papers were exchanged and compliments passed. I went down and exchanged papers with several of the Yankees, or rather Federal Kentuckians. They asked many questions about friends and acquaintances in our army and we parted at Sundown." Some Yankees in Palmer's division bantered with a Reb picket, dressed in a stovepipe hat and a white duster that reached to the round. "Does your mother know you're out?" they laughed. The vedette appeared to love it, but then showed his true intent as he ran from tree to tree taking pot shots. A friendly fire incident occurred when the troops of Colonel James P. Fyffe's brigade fired on a returning patrol of the 51st Ohio.[42]

As Bragg positioned his army for battle, Rosecrans continue to wonder if a battle would be fought at all. The Confederates had made no serious resistance at Stewart's Creek—a logical defensive position. Indeed, Hazen reported "no strong force this side of Murfreesboro." Contraband swore the Rebels were leaving Murfreesboro. Adding to the enigma, McCook lost sight of Hardee's corps. If Hardee retreated due south to Shelbyville, Bragg would surely abandon Murfreesboro and retire to a defensive line along the Duck River. Indeed, the lack of activity by Rosecrans this Sunday may not have been totally related to religious considerations, as much as to his desire "to hear more of Hardee's movements before moving on Murfreesboro with the left and center."[43]

The task of ascertaining Hardee's whereabouts fell to Willich's brigade, screened by the 3rd Battalion, 3rd Indiana Cavalry, and a detachment of the 15th Pennsylvania Cavalry. The column moved south of Triune at 7:00 a.m. Captain Horace Fisher ruthlessly rounded up a dozen local farmers as guides, assuring them that, if they led the Federals into a trap, they would all be shot and left on the roadside. At 11:00 the brigade arrived at Rigg's Crossroads, seven miles south of Triune. Prisoners (forty-one stragglers were rounded up) and the condition of the roads indicated that Hardee had veered onto a four-mile dirt road which lead into the Salem Pike and thus to Murfreesboro. Evidence indicated that six brigades had been at College Grove, but they had now totally vanished. At 1:30 McCook forwarded a Willich dispatch to army headquarters at La Vergne—"The enemy is no more here; all gone to Murfreesboro."[44]

At noon Thomas received orders to march Rousseau's division to Stewartsboro. Unfortunately, the order did not arrive until 4:00, and most of the division did not get off until after dark. The exhausted troops arrived at 11:00 that night. Rosecrans made his plans for the morning. At daylight Crittenden would move in force across Stewart's Creek. McCook would proceed to Murfreesboro via the Bole Jack Road, leaving a brigade (Baldwin's) at Triune to cover the rear. The Right Wing commander, nervous to leave his wagons at Triune, decided to take his train with him. The troops greeted the sun "with a cheer from one end of the line to the other." Fires quickly sprang up as the troops began hanging overcoats and blankets to dry out. The supposed five days' rations had already given out.[45]

I HAVE THE DEAD ON HIM

A light frost covered the ground on Monday morning, December 29. A little after 6:00 a.m. Cheatham's division filed into line. "We marched out on the RR towards Nashville and crossed Stones River on the RR Bridge (upon which plank had been laid for the purpose)," Tennessee Captain Alfred Fielder wrote. "We then filed left and marched up the meanderings of the River for a mile or two—and were marched back and forth for some time getting a suitable position and finally formed in line of battle in a clear thicket and were ordered to stack arms and rest in place at 10 O'clk. . . . [A]t this writing 101/2 [10:30] all is quiet and there fore this is one of the prettiest winter days I ever saw."[46]

Cheatham came into position 500–800 yards behind Withers's division, the over-stretched 1,700-yard line extending between the Wilkinson Pike and the Franklin Pike. Colonel A. J. Vaughn's brigade held the left in support of Loomis, Brigadier General George Maney's brigade formed in rear of Manigault, Brigadier General Alexander P. Stewart's brigade lined up behind Patton Anderson, but close enough to the river to be in supporting distance of Chalmers, and Brigadier General Daniel Donelson's brigade formed behind Chalmers, his left resting on a ridge 200 yards southeast of the Widow James House. Polk and Cheatham made a hurried inspection of the lines. The Bishop made a brief speech and then turned to Cheatham and said: "General, talk to them in your way." The Tennessean straightened his legs in his stirrups and shouted: "Men, give them hell!"[47]

Meanwhile, Cheatham received a small accession with the arrival of Colonel Sidney S. Stanton's 84th Tennessee. Comprised of about 276 men, the regiment had been organized only weeks earlier and had been kept at McMinnville. The troops arrived in Murfreesboro hardly equipped for battle—no blankets, no arms. Receiving muskets upon their arrival, Stanton relentless drilled his men throughout the day. The regiment went to Donelson's brigade. A mishap occurred when Wharton's brigade approached to take its rightful place on the left of Polk's corps. As it neared the dogleg of the Franklin Pike, near the Widow Smith House, Robertson's Alabama Battery, mistaking them for the enemy, opened fire, killing and wounding several troopers. Wharton dispatched an orderly (a German who spoke little English) to inform them of the error, but the skirmish line opened on him, riddling him with bullets. "It took an hour or so to recover from the confusion," admitted Lieutenant W. R. Friend of the 8th Texas Cavalry.[48]

• • • •

At 10:00 a.m. on this crisp and sunny day, Rosecrans moved his headquarters from La Vergne to the Bridge House at Stewartsboro, where he spent most of the day with Thomas. He immediately ordered the crossing of Stewart's Creek in force—Wood's division to the left of the Nashville Pike and Palmer's division to the right of the highway. Negley's division crossed at a ford two miles southeast of the turnpike bridge. Van Cleve's and Rousseu's divisions remained in support, the last at Stewartsboro. Shortly before 10:00, Lieutenant Charles C. Parson's eight-gun Battery H/M, 4th U.S. Artillery, unlimbered on a ridge overlooking the east bank and opened with a brief but intense barrage, easily dislodging Wheeler's dismounted troopers. The blue infantry waded the waist-deep water along a broad front, with Wood encountering the stiffest resistance. Wheeler conceded in a 1:30 dispatch that he was "falling back gradually" as the enemy advanced "very handsomely" in three columns.[49]

The Federals continued their drive toward Overall Creek (named after Robert Overall, an early settler), which crossed the Nashville Pike only five and a half miles northwest of Murfreesboro. The Hoosiers of the 57th Indiana quickly gained a beachhead. By 4:00 Wood's and Palmer's divisions closed to within three-fourths of a mile of Stones River, expecting to find Murfreesboro abandoned. On the east bank the enemy could clearly be seen "in full view." With Negley's division seven miles in the rear, Van Cleve behind him, and with the afternoon "well nigh spent," the two generals decided to deploy and await orders. Wood formed two lines west of the Nashville Pike, with George Wagner's brigade on the right, its right on the pike, Harker in the center, and Hascall on the left, his left on the river. Palmer deployed his two brigades (Hazen had not yet come up) to the right of the road, with Cruft's left connecting with Wagner, and William Grose to Cruft's right. Crittenden sent for orders, but was told only to open with artillery "if you see a good chance."[50]

An episode now occurred—either a misunderstanding or an overt coverup. Rosecrans claimed in his after-action report that at 3:00 he received a signal from Palmer stating that he was within sight of Murfreesboro and that "the enemy were running." Palmer had apparently mistaken the withdrawal of Wheeler. The army commander thus ordered Crittenden to occupy the town with one division. Palmer gave a very different account. He adamantly insisted that he never sent any dispatch. According to him, Rosecrans's order to Crittenden essentially read: "Stanley reports from Triune that the people saw that Bragg has abandoned Murfreesboro. You will therefore occupy the place with one division, and camp your others near them." In truth, the dispatch read: "Occupy Murfreesboro, if you can, with one division. Encamp main body of troops on this side as directed before."

Yet, if Rosecrans received Palmer's dispatch at 3:00, why did he not reply until 5:15? Also, how could Palmer claim that he was within sight of Murfreesboro at 3:00 when he did not cross Overall Creek till 4:00?[51]

Both Wood and Palmer protested the order, Palmer stating that "the information which purported to come through General Stanley was erroneous." Although Rosecrans had left some discretion in his words "if you can," Crittenden strictly obeyed and ordered his divisions to advance. Even as the infantry began forming, Wood and Stanley again rode up and protested. Wood even went so far as to suggest that the corps commander take personal responsibility for disobeying the order. In a 5:25 dispatch to Rosecrans, Crittenden explained their concern of advancing at dusk over an unknown ground against an enemy of unknown size. Furthermore, a citizen had advised that the crossing of Stones River would be difficult, even if unopposed. The corps commander also questioned the phrase "as previously ordered," as he had received no other dispatch. At 5:40 an increasingly nervous Crittenden, obviously not wishing to take responsibility for a potential disaster, notified army headquarters that he had suspended the movement for an hour.[52]

In a letter to his wife, a furious Palmer insisted that Stanley had been the source of the faulty intelligence and that Rosecrans had covered for a fellow Catholic and Regular. "You perhaps have seen the official reports of Rosecrans and Crittenden," he explained on March 5, 1863. "You will see that Old Rosy pretends that I sent him a message that the Rebels had evacuated Murfreesboro and makes the message an excuse for a foolish order which, if executed, would have sacrificed the whole left of the army. The truth is, I sent him no message whatever and, in his order, he states that he received the information from General Stanley. I have the dead on him. He selected me because he thought that as I was the only civilian, he might destroy me with impunity. He will find that a harder job than he imagines." In a subsequent letter dated March 23, Palmer continued his denunciations: "He [Rosecrans] knows his [Stones River] report is false so far as I am concerned and he knows my opinion of him, no doubt, as a man of truth and honor."[53]

While Crittenden deliberated the occupation of Murfreesboro, Harker, in response to the original order that had never been cancelled, moved his brigade out; a potential disaster was in the making. Unknown to him, Breckinridge's entire division lay ahead. Harker crossed his first wave of infantry, the 51st Indiana, 13th Michigan, and 73rd Indiana, in waist-deep water on either side of what today is Harker's Crossing, 250 yards northeast of Wayne's Hill. Rebel pickets feebly contested the crossing at a fence near the wooded riverbank, disappearing into a nearby cornfield. Eyeing strategic Wayne's Hill, Colonel Abel Streight of the 51st Indiana determined "to seize the crest before the enemy could get there, if possible." As he surged ahead, Confederate reinforcements could be heard approaching in the darkness. Streight had his men lie down as the enemy closed to within thirty paces, when his Hoosiers unleashed a volley, sending them reeling. Sensing victory, Streight ordered his 51st up the hill.[54]

Unfortunately for the former Indianapolis book publisher, the hill was in fact occupied, but only barely. At 4:00 Breckinridge belatedly ordered a detachment of Hanson's brigade to the summit. Cobb's Kentucky Battery unlimbered on the hill behind a small earthwork, with the 41st Alabama in support, the 9th Kentucky on the left, and the 6th Kentucky in the woods two hundred yards to the right. John Jackman could not understand "why we were not ordered to a position on the hill in the beginning." The Indiana troops rushed blindly toward the muzzles of the guns. "One of the 'Feds' hallowed out, 'Boys here is a cannon, let us get away from here' and they all skeedaddled," contended Jackman. Major Rice Graves, Breckinridge's artillery chief, ordered his cannoneers to lie down, but one gun detachment, never hearing the order, remained standing and were "all either killed or wounded."[55]

The 51st Indiana withdrew into the cornfield, where it reunited with the 73rd Indiana and 13th Michigan. Harker learned from a prisoner that he fronted an entire division not five hundred yards distant. When Rosecrans arrived at 9:30, Crittenden, still not grasping the gravity of the narrowly diverted disaster, offered his immediate apology for not having taken the town. Harker's three regiments silently retired across the river after 10:00, miraculously having sustained only five casualties. Harker's brigade and Van Cleve's division arrived later that night. Rosecrans and Crittenden, with their staffs, squeezed together in a rickety Daniel Cabin by the pike for the evening.[56]

The Wood/Palmer debacle proved an embarrassment to both army commanders. Rosecrans had maintained his headquarters at Stewartsboro all day which, though the center of the army, was not the center of the action. He continued to embrace the belief that Bragg would not fight a battle at Murfreesboro, but instead retreat behind the Duck River. Why? Because that is what he would have done had he been the Confederate commander. Stanley's faulty intelligence (which Rosecrans ungracefully attempted to pin on Palmer) had served to confirm his preconceived notion. Crittenden displayed a pitiful lack of leadership at a crucial moment. It was clear he did not know what to do. Wood's influence had saved the day. In September 1863, at the Battle of Chickamauga, Wood's career would forever be tarnished for creating a breach in the Federal line. On this day, he may have saved his division.

The virtually unopposed crossing of Stones River by Harker's three regiments, and the nearly subsequent capture of Wayne's Hill, had been accomplished with shocking ease. Despite having been in Murfreesboro for six weeks, Bragg was not prepared. Had Breckinridge's division been on the west bank of the river, it would have been in position to strike Wood's division in flank and drive it east, away from the Nashville Pike. Even so, permitting three isolated Federal regiments to brashly remain unmolested on the east bank for over three hours, within a ten-to-fifteen-minute march of Breckinridge's entire division, typified the confused state of command.

· · · ·

That night Polk rode about and "made a very nice speck [*sic*] to the men that they might be encouraged while fighting," a Mississippian noted in his diary. Later in the evening the men "commenced building up a breast work and soon had it high enough to kneel behind and shoot. During the day we lay behind our breastworks, and slep[t] only tolerably well." No fires were permitted and, according to a Mississippi gunner, the night "passed wearily away."[57]

The southerners accidentally set fire to the large brick house owned by Varner Cowan in an open field west of the Nashville Pike. Bragg ordered the destruction of the several outhouses which obstructed a direct line of fire but gave implicit instructions not to harm the house. Unfortunately, brisk winds carried the sparks, and the flames gutted the house. "[H]igh up leaped the flames, mingled with an inky column of smoke, which pierced the very heavens. Gloomy sight at such a time as this," observed Jackman. At 8:00 p.m. Loomis's brigade of Withers's division, which had been on outpost duty at Black Mills, seven miles from Murfreesboro on the Lebanon

Pike, was recalled. It rejoined the division between 2:00 and 3:00 a.m., forming between the left of Manigault's brigade and the Franklin Pike.[58] In the Union ranks, an artilleryman in Palmer's division expressed concern about "looseness and want of caution" that night. He noted that, in the rain and darkness, the Rebels could have approached to within three hundred yards before being noticed. As he strolled along the division line, he saw large campfires and men singing in groups "with no thought of tomorrow." A fiddler in the 79th Pennsylvania, sitting on a cracker box and under an oilcloth to protect his instrument, attracted a crowd. Somewhere in the darkness, some seven hundred yards distant, the enemy waited in silence.[59]

THE MOST GOD FORSAKEN WILDS I EVER SAW

McCook's corps (the corps commander having recovered from his previous day's illness) marched due east along the wretched Bole Jack Road, which ran through cedar thickets and over rugged hills—"one of the most Godforsaken wilds I ever saw," described a Wisconsin soldier. Once past Stewart's Creek, the road intersected with the old Nashville-Shelbyville Stage Road, which ran north-south. Beyond this road juncture called Wilkinson's Crossroads (today called Blackman's, at the intersection of Blackman Road and Manson Pike), the Bole Jack Road became the improved Wilkinson's Pike for the final six miles into Murfreesboro. Stanley's reserve brigade screened the advance, with Davis's division in the lead, followed by Sheridan and Johnson. At 8:30 Davis's division arrived at Lane's Store, just beyond Stewart's Creek. Warned of enemy activity in the area, McCook ordered a halt for the column to close up. Nothing had been seen of the enemy, save three captured stragglers.[60]

Major Adolph Rosengarten's 15th Pennsylvania Cavalry, leading Stanley's advance, cleared the road of Wharton's troopers. Some 397 members of the regiment remained in Nashville under arrest, claiming that they had been recruited under false pretensions, thus leaving only 250 active men. The Pennsylvanians made contact on the Wilkinson Pike at 2:00, and a running fight commenced. The lead battalion, under Major Frank B. Ward, chased the enemy past the Overall Creek bridge and into the woods beyond. "There they go! Charge them! Go for them!" the excited troopers shouted. "No, don't go. My orders are to go only this far," Ward yelled. A number of hotheads spurred ahead anyway, prompting Ward to yell, "Damn you! If you will go, I'll go too, charge!" The battalion filed by fours through a fence and into a woods, on either side of which lay a cornfield. Three-fourths of a mile beyond the bridge, the troopers charged, striking Company A, 10th South Carolina, on picket duty, throwing the unit into confusion. Content on finishing the job, the Yankee troopers then advanced toward a fence. By this time the Carolinians had rallied and, reinforced with two more companies, unleashed a volley, dropping a number of troopers and mortally wounding Ward. A messenger related the news to Rosengarten back at the ridge; he recklessly ordered his battalion to the rescue. He thus rode into the same ambush, the enemy firing "right into the faces of our boys." The 15th sustained forty-five casualties, among them the dead Rosengarten, who had been struck seven times. One of Stanley's staff officers rode forward and angrily ordered the decimated regiment back.[61]

To the south, Zahm's brigade on the Franklin Pike (which ran parallel to the Bole Jack Road) protected McCook's right flank. The 4th Ohio Cavalry moved into column along the pike, the 1st Ohio Cavalry on the brigade left, within sight of the Bole Jack Road, and the 3rd Ohio Cavalry going cross-country in the center. A mile west of Stewart's Creek, the Buckeyes brushed with Wharton's troopers; sharp skirmishers and squad-size sorties continued all the way to Overall Creek. At one point the Texas Rangers struck the 3rd Ohio Cavalry and quickly moved off to the left, but "to their great surprise," the 1st Ohio Cavalry "gave them a broadside." The 4th Ohio Cavalry ran into an ambush against two cannons. In the fray that followed the Ohioans captured seven prisoners but sustained fifteen casualties. The Rebels withdrew beyond Puckett Creek, where Wharton made one last counter-attack. Modern historians have wrongly claimed that Zahm viewed Bragg's army drawn up in line of battle, from the Franklin Pike to the Nashville Pike. In truth, they merely garnered the information from "prisoners and negroes." Zahm's cavalry camped for the night at Begsley Lane Church, on a country lane that connected the Franklin Pike with Wilkinson Crossroads.[62]

At dusk, two of McCook's divisions camped in the west bank of Overall Creek, Davis on the right of the Wilkinson Pike and Sheridan on the left around the magnificent Washington Plantation, which still survives. One of Johnson's brigades (Willich's) sat in reserve, while a second (Kirk's) guarded the ammunition train, and a third (Baldwin's) brought up the rear at Wilkinson's Crossroads, where McCook made his headquarters, a mile and a half from Overall Creek. A 5:30 dispatch from Rosecrans ordered McCook to connect with Negley's right, but at 10:20 the corps commander replied that his cavalry had not yet made contact. Little wonder, for Negley's division camped behind Palmer's division three miles away. Had Wharton properly apprised Bragg of this gap between the Union Right and Center, argues one modern historian, Bragg could have "launched a decisive attack while the Federal wings were still separated and vulnerable to defeat in detail."[63]

Did Bragg fail to exploit his greatest opportunity? It would clearly have been advantageous to deal with five rather than eight enemy divisions, although Bragg would have to have committed one division (presumably McCown's) to contest McCook's crossing of Overall Creek if he planned to attack Crittenden and Thomas. Yet there is no indication that he ever considered such a plan. Although he never addressed the issue, his tepidness presumably related to his concern about the potential force on the Lebanon Pike. Until Rosecrans revealed his intentions, Bragg felt that he could not risk being attacked in the rear by a Yankee column approaching from Gallatin, as he assaulted between the Nashville Pike and Wilkinson Pike. "Fully aware of the greatly superior numbers of the enemy . . . it was our policy to await attack," Bragg wrote. He would remain on the defensive "until the real point of attack should be developed."[64]

At 1:00 a.m. McCook received word to report to Rosecrans's headquarters on the Nashville Pike; he arrived at 3:00 a.m. Rosecrans never mentioned the conference in his report. Bickman makes passing mention of it, but it seems clear he was not present. Although it has been suggested that McCook was being called on the carpet for his failure to connect with Negley, such does not appear to be the case. McCook described the meeting simply as receiving his orders for the next day, which remained to connect with Negley in the morning and bring his right forward until it paralleled Stones River. Indeed, if Rosecrans was truly worried about the gap in the Federal line, he could have closed the distance a half-mile or more by moving Negley's division to Crittenden's left, which he never did.[65]

4

EVE OF BATTLE

OPPOSITE PLANS

The weather continued dismal on Tuesday, December 30. It rained nearly all night, and a morning mist obscured observation. In the early morning Breckinridge reoccupied Wayne's Hill with three regiments of Hanson's brigade and Cobb's battery. At 8:00 a.m. Cobb found himself in a spirited duel with the 10th Indiana Battery in the Round Forest and the 6th Ohio Battery. Seeing Cobb outgunned, Major Graves ordered two sections of rifled guns, one each from the Washington Artillery and Lumsden's battery, to his support. Despite protest from Cobb, Graves directed Lumsden to fire two shots from each of his guns. Unfortunately, Cobb received the return fire. A shot completely gutted all six horses of a limber parked below the crest of the ridge, but the riders miraculously escaped injury.[1]

Rosecrans stood in front of his headquarters, some 1,500 yards from Wayne's Hill, as the duel commenced. One of Cobb's shells suddenly ricocheted in the pike. A second shot exploded dangerously near the general. A third shot carried away the head of an orderly. The general and his staff hurriedly mounted and rode up a slope out of range, re-establishing headquarters to the left of the pike. As it began to rain, staff officers set up a makeshift shelter of blankets stretched between two trees so that orders might be written. Crittenden soon arrived at army headquarters, as the 4th U.S. Cavalry stood in line behind a crest 300–400 yards in the rear. As an occasional shell burst, the band of the 4th struck up to the "Star Spangled Banner."[2]

McCook reported that his corps did not take up the march until 9:30, which, given the three-mile gap that existed between his and Thomas's corps, made him liable to censure. Yet he clearly erred about the starting time. Sheridan's division roused at 4:00 a.m., formed in line of march at

6:00, and Colonel George W. Roberts's lead brigade crossed Overall Creek Bridge at 7:00, passing the General Smith House ("Fairfield"), still in existence today. The congestion at the bridge delayed the next brigade, that of Brigadier General Joshua Sill, until 9:00. "As we marched out the pike [Wilkinson,] Genls. McCook & Sheridan sat on their horses looking at us, McCook burly & robust with a full red face indicative of plenty of good beef & brandy, Sheridan with a small diminutive figure presenting a strong contrast to McCook," one of Roberts's men recalled.[3]

At 9:00, as Roberts pushed east down the Wilkinson Pike, light skirmishing commenced, with the shooting intensifying as the Confederates fell back. To relieve the hard-pressed 19th Illinois, Sheridan threw forward the 22nd Illinois as skirmishers to the left of the Wilkinson Pike and the 42nd Illinois to the right, resulting in an approving cheer from the men. At noon, in the midst of a drizzling rain, Roberts connected with Negley's right. Having been given no orders to halt, the 22nd continued to advance far beyond Negley's line and nearly to Patton Anderson's breastworks before being recalled. The 51st and 27th Illinois formed line of battle in a cornfield in the rear, while Battery C, 1st Illinois Light Artillery, took a position in a point of timber on high ground a little farther to the right of the road.[4]

By noon Sill's brigade had advanced as far as the Harding House. At 3:00 Sheridan ordered Sill across a cottonfield to come up on Roberts's left. The blue infantry came under the fire of Waters's Alabama Battery, sheltered in woods 600 yards distant. "We . . . had gone about half way across when a masked Rebel Battery opened on us with shot and shell," Lieutenant Howard Greene of the 24th Wisconsin related. The fragments came "so thick, that it was almost useless to cross in face of the fire, so we were ordered to halt and lie down." Captain Asahel Bush's 4th Indiana galloped to a wooded hill 450 yards distant and engaged the enemy guns, with Sill posting five companies of the 24th Wisconsin in support. No sooner had the Badgers come to attention, wrote Greene, than a shell "came crashing toward us striking a man about 20 pcs [paces] from me in the forehead taking the top of his head completely off & scattering his Brains in all directions." Battery G, 1st Missouri Light Artillery, took Bush's former position, and together the twelve guns blasted away for two hours.[5]

Waters found his four smoothbores badly outmatched and requested a section of rifled pieces. A. P. Stewart sent two guns from Stanford's Mississippi Battery under the command of Lieutenant Ancil A. Hardin. As soon as the section got into position in an open field to the left of Waters, the Alabama gunners withdrew, for what reason was not certain—"I fear no good one," commented "Leigh," one of Stanford's men. "Here we remained for a few minutes for orders while the shells were exploding among us every minute," he continued in a letter to the *Appeal*. "There was scarcely a tree to be seen which was not shattered by these terrible missles." He counted a dozen guns concentrated on his two—"at least a dozen shells passed within ten feet of my head." In the words of cannoneer John Magee: "We had no infantry to protect us, and the enemy's sharpshooters opened on us." He concluded in disgust: "Our infantry seemed paralyzed." Each gun having fired thirty rounds, the section retired under heavy fire, two men having been wounded and Lieutenant Hardin killed by a solid shot that cut off his arms as it passed through his body. Waters later reported three wounded and an artillery wheel damaged.[6]

Davis's division extended McCook's line to the southeast. At 11:00 Woodruff came up on Sill's right, on the edge of a large cottonfield. On Woodruff's right, Carlin's brigade fought its way through dense woods, encountering stubborn resistance from Rebel skirmishers, with Post's deploying brigade on his right. At 2:00 McCook ordered a general advance. Carlin drove the enemy back to the Franklin Pike near the Widow Smith House, when the brigade came under fire from Felix Robertson's six-gun battery west of the house. "The Rebel lines were broken and we were moving on in victory in the full tide of victory when we were opened on by a masked battery on our right," contended John Russell. Upon his own authority, and without Carlin's knowledge, Davis ordered Colonel W. S. Alexander and his 21st Illinois to take the battery. "Men we must have these guns. Charge!" Alexander shouted as he waved his men forward. The regiment, along with the 15th Wisconsin to its left, set a double quick pace over 200 yards of open ground, closing to within 80 yards. The cannoneers could be seen abandoning their pieces, and it appeared as though the 21st had victory within their grasp when "a line of infantry arose from the sunken Road [Franklin Pike] and poured a volley into his [Alexander's] line," Carlin recalled. In the 15th Wisconsin, Sergeant Nils J. Gilbert thought that "all Hell had been poured on us."[7]

According to a Confederate, at 3:00 Alexander's men "came yelling and howling like demons." Having sustained several killed and fourteen wounded, Robertson's gunners abandoned their six 12-pounder Napoleons, all cast by Leeds & Company of New Orleans. The 9th Texas and 154th Tennessee of Vaughn's brigade, lying in the roadbed in support, prepared to charge, when the 26th and 29th Alabama of Loomis's brigade suddenly "arose from behind a fence and poured to their [Federal] ranks such a well directed fire that they were compelled to retire leaving the ground literally black with their wounded and dead." The 25th Alabama advanced to the stone fence of the Widow Smith House and assisted in repulsing a second sortie by the 21st Illinois. The Eufaula (Alabama) Light Artillery unlimbered north of the house and opened a crossfire. Seeing the 21st Illinois break to the rear, Colonel Hans Christian Heg ordered his Scandinavians back a hundred yards behind a rail fence. Cheatham placed losses in Loomis's and Vaughn's brigades at about seventy-five.[8]

On the Confederate right flank, sniping continued throughout the day around Wayne's Hill. One of Hansen's Kentuckians, writing under the pen name "Volunteer," expressed his chagrin that the Yankees had trees to hide behind, while Hansen's men had only tall grass. Throughout the afternoon the bluecoats gave taunting shouts to draw out the enemy: "Rebs get off the wet ground, you will catch your death cold." To the shout, "Rebs have you had your breakfast?" one wag answered, "yes, but the Hartsville brave didn't." The Yankees quickly unleashed fifty shots.[9]

. . . .

Bragg, fully anticipating the battle to begin this day, spent the morning on the field. Initial intelligence reports led him to believe that the enemy would cross Stones River on the right and attack Hardee. This threat dissipated by early afternoon. As McCook's corps inched south toward the Franklin Pike, where Polk's line ended, Bragg became increasingly alarmed that Rosecrans was "extending his right, so as to flank us on the left." He had little choice but to order forward McCown's division, the army's only reserve, and place it on Polk's left, below the pike. By 3:30, Bragg also ordered Hardee, with Cleburne's division, from the far right of the army to the far left, in support of McCown. McCown's three brigades, positioned near Murfreesboro, crossed the Franklin Pike ford of Stones River, arriving before sunset.[10]

Hardee arrived on the left near sunset and requested McCown and Cheatham to explain their relative positions. The division commanders im-

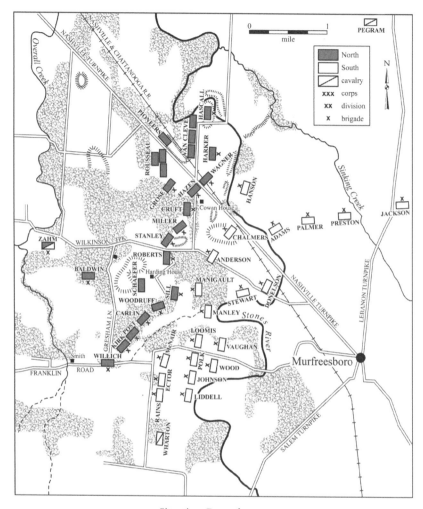

Situation, December 30

mediately disagreed as to the nature of the ground in their front, where Mc-
Cown's right would connect with Withers's left. Hardee accepted Cheatham's
interpretation (which turned out to be correct), meaning that McCown
would have to advance Evander McNair's brigade 150 yards through woods
and form diagonally in the dogleg of the Franklin Pike, McNair's right resting at the Widow Smith House. Not wanting the responsibility of advancing too far in the darkness (only 300 yards separated the lines at that point)

and igniting a night engagement, McCown requested that he be shown the precise location. Hardee ordered Cheatham to go with him and show the position. Bragg and Hardee would later both wrongly criticize McCown for waiting to position McNair's brigade till in the morning, thus delaying the attack one hour. Cleburne's division arrived later that evening. The river fording proved rough, the Irishman admitted, and all of his troops did not get into position till midnight. "We had the river to cross, which made it so late going five miles[.] We had it to cross on rails & rocks," E. J. Wall of the 2nd Arkansas explained to his brother and sister. His brigades extended Cheatham's line to the left and formed 400–500 yards in McCown's rear.[11]

That night Bragg returned to his Murfreesboro headquarters and held a council of war. According to Brent, the army commander proposed an assault the next morning up the Nashville Pike. Precisely why is not known, but presumably he thought that Rosecrans had weakened his left in order to attack with his right. If this was his thinking, he could not have been more wrong. Polk balked and suggested to "turn the enemy's right where we out-flanked him." Bragg agreed, and the plan was set. Yet there is documented evidence that, as early as 1:50, Bragg had issued orders for an attack on the Union right on the morning of the thirty-first. In order to square the 1:50 order with the evening council of war, one must assume that Bragg, up to the last moment, remained uncertain as to precisely what to do.[12]

The morning's attack plan called for a grand right wheel, in succession of brigades, from left to right, with four of the army's five divisions and Wharton's cavalry swinging northwest like a giant jackknife, forcing the enemy's right past the Nashville Pike and pinning it against Stones River. Such a tactic would sever Rosecrans's line of communications, if not his line of retreat. The plan has been universally panned by modern historians as overly ambitious. A pivot maneuver, it has been argued, was not well suited for the broken terrain and cedar thickets of the Middle Tennessee countryside. Too much reliance would be placed upon McCown, the army's weakest division commander. Breckinridge's lone division would remain to hold the right, making for "easy prey" if Rosecrans attacked that flank. Moreover, as the Federal right fell back, it would pick up strength "like a snowball," from the debris of battle, while the Confederates would unwind "like a ball of string" as they advanced. The council of war adjourned.[13]

• • • •

At 2:00 on Tuesday, General Stanley sent a citizen under guard to Mc-Cook's headquarters. The farmer, who lived on the Franklin Pike, related that he had gone up to the Confederate lines twice on Monday, the twenty-ninth, and once on the thirtieth to get stock taken from him. According to him, the right of Cheatham's line rested on the Wilkinson Pike and Withers's division was to his left, extending to the Franklin Pike. Hardee had deployed entirely beyond the pike, stretching all the way to the Salem Pike. The informant was either misinformed or openly lying, for McCown's division did not come on line until sundown of the thirtieth. McCook was nonetheless alarmed. He sent the farmer to army headquarters, along with an aide, Captain Horace N. Fisher, to report that his right rested directly in front of the enemy's center. McCook alerted his division commanders, and posted Willich's and Kirk's brigades of Johnson's reserve division on the corps right—the far right of the army. Kirk's brigade arrived in the late afternoon and deployed facing south along the Franklin Pike. At sunset Willich formed at a right angle to Kirk.[14]

Upon receiving McCook's information at 4:00, Rosecrans ordered him to build large fires that evening far beyond his right flank, inducing the enemy to believe that troops were massing in that sector. Major R. H. Nodine, an engineer on McCook's staff, carried out the task, but there is no evidence that the ruse in any way affected Bragg's plan. Learning that McCook's corps faced nearly east, Rosecrans related that, with the exception of the corps left, the line should more properly face south, although he left discretion to the corps commander. Before Captain Fisher returned to McCook's headquarters, Rosecrans related: "Tell General McCook, that if he is assured such is the fact [confronted by Hardee's corps] he may drive Hardee sharply if he is ready. At all events tell him to prepare for battle tomorrow morning. Tell him to fight as if the fate of a great battle depended upon him. While he holds Hardee, the Left, under Crittenden, will swing round and take Murfreesboro. Let Hardee attack if he wants to. It will suit us exactly." Moving around to the fire, he then said, "It is looking better." At 6:30 Captain R. S. Thoms arrived at McCook's headquarters, bringing instructions for in the morning: McCook would retire slowly if attacked, contesting every inch of ground. If not attacked, he would make his own slight but convincing demonstration.[15]

Rosecrans claimed that he called a council of war that evening. Thomas arrived early, received his instructions, and retired. An exhausted Crittenden, who had spent most of the afternoon with the army commander and apparently knew the plan of battle, begged off. Crittenden would later testify before the Committee on the Conduct of the War that he had never been given a specific plan concerning his role during the upcoming battle. McCook and Stanley arrived at 9:00. In March 1863, when the issue of the conference became a matter of dispute, Thomas reported that Rosecrans actually came to his headquarters that evening. The Virginian accompanied him part of the way back to army headquarters, at which time he was told his role in the morning's battle. McCook and Stanley arrived at 10:00, according to Stanley, and remained for half an hour. McCook adamantly wrote that he never received any word about a council of war and went to army headquarters that evening "through a sense of duty." He further insisted that the details of the battle were never explained to him, nor did he fully know them till he read an article in the *Cincinnati Commercial* two months later. The latter assertion was not entirely true, however, for Stanley, who overheard a part of the conversation between the generals, gave the following details: "That General McCook was to attack the enemy in the morning with vigor, but mainly with a view to engage him whilst Crittenden's corps marched upon Murfreesboro. If the enemy attacked McCook's corps, he was to contest the ground, and refuse to engage his right flank, as far as possible."[16]

Rosecrans's plan of attack, virtually identical to Bragg's but in reverse, would be a grand wheel on the enemy's right. Van Cleve's division would initiate the attack by crossing McFadden's Ford and assaulting Breckinridge's division. He would be joined on the right by Wood's division, who would plant his artillery on the ridge east of the river as he advanced. Palmer's division and Thomas's corps would take up the assault, drive across Stones River, sweeping the enemy through Murfreesboro, past the Franklin Pike, towards Salem, with the prospect of cutting off their line of retreat. In order to insure overwhelming force on the Union left, McCook had to hold his position at least three hours. "You know the ground; you have fought over it; you know its difficulties. Can you hold your position at least three hours?" the army commander queried. "Yes, I think I can," McCook answered. As for McCook, he later said that he had no recollection of "three hours" having been mentioned, but to the question of whether or not he could hold his line, he answered "I think I can," meaning, he later contended, he could hold against the same force that had opposed him throughout the afternoon.[17]

Rosecrans trusted that McCook would "make things sure" and thus never rode to the right for a personal inspection. Whether or not the army commander's appearance at this late hour would have revealed the inherent weaknesses on the right is doubtful. He trusted McCook to do what he had to do; "it was a mistake," he would later admit. The larger mistake belonged to the army commander himself, by clustering five of his eight divisions between the Wilkinson Pike and Stones River. Rousseau's reserve division should have been placed by the Wilkinson Pike. Once it had been determined that McCook was secure, it could have been shifted toward the Nashville Turnpike to join in the attack. Bragg, of course, had taken the same risk in reverse, by leaving only one division on his right flank.

· · · ·

McCook had reason to worry; after all, it was his corps that had been surprised and routed at Perryville. He nervously related to Johnson that he feared that he would be attacked in the morning "by the entire rebel army." Yet, his powerful 15,700-man corps appeared to be strongly posted in a double-line formation generally along a wooded edge. He had met with all three of his division commanders and given them instructions. The lines nonetheless remained dangerously close at places—three hundred yards, and no attempt had been made to construct barricades. In a glaring mistake, McCook maintained Colonel Philemon Baldwin's reserve brigade of Johnson's division, in the center of the corps, a mile away from the vulnerable right flank.[18]

At about 10:00, Brigadier General Sill of Sheridan's division became anxious. In the darkness, large bodies of enemy troops could be detected marching toward Overall Creek in an apparent massing against the corps right. He sent three warning messages to division headquarters and finally rode himself to see Sheridan. Realizing the potential danger, the two officers proceeded to corps headquarters, where they found McCook asleep on some straw by the Gresham House. McCook appeared amazingly unconcerned and answered: "General Rosecrans is fully advised of the fact that the enemy is massing troops in my front, but he explained to me his attack upon their right in the morning will be so vigorous that they will be compelled to withdraw their forces to support that portion of the line. I am only to hold my line, and wait for orders from headquarters." He did not find it necessary to go to the front himself, nor did he notify army headquarters of this intelligence. Later that evening McCook was again awakened, this time by Stanley, who had been ordered to take his cavalry to the rear to protect the wagon trains. He warned the corps commander that he had ridden with an escort beyond the Federal right and found the enemy line far beyond McCook's right. "Old Gut" seemed "utterly indifferent and laughed, joked, and rolled around his rail pen—filled with fodder to make a soft bed."[19]

In the quiet of the night, bands on both sides struck up to their favorite music—"Yankee Doodle" and "Hail Columbia" for the northerners and "Dixie" and the "Bonnie Blue Flag" for the southerners. One of the Federal bands then began playing "Home Sweet Home." As if by orchestration, a Confederate band joined in, creating a surreal moment of harmony. "We could hear the sweet refrain as it died away on the cool frost air," a member of the 19th Tennessee recalled, as thousands momentarily reflected on home and family. The cold drizzling rain was the only thing that consumed the thoughts of Sergeant Squire N. Bush of the 6th Kentucky (C.S.), who wrote in his diary that evening: "I have never suffered so from cold in any one day in my life."[20]

· · · ·

During the early morning hours of the 31st, McCook, no longer nonchalant, ordered his division commanders to get their men under arms. Sheridan began to personally inspect his lines. Concerning the night's activities, Colonel William Wallace of the 15th Ohio would later write his wife: "I felt uneasy all night. Gen. Willich allowed the men to put up their shelter tents, I was much opposed to it. I felt they might be attacked very early, and their shelter tents would be in their way. I remained up myself all night, and had a sentinel from each company, who was relieved every hour, march up and down their company line." McCook instructed his division commanders to rouse their men early. Sheridan, unattended and on foot, personally inspected his lines. As Willich ate breakfast, he received a dispatch from Johnson: "General McCook is apprehensive that an attack will be made upon your line at daybreak. See that your men are under arms and on the alert." The Prussian laughed and uttered in his broken accent: "They are so quiet out there I guess they are no more here." He nonetheless made a personal inspection, during which time he received another message, this one directly from corps headquarters, admonishing him to keep a sharp eye. The tension mounted.[21]

WHEELER UNLEASHED

On the afternoon of December 29, Wheeler's jaded troopers, having done all they could in slowing the Union juggernaut, crossed Stones River and took their place on the right flank, east of the Lebanon Pike. Orders arrived for the cavalrymen to rest their mounts and be ready to move at midnight. "I was certain we were going to evacuate the place," admitted Captain Miller. In truth, "Fighting Joe" had received orders to completely ride around the Federal Army. He would have his own brigade—the 3rd Alabama Cavalry, 51st Alabama Cavalry, 8th Confederate Cavalry, two Tennessee cavalry battalions, and two guns of Wiggins's battery, as well as the 1st Tennessee Cavalry of Pegram's brigade, in all 1,600 horsemen.[22]

As early as the twenty-eighth, Bragg had planned such a venture. Was this the time to be conservative or bold? If he genuinely feared a threat on the Lebanon Pike, the army commander could have drawn Pegram's brigade south from Fall Creek to the East Branch of Stones River, watching to the north and west. In such a scenario, Wheeler would have remained with the army. In short, Bragg could have used his cavalry in the traditional role of intelligence gathering and flank protection. By going bold, on the other hand, Bragg could seriously disrupt Rosecrans's communications. Yet, what if Wheeler failed to inflict serious damage and in the process rode himself out of the battle, or, worse yet, got the brigade cut off and surrounded? Bragg gambled on Wheeler—and luck.

The troopers mounted at midnight and proceeded up the Lebanon Pike. "It was raining and so dark that one could not see the trooper by his side. When we struck the ford at Stone's River, we only knew we were riding in water by the splashing of our horses' feet," Miller described. After crossing the West Fork of Stones River at the Sharps Spring Ford, the graycoats continued up the Lebanon Pike at a "full gallop." At 4:00 a.m. Wheeler sent a dispatch to Brent at army headquarters: "We have now crossed Stones River and are now on the Jefferson Pike. The Enemy's camp fires are very dense on my left and apparently extend as far back as Stewart's Creek. We are getting along well. I have about sixteen hundred men in my command."

He added a postscript: "We will be in position by daylight, unless we are opposed by too heavy a force."[23]

The cavalry column entered the Jefferson Pike opposite Espey Church. At 9:00 a.m. Wheeler attacked the train of John C. Starkweather's brigade, comprised of sixty-four wagons of rations, officer's baggage, knapsacks, and stores. Starkweather's brigade had arrived at the pike the previous night. That morning found the men casually standing about talking, cleaning up after breakfast, and drying out blankets. The head of the train had already entered the camp, when Wheeler struck the rear. The 21st Wisconsin, the closest regiment, immediately came to arms and rushed to rescue their comrades. They encountered dismounted cavalry, and long-range skirmishing ensued. Until the balance of Starkweather's men came up, the 21st took position on a hill with a schoolhouse surrounded by a fence. Yet, it was clear that Wheeler did not want a fight and, as Union reinforcements began to arrive, his forces disengaged. The Federals, who grossly overestimated the enemy at 3,500, conceded the loss of twenty wagons (eighteen from the 24th Illinois), and Wheeler claimed 60 prisoners, all paroled. Starkweather later reported 9 killed and wounded and 113 captured or missing, meaning that a number of his men scattered. Wheeler made no casualty report, but 8 are known to have been captured, including 2 mortally wounded.[24]

The raiders continued west on the Jefferson Pike, swooping up two Yankee foraging parties along the way, and striking at La Vergne. Advised of a large wagon park in a nearby field, Wheeler divided his brigade in three columns, striking from the southwest, north, and northwest. The stunned Federals surrendered after only a few shots. Wheeler had bagged McCook's reserve quartermaster and commissary train—200 wagons (by Wheeler's first estimate, but he would later raise the number to 500), 100 horses, nearly a thousand mules, and 700 prisoners. The men torched the wagons and scattered the mules—"It was a sight that would have made all rebeldom glad to see," wrote a gleeful Miller. A Federal officer later saw the turnpike filled with destroyed wagons "as far as the eye could see." Yet, the effects of the La Vergne raid, though highly touted, may have been exaggerated. Union reports claim only 103 destroyed wagons, mostly in Sheridan's and Davis's divisions and corps headquarters. The next day Walker's brigade gathered up the mules, saved some of the stores, and, according to one source, "recaptured" the prisoners. An arriving Ohioan noted that

132 wagons had been destroyed and "several hundred mules were running around loose with the harness on."[25]

Deep within enemy lines, the gray horsemen could not afford to tarry long. They galloped to Rock Springs, northwest of Stewartsboro, where they captured and burned a brigade train, and, applying the spurs, raced two hours to Nolensville. Miller estimated the take at 150 destroyed wagons and several fine ambulances, the last being taken. After paroling 200 prisoners, Wheeler moved west six or eight miles toward Franklin. Along the way they encountered several foraging parties. "We relieved them of their plunder, put the prisoners bare back on mules, burned their wagons and rode on." The men rested five hours that night west of Nolensville, having ridden a circuit of fifty-five miles. At 2:00 a.m. they returned to Murfreesboro via the Bole Jack Road.[26]

5

THEY'RE COMING!

The troops of Johnson's division began to quietly stir at 4:00 on the cold, misty, overcast morning of December 31. An order came down from division to build fires and make coffee. "I could do nothing but obey," lamented Colonel Wallace, who remained apprehensive. At first light the men began to scan their surroundings. An eight-yard-wide wagon road known locally as Gresham Lane, which connected with the Wilkinson Pike one-and-one-third miles distant, ran perpendicular to the Franklin Road. In 1855, Amossa and Jane Gresham built their log cabin near the turnpike. Open and gently sloping ground characterized the terrain south of the Franklin Road.[1]

Kirk deployed his brigade, absent the 79th Indiana guarding the ammunition train, in the woods (described variously as a "cedar thicket" and a "dense cedar grove") 230 yards east of Gresham Lane, in a line running northeast to southwest. The 77th Pennsylvania anchored the left, with the 30th and 29th Indiana in the center, with pickets extending 150–200 yards. The 34th Illinois, which fronted open ground, arrayed on the far right facing due east, forming an angle with the balance of the brigade. The six guns of Warren P. Edgarton's Battery E, 1st Ohio Light Artillery, camped in the left rear of the 34th Illinois. With the exception of the 34th, the troops had no clear field of fire. Why Kirk settled on such a seemingly flawed deployment is not known; he never addressed the issue in his after-action report. He apparently believed that advancing his right two regiments the additional 270 yards necessary to get them out of the cedars would expose his left flank unless Sheridan, on his left, did the same.[2]

Willich deployed three regiments facing south behind the rail fence of the Franklin Road—the 49th Ohio a hundred yards west of Gresham Lane in a wooded field, and the 32nd and 39th Indiana east of the lane, with pickets extended 700 yards. Willich refused his line on the right of the 49th Ohio, posting the six guns of Battery A, 1st Ohio Light Artillery, facing west, and to their right the Buckeyes of the 15th Ohio, which "curled around like a dog's tail until some of us fronted to the rear (north)," described R. B. Stewart. The 89th Illinois camped in a double column in the woods behind the 15th Ohio. "I think the general understanding among our soldiers was that the most of the rebel army was in front of our [brigade] *left*," Lieutenant Morris Cope remembered—a correct assumption, but the enemy line lay oblique to the Franklin Road, not parallel. The right angle of the two brigades (the 39th Indiana and 34th Illinois) remained vulnerable.[3]

A remarkable passivity permeated Johnson's division. Soldiers stacked arms and cooked breakfast, and the horses of both batteries had been sent to the rear for watering. Although perfunctorily sending a message to Johnson to be vigilant and have his men under arms, McCook, back at corps headquarters, proceeded to leisurely shave. Willich confided to Wallace that he believed that the Rebels had fled. Surgeon Solon Marks, the division medical director, worried that the hospital at the Smith House was too far beyond the right of the Union lines, but the abundant water of Overall Creek and the size of the house, with numerous log cabins (slave quarters), made it the logical choice. When advised of the situation, Johnson expressed no concern. Captain Edgarton also rode to Johnson's headquarters that night, suggesting that his guns be placed action-front with double-shots of canister. "Never mind, you won't be attacked," the division commander answered.[4]

The officers commanding the two front-line brigades were a study in contrast. Thirty-four-year-old Kirk had been a schoolteacher and Illinois lawyer prior to the war. Having fought at Shiloh, where he fell wounded, he proved able, if not stellar. Fifty-two-year-old Willich, on the other hand, was a hardened veteran and fierce fighter. Born to Prussian aristocracy (a rumor wrongly labeled him "the illegitimate son of the King of Prussia"), he quit the Prussian Army and sided with the revolutionists in an 1848 uprising. After the defeat at the Battle of Candarn, he fled to Switzerland and, in 1853, to the United States. He ultimately became the editor of a communist newspaper and a respected member of the German community in Cincinnati. He had fought at both Shiloh and Perryville.[5]

Both at Shiloh and Perryville the Confederates had demonstrated a penchant for first-strike attacks. Yet, as the sun began to rise, not a single bluecoat in Johnson's division stood in line of battle. Indeed, the stillness in the air belied the horrific violence that would soon erupt. William F. G. Shanks, a reporter of the *New York Herald,* had spent the night with the gunners of Wilbur Goodspeed's battery on the far right. The correspondent was in search of a good story; he would soon have one.[6]

. . . .

McCown's troops, camped 150 yards east of the Triune Road, also roused at 4:00 a.m. There would be no fires, no breakfast, no talking or laughing. The rail fence on the west side of the Triune Road had been removed and stacked against the other side to use as a breastwork if the attack failed. At 5:30, some reports claim as early as 5:00, the troops moved up to the road and began forming in double line—Evander McNair's 1,484 Arkansans on the right, Matthew D. Ector's 1,407 Texans in the center, and the 1,555-man mixed brigade of James Rains on the left, the last having left his sick bed to lead his men. The 300-man 29th North Carolina, in the last, arrived shortly before the advance, having force-marched from McMinnville. Having kept silent and in position for two days, an electric atmosphere now swept the ranks. Colonel Matthew F. Locke, of the 10th Texas, conceded the difficulty in restraining his men. The troops passed about whiskey in some companies, ostensibly to take the bite out of the morning coldness, but perhaps also to strengthen their fortitude. Some imbibed freely, although one of Locke's Texans remembered that over half of the men in his company took a pass. In the 14th Texas, Private S. M. George turned to his friend John Wyche and threatened to write his family if he ran. Before the day ended, Wyche would have his name entered on the regiment's honor roll.[7]

Though veterans, none of the brigadiers leading the division were professionals—Ector and Rains had been lawyers, the last a talented Yale graduate, and McNair in the mercantile business. Rains, at age twenty-nine the youngest, had a wife and three-year-old child, but Ector, at forty, remained a bachelor. Ector and McNair would both survive the war, but not without wounds. All three showed more talent than their division commander.[8]

The terrain over which the troops would advance appeared forbidding: 600–800 yards of flat rolling land and cornfields, with fences occasionally running at right angle, and sometimes parallel to their lines. At 6:00 the order "Forward, March!" sounded, and the division, with skirmishers only fifty yards in advance, surged silently ahead at the quick time—no drums, no clanking, no shouting. Soon the crack of the Yankee pickets could be heard, but officers admonished their troops to withhold their fire. Texan Henry Watson noted that the men "got over the [Triune Road] fence and marched slowly along for about a hundred and fifty yards and the yanks began to fire on us." When 200 yards from Kirk's battery, the enemy guns opened a "most terrific fire." Private Billy Melton of the 14th Texas was one of the first to fall, causing nearby Captain James A. Howze to turn pale. Determined, he raised his sword and encouraged his men forward. At a hundred yards the order "Charge!" rang out; the troops unleashed a crashing volley and ran screaming forward. The Battle of Stones River had been joined.[9]

· · · ·

Sergeant Major Lyman Widney of the 34th Illinois finished his coffee and, in the semi-darkness, strolled leisurely forward toward the picket line. Halfway there, a soldier ran past him, shouting, "They're coming!" As no shots had been fired, Widney felt decidedly skeptical and continued walking. He suddenly bolted in open-mouthed amazement; sweeping before him was a line of gray as far as the eye could see. The time was precisely 6:22. Soon wounded pickets of the 34th came hobbling back, some of the first casualties of what would become a bloody butcher's list.[10]

The alarm sounded back at Kirk's brigade camp. Thirty-two-year-old Colonel J. B. Dodge, a rebellious preacher's son who had run away at age sixteen, commanded the 30th Indiana. Having difficulty seeing in the twilight and mist, he climbed to the top of a nearby fence rail and peered ahead; the Rebels came into view. "They're they were! It was a magnificent but fearful sight. Their lines extended as far as we could see in the dim light," he recalled. Major Alexander P. Dysart, commanding the 34th Illinois at the crucial angle, sent an urgent message to Kirk and then frantically galloped to Willich's headquarters, about 165 yards in his rear. To his dismay, he discovered that Willich was away at division headquarters. Kirk had by now sighted the well-ordered gray masses surging toward him, "without music or noise of any kind." W. H. Carman, a gunner in Edgarton's battery, wrote his father on January 5 that "some of the men had gone to water their horses, some had gone to get water for breakfast, some had not yet got up. The man that sleeps with me had just got up and told me to sit

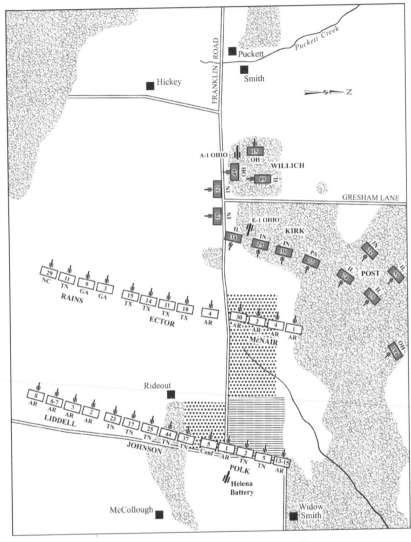

December 31, 6:22 a.m., McCown's Attack

up, when a lieutenant colonel rode through our camp and told our captain that the rebels were coming about one hundred rods (500 yards) from us."[11]

Edgarton faced four of his guns behind the 34th Illinois, with two fronting the Franklin Road. With half of their horses watering at Puckett's Creek, some 500 yards distant (for which the captain would later be censured), Kirk frantically attempted by buy time. After sending a courier to division headquarters, he ordered the returning Dysart to advance his 34th Illinois. It proved as valiant as it did futile. As Lyman Widney raced back to his brigade, he encountered his regiment, 354 strong, marching in line across an open field. "Our only salvation was to lie as flat as possible on the ground, for the air freely seethed with the 'Zip' of bullets and grape shot over our heads. It reminded me of the passage of a swarm of bees. . . . [Bullets] plowed little furrows around us, throwing up tufts of grass and hands full of soil into our faces," Widney related, who had a bullet pass through his coat collar, momentarily causing him to think that he had been mortally wounded.[12]

Slugging it out with the 34th was Locke's 10th Texas, the far-right regiment of Ector's brigade. The thirty-seven-year-old Locke, a native of Murfreesboro, had a grandfather who had commanded the Murfreesboro Blues during the 1814 Battle of Horseshoe Bend. As the regiments closed to within a hundred yards, noted Henry Watson, "they ris a running." In the brief (no more than five minutes) stand, the Illinois troops sustained twelve killed and sixty wounded—20 percent of the regiment. At the height of the exchange, the flag bearer of the 10th Texas ran up to the color bearer of the 34th and defiantly attempted to snatch his banner; both men fell dead. A vicious struggle now ensued for the Illinois flag, with men falling on both sides, before a Texas private claimed the trophy. The fight became "too warm for them," confessed 34th member Lon Payne to his brother, and the regiment fell back to their camp. As Dysart's men fought desperately, Kirk rode to Willich's headquarters; the Prussian was nowhere to be found. Desperately he pleaded with the officers of two regiments to come to his aid, but they refused without an order from their brigadier. It made no difference; within minutes they too would be under attack.[13]

The 10th and 11th Texas now swarmed over Edgarton's battery. Blasts of canister tore gaps into the gray line, but the troops quickly closed. Twenty-seven-year-old 11th Texas Colonel John C. Burks, a former lawyer and politician, fell just as he yelled, "Forward, boys!" He died two days later and, in 1895, the veterans of his old regiment would have his remains brought home and buried next to his wife. Edgarton, a twenty-six-year-old law professor and famed teacher of elocution in civilian life, berated the 34th Illinois, which "ran almost with the first volley." Within minutes, seventy-five of his returning horses lay dead in heaps, making it impossible to remove his guns. One caisson got lodged in a tree. He managed to get off seven rounds (his claim of sixteen rounds is not substantiated) before being over-run, with Edgarton among the captured. As an artilleryman put it, "The [enemy] front rank fired and fell, and then the next ranks kept doing so until they got up within five rods of our pieces, then they charged and took them." The gray line literally absorbed the battery, with Edgarton losing twenty-eight killed and wounded, twenty-two captured, and all six guns—the battery was wrecked. "The gun (a howitzer) I belong to had all the men killed but myself[,] . . . and I was shot in the head and leg but not bad," G. H. Stacy, one of the Ohio gunners, explained to his father. According to cannoneer Alfred King, "Our supports scattered back like sheep. We lay by our pieces till the Captain told us to take care of ourselves, and all that could, followed the infantry to the rear." Nine months earlier at Shiloh, the Rebels tarried to ransack the Federal camps, but not today. The disciplined veterans steadily advanced, never breaking ranks.[14]

In the midst of the melee, a bullet struck Kirk in the hip, penetrating almost to his spine. Having had two horses shot from under him, and now profusely bleeding, he nonetheless fell back with his men. Eventually placed in an ambulance, he would be captured and later exchanged. He lingered for seven months at his Ohio home before dying. Command of the brigade fell to Colonel Dodge, who also got caught up in the dash to the rear.[15]

McNair's Arkansans struck the rail fence bordering the Franklin Road simultaneously and with such force that it "knocked it flat to the ground," recalled a Razorback. They then began clawing their way through the thickets. A bullet severed the staff of the 4th Arkansas Battalion flag, and so jarred the arm of the bearer that he dropped the banner. Sergeant J. C. Davis immediately snatched it up and ran forward. The Arkansans en-countered a brief but lacerating fire. Lieutenant Colonel J. A. Williamson, writing to "Miss Muldrow," marveled at his close calls. "Every Field and Staff officer in my Regiment except myself was wounded, and all of them were wounded within fifteen feet of me. My horse was struck with a piece of shell within a foot of my leg. Of seven Captains in my Regiment, all were killed or wounded. Of three Lieutenants commanding Companies, all were killed or wounded." The 30th Arkansas lost seven company commanders (three killed, four wounded) and several lieutenants.[16]

Kirk's center, the 29th and 30th Indiana, soon gave way, the 30th, to its embarrassment, losing only two wounded before breaking to the rear.

Lieutenant Colonel David M. Dunn of the 29th did something, but he did the wrong thing; he advanced Company C to strengthen the picket line in the cedars. The regiment could thus not fire, for fear of hitting their own men as they came running back. This dilemma, coupled with the thickets that obstructed vision, meant that the southerners closed to within twenty yards before they came into full view. The 29th, lying in a prone position, held briefly, unleashing four or five volleys, before joining the exodus to the northwest. Everywhere the Arkansans saw frying pans on the fire and coffee pots smoldering, evidence of the total surprise.[17]

On the brigade left, the undermanned 77th Pennsylvania, only 288 strong, advanced in a left swing as their picket line returned, placing the regiment almost parallel to the Franklin Road and in perfect position to enfilade McNair's right, the 1st Arkansas Mounted Rifles. The two right companies of the 1st had been delayed in scaling a fence, and they now came under a blistering fire, causing them to flee through a cornfield. The 77th continued its unobstructed advance south toward Edgarton's guns, McNair's brigade having passed into the cedars. At that moment, Douglas's Texas Battery approached at a trot from the east. The Keystone boys, believing it to be a Federal battery, cheered and waved their flag. Admitting that he was "a little surprised" to see Yankees 150 yards on his right, Douglas nonetheless determined to create a ruse. He unlimbered his four pieces at the site of Edgarton's abandoned guns and aligned them obliquely. After loading double canister, he had his pieces suddenly swing to the right. Writing to his parents on January 9, artilleryman John A. Templeton related: "As soon as we got our guns ready they took to their heels, but our canister shot overtook a good many of them." The Pennsylvanians hurriedly withdrew toward Post's brigade to their left.[18]

Kirk lay mortally wounded and his brigade shattered. In his after-action-report, claims would be made of overwhelming enemy numbers. At the point of contact, however, Kirk's 1,650 men held near parity of strength with McNair's Arkansans and the 10th Texas, together 1,834 troops. The surprise nature of the attack, the oblique formation (which served to neutralize the Federal fire), momentum, and the sheer discipline of the Rebels had spelled Kirk's doom. Could the breached dike now be plugged?

· · · ·

As the men of Willich's brigade prepared their breakfast, according to Francis Kiene, there suddenly came "considerable musketry but no one seemed to mind it." The first indication of trouble came not from the Rebels, but from Kirk's men fleeing in their direction. The raw recruits of the 89th Illinois, the so-called Railroad Regiment, because it had been sponsored and largely recruited by ten Chicago-based railroad companies, camped in an open woods behind Willich's main line. As they prepared their breakfast, firing erupted on Kirk's front. A soldier suddenly came running toward George Sinclair. "Thinking that he was getting scared rather early, I tried to stop him, but he says, 'I [am] shot in the bowels, I can't.'" Moments later a second wounded man passed him, but even then Sinclair "could not believe that they were anything more than spent balls that were over shot from where they were at it on the left of us." Joseph Buckley had just picked up his coffee pot, when the enemy rushed into camp. "We had not time to get into line of battle as the Rebels were only ten rods [150 yards] from us, and we had all our traps [cartridge boxes and canteens] to pick up." Lieutenant J. S. Rea of the 39th Indiana stood spellbound: "Emerging from the woods, a short distance in front of us, were the advancing columns of the enemy moving in line of battle, five and six deep." Frederick Goddard no sooner stepped into line than he fell with a bullet wound in his side. He ran behind a tree and had another bullet strike him in his left leg. Lieutenant Colonel C. T. Hotchkiss immediately ordered his men to lie down, a task impeded by Kirk's men running pell-mell over them.[19]

Ector's Texans obliquely struck Willich's three front-line regiments facing south along the Franklin Road—the 49th Ohio, 32nd Indiana, and the 39th Indiana. As the men grabbed their rifles and stumbled into line, Kirk's men stampeded into them. "We barely had a fence for protection and were nearly run over by the fleeing [men] and by the run away artillery horses," attested a member of the 32nd. Private James Cole witnessed "men running every way and no one knew where to go but to try and get out of danger." The Texans began to interpose between the pickets and the brigade line. In the chaos, Lieutenant Colonel Milton Miles of the 49th Ohio rode into the Confederate lines. Wearing his overcoat, the Rebels mistook him for one of their aides, and an officer ordered him to place a regiment into line. He saluted, rode in that direction, and then cut back through a cluster of bushes and made his way back. Lieutenant Colonel Fielder A. Jones of the 39th Indiana assembled about sixty men behind a rail fence facing east-west at the Hickory House, south of the Franklin Road, but at the first volley the Texans dropped half of them.[20]

The men of the 89th Illinois hastily formed into line and managed to get off a single volley at fifty yards, but Hotchkiss ("he was a brick I tell you," one soldier observed) could see that the brigade was breaking apart all around him and ordered a withdrawal by the right flank. "The whole brigade run for life[.] in ower Regiment we lost [a] good many men. . . . I saw men shot down on my left, on my right and in forward of me," George Barry related to his wife. Private Theodore Whitney confided to his family: "I found out who the brave boys are. Some of them run five miles before they stopped. . . . But you mustn't say anything." One incoming shell made a direct hit on a stack of guns, shattering it to pieces.[21]

A stunned Johnson quickly mounted and rode to Baldwin's brigade, a soldier shouting to him: "Don't go there general, or you will be captured." As Willich galloped back from division headquarters, he stumbled into Ector's Texans. When a Rebel ordered him to surrender, the Prussian smiled, gave a friendly greeting, wheeled about and attempted to escape, with bullets zipping all about him. He would have made it, he asserted to a fascinated Cincinnati audience five months later, after his prisoner exchange, but his horse became entangled in the underbrush and stumbled. Command of the brigade fell to forty-one-year-old Colonel William H. Gibson, a former attorney and Ohio state treasurer. At that moment, however, Gibson's horse had been shot and he was on foot. He turned to Lieutenant Woodward and said: "Go back and tell General Johnson that my right flank is being turned, and I must have reinforcements."[22]

The battle rolled west, toward Colonel Wallace's 15th Ohio, which faced west and south. The Buckeyes tumbled over each other to get in line—"we could distinctly hear the rebels cheering," said Samuel S. Pettit. Sergeant Alexis Cope heard Colonel Gibson shout out: "Fall in 49th and 15th Ohio! Hook up them battery horses!" Wallace understood that he had to swing his regiment right in order to face the enemy, but what ensued was a series of nonsensical commands—a "rear in front," through a cottonfield, a "change front" by countermarching, then "Forward," only to ultimately order the men to "Lie Down!"—all under fire, which served only to entangle the troops. Even then Wallace would not order his troops to fire, sensing that the oncoming regiments were Federal. "Damn it, don't you see the rebel flag? Fire!" shouted Lieutenant Colonel Frank Askew, a law student at the

University of Michigan when the war commenced. Conveniently leaving out a few of the details, Wallace later wrote his wife: "I opened fire on them when they were not twenty yards from us. We gave them about six rounds."[23]

The Ohioans bounded west toward the Smith House ("all were trying to get out of the way the best they could," admitted Pettit), where wounded had already begun to arrive. An orderly came to Surgeon Marks and quietly whispered that the division was falling back. Having previously spoken to Johnson, however, Marks believed this to be according to plan. A few moments later he stepped out of the house to see for himself. "I was not only surprised, but paralyzed," he admitted; the division had obviously been routed, and the fight was coming toward him. He went back inside and advised the surgeons of the situation and gave them permission to leave; all remained.[24]

The Buckeyes fell back to the Smith House in decent order, where they encountered a high fence running north-south—not a rail fence, but pine poles tied closely together—which would prove a death trap. "I could not get to it for the crowd that was ahead of me," recalled R. B. Stewart. While waiting he managed to get off a couple of shots, but his numb fingers could hardly tear the cartridge paper. Many of the men attempted to pull down the poles; a few squeezed through and made it to Overall Creek. Some men even ran south, toward the enemy, in an attempt to get around the fence. "We lost heavily in crossing the fence," Wallace admitted to his wife. In the end, as many as a hundred of the Ohioans surrendered. Askew fell with a bullet in his hip, Major John McClenahan with a slight shoulder wound. The major would later be court-martialed for prematurely leaving the field, but he was found innocent. A team of riderless artillery horses attempted to get between two gate posts, with one of the animals being killed as it careened into a post.[25]

William F. G. Shanks, the *New York Herald* reporter who had camped with Goodspeed's battery in order to get a story, now had a front-row seat. "Here, for the first time, I got a good view of the advancing columns of the enemy," he told his readers. "Two columns deep, with a front at least three-quarters of a mile, the line tolerably preserved, advancing with great rapidity, on came the whole rebel left wing, the bayonets glistening in a bright sun which had broken through the thick fog."[26]

Captain Wilbur F. Goodspeed, a twenty-six-year-old former Cleveland wholesale shoe salesman, frantically attempted to remove the six pieces of his Battery A, 1st Ohio Light Artillery. Like Edgarton, he had sent some of his horses to the rear for watering; the animals had returned and were in the process of being hitched when the attack began. The cannoneers wheeled one gun around and managed to get off three rounds in an enfilade fire. Everywhere the horses began to drop (seventy-three, to be precise); two caissons were never even moved. A. S. Bloomfield managed to jump on one escaping caisson, with bullets "whizzing on all sides." Goodspeed noticed a slight knoll to the west, a good position for artillery, and he sent two of his guns there. One of his sergeants came running back, hatless and out of breath, stating that the Rebel cavalry had overrun the knoll and captured the section. Three guns fell into enemy hands, but the remaining three pieces miraculously made it out.[27]

On McNair's left, Rains's brigade swept across the Franklin Road virtually unopposed, capturing two guns and three wagons, one filled with band instruments. Seeing the Yankees flee toward Overall Creek, Rains's men instinctively pursued. It would prove the first Confederate mistake of the day. By veering northwest, away from the battle, Bragg's line would be stretched and gaps inevitably made. McCown had nonetheless accomplished much. Johnson's two front-line brigades, 3,750 men, had been shattered, with a carpet of 800 killed and wounded and 1,000 men and nine guns captured. Running like madmen through the timbers, the bluecoats shouted, "We are sold again! We are sold again!" Most of the blame fell to McCook and Johnson—"The army is hostile to both at the present," a correspondent related. Wrote one of Johnson's disgusted soldiers: "And General Johnson was—God knows where." Many in the division, he asserted, prayed that "he would never get off the field alive."[28]

Back at Bragg's Murfreesboro headquarters, a courier galloped up, touched his hat, and reported: "General Hardee desires to report that he has captured two batteries and the enemy are flying before him." A cheer immediately arose from the army staff and escort. Bragg, never changing expression, answered: "Tell General Hardee to keep at them."[29]

CLEBURNE'S DIVISION ATTACKS

Shortly after sunrise, the 6,000 veterans of Cleburne's division silently stepped off in support of McCown, continuing the gate-like swing to the left—Brigadier General St. John Liddell's Arkansans on the left, Brigadier

General Bushrod Johnson's Tennesseans in the center, Brigadier General Lucius E. Polk's mixed Arkansas-Tennessee brigade on the right, and Brigadier General S. A. M. Wood's brigade in reserve. From the outset, the awkward swinging movement created problems, with Liddell's men on the left having to advance considerably faster than the far-right brigade. Liddell also had to oblique to the left in order not to crowd Johnson, resulting in an even wider swing. Occasional halts had to be made to adjust alignments. Further complicating the advance was Cheatham's far-left brigade (J. Q. Loomis's), which did not advance concurrent with Polk's brigade on its left, resulting in a considerable gap on Cleburne's right. Seeing Cleburne's flank in the air, Hardee did the only thing he could—he pulled Wood's brigade from the reserve and placed it in line.[30]

Johnson's and Liddell's brigades, advancing in relatively open country, had little difficulty as they passed Hardee's headquarters at the McCullouch House. As Johnson's brigade advanced to within 150 yards of the Triune Road, however, Yankee sharpshooters posted along the fence line in the woods seventy-five yards to the right took aim. The Confederates quickly learned that even nameless sharpshooters could be lethal; several men in the 44th Tennessee dropped from wounds, as did Colonel Moses White and Lieutenant Colonel R. D. Frayser of the 37th Tennessee. The 37th immediately fell back twenty-five yards to a rail fence, but Johnson would have none of it. He immediately ordered out skirmishers and advanced the regiments. The brigade cleared the sharpshooters and marched to the Triune Road "in a beautiful line." Similar reports of sniper fire came in from Lucius Polk's brigade. "I did not believe at first the enemy could be so near us," Polk admitted. With reports slowly coming in, Cleburne could come to only one conclusion—somehow in the mist McCown's line in his front had "unaccountably disappeared." McCown, of course, had "disappeared" by drifting west rather than continuing north, meaning that Cleburne would not be advancing in support, but as a front-line division with no reserve! There would be no time to hunt up McCown and make adjustments. The attack must continue, if not in two waves, then in one.[31]

• • • •

Colonel P. Sidney Post, a twenty-nine-year-old former Illinois lawyer with a penchant for the classics, led a four-regiment brigade in Jeff Davis's division. His troops, facing northeast to southwest, deployed in cedar woods so thick that on the right Post did not even have visual contact with Kirk's brigade. Fearing an attack, Colonel Jason Marsh of the 74th Illinois ordered his men not to put up tents and to lay down. At 4:00 a.m., still suspecting trouble, he roused them. For a half-hour Post's pickets watched as they saw at a distance of 350 yards an immense force of Rebels sweeping around to their right. "It was plainly seen that the fire of my skirmishers took effect upon their ranks," Marsh reported, yet "the enemy seemed to pay no attention." As the sounds of battle neared and the advancing cheers of the enemy rolled around Post's right and rear, it became evident that he had been outflanked. The colonel had no choice but to withdraw 475 yards northwest to a second position, parallel to the Franklin Road and straddling Gresham Lane. The 74th and 75th Illinois posted behind a rail fence west of the lane, and the 59th Illinois and 22nd Indiana deployed east of the lane. Davis arrived on the scene, ordered the skirmish line strengthened, and had the six guns of Pinney's 5th Indiana Battery unlimber in a field between the 59th and 22nd. Kirk's 77th Pennsylvania and 29th Indiana, having withdrawn relatively intact amidst Johnson's debris, came in line on the far right of Post's brigade.[32]

Post had been in his second position only minutes when Johnson's Tennesseans emerged from the cedar thickets and onto open ground. Alexander Pippen of the 59th Illinois remembered: "We was standing up in line when the enemy came out of the timber into the . . . field, they was three or four lines deep. I could see the rebel officers riding behind their lines. There was no firing going on yet. The first order we got was to fix bayonets and then the command to march forward. . . . The next order was to lie down; then we opened fire with every musket in the brigade. . . . My hands was cold and numb and their bullets was coming pretty thick and fast. . . . I looked up in the corn row that I was on and saw the corn stalks clipped off with their bullets."[33]

The 17th and 23rd Tennessee, 900 strong, erupted from the cedars west of the lane. Pinney's battery opened a blistering fire. Only hours earlier Pinney had turned to one of his officers and said: "Lieutenant, look well to your section, for I am confident that this will be a day when our very souls will be tried." The redlegs so rapidly discharged their pieces that they ran out of water in the sponge buckets, so they emptied their canteens into the buckets and continued swabbing. "Every time we discharged our gun, it

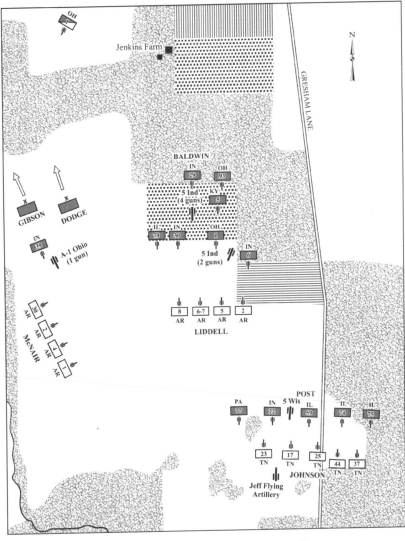

December 31, 7:30 a.m., Johnson's Division Collapses

seemed to me that it made a gap 20 feet wide where every man went down," a gunner recalled.[34]

The Tennesseans closed to within 150 yards before being checked by the raking fire of the 59th Illinois and 22nd Indiana. As his infantry laid down to return fire, Johnson summoned Captain Putnam Darden's Jefferson

(Mississippi) Flying Artillery to the western portion of the field to establish counter-battery fire at a range of 400 yards. A half-hour duel ensued, during which the Mississippians disabled one of Pinney's 12-pounder Napoleon guns. The 59th fixed bayonets and prepared to defend the battery, but with eighteen horses down Pinney had to pull back while he still could. Sensing the moment, twenty-seven-year-old Colonel Albert S. Marks of the 17th Tennessee shouted, "Boys! Do you see that battery? It is ours, is it not?" During the subsequent charge, canister so badly mangled Mark's right leg that it had to be amputated. The colonel would survive the war to become governor of Tennessee in 1879. "On and on they came, nothing daunted at the heavy charges of canister and grape the battery . . . was pouring into their ranks," testified Colonel Michael Gooding of the 22nd Indiana. The men of the 59th Illinois dragged Pinney's guns to safety, but two pieces and two caissons had to be abandoned. A bullet left Pinney mortally wounded. Eighteen-year-old Jimmy Fitzpatrick, Mark's adjutant, arrived at the abandoned guns first and, laying his sword across one, claimed them. A bullet instantly struck him in the thigh, leaving him severely wounded. Post ordered a withdrawal, but the staff officer delivering the message was shot. So, too, a second and third messenger. An orderly finally got the dispatch through, and the bluecoats slowly retired, firing from behind logs and trees as they withdrew. The fighting had been savage; twenty officers in the two Tennessee regiments lay dead or wounded.[35]

Bushrod Johnson's three regiments astride and east of Gresham Lane, the 25th, 44th, and 37th Tennessee, a thousand strong, finally emerged from the cedars and into a narrow field, where they collided with the 74th and 75th Illinois. The right flank of the 25th Tennessee came under an enfilade fire from Pinney's guns. The Tennesseans surged into the field for what would become a twenty-minute blood-letting. The grays managed to get off twenty volleys, but the boys from Illinois stubbornly held. Twenty-six-year-old Captain Robert B. Snowden, a member of Johnson's staff, had grown up in Nashville and attended the Western Military Institute. Seeing the 25th Tennessee stall after the loss of its field officers, Snowden, to the point of reckless, rode up and down the line, urging it forward. After the battle, he would be promoted to lieutenant colonel and given command of the regiment. Not until the 59th Illinois, west of the road, fell back, did the two Illinois regiments slowly withdraw into the cedars, losing fifty prisoners in the process. The Tennesseans gained the field at a horrible cost—among the dead and wounded lay the colonel and six officers of the 25th Tennessee and the major and eight officers of the 44th Tennessee.[36]

. . . .

Nearly a thousand yards north of Post's second position sat Colonel Philemon P. Baldwin's 2,500-man brigade—the reserve of Richard Johnson's division. In a year and a half, the twenty-six-year-old colonel, who had begun the war selling agricultural instruments, had risen from first lieutenant to brigade command. His troops, camped in the cedars west of Gresham Lane, routinely stirred about on the morning of December 31—some fetching water, some cooking, some still sleeping. At 6:22 the unmistakable sound of heavy musketry could be heard on the right; the long roll sounded amidst "great confusion." Colonel Granville Moody, the "Fighting Parson" of the 74th Ohio, rode his regimental line, exhorting: "Say your prayers, my boys, and give them your bullets as fast as you can." McCook, casually shaving at his headquarters near the Gresham House, also heard the distant roar. Thinking that his troops had prematurely engaged, he threw down his razor and blurted: "That is contrary to orders!" An aide soon arrived, explaining that the Confederates had initiated the battle. With shaving lather still on his face, the corps commander mounted his horse and galloped to the front; he would not have to ride far.[37]

Post initially deployed his men on the edge of the woods near his encampment—three regiments on the front line and one regiment and the battery in reserve. Johnson arrived on the scene and, about 7:00, strangely ordered Baldwin to push forward the 1st Ohio 300 yards across an open field in his front to the rail fence on the southern edge of the field—why, he never said. Perhaps with terrified stragglers now rushing in and the approaching sounds of battle, Johnson simply felt that he must do something—anything. The 6th Indiana now had to be similarly advanced to the left of the 1st, the Hoosiers facing south and fronting a field. In the seventy-five-yard gap that separated the right of the 6th Indiana and the left of the 1st Ohio, a section of 12-pounder Napoleon guns from Captain Peter Simonson's 5th Indiana Battery unlimbered. The 5th Kentucky (the Louisville Legion) remained in support in the middle of the field, a hundred yards in the rear of the Buckeyes, and the 93rd Ohio in reserve, on the northern edge of the field, thus giving a stacked formation in depth. Simonson's four 10-pounder Parrott rifles dropped trail in the center of the field. Some 500 yards separated Baldwin's front line from Post's brigade.[38]

Johnson rallied fragments of two regiments—Kirk's 30th Indiana and Willich's decimated 39th Indiana, and placed them to the right of the 1st Ohio. Lieutenant Colonel William W. Barry of the 5th Kentucky later noted "some regiment," he did not know which, came in line on the right of the 1st Ohio, indicating the dwindled size of the two regiments. Opportunely, Colonel Sheridan P. Read arrived with his 79th Illinois, having force-marched two miles from the rear, where he had been guarding the ammunition train. Colonel Dodge, who took charge of the three-regiment extended line on Post's right, strongly suggested that Read dismount, which he did under objection. Dodge's line took cover behind a rail fence on the top of a slight ridge, with ground gently sloping toward the enemy.[39]

Liddell waved his 1,700 Arkansans forward toward the Franklin Road. There he halted his fagged troops and went to consult with McCown. The North Carolinian conceded that his division had been "considerably cut up," and that McNair's brigade was still under fire on its right. Indeed, Yankee snipers had gotten in his rear and were reportedly shooting the southern wounded. McCown desired Liddell to replace McNair's exhausted men. Liddell answered that he had orders to be in support, but that he would compromise by coming up on McNair's right. The plan had been set. Riding back to his brigade, Liddell told his Razorbacks that they were "about to go in," and he admonished them to leave prisoners to the cavalry and not break ranks. The hot-tempered Arkansan was not one to be trifled with. Back in 1851, at the age of thirty-six, he had been badly burned and almost died in attempting to save a small black child. The next year he killed two men in a feud. In the spring of 1862 he contracted typhoid fever and almost died. In a foul mood on this particular morning, he had cursed at Yankee prisoners who pleaded for mercy, and he later cursed a Federal surgeon at a hospital—"He [Liddell] gave me an awful cursing and said if he could have his own way, he would kill every one of us and other abusive language," Surgeon J. B. Blount claimed. Liddell would survive the battle and the war, only to be murdered in 1870, a continuation of the 1852 feud.[40]

While moving through a large open field in battle formation, the Arkansans suddenly began to take artillery fire—Simonson's guns. As the troops continued under fire, they could see the Yankees in the distance (the 1st

Ohio) making for a rail fence at the top of the ridge. At two hundred yards the bluecoats unleashed a devastating fire. Liddell's men laid flat to return fire—"I thought they would kill us all," a member of the 8th Arkansas remembered. Liddell's battery, the Warren (Mississippi) Light Artillery, unlimbered their four guns on an eminence in an open field and attempted to neutralize Simonson's guns. Shells landed indiscriminately in the nearby 5th Kentucky (U.S.), killing and wounding many. The Mississippi gunners unfortunately failed to compensate for the upward sloping terrain and also inflicted several casualties in the 6th and 7th Arkansas.[41]

Simonson's guns, the 1st Ohio, and Dodge's makeshift line checked Liddell's Arkansans for fifteen minutes, but McNair's brigade, almost certainly reduced to a thousand men through casualties and exhaustion, but still a powerful force, eventually swung around the Federal right flank, dooming the position. Dodge's regiments buckled first. Colonel Read fell dead almost at the first volley. Lieutenant E. R. Stribley, a staff officer, leaned forward on his horse, hand on knee, and shouted so that Colonel Dodge could hear him, when a bullet struck the lieutenant in the heart. A bullet hit Dodge's horse, causing the animal to jump thirty feet in the air and run uncontrollably away. Dodge wanted to get off, but he did not know how; he eventually fell off, badly shaken. The colonel nonetheless made it to Captain Simonson and warned him of the impending danger. Although two guns had to be abandoned due to dead horses, the other four pieces escaped.[42]

The 1st Ohio fell back in confusion. "The first thing we know, every regiment on our right had gone, and the rebels were pouring it into us from both sides," S. P. Simmons of the 1st wrote his parents. Due to an intervening ridge, Lieutenant Colonel Barry could see no Confederates and concluded that the Buckeyes had exhausted their ammunition. Suddenly, "to my utter amazement," he reported, a large force of grays appeared on his right flank. He attempted to refuse his right companies to receive the enemy when the 1st Ohio came running through his men in "great confusion." (Major J. A. Stafford of the 1st carefully chose the word "entangled" to describe the chaos.) Barry then glanced to his left to see the 6th Indiana give way, although Lieutenant Colonel Hagerman Tripp, commanding the 6th, insisted that the Kentuckians quit the field first, causing *his* withdrawal. It mattered not—the dominoes were all toppling. Jerome P. Holland of the 6th Indiana admitted to his brother and sister: "The men was so confused they just ran in every direction." Even in the midst of the disaster the Hoosiers could not help but laugh at a particular captain who had been complaining about rheumatism and limping about for days with a cane. "My God, look yonder at Captain — —, going across the field, he is just touching the high places."[43]

Baldwin's men ran back to the woods and their reserve regiment, the 93rd Ohio, but, according to a member of the 1st Ohio, they found the cedars so "full of panic stricken stragglers" that it became impossible to form a new line. To the utter disgust of Colonel Charles Anderson of the 93rd Ohio, Baldwin ordered a withdrawal in the face of an imminent attack. Anderson about-faced his men and "in slow time" marched to the rear. As the screaming Texans and Arkansans came tearing through the woods after them, however, the regiment "much increased its speed" until the pace "degenerated into a run." Samuel Hughes of the 93rd, who had no military career to defend, admitted that "our brigade got into the confusion." "I saw men killed as they were running. I saw some wounded, and I expected every moment my time would come next." Captain Henry Richards of the 93rd wrote contemptuously: "They were old [veteran] regiments, too, and we expected better things of them. Our regiment took the panic and followed suit."[44]

Liddell continued north, with his right regiment, the 2nd Arkansas, passing through the front yard of the Gresham House, now serving as a Union hospital. The 2nd gathered up 250 prisoners, an abandoned cannon, and some wagons. When Liddell arrived on the scene he began barking so many orders at once that he got ahead of himself. He admonished a soldier to rejoin his regiment, to which the man replied: "You, General Liddell, just placed me here on guard." "Well, remain there," he snapped.

In truth, the 2nd had not captured the hospital, but rather the 17th Tennessee of Bushrod Johnson's brigade, which was a hundred yards and a half-hour ahead of the Arkansans. When the Tennesseans marched north, they first came under fire from Yankee snipers in a cotton gin seventy yards south of the Gresham House. After chasing them off, the Tennesseans moved past the house, seven companies on the right and three to the left. The regiment then oblique-marched sharply right, leaving the prisoners and cannon captured at the Gresham House hospital for the cavalry to mop up. The commander of the 2nd Arkansas claimed that his regiment captured the hospital, as the vicinity in his direct front had not been cleared of the enemy (which was true) and because no Confederates came behind him (also true). A post-battle row thus developed between Johnson and Liddell as to which unit should get the honors—the 2nd Arkansas or 17th Tennessee. Liddell never backed down, but concluded sardonically that, if the facts "get in the way of General J[ohnson]'s glory, I am willing to let it go."[45]

· · · ·

Advancing to the left of Liddell were the mixed brigades of two veterans— Lucius Polk, a Tennessee planter and nephew of the Bishop-General, and Sterling A. M. Wood, a Florence, Alabama, newspaper editor. Both had been unlucky in previous engagements, Polk having been wounded in the face at Shiloh, head at Richmond, Kentucky, and foot at Perryville, and Wood, thrown by his horse and dragged at Shiloh and wounded in the head at Perryville. This day would be different; both would emerge unscathed. The two brigades had marched out at dawn, Wood's 1,100 men moving up from its reserve position to fill the gap on Polk's right, created when Cheatham's division lagged behind. Wood's 16th Alabama and 45th Mississippi had not gone a hundred yards when they came under artillery fire. Polk had his own problems. Colonel Benjamin J. Hill of the 5th Tennessee, on the far right of the brigade, approached the brigadier with the startling news that he had come under small-arms fire. Polk could hardly believe it; McCown was supposed to have passed over the ground and cleared it. He would soon discover that the only ones before him were Yankees drawing a bead. As Polk rode over to investigate, he too suddenly came under fire, his orderly falling severely wounded.[46]

Waiting in the cedar glade and rocky crevices were the troops of Colonel Billy Carlin. He could have passed for much younger than his thirty-four years. A graduate of West Point, he had fought Sioux and Cheyenne out west, helped keep the peace in Kansas, and later served in the Mormon expedition, for which he had little stomach. He had a superb combat record, having distinguished himself at Perryville, but he proved politically inept. He could not refrain from showing his contempt for certain officers, notably his division commander, Jeff Davis, who held anti-abolitionist views and whom Carlin blamed for getting the 21st Illinois needlessly shot up on December 30. He also detested Colonel Woodruff, who he believed illegitimately passed himself off as a brigadier.[47]

Colonel Leander Stem's raw 101st Ohio and the 38th Illinois waited in ambush in the dense bushes, trees, and rocky sinkholes. Carlin had earlier found Stem, pipe in mouth, preparing to mount, but he discouraged him, fearing he would be too much of a target. The two regiments had deployed a hundred yards in advance of the 21st Illinois and 15th Wisconsin. Yet another hundred yards in the rear of that line, the 2nd Minnesota Battery unlimbered. The 101st and 38th now unleashed a horrific fire "for several minutes," causing Wood's brigade to recoil. Indeed, little could be seen of the Federal line. The 33rd Alabama returned fire at 140 yards, although the commander noted with some disgust that the 16th Alabama, contrary to orders, had already uselessly discharged two or three rounds. Wood decided to simply wait while Polk came up on Carlin's right flank.[48]

During a momentary lull, Carlin removed his two front-line regiments. As the enemy renewed their attack, Carlin called up the 21st Illinois. An orderly arrived with the "startling intelligence," however, that the 21st was under heavy attack—Polk's Tennesseans and Arkansans had made their way around to the flank and rear. Carlin's entire line teetered on collapse. "The air was filled with condensed smoke, the rattling of musketry and the roar of cannon was deafening," W. H. Williams of the 101st Ohio explained to a friend. At the height of the fighting, Carlin's lower right leg suddenly received a severe jolt. Believing that he had been wounded, the colonel nonetheless attempted to make it to the right to ascertain how the 21st Illinois fared. In so doing he heard the thud of a bullet striking his horse. He dismounted, removed his boot, and to his amazement discovered that he had not been hit. The jolt and subsequent blood on his leg came from one of the four wounds his horse had received. He gave his mount to an orderly to take to the rear, but in the process the young private fell, severely wounded.[49]

The Yankees fell back under the combined weight of Polk's and Wood's brigades. "Our regiment became so confused and scattered it was useless to try to rally them," Ohioan Enos Lewis admitted. Jay Butler related that the Rebels came "firing upon us and yelling like Indians." The 38th Indiana held till the enemy came within five steps, but finally gave way. As the brigade fell back toward the Gresham House, explained Lyman Parcher, it withdrew "out of the woods into a cornfield, then a cotton field." Lieutenant Thomas J. Key, the thirty-one-year-old former militant editor of a Helena, Arkansas, newspaper, unlimbered his four-gun battery in a field and exchanged shots with the 2nd Minnesota Battery, in woods two hundred yards east of the Gresham House. For the Rebels, the retreat became a turkey shoot—"Dead bluecoats were thick in every direction," Arkansan William Bevins remembered. Yankees dropped by the dozens in the chaotic retreat; the 101st Ohio would be reduced to a hundred men. As thirty-seven-year-old Tiffin, Ohio, lawyer Colonel Stem shouted, "Stand by your colors, boys, for the honor of the good old state of Ohio," a bullet lodged in his kidney, leaving him mortally wounded.[50]

The 15th Wisconsin, the famed Scandinavian regiment (90 percent Norwegians, the balance Danes and Swedes) held long enough for the 38th Indiana to escape. A captain in the 38th, although wounded three times, stayed back and fought with his revolver till he fell dead. After the 21st Illinois retreated, Colonel Hans Heg explained to his wife that little remained for the Scandinavians to do but also pull back: "I fell back only one Hundred yards to a rail fence, giving the enemy two solid volleys as we retreated." A bullet struck Lieutenant Colonel David McKee of the 15th in the head, killing him instantly. "I believe he expected to be killed," Heg confided. "He was very gloomy the day before, and in the morning before the fight began, he asked his hostler to take his horse—and wanted him to take his watch, and also gave Dr. [Stephen] Himoe most of his money. I did not see him fall, but he was not more than two or three hundred feet from me. The smoke, and noise was so heavy, that little could be seen or heard." Private Lars O. Dokken fell wounded, shot in his thigh. He laid still as the Rebels passed by him, one of them saying: "Here lies a damn Yankee." They proceeded to steal his blanket, canteen, wallet, and pin-and-needle kit.[51]

His men escaping through open country north toward the Wilkinson Pike, Carlin had no place to make a stand. The troops passed through two fields and attempted to form a new line in open woods. This position offered little protection, and the grays soon appeared behind a fence on the east side of a cottonfield, their sharpshooters taking particular aim at mounted officers. In the middle of the brigade sat a collection of high-ranking officers—McCook, Davis, and Carlin, the last having remounted, and their staffs, thus making an inviting target. A sniper's bullet suddenly struck McCook's horse in the shoulder, shooting out a stream of blood. "McCook was a large and fleshy man, but the agility he displayed in leaping from that wounded horse was truly wonderful to behold," Carlin recalled. Unable to hold the line, Davis ordered the brigade back once again.[52]

. . . .

Between 6:30 and 8:30 the Confederates had launched a vicious surprise attack (totally predictable given their past performance at both Shiloh and Perryville) that rolled up five Federal brigades, capturing 1,500 prisoners and eleven guns. To accomplish this stunning success, however, Bragg's plan was already unraveling. McCown's failure to stay on course meant that the battlefield was spreading out. A brigade gap developed on McCown's right that Cleburne had to fill. Because Cleburne outran the dilatory Cheatham, yet another reserve brigade had to be committed. A planned five-brigade front had thus become a seven-brigade front! As at Shiloh, it did not take long for successive waves to become the front line. The benefit of this mishap is that the Confederates constantly overlapped and outflanked the Yankees. Inevitably, however, the thinned southern ranks would have to encounter Rosecrans's reserves. Bragg, on the other hand, would already have every man in two divisions on the front line. Additionally, the initial momentum gained by the surprise attack was already beginning to lose impact, as the alerted Federals began to resist fiercely. While Kirk's and Willich's brigades lost 1,000 prisoners, the brigades of Baldwin, Post, and Carlin sustained losses of only 500.[53]

6

CAVALRY ON THE FLANK

By 7:30 a.m., Wallace's and Gibson's brigades had been all but knocked out of the battle and were clinging for life. After the slaughter at the Smith House, the remnants of the 15th Ohio crossed Overall Creek. It appeared to one member to be "a disorganized crowd" with no one commanding. Following the creek bed north, the Buckeyes eventually formed behind a fence in an open field east of the creek, their right resting on a wooded area. The troops, fearing a cavalry attack, had fixed bayonets, but a sergeant went along the line yelling to detach them, thus making it easier to fire over the rails. Lieutenant Edmund B. Balding, escaping with a single gun from Goodspeed's battery, took position on the left of the regiment. Eventually fragments of the 49th Ohio and 32nd Indiana also came on line. A few shells from Belding's gun kept the enemy at bay, but Wallace realized he could not hold long. He again moved his command, this time to the northeast.[1]

As Wallace's men approached the Wilkinson Pike, they saw a "devil's lane," two fences close together. Crossing them, a member of the 15th Ohio could not help but notice another unit which had linked up—the 89th Illinois, one of Willich's regiments. It appeared to be the only regiment close to being intact, with Colonel Charles T. Hotchkiss calmly conducting a retreat. As the brigade crossed Wilkinson Pike and entered some woods filled with stragglers, a flag was raised and a few voices shouted for the men to rally. "In a moment, almost, the tide of the retreat turned and everyone was cheering and rushing wildly back," a Buckeye remembered. They formed along the fence row, firing at the pursuing Rebels, momentarily checking their advance.[2]

• • • •

The Confederate cavalry was on the prowl, specifically Wharton's 2,000 troopers, reinforced with one of Pegram's regiments. Positioned on Hardee's left, the brigade crossed the Franklin Pike and Puckett's Creek, riding north along the east bank of Overall Creek. Wharton, a hard-fighting former Texas lawyer who had worked his way up through the ranks from captain in the 8th Texas Cavalry, had been plagued with wounds and sickness and had returned to duty only three months earlier. As for his Texas Rangers, known for their wide-brim hats with a single lone star and their six-shooters, even an Alabamian had to admit they were "certainly a hard looking set." Somewhat taken aback by the rapid advance of the infantry, Wharton quickened the pace from a trot to a gallop.[3]

Blocking Wharton's advance were the 950 troopers of forty-two-year-old Bavarian-born Colonel Lewis Zahm's Ohio cavalry brigade, reinforced with the 2nd East Tennessee Cavalry from the reserve brigade. Since 6:00 a.m., Zahm had been scouting along Overall Creek. Seeing refugees streaming north from the front line, it became clear that a disaster had befallen Johnson's division. The nervous troopers formed east of the creek. "Never mind boys—keep steady and keep your carbines ready!" an officer shouted. Peering into the distance and seeing what appeared to be a force twice his own, Zahm pulled his line back toward the Wilkinson Pike. "We fell back a little, and changed front to suit their line, when 'boom' comes a shell from the woods in our rear . . . coming from the direction we had supposed occupied by our friends." The stunned troopers turned in horror to see "long lines of gray-backed infantry." Wharton unlimbered the three guns of White's Tennessee Battery and began shelling "pretty lively." Zahm withdrew with the loss of three men, including Major D. A. B. Moore of the 1st Ohio Cavalry, who fell mortally wounded from a shell fragment. Several shells burst within two feet of Zahm, but he escaped harm. Ironically, after the battle, his horse fell on him, leaving the colonel seriously injured. He had to take a furlough and never returned due to ill health.[4]

Zahm's hard-pressed brigade finally connected with Gibson's makeshift infantry line, only a few hundred men and Belding's rifled gun, in a cornfield a little over a half-mile south of the Wilkinson Pike near Overall Creek. Wharton prepared his battery for action, while Colonel John T. Cox's 1st Confederate Cavalry formed for a charge. A few well-placed shots from

White's guns created consternation in the blue ranks; the gray horsemen overran Gibson's feeble line, with Zahm's cavalry fleeing. In one of his few aggressive moves this day, Zahm rallied his men and launched a counterattack that threw Cox's regiment into confusion and recaptured most of the infantry, Gibson included. As the Federals pulled back, four companies of the Texas Rangers captured what Wharton called a complete four-gun battery, probably three of Goodspeed's escaping guns and one of Pinney's.[5]

The blue-jacketed troopers continued their withdrawal through a large strip of woods to a cornfield southeast of Asbury Church, at one time paralleling a column of Rebel infantry not twenty yards distant. Captain Gates P. Thruston arrived and frantically informed Zahm that the entire ammunition train of McCook's corps, seventy-six wagons, was approaching Asbury Road, which ran east-west (as opposed to Asbury Lane, which ran north-south), attempting to get to the Nashville Pike, and must be saved "at all hazards." How the wagons arrived to this point was a story in itself. Initially parked near McCook's headquarters on the Wilkinson Pike, Thruston had taken them cross-country through ravines, cedar thickets, and fences toward the east-west juncture of Asbury Lane. Along the way he fought off pesky Rebel cavalry with a seventy-five-man train guard and Davis's escort company. Now they were caught out in the open fields south of the Widow Burris House with no place left to run.[6]

Zahm formed his brigade in the cornfield, with the wagons parked behind it. The 4th Ohio Cavalry and 2nd East Tennessee Cavalry held the right, along and near the bend in Asbury Lane, southeast of Asbury Church. The 3rd Ohio Cavalry anchored the left, with the 1st Ohio Cavalry held in reserve. Wharton's brigade probably approached from the southwest, as it followed Thurston's wagons. Once again, White's guns turned the trick. A few shells bursting and the 2nd East Tennessee Cavalry, in Zahm's words, "broke and ran like sheep." The 4th Ohio Cavalry, having sustained only a few casualties in the shelling, also quit the line "at a lively gait." The 3rd Ohio Cavalry repositioned closer to the Widow Burris House, somewhat sheltered by the house and barn.[7]

The Texas Rangers, according to Thruston, "charged down upon us like a tempest . . . yelling like a lot of devils." The Texans overran McCook's baggage train and then turned their attention to the real prize—the ammunition train, which had been left "high and dry in a corn field." The teamsters fired a volley, then ran for cover behind a fence and in a nearby thicket. "Our teamsters outran the cavalry," Thruston admitted. John C. Zollenger, one of the teamsters, witnessed Wharton's men bear down on Zahm's troopers. "Our cavalry broke and ran," he wrote, while "our infantry threw down their arms and run for dear life." A Texas Ranger denounced the Federal cavalrymen as "the poorest horsemen I ever saw."[8]

Amandus Silsby coincidentally found himself with the wagons as the Texans struck. As he was a member of the 24th Wisconsin, his shoes had played out before he got to the battlefield. Useless in his sock feet and in pain, officers sent him to the rear. He now shuddered as he saw the teamsters panic. "The ground was strewn with pots and kettles, pans, camp stoves, tents, and boxes," he explained to his father. "Our cavalry fled. [C]losely following the wagons galloped the Texas Rangers cheering & shouting to the teamsters to halt. Another moment and they were alongside the wagons shooting them down from the backs of the horses and mules. The driver of the wagon I was in fell dead from his horse. One of the butternuts seized hold of the horses head & stopped them." As Silsby was taken to the rear as a prisoner, he noticed a Texan riding with a beautiful Federal flag draped on his shoulder—a Stars and Stripes silk flag with gold fringe.[9]

Sergeant Alexander S. Johnston, a wounded gunner in Battery H, 4th United States, who had been placed in the Widow Burris House, witnessed the capture of the train. A corporal in the 6th Ohio, also wounded, peered out the window and yelled: "By God, sergeant, look here! I believe our whole army is retreating." As the southerners approached the house, the Buckeye grabbed his rifle and took aim through the window, but, being under a hospital flag, Johnston discouraged him from firing. Soon the Texans came into the front yard, dismounted, and swarmed in and around the house, taking blankets, overcoats, rations, and the surgeon's horses.[10]

The Texans momentarily became distracted from the wagons and instinctively began chasing fleeing teamsters. Wharton eventually re-directed his brigade right, crossing the Wilkinson Pike between the Smith and Jenkins houses. Colonel Minor Milliken, his 1st Ohio Cavalry in reserve, made a decision, partly out of desperation and partly because he had always had an ambition to make a saber charge. He ordered Major James W. Paramore's battalion of five companies to wheel about in column of fours, draw sabers, and charge. Brandishing the sword that his father had given him at Christmas, Milliken led the way. A chaplain, Albert G. Hart, in the Widow Burris House, witnessed the event. "Then down they [Paramore's battalion] went, every horse plunging forward, every man yelling like a mad man, every saber flashing in the bright sunlight. I could see the wounded falling from the saddles. It was a never-to-be-forgotten sight."

The Buckeyes slashed their way through the startled Texas Rangers and the 2nd Georgia Cavalry, throwing them in disorder. In the words of Ranger B. F. Batchelor: "As we rose the hill an exciting scene presented itself—the poor Georgians who were mostly armed with long Enfield Rifles & nothing less had fired & unable to load in face of the advancing foe had turned & with heads smartly stretching forward like 'Turkeys in a drive' were kicking their horses for dear life." Although momentarily successful, Milliken realized that he could not possibly hold his position and ordered a recall. Falling captive to a private in the Rangers, the colonel exclaimed: "I will never surrender to a rebel." He was instantly shot in the neck and killed. In the subsequent counter-attack, the Texans engulfed the Ohio battalion, killing and wounding fifteen and capturing another fifteen. The Federals later recovered Milliken's body, less his overcoat and sword. The gleeful southerners began collecting the captured teams and wagons. In the distance, however, Colonel James P. Fyffe's brigade, sent earlier by Rosecrans when he received word that the train was in trouble, began to arrive. Captain George R. Swallow unlimbered the guns of the 7th Indiana Battery and began shelling the graycoats as they attempted to remove the wagons across the field.[11]

Federal cavalry reinforcements were also on the way. Fearful of matters on his right, the army chief of staff had sent Captain Elmer Otis's 4th United States Cavalry, six companies of 260 men, from army headquarters toward Overall Creek. "Otis, there is cavalry on our flank—go and look after them," Garesche said. Joining the Regulars would be two companies, about 80 men, of the 3rd Kentucky Cavalry, sent by Colonel Kennett, the division commander. The Ohio corporal watching events unfolding from within the Widow Burris House turned to Sergeant Johnston and uttered: "Now you will see some fun, here comes the Fourth Regular cavalry." Johnston glanced out the window and saw them forming for an assault. Arriving at the opportune moment, Otis shouted to his men: "Don't you fire a shot until you take each your man by the scalp. Forward—trot!" The troopers slammed into the flank of the 2nd Tennessee Cavalry, scattering it, capturing 100 men, retaking 250 Union prisoners, Goodspeed's and Pinney's four guns, and most of the ordnance train, and capturing 50 to 60 Rebels in the process. To his father Silsby wrote: "Ten minutes more another shout & the 4th Regular Cavalry came dashing down, commenced shooting at them. . . . The Rebels turned to skeedaddle but found the [2nd] East Tennessee Cavalry coming down on them from the other side, so they were compelled to stand. 'Draw sabers! Give them hell!' And for once I had a chance to see a cavalry charge."[12]

The brilliant charge would propel the career of twenty-seven-year-old Captain Eli Long, a graduate of the Kentucky Military Institute and a lieutenant in the Regular Cavalry prior to the war, where he fought Indians in Kansas. Before war's end, he would command a brigade. The 3rd Ohio Cavalry provided a screen, giving time for the ammunition wagons to move toward the Nashville Pike. Having routed the 4th Tennessee Cavalry, Otis sighted White's battery four hundred yards in the rear. In the chaotic charges and counter-charges that had occurred, only 125 troopers of the 2nd Tennessee Cavalry remained as a support. Otis's 230 Regulars attempted to take the guns but were checked by several rounds from the cannoneers. Otis sought the help of the 3rd Ohio Cavalry, but an officer refused, stating that the removal of the train took precedence. He was right, but Otis later wrote with disgust: "I have no doubt I could have taken the artillery." Nonetheless, the ordnance train, save five wagons, had been secured.[13]

Thruston reported to Rosecrans. "Are you the officer who says McCook's ammunition train was saved?" the general inquired. Thruston saluted and nodded affirmatively. The general asked where the wagons were, whereupon the captain took him but a few yards towards Stones River and pointed. "How did you manage to get it away over there?" the general queried. "Well, General, we did some sharp fighting, but we did a great deal of running," the captain answered. Rosecrans smiled, slapped him on the shoulder, and said: "Captain, consider yourself a major from today."[14]

As for Wharton, his flank attack had been largely a bust. He returned with only 400 prisoners and five wagons. Hardee's escort also captured a small herd of 327 beeves. The Federals simply had enough troops in the rear and plugged the breach within a few hours. Wheeler's jaded troopers, operating west of Overall Creek, accomplished even less. In the afternoon he crossed to the east bank and withdrew to the Wilkinson Pike.[15]

IN THE REAR

About 1:00 a.m. on the thirty-first, Garesche sent David Stanley a dispatch to proceed to Stewart's Creek, where the enemy had reportedly attacked a wagon train. Stanley took with him the 1st Tennessee Cavalry (U.S.) and 15th Pennsylvania Cavalry in what amounted to a wild goose chase. Arriving around 5:00 a.m., he found Colonel Joe Burke, commanding the 10th Ohio, which served as provost guard at the creek. Stanley joined Burke and the regimental chaplain (a Father O'Higgins) in eating breakfast and imbibing on a jug of whiskey. Scouts arrived at daybreak and brought assurances that the train was secure. From a casual view, the scene appeared damaging—the cavalry chief in the rear drinking, while the army's right was being routed. He had been sent under orders by the army chief of staff, however. As for the inconsequential drinking incident, criticized by modern writers, the cavalryman told the incident on himself.[16]

Later that morning, Colonel Moses Walker's brigade, along with Minty's 4th Michigan Cavalry and 1st Battalion, 7th Pennsylvania Cavalry, arrived from La Vergne. At this point, Stanley received Garesche's urgent message to "hasten to the right and do your best to restore order." For the first time the magnitude of the disaster became apparent. Leaving 120 troopers of the 4th Michigan Cavalry and a section of Battery D, 1st Ohio Light Artillery, at Stewartsboro to guard the trains, and the 10th Ohio at Stewart's Creek, Stanley and Walker proceeded to the front. The cavalry arrived about 2:00 p.m.—a welcome sight. A line formed along Asbury Road, with the 4th Michigan Cavalry, supported by the 1st Tennessee Cavalry (U.S.) on the left, and the 1st Battalion, 7th Pennsylvania Cavalry, two companies of the 3rd Kentucky Cavalry, and the 15th Pennsylvania Cavalry holding the right— in all 950 horsemen, but fighting dismounted, meaning that probably no more than 700 men held the line. For now they waited.[17]

Late in the afternoon, Wheeler drove Stanley's cavalry behind a wooded ridge along the Nashville Pike. He planned an attack, but before his horsemen got into position, Stanley led a saber charge with two companies of the 4th Michigan Cavalry, 50 men of the 15th Pennsylvania Cavalry, and a battalion of the 7th Pennsylvania Cavalry. Caught in flank, Wheeler's men scrambled to the rear in disorder. Colonel William W. Allen of the 1st Alabama Cavalry had his right hand shattered and his horse killed. Remounting behind his bugler, he went back into action with his hand raised, yelling to his men to "Avenge this!" Minty meanwhile assaulted with the balance of the 4th Michigan Cavalry and 15th Pennsylvania Cavalry and the 5th Tennessee Cavalry (U.S.). With dusk approaching, Wheeler withdrew.[18]

Modern historians have criticized Bragg's use of cavalry. Wheeler "almost rode himself out of the battle," "chose not to support Wharton," and "accomplished nothing" on the first day's battle. Had Wheeler operated with a unified command—that is, his, Buford's, and Wharton's brigades— the Nashville Pike might have been severed. At the very least, a thousand-or-so dismounted troopers could have provided Hardee with reinforcements on his weak left.[19]

7

SHERIDAN HOLDS THE LINE

DRIVE THEM WITH THE BAYONET

Something had gone wrong in Cheatham's division. Six o'clock had come and gone, and no movement had occurred; nor would it for nearly an hour. The cause would not come to light until after the battle. In a word, the division commander labored under the influence of alcohol, if not out-and-out drunk. Cheatham had ridden along the line of Maney's and Vaughn's brigades that morning, waving his hat to inspire his troops, when he unceremoniously fell off his horse, to the utter horror of his on-looking Tennesseans. He laid on the ground "as limp and helpless as a bag [of] meal." Other eyewitnesses would give testimony to his inebriated state this day. The Tennessean never contested Bragg's later allegations of drunkenness. If McCown's failure to incline right caused the first gap in the Confederate line, it was Cheatham's intemperate state that caused the second gap.[1]

This appalling state of affairs would not in and of itself have delayed the attack, since Cheatham's division formed in reserve behind Withers's front line. At the last moment, however, Polk had adjusted the command structure. Due to the rugged terrain and length of the line, the Bishop determined to give the left two brigades in both the front and rear lines to Cheatham, and the right two front and rear brigades to Withers. Given the terrible confusion and mixing of lines that had occurred at Shiloh, the concept was not a bad one, but the time had passed for implementation. Withers and Cheatham should more properly have stacked their brigades in a two-two formation. Polk's ad-hoc structure would cause confusion and, in the case of Withers's left two brigades, now under Cheatham, also a delay. None of this seemed to matter as Bragg passed Cheatham's division on the way to see Polk. In a rarely recorded scene of affection, the Tennesseans greeted the army commander with loud cheers and pressed forward to see him.[2]

The troops stood patiently in line, listening to the din of battle off to their left. At 7:00 thirty-seven-year-old Colonel John Q. Loomis, like so many other colonels a former lawyer, led his 2,400-man-brigade en echelon—one Louisiana and five Alabama regiments, northwesterly from a strip of woods east of the Widow Smith House and into a two-hundred-yard-wide cottonfield. The enemy, supported by artillery, held the wooded area lining the opposite end of the field.[3]

Loomis fell against the left of Davis's division, Colonel William E. Woodruff's brigade of three regiments—the 35th and 25th Illinois, 81st Indiana—as well as three guns of Captain Stephen J. Carpenter's 8th Wisconsin Battery and the 24th Wisconsin, the last in Joshua Sill's brigade of Sheridan's division. Earlier that morning Woodruff had expressed concern about the gap that existed between Carpenter's guns and the 24th Wisconsin. He requested that Sill bring forward additional regiments from the reserve. Sill, a thirty-one-year-old Ohio-born West Pointer described as "reserved almost to a fault," agreed, but hardly had the 15th Missouri and 44th Illinois moved up than they were recalled. Davis told Woodruff that he would have to do the best he could with what he had.[4]

The battle on the far right had been raging for half an hour, and Woodruff's men stood full alerted. The blue-coated infantry came on line behind a fence at the edge of a wood, fronted by a large cottonfield—the very one that Loomis would be diagonally crossing. "We waited till they got near enough and gave them a sudden volley which staggered them and they had to stop, but tried it again; as we were behind a fence we had a little advantage," James K. Wier of the 25th Illinois told his mother. Colonel Loomis, who had been wounded at Shiloh, did not even clear the woods before a cannonball struck a large limb that fell on his shoulder, so injuring him that he had to quit the field; he would resign after the battle. Command fell to thirty-five-year-old Colonel John G. Coltart, formerly proprietor of Coltart & Son, a Huntsville book dealer and publisher. Suddenly the Alabamians came under a raking fire, as Carpenter's guns had them "mowed [them] down as grass beneath the sickle." In later describing the cottonfield to his wife, 19th Alabama Sergeant Ambrose Doss wrote: "I saw more dead men in one field than I saw in the hole Shilow battle." The 25th Illinois and 81st Indiana eventually fell back 150 yards under the onslaught. Colo-

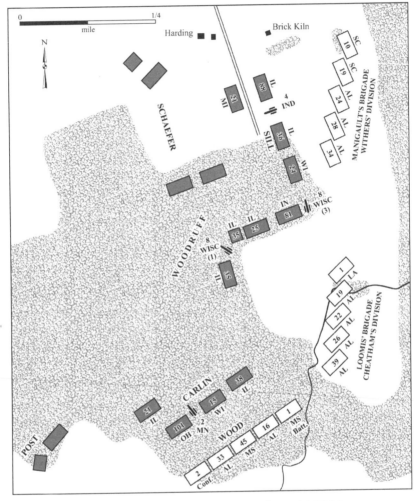

December 31, 7:00 a.m., Woodruff's Brigade, Davis's Division

nel Thomas Williams of the 25th Illinois grabbed his regimental flag and shouted, "We will plant it here, boys, and rally the old Twenty-Fifth around it, and here we will die"; a ball suddenly struck him dead. Captain Carpenter also fell mortally wounded. The fire "came nearer and directly it was one sheet of flame and smoke on our right so we had to run to save ourselves from being cut off. . . . The whole line of battle was running for life," Wier admitted. "I thought everything was lost. I thought it was a stampede and a Manassas affair."[5]

As the 25th Illinois and 81st Indiana fell back in disarray, the Alabamians gave chase. This exposed their left flank to the 35th Illinois, which faced easterly along a ridge at right angle to the brigade, placing it in perfect position to enfilade Loomis's line. The colonel of the 26th Alabama stated that the Union fire "raked down our lines with heavy damage to us." The 25th Illinois and 81st Indiana rallied and made a counter-attack with the bayonet, driving the Alabamians back past the cottonfield and beyond, reclaiming Carpenter's abandoned 10-pounder Parrott rifle. Captain A. H. Flewellen of the 39th Alabama, writing only days after the battle, related: "We reached the battery [8th Wisconsin], or very near it, and captured one piece, but we were compelled to fall back under a heavy fire to where we first started."[6]

At 7:15, Coltart's three right-wing regiments—the 1st Louisiana, 19th Alabama, and 22nd Alabama—came under a blistering fire from Bush's guns and the 24th Wisconsin. The regiments executed a left half-wheel and then came straight forward. The raw Milwaukee regiment nervously braced for the assault, with the flag bearer rolling up his banner and skulking behind a tree. "Their banners flying, and uttering a horrid yell, they advanced heeding neither shot, shell or bullet. Our men were firing and loading as quickly as possible and picking them off fast," wrote Lieutenant Robert Chivas. Major E. C. Hibbard gave the order to "break to the rear," but not all of the companies received the order simultaneously, thus making for a chaotic withdrawal. The regiment fell back to the open ground south of the Wilkinson Pike.[7]

With the 24th Wisconsin in retreat, the right of the 36th Illinois became exposed. Colonel Nicholas Greusel and his Prairie State veterans of Pea Ridge and Perryville held firm. When the Greusel family arrived in America from Germany in 1833, sixteen-year-old Nicholas, along with his brothers and sisters, was given his father's blessing and literally turned out on the street, knowing no English. He would be in and out of many jobs, but ultimately ended up in the railroad business. Greusel commanded a company of Michigan volunteers during the Mexican War. The battle had now come to this hard-life German immigrant, and he refused to budge. Ironically, the colonel would have to leave the army after this battle, due to rheumatism contracted from sleeping out in the open. In 1864 he and his wife would give birth to their twelfth child—a son name Philip H. Sheridan Greusel.[8]

For half an hour, the 36th Illinois stubbornly held its ground with Coltart's right approaching to within fifty yards. Supporting the regiment were the batteries of Captain Charles Houghtaling's C, 1st Illinois Light Artillery, and Captain Henry Hescock's G, 1st Missouri Light Artillery, firing obliquely from a high ridge in the rear of Sheridan's line. The Confederates briefly withstood the punishing fire, but then wavered and fell back. Greusel ordered his men to fix bayonets and charge. The advance came simultaneously with Woodruff's counter-attack; all along the line Coltart's Alabamians fell back. By the time the 36th Illinois had been recalled, the 24th Wisconsin had also returned to its former position, thus re-establishing the original line. Woodruff and Sill had soundly repulsed the first wave hurled at them.[9]

Victory had come with a price. In charging with the 36th Illinois, Sill had been fatally shot near the guns of Bush's battery, the bullet entering his mouth, then the brain, and exiting the skull. Cannoneer Ed Abbott was within ten feet of Sill, the brigadier's out-of-control horse nearly trampling him. "He was still breathing and as the air bubbled through the stream of blood he seemed like a drowning man," wrote Lieutenant John Mitchell of the 24th Wisconsin, who almost stumbled over Sill's body as he searched for him. An adjutant removed the brigadier's sword and handed it to Mitchell, as several men placed the limp body on a blanket and carried it to the Gresham House. There the gray infantry of both Johnson's and Liddell's brigades would find his body and argue over who killed him. In truth, he was already dead and the body abandoned.[10]

The bloodied and exhausted Alabamians fell back to the woods to regroup. Major John Marrast of the 22nd Alabama singled out a particular lieutenant who cowardly ran, but noted that most of his men behaved well. The flag bearer, a Sergeant Austin, fell mortally wounded in a hail of bullets. Three times, as he lay prostrate on the ground, he waved his hand over his head and shouted: "Victory or Death!" The regimental flag momentarily passed to Marrast. The Alabamians retreated in some disorder under the galling fire to the edge of the woods where the attack began. There some 75 to 100 men rallied and advanced to the support of the troops still engaged. As they reached them, however, "they too gave way and we again fell back to our first position."[11]

. . . .

At 7:30 a.m., as Coltart's brigade retreated in disarray, Cheatham brought up one of his supporting brigades from three hundred yards in the rear—Colonel Alfred J. Vaughn's 1,773 infantry, all Tennesseans except for the 9th Texas. Brigadier General William Preston, the brigade commander, had gone to visit his sick wife, leaving the thirty-two-year-old Vaughn, a graduate of the Virginia Military Institute and former Mississippi farmer, temporarily in command. The men came in line and began dropping their knapsacks into piles, prompting several to say: "You know what that means." Indeed they did; the brigade would soon be going in. As Coltart's Alabamians fell back, they withstood some smug jeers from the Tennesseans, prompting an angry retort: "You'll soon find it the hottest place you ever struck." Nonetheless, a Tennessean wrote critically in his diary that evening that Loomis's men "disgracefully fled."[12]

When the Alabamians cleared the front, Vaughn's Tennesseans marched out of the woods, between the Burgess House on the right and the Widow Smith House on the left, and into the same cottonfield. Cheatham gave an order to fire an initial volley under the smoke of the enemy's guns, and then load and fire advancing. "We fired all at once and rose yelling," W. J. M'Dearman of the 12th Tennessee recalled. The Tennesseans ran into the same meat grinder that the Alabamians had encountered and with the same results. In the 13th Tennessee, Lieutenant Colonel William E. Morgan and Major P. H. Cole both fell mortally wounded. As casualties mounted, the Tennesseans fell back under the staggering fire, having lost a third of their men and every horse in the brigade save two. A company in the 12th Tennessee lost 22 of 44 men in the initial charge. "The enemy cheered like a lot of little schoolboys," one of Vaughn's men bitterly recalled.[13]

Cheatham continued to commit his brigades piecemeal. Although there are discrepancies, it would appear that Arthur M. Manigault's brigade had not moved in tandem with Loomis 7:00 assault, as the battle plan had stipulated. Indeed, from the amount of enfilade fire Vaughn received on the right, it is highly possible that Manigault failed to support even the 7:30 attack. In his rough draft and final report, Cheatham submitted two times for Manigault's first advance—7:30 and 8:00, the last being the official time. It is highly possible that neither Loomis nor Vaughn was properly supported.[14]

Although not college educated, Maniagult (pronounced *manny-go*) had toured Europe and fought in the Mexican War, during which he fell wounded on two occasions. Both he and his wife, Mary, came from distinguished

Charleston families. At the start of the war the family lived in White Oak, their rice plantation near Georgetown, South Carolina. As a member of a militia company, Manigault had help construct the batteries that would open fire on Fort Sumter. His brigade counted five regiments—three Alabama and two South Carolina, in all some 2,200 men.[15]

Manigault struck Sill's line en echelon. The leading regiments on the left, the 34th and 28th Alabama, cleared the woods and moved into a cottonfield, where they came under a withering fire. The Alabamians suddenly found their left exposed, as Loomis's brigade fell back in disorder, causing them to likewise flee. Heavy-set Colonel Julius Caesar Bonaparte Mitchell, the wealthy forty-three-year-old planter who had equipped his 34th Alabama, had dismounted before leaving the safety of the woods. As the brigade fell back he became winded, prompting a burly soldier to say: "You'll be taken prisoner, Colonel, if you don't get away from here in a hurry." Taking his advice, the exhausted colonel unceremoniously rode piggyback and made good his escape.[16]

Having to contend with no counter-battery fire, the guns of Captain Asahel K. Bush's 4th Indiana Battery, on the front line in an open field between the 36th and 88th Indiana, and Houghtaling's and Hescock's batteries in the rear, zeroed in on the "fresh brigade of the enemy," coming "in a splendid order." On Sill's left lay the 88th Illinois, the so-called Second Board of Trade Regiment—another raw unit outfitted by the Chicago Board of Trade. Colonel Francis T. Sherman, commanding the 88th, was perhaps best known for his famous father—Frances T. Sherman, the antiwar Democratic mayor of Chicago. After the battle, the young colonel would create quite a stir by writing a prowar letter that found its way into the Republican *Chicago Tribune*, which caused a rift between father and son. Although embarrassed by the episode, the colonel refused to back down. He intensely disliked two of his fellow regimental commanders in the brigade—Colonel Charles H. Larabee of the 24th Wisconsin, who was "drunk half the time," and Colonel Greusal of the 36th Illinois, who was "not entirely free from this vice."[17]

Sherman now watched as the enemy came into full view. For a few moments, "everything was still as death," as the Rebels approached "with flags flying as if on parade ground." They approached to within a hundred yards and then, with a yell, charged. At seventy-five yards, Sherman ordered the regiment to open fire. "Like the grass before the scythe of the mower[,] the ranks of the enemy went down as that volley went crashing and tearing through their ranks," Sherman described to his father. "It brought them to a dead halt for a moment, and then on they came again. The halt was fatal to them; it gave my men time to reload. Again another crashing volley tore through their decimated ranks. Still stubborn, these brave but infatuated [*sic*] men lay down and attempted to return fire, but the advantage was ours. . . . 'Twas now that I ordered the battalion to rise and give them hell. At that word every man sprang to his feet and we poured in such a fire upon them that they were forced to leave the ground on the double quick and retire to the timber beyond." William McGregor, one of those fighting in the ranks of the 88th Illinois, related to a friend: "We gave them the best we had[.] they made a right face and sought shelter in a piece of timber where they lay down but still in sight[.] we made it too hot for them[.]"[18]

Manigault admitted that the artillery fire proved terrible and that no troops could have withstood it. With no support to relieve the pressure on his right, the brigade did not get 150 yards. According to Lieutenant Colonel William B. Dennett of the 24th Alabama: "The enemy's guns were playing upon us with such terrible effect when an order was given by some one to march in retreat. The Regt. fell back to the breastworks." In this charge, Colonel William A. Buck of the 24th fell wounded, Major Newton N. Davis disabled by a shell, and Dennett stunned by the concussion of a shell.[19]

. . . .

All along the line Cheatham's provisional division had been bloodily repulsed in piecemeal assaults—first Coltart, then Vaughn, followed by Manigault. About 8:15 (Cheatham had apparently sobered up, or at least sufficiently so), a coordinated attack was at last made by Vaughn and Coltart; whether it was precisely planned that way is murky. After Vaughn's repulse, his men retired to the Triune Road. Having rested ten minutes and replenished ammunition, another assault was attempted a little to the left across the same field. This slight westward shift enabled the far left of Vaughn's brigade, the 9th Texas, to walk into the gap which had been recently created by the withdrawal of Carlin's brigade.[20]

Led by twenty-two-year-old Colonel William H. Young, who had only a year earlier graduated from the University of Virginia, the Texans marched unopposed to the top of a hill, where they spotted Woodruff's brigade, obliquely to the right 200 yards. Two volleys proved ineffective, so Young moved by the left flank, to a six-foot-tall rail fence only 100 yards distant. Scaling the fence, the Texans stopped fifty paces short rather than continue their assault. It became a killing field, as the 35th Illinois unleashed a murderous fire; over a hundred Texans dropped within five minutes. His horse shot, Young's frantic orders to advance could not be heard. "At this critical moment the color bearer was shot down when Colonel Young seized the colors and bore them almost within the abolitionists ranks and the boys rushed forward yelling and shouting at the top of their voices and the enemy broke and fled in wild confusion," Texan J. K. Street described to his wife, concluding, "[I]t is enough to say we gave the miserable abolition invaders one of the worse whipings [*sic*] they ever had."[21]

Woodruff's ammunition supplies had reached a critical state. Coupled with what appeared to be "fresh troops on our right," in truth Vaughn's repositioned brigade, Woodruff's men began to break toward the Wilkinson Pike. Whether or not Woodruff was actually present at the time has been questioned. The colonel stated that he placed the 8th Wisconsin Battery near the Wilkinson Pike, a quarter of a mile distant, to cover his brigade's withdrawal; whether he returned is uncertain. Regimental commanders seem to imply that they took it upon themselves to withdraw.[22]

As Woodruff's men gave way, the 15th Missouri and 44th Illinois, from Colonel Frederick Schaefer's brigade, in reserve behind Greusel's (late Sill's) brigade, received orders to rush 250 yards south to his support. By the time they arrived and entered the woods north of the now infamous cotton-field, Woodruff's men had passed. The two reinforcing regiments suddenly found themselves not in support, but facing an enemy "six columns deep." Worse yet, the 36th Illinois of Greusel's brigade, their ammunition finally exhausted and, having lost a staggering 212 casualties (including Major Silas Miller who had cursed till his voice gave out, now wounded and a prisoner), "broke and ran" to the left of the fresh regiments. It proved too much; the 15th and 44th also fell back.[23]

Even before the 36th Illinois gave way, the Chicago 88th Illinois had disintegrated, running through the ranks of its supporting regiment, the 21st Michigan. Writing to his friend days after the battle, Arza Bartholomew of the 21st explained the chaos:

The first fire was on our right, and before we knew it, they drove the brigade we were supporting. A regiment [88th Illinois] ran right through our ranks and broke us all to pieces. When we reformed, we were nearly surrounded, so we gave them one last volley and fell back twenty yards to a fence. Every man fought on his own hook to the best advantage until they drove us into a swamp. Our unit was nearly surrounded and cut to pieces. They fired into us from front and rear and piled our men in heaps. The balls were thick as hail. Shot and shell cut down trees like scythes cutting grain. It was awful to see trees falling and riderless horses running around. I hope never to see such a desperate time again.

At the end of the day, according to Bartholomew, the regiment counted only 85 of 300 men.[24]

Slicing through Greusel's line were Manigault's Alabamians and South Carolinians, who at 8:30 had returned for a third assault, this time supported by Maney's Tennesseans. Maney, and for that matter his regimental commanders, insisted that they moved out promptly at 8:00 a.m. Well and good, but Manigault unquestionably attacked twice without them. On this, the third attempt, the crumbling Yankee line made "but feeble resistance."[25]

Colonel George Washington Roberts, the twenty-nine-year-old Yale graduate and Chicago lawyer commanding Sheridan's left brigade, sensed an opportunity. Finding the division commander on the ridge at Hescock's battery, he requested permission to change front—from east to south, in order to strike Manigault's right flank as it entered the woods vacated by Nick Greusel's brigade. Sheridan enthusiastically approved the plan and suggested that he try the bayonet. Roberts returned and formed his four Illinois regiments in two lines in a field south of the Harding House. In the first line, the 51st Illinois held the right, the 42nd Illinois the left, with the 22nd Illinois in the rear of the 42nd. The 27th Illinois, never officially accounted for, was apparently held in support. Strict orders came down not to fire until ordered, and with that the command "Forward, march!" rang out. The brigade had not tramped far before it encountered the 88th Illinois and 21st Michigan, firing from behind fences along Harding Lane and thus blocking his path. Roberts sent his adjutant to instruct the regiments to cease firing and lie down—his troops would literally be marching over them. So loud was the din of battle that Colonel Sherman could not make out the adjutant's words. The adjutant thus rode to the fence and by motions got the men to level it and then to lie flat. The 42nd Illinois stepped over the troops of the 88th Illinois and cleared the fence first (the 51st Illinois got delayed in rugged terrain). Without waiting, Roberts realigned his old regiment, ordered a "Charge bayonet!" and rode the length of the regiment waving his hat and yelling, "Don't fire a shot! Drive them with the bayonet!" Corporal Dwight A. Lincoln described the scene thus in a letter to his father: "On we went, the boys cheering, and the enemy peppering us and falling back. We drove them and regained the old ground, which was covered by dead and wounded." According to Thomas J. Maxwell of the 42nd Illinois, the Rebels laid down on a slight rise in a field, but "when we came within about 30 rods [165 yards] of them, they broke and ran like a flock of sheep."[26]

The audacious Illinois riflemen slammed into Manigault's right flank—the 10th and 19th South Carolina—completing routing it. By the time Dennett's 24th Alabama came up, he found the Carolinians "falling back in confusion, running through our ranks and breaking our line," causing his regiment to fall back fifty yards. Although buying much needed time for Sheridan, Roberts's solo attack ultimately could not have succeeded. Indeed, S. A. M. Wood's brigade had already worked its way into the rear of their position. Waters's Alabama Battery came up in support of Manigault's Carolinians and opened with canister, but the gunners fired too high and merely struck limbs. Sheridan had Roberts recalled.[27]

A lull now occurred, during which Sheridan attempted to piece together a second defensive position along the ridge north of the Harding House, where he had his artillery posted. He requested Davis to form on his right, but to no avail. So demoralized was the First Division that most of the troops drifted back past the Wilkinson Pike and reformed behind Thomas's corps. Sheridan did take note of the demeanor of Billy Carlin, calmly smoking a stumpy pipe, which stood in stark contrast to Davis's "excited manner." Seeing Cleburne's and Cheatham's divisions moving in concert, the first toward the Gresham House and the last toward the Blanton House on the Wilkinson Pike, Sheridan realized that his second line could not possibly hold long, so he drew back to the ridge, where Hescock and Houghtaling were engaged.[28]

Maney's and Manigault's brigades regrouped southeast of the Harding House. Giles and Mary Harding had constructed a two-story frame house, surrounded by a log-cabin cook house and slave cabins, with a barn and

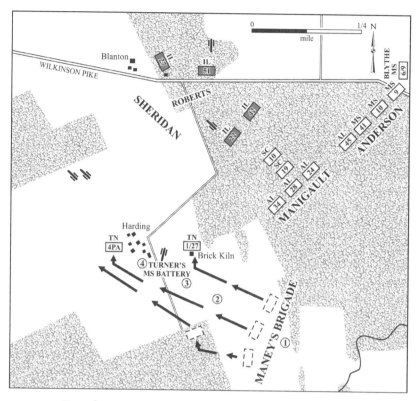

December 31, 9:00 a.m., Maney's Brigade at the Harding House

cotton gin a little distant. Harding's family had escaped, but the old man hid in the basement during the battle. Although known to be "Secesh," a Union surgeon contemptuously declared that he cared more about his chickens than he did either the northerners or southerners. Harding had a brick kiln constructed with the purpose of bricking his house—a project in-terrupted by the war. The structure would actually survive the battle, as well as a grand piano which had one of its legs shot off by an artillery round.[29]

Sheridan's two batteries, Hescock's and Houghtaling's, on the high ridge northeast of the Harding House, with a mutually supporting crossfire, had been bedeviling Manigault, who had already been forced back under their fire. As Maney's brigade approached the brick kiln, he also came under fire from a battery on "quite a high ridge obliquely to my front and right" (Houghtaling's), and a masked battery "directly to my right" (Hescock's) in a cedar glade, the last, according to Colonel Hume R. Field of the 1st and

27th Tennessee, only two hundred yards from the kiln. Field's men, on the far right of the brigade, sought shelter in the brickyard.[30]

At this moment, the fog of war took over. Maney (and many others) believed that they had been mistakenly fired upon by a friendly battery, despite the frantic shouts of the skirmishers who yelled back otherwise. Chaos reigned as the shelling continued amidst the arguing Tennesseans. Maney had his men lie down behind a ridge. Impatient to get a view of the Rebels, Colonel Roberts, his brigade supporting Hescock, turned to his adjutant and said: "Let us see what they are doing." The two rode toward the ridge and glanced over, where they clearly saw the Confederates resting, apparently waiting for orders. They quickly wheeled about and rode off, not a shot having been fired.[31]

Even sheltered by the ridge, the Tennesseans took casualties from the shelling—the 6th and 9th Tennessee alone sustained three killed and three wounded. The identification of the battery in the woods had to be determined and quickly. Lieutenant Fred R. James, a Cheatham staff officer, rode toward the outfit and, within forty yards, toppled from his horse from infantry fire. James ironically fell not far from his home, now being used as Polk's headquarters. Another staff officer, Lieutenant John H. Marsh, narrowly averted being shot. All along the line Confederate battle flags conspicuously waved, the men still believing the battery to be their own. A Sergeant Oakley of the 4th Tennessee waved his banner for ten minutes under a murderous fire, which only seemed to increase the fury. Sergeant M. C. Hooks of the 6th and 9th Tennessee climbed to the top of one of Harding's outhouses and waved his flag. Captain Thomas H. Malone, Maney's adjutant, rode around to the right to within thirty yards of the battery and, although bullets ripped his clothes and struck his horse, he uncovered the enemy's true identity. Colonel Field had already seen enough. He ordered his men to "fire on that battery, anyhow," although even then "the major part of my men thinking it was our own people."[32]

Malone, the one-day governor of Tennessee, rode to Captain William B. Turner, commanding a Mississippi battery, with orders to "knock to pieces that Yankee battery that is playing on our lines so!" "They are Yankeess, and I've known it all the time," Turner answered. The battery rumbled forward to the kiln with its two 12-pounder Napoleon guns (trophies from Perryville) and two 12-pounder howitzers, set fuses for five hundred yards, and opened a rapid fire—two hundred rounds in forty minutes. When one of the gunnery sergeants, a former preacher, made a direct hit on a caisson, Turner forgot himself and yelled, "Parson, Give 'em hell, G[od] d[amn] 'em!"[33]

A lull eventually came, and Cheatham rode out a hundred yards in advance of the line, shouting, "Come on, boys, and follow me." Sam Watkins, a wounded soldier in the 1st Tennessee, yelled back: "Well, General, if you are determined to die, I'll die with you." Vaughn, who had by this time come up with his brigade, and Maney began their right wheel west of the Harding House, a Federal observer admitting: "It was a grand sight; seldom has it been executed in a finer manner." Sheridan pulled his division back to north of the Wilkinson Pike, where he formed his third line.[34]

THE SLAUGHTER PEN

The Wilkinson Pike had been in existence only four years at the time of the battle. It now became a focal point as Sheridan pulled back mostly north of the road to his third position. Sheridan's line would take the shape of an L tilted at the angle toward the northwest. Negley's division of Thomas's corps extended Sheridan's left. Schaefer's brigade pulled back first, then the batteries, then Roberts's and Greusel's brigades. The terrain they entered appeared to be a kind of green island surrounded by brown plowed tracts. Although pocked with occasional openings, or glades, for the most part the area was heavily wooded and surfaced with rocks and boulders. At places it proved impossible to move through the morass, and typically one could not see even the length of a regiment. A Confederate would write of the gnarly cedar trees, limestone rocks, and stub arms sticking out of the ground. Variously referred to as "the cedars" and the "cedar swamp," some Chicago artillerymen, thinking of the stockyards back home, labeled it the "Slaughter Pen." Rosecrans sent a message that a new line was being formed in the rear, and that Sheridan should hold "no matter what the outcome." The division commander interpreted the order to mean that his command was to be sacrificed.[35]

Half of Colonel Frederick Schaefer's Second Brigade (the 2nd Missouri and 73rd Illinois) had been held in reserve and had not been heavily engaged. Schaefer first tasted military life in his native Germany when he engaged in an 1848 insurrection. Like Willich, he found himself on the losing side and came to America. Tall, slender, and student-like in appearance, the colonel would invariable become nervous and excitable under stress, although he would regain his composure. During the afternoon fighting at the Round Forest, Schaefer would be killed. Some would swear that his own men in the 73rd Illinois murdered him, for previously hanging up two men of their regiment by their thumbs for stealing fence rails for fire wood. Earlier in the morning, the men of the 73rd Illinois, the so-called "Preacher Regiment," due to a heavy infusion of Methodist ministers, had been listening to Major William A. Pressman admonish them, "Murfreesboro or die!" when the sudden appearance of wounded streaming to the rear cut short his speech. Although somewhat scattered (the 15th Missouri and 44th Illinois had gone to Greusel's support) the brigade eventually reunited at Sheridan's second position and fell back to the cedars, deploying along the edge of woods facing southeast, its left extending not quite to the pike. The remains of Greusel's brigade, minus the 36th Illinois (down to 140 men) and the 21st Michigan (supporting Hescock's battery), formed on Schaefer's right, extending the line to the northwest. The 81st Indiana of Woodruff's brigade extended Greusel's line to the right, the rest of the brigade having gone to the rear for ammunition.[36]

Roberts's brigade split, with the 27th and 51st Illinois along the pike facing south. The 22nd and 42nd Illinois came on line diagonally in the cedars south of the pike and facing southeast, the two regiments connecting the Wilkinson Pike on the left and Harding Lane on the right. Bush's and Hescock's batteries retired to a rocky elevation on the northwest corner of Wilkinson Pike and McFadden's Lane. Houghtaling's six guns unlimbered in the edge of woods south of the pike, facing southwest along Harding Lane. Although it was never stated, Sheridan obviously worried that the Rebels would plant artillery on the same ridge and, at a range of three hundred yards, blast the obtuse angle of his line.[37]

From his dispositions, Sheridan clearly anticipated Cheatham's attack from the south, but at about 10:45 adjustments had to be made to the west, where the Confederates (Cleburne's division) were unquestionably moving in force east along the Wilkinson Pike toward the Benjamin Blanton House. Sheridan, realizing that an attack from the south would inevitably come, reinforced Houghtaling's battery with two 10-pounder Parrott rifles under Lieutenant C. M. Taliaferro of Hescock's battery and two guns under Lieutenant D. Flashburg from Bush's battery. To address the new threat from the west, Roberts had the 27th Illinois change front from south to west, facing the Blanton House, thus forming a right angle with the 51st Illinois, which spread out to fill the space.[38]

The Federals had spotted Wood's brigade, which had moved up from the woods northeast of the Gresham House toward the Blanton House. Wood launched a half-hearted piecemeal assault across a large field (probably north of the pike), exchanging desultory fire with Schaefer's and Roberts's troops. Vaughn's Tennessee brigade had not yet advanced from the ridge south of the Harding House, leaving Sheridan's ten guns on Harding Lane to wheel northwest to enfilade the brigade. Wood retired toward the Blanton House and the safety of Darden's Mississippi Battery and the Helena Light Artillery, where his regiments replenished ammunition.[39]

Lucius Polk's brigade, to Wood's left, also came under the enfilade fire of Sheridan's artillery on Harding Lane. Polk pivoted his troops right so as to directly face the enemy batteries. He dispatched his two smallest regiments to support the division artillery. Cleburne faced a quandary. Bragg, back at his Murfreesboro headquarters, could offer no guidance. The whereabouts of Hardee at this precise moment was not known. The only thing Cleburne knew for certain was that the enemy had taken refuge in the thick cedar brakes north of the Wilkinson Pike and that he had advanced far beyond the line of Cheatham and Withers. He instinctively desired to pursue, but could he do so without endangering his flanks and becoming isolated? Cleburne momentarily hesitated.[40]

Moving en echelon across the Wilkinson Pike northeast of the Blanton House, Bushrod Johnson's brigade came up in piecemeal fashion on Polk's left. When Polk's brigade fell back, Federal skirmishers brazenly reoccupied the Blanton House, firing from behind the garden fence. Johnson quickly chased them off, capturing about sixty. As Johnson wheeled his brigade, his left suddenly came under fire from Greusel's men in the cedars. Hidden in the trees as they were, all that could be seen was the smoke of their muskets. Johnson, thinking that he had come under friendly fire, rode to the front and ordered his men to cease firing. The real surprise came on the brigade left, however, where the 37th Tennessee came under such a sudden fierce fire that it broke to the rear, the men screaming that they had been flanked. In the process, Major J. T. McReynolds, the sole remaining field officer of the 37th, fell mortally wounded. The brigade fell back, but soon sallied forth in a second attempt. Again the brigade right (presumably the 37th) fell back in disorder. Believing that he might indeed be in danger of being flanked, Johnson retired. In truth, the Yankees were clinging for dear life.[41]

The time approached 10:15. Cleburne had made three attempts at the cedars (one by Polk and two by Johnson), and although none of the assaults had risen to the level of impressive, the Irishman was not willing to risk more. The troublesome Federal guns along Harding Lane had to be neutralized. Until Cheatham and Withers could come up from the south and take the position in reverse, Cleburne contented himself with counterbattery fire.

The scene was set for what would become the most vicious artillery duel of the day. North of the pike were the four guns of the Helena Light Artillery, and south of it would be the four guns of Darden's Jefferson Flying Artillery. Joining Darden would be Captain John T. Humphreys's 1st Arkansas Artillery of McCown's division. For the next half-hour it would be ten guns on ten in a death struggle. Very soon superior Federal armament and marksmanship tipped the scale. Taliaferro's two 10-pounder Parrott rifles quickly caught the attention of Lieutenant Thomas Key of the Helena Light Artillery. Command had fallen to the thirty-six-year-old former newspaper editor because its captain, J. H. Calvert, had been cashiered for drunkenness during the Kentucky Campaign. "Their rifle guns could throw canister as far as ours could spherical case," he reported. His two 6-pounders and two 12-pounder howitzers simply not cope with the Taliaferro's Parrotts. One of the Arkansas gunners was decapitated, and another had his hand blown off. Key had no choice but to withdraw. The Federal guns now zeroed in on Humphreys's position. Two of his guns received direct hits, one shell killing five horses. Adding to Humphreys's woes, faulty ammunition jammed the bores of two of his pieces, disabling both. Lieutenant William H. Gore, wounded by a shell, got up and rallied the men to their posts. A cannoneer fell wounded, and Lieutenant John W. Rivers snatched up his rammer and took his place. When the flag bearer had his banner shot down, he calmly remarked that the Yankees appeared to be "shooting a little close." Nonetheless, Humphreys continued the one-sided fight. As for the Federals, huge broken limbs so covered their guns that Colonel Roberts himself rushed over to help clear them.[42]

At this time the rather strange case of Lieutenant Edward W. Wright of Houghtaling's battery occurred. In the midst of the intense shelling, the mind of the "always jolly" lieutenant seemed to snap. He began "shouting like a mad man," and his actions to eyewitnesses became "unnatural." As men fell all around him, he became even more animated. He was "never right" after that time, although he would for a while command the battery. He would at times appear wild and incoherent, a problem that continued in postwar years, as he attempted suicide. By the time of his death in 1869 he had become utterly insane—a distant casualty of Stones River.[43]

. . . .

Manigault regrouped his brigade southeast of the Slaughter Pen. His regiments had been badly chewed up in the attacks upon Sill's line, but now he faced an even more daunting task—breaking the angle of the Slaughter Pen and knocking out Sheridan's artillery "at all hazards." He could not do it alone. At about 10:00 the South Carolinian conferred with the brigade commander to his right—forty-four-year-old former U.S. Marshal Patton Anderson. Actually, Anderson had up until a few days earlier commanded Manigault's brigade, but Brigadier General Edward Walthall had taken sick. Walthall's brigade, comprised of Mississippians and a single Alabama regiment, requested Anderson as their commander. In the days following the battle, Anderson would be given a division command, but he confided to his wife: "I would prefer the Brigade of Mississippians, which I had in the Murfreesboro fight to my Division in the Army. It is true, it composes a part of the Division, but the other Brigades are not [at] all like it."[44]

Now was the time to attack, while the Yankee gunners busied themselves with Confederate artillery west of the Blanton House. If Manigault could overwhelm their infantry support, the 22nd and 42nd Illinois, facing southeast in the woods between Harding Lane and the Wilkinson Pike, he could take the Union batteries in reverse. Manigault planned to assault with his two right regiments, the 10th and 19th South Carolina, and the two left regiments of Anderson's brigade, the 45th Alabama and 24th Mississippi. He also sent Colonel Walker of his staff to Maney, asking for a demonstration on his left.[45]

Sheridan was making plans of his own. He rode to General Thomas and pleaded for one of his divisions to come up so that together they could go on the offensive. The corps commander refused, and thereafter Sheridan apologists would claim a golden opportunity missed. It made a good story, but it was hardly the truth. Thomas could clearly not pull Negley out of line, who any moment would certainly be attacked. Thomas's only remaining division, Rousseau's, had been commandeered by Rosecrans to buttress the Union left. So much for old veterans' tales.[46]

What resulted was a disjoined assault against Houghtaling's battery, in which Walker insisted that Anderson's two regiments never came up "as had been promised." Thus advancing alone, the two South Carolina regiments came under a galling fire from Roberts's infantry and doubtless enfilade fire from Bush's and Hescock's batteries north of the pike. The 10th South Carolina advanced with its new regimental banner flapping in the breeze—a Palmetto tree and crescent on a field of blue, the very flag that Withers had not permitted them to display during the presidential visit. Bullets now shredded the banner. The Carolinians closed to within 120 yards, but could take no more. The wrecked 10th South Carolina left behind eighty-five killed and wounded in this single attack. What had gone wrong? There were three possibilities: the commanders of the 24th Mississippi and 45th Alabama understood themselves to be in support of the attack, they got a belated start, or they became delayed as they struggled through the thickets. It is clear in the reports of the 10th and 19th South Carolina that they received no support. The rout of the two regiments rippled down the line. "The first charge my Regiment advanced as far as the pike and I observed that my support on the left [10th and 19th South Carolina] was giving way and I here ordered my men to fall back," 24th Mississippi Lieutenant Colonel R. P. McKelvaine reported. Colonel James G. Gilchrist of the 45th Alabama pointed to the rout of the 10th South Carolina, which caused "some confusion and eventually carried my command with it." Anderson's two regiments reformed and picked up the assault, but "a second time some of my men fled back about 100 yards causing some confusion in the regiment," Gilchrist wrote.[47]

Manigault pointed his ire at Maney as much as the Yankees. Convinced that he had not been properly supported on his left, Manigault sent a staff officer to the brigadier informing him of the abortive assault and that a second attempt would be made. Maney assured his cooperation. (After the Battle of Perryville, Maney had been accused of hanging back in the rear and had even fought a duel to defend his honor.) The Tennessean sluggishly advanced his brigade north on either side of Harding Lane toward the Wilkinson Pike, about five hundred yards distant. Again the Carolinians and Alabamians surged forward, this time not even getting as far as the

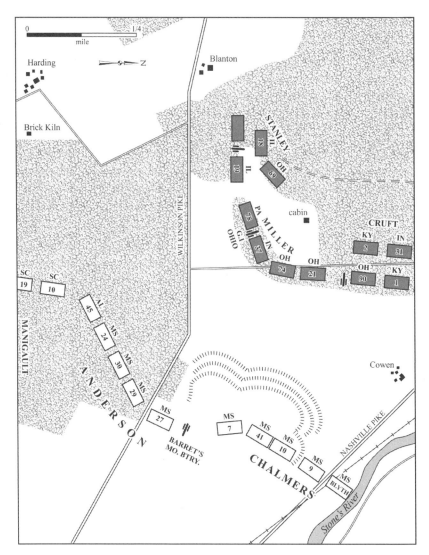

December 31, 10:00 a.m., Assault of Anderson's Brigade

first attempt. Captain Daniel E. Hugar, Manigault's brother-in-law and a member of his staff, sensing confusion in the ranks of the 24th Alabama due to the loss of field officers, gallantly rallied the regiment. Manigault again pointed the finger at Maney, who was "still tardy" in moving up.[48]

Roberts's command had likewise been whittled away. "I got rather gritty seeing all our best Boys fall to the ground. I could not look but what I see the boys a falling," William E. Garlock of the 42nd Illinois related to a friend. As Lieutenant Colonel Nathan H. Walworth of the 42nd Illinois steadied his line, a Corporal Smith reported to him: "Colonel I come to return my gun to you, for I suppose I shall go on furlough now." "Why, what is it?" Walworth asked as he looked at the musket. "Look," the corporal answered, as he removed his hand from his gut, revealing his intestines flowing out. "To what hospital can I go?" "Go that way," Walworth said, pointing to the Blanton House, now in no-man's land. "When the battle is over I will see you," the colonel promised, but the young corporal never made it.[49]

Anderson realized that, to take the Union artillery along Harding Lane, he first had to eliminate the eight guns (Bush's and Hescock's batteries) on the wooded high ground northwest of Wilkinson Pike and McFadden's Lane. Lieutenant Colonel J. J. Scales of the 30th Mississippi knew that it had to be done, but he frankly considered the mission "a hopeless undertaking." Indeed, after clearing 200 yards of woods south of the pike, the right regiments would have to make a head-on assault over a 500-yard-wide cornfield, which offered no more cover other than plowed furrows between the rows. All formation was lost as the regiments clawed through the thickets. As the troops reformed before entering the field, Anderson sent a dispatch to take the guns "at all hazards." While most of the regiments struck Roberts's line in the cedars, between Harding Lane and the Wilkinson Pike, the 27th and 29th Mississippi stepped out into the cornfield. A surreal silence prevailed as the Mississippians approached to within 75 yards of the base of the knoll. A wall of flame savaged them. "They were among the trees, while we were in an open field, so they were just mowing us down like weeds," J. E. Robuck of the 29th remembered. The men instinctively hit the ground, oblivious to officer's shouts of "Forward!" "Men fell around on every side like autumn leaves," Scales reported. "To lie there was death to the last man, but my order to retreat repeated again and again met with the same fate." Timothy Stanley's brigade and the two right regiments of John Miller's brigade poured a searing fire into the Mississippians. After hideous losses, the two regiments fell back to the safety of the wood line. On the right, Lieutenant Colonel James Autry, a former county judge commanding the 27th Mississippi, fell dead, a bullet piercing his head; his regiment fell back in confusion. On the left, the 30th Mississippi had been cannibalized, losing 62 killed and 130 wounded in an area less than an acre. Lieutenant Colonel Scales fell, stunned by the concussion of a shell.[50]

Back at Anderson's temporary breastworks, east of McFadden's Lane, Brigadier General Alexander P. "Old Straight" Stewart's brigade of 1,635 Tennesseans had moved up and taken their place. Withers had actually requested only two of his regiments, but Stewart, seeing the debris of Anderson's shattered regiments streaming back (Major L. W. Findlay of Stewart's staff succeeded in rallying the 27th and 29th Mississippi), wisely suggested that he bring up his entire command. Reserved, unflappable, thoughtful, "Old Straight" had the demeanor of a college professor, which he in fact had been. Although a West Point graduate, he had been out of the Regular Army for eighteen years at the start of the war. Stewart would ultimately rise to corps command and in postwar years would become the chancellor of the University of Mississippi and later the first superintendent of the Chickamauga and Chattanooga National Battlefield Park. Even while huddled behind Anderson's slight rock-and-log breastworks, the Tennesseans came under artillery fire from the Slaughter Pen. The troops sustained several casualties, but it was the explosion of a single shell in the ranks of the 19th Tennessee that created the greatest damage—6 wounded, 1 of those mortally. The brigade now replaced Anderson's line in another attempt to crack the Slaughter Pen salient.[51]

As Stewart's men advanced up the Wilkinson Pike, Stanford's Mississippi Battery, under direct orders from Polk, unlimbered next to Barret's Missouri Battery (C.S.A.), in a field east of the pike. Together the eight guns opened on an enemy battery "in the cedars" (the three guns of Battery B, Kentucky Artillery) and another "in the left of the field" (Battery G, 1st Ohio Light Artillery, on Miller's left). Barret would later fume about his inferior fuses, which caused nearly all of his 6-pounder spherical case shot to burst short.[52]

The salient teetered on the brink. Casualties had been horrific; Sheridan had lost one-third of his division, with the 22nd and 42nd Illinois reduced to half their number. Colonel Roberts dashed along the line, his sword high in the air. When passing an officer he smiled, saluted him with his sword, and galloped toward the left, cheering on his men. The sudden thud of three bullets striking his body was heard. He collapsed from his mount, and as his men ran to him he spoke in a husky voice: "Boys, put me on my horse again!" The attempt proved futile; he soon died. Colonel Luther L. Bradley placed the time at 10:45. Command fell to Colonel F. A. Harrington of the 27th Illinois, but within minutes an artillery shell blew away both of his jaw bones. "I tell you poor fellow. I fear he has gone to a worse world than this for he [was] an awful wicked man but he was a first rate colonel," a member of the regiment related to his brother. As the 22nd and 42nd fell back north of the Wilkinson Pike, Sheridan, chomping a cigar, approached Walworth and said in a slow manner: "Colonel, when you cannot hold this point any longer, and are out of ammunition, move the regiment in this direction," pointing to the northwest. "This is about the only place for us to get out; they have nearly surrounded us." When the division commander later saw the lieutenant colonel, he asked: "Colonel, where is the balance of the Forty-second?" "General," he answered, pointing to the remnants, "this is all there is left of the Forty-second *and* Twenty-second."[53]

The Confederates began to close the vice on the Slaughter Pen—Manigault's brigade fighting east of Harding Lane, Maney's brigade left of the lane, and Vaughn's Tennesseans on Maney's left—all three brigades attacking north. At the Harding Lane artillery position, dead and dying horses, eighty from Battery C, 1st Illinois alone, could be seen everywhere. Houghtaling fell badly wounded, and Taliaferro lay dead. Attempts to manhandle the guns through the cedars proved fruitless. Houghtaling's six pieces had to be abandoned. In four hours Sheridan's three batteries had expended a staggering 3,436 rounds! A member of the 27th Illinois attempted to describe to his hometown readers the "mass of spokes, hubs, axles, and bleeding horseflesh." A member of the 51st Illinois noted that the men had not seen Sheridan for two hours. Finally the order came to fall back. "I had no idea of where we were going when we started & very little expectation that we would get out," 57th Illinois Lieutenant Otis Moody recalled. Captain John H. Phillips, of the 22nd Illinois, thought "we would all be killed or captured." Negley rode up and ordered them back, "so we started a perfect mass of companies and came out to the Nashville Pike." As Roberts's men withdrew, Schaefer's and Gruesel's brigades, their ammunition utterly exhausted, prepared to fix bayonets as they awaited the inevitable next assault.[54]

The anticipated attack was even then forming in the woods south of the pike, as Stewart's Tennesseans replaced Anderson's brigade. They marched "in splendid order and with a cheer," with the 31st and 33rd Tennessee (consolidated) and 4th and 5th Tennessee (consolidated) on the right, emerging diagonally across the same cornfield where the 27th and 29th Mississippi had been shredded. Approaching south of the pike (from left to right) came the 29th Mississippi, which had rejoined the fight and formed on Stewart's left, 19th Tennessee, and 24th Tennessee. Seeing the approaching Tennesseans, Anderson dashed in front of the 24th Mississippi with his hat off, yelling, "Mississippians, follow me." Roberts's regiments, in the midst of withdrawing, did not even see the Rebels barreling down until they were nearly on top of them. The blue line cracked and fell back in disorder. The 23rd Mississippi overran Houghtaling's guns, with "the enemy falling before us," Lieutenant Colonel McKelvaine reported. In the words of Robert Masten of the 24th Mississippi, "we soon frightened the enemy and making them leave it [battery] we took possession of it." On the right, the 31st and 33rd Tennessee overran the knoll, capturing two of Bush's guns—a 6-pounder and a James rifle. Everywhere Sheridan's troops fell back—in places a fighting withdrawal, but retreating nonetheless.[55]

The press gave Stewart's Tennesseans the credit for breaking the salient and, although technically correct, the position was in the midst of dissolving at any rate. A chagrined Anderson complained to his wife: "Well, they [Tennesseans] may have *taken* them [Houghtaling's guns], but it was after my Brigade had driven the enemy from his guns and were pursuing him two hundred yards in advance of the Tennessee troops! Who will ever write a *truthful* history of the war." A dispute also arose over the capture of Hescock's four Napoleon guns. The 10th and 19th South Carolina, supported by the 45th Alabama of Anderson's brigade, captured the pieces, but were driven back by the 21st Michigan—but only momentarily. Anderson's men thus claimed the battery "that was rightly ours," bitterly complained a Carolinian. Bragg later sent the guns to General P. G. T. Beauregard in South Carolina.[56]

With Roberts dead and Harrington seriously wounded, command of the Illinois brigade fell to forty-year-old Colonel Luther L. Bradley, a former Chicago businessman with a long background in the Connecticut militia. Exactly where he injured his foot on the battlefield is not known, but for a month afterward he would have to wear a moccasin and could not ride a horse. As the 27th and 51st Illinois withdrew into the cedars, they were met by Negley, who informed them that they were surrounded and would have to fight their way out. The two prongs of the Confederate attack were fast beginning to close. An order went out to counter-attack, which the Illinoisans did in "one continuous yell," so stunning the pursuing Rebels that they "turned about, and we had the pleasure for once to see them skee-daddle," wrote Lazenby. Recounted yet another: "The whole length of the two regiments, at a full run, scaled the hill, yelling at the top of their voices, loading and firing as we went. The enemy soon became confused and began to break ranks and scatter before us." Audacious as it was, the Federals only momentarily stalled the inevitable and continued their retreat to the rear.[57]

With Sheridan's position crumbling, Timothy R. Stanley's 1,800-man brigade of Negley's division, to the left of Roberts along the ridge in the northwest corner of the Wilkinson Pike and McFadden's Lane, found itself in a precarious position. Already the enemy was fast closing in on their rear. His communications with Thomas severed, Negley ordered Stanley's men to cut their way out. The bluecoats fell back a hundred yards to the bottom of a hill to the wooded edge of a cleared field. The 11th Michigan and 19th Illinois were given orders to charge back into the cedars to slow the enemy. An aide rode up to Colonel Joseph R. Scott of the 19th and said: "Colonel, General Negley's compliments, and orders your Battalion to hurry to the support of yonder guns," pointing to Captain Frederick Schultz's Battery M, 1st Ohio Light Artillery. Related Ira Gillaspie: "The rebils kept coming and the 19th Illinois and ours [11th Michigan] charged on them pouring a hole voley into them and then keeping up the fier we drove back a whole division of gray backs." Bugler J. W. Slater of the 18th Ohio sounded the retreat and then headed for the rear. In the process he met a staff officer who demanded that he go back in. Said Slater: "I'll die first. I've been there."[58]

The battle was fast coming to thirty-one-year-old Colonel John F. Miller, a former South Bend attorney. As part of Negley's division, his brigade had been committed at the edge of the cedar forest, straddling McFadden's Lane and to the left of Stanley's brigade. The 21st Ohio held the left at a rail fence; then came the 74th Ohio in an open field, the 37th Indiana, and atop a hill on the far right the 78th Pennsylvania, its right resting on Battery M, 1st Ohio Artillery, of Stanley's brigade. On a small hill in an open field near two log cabins, between the 37th Indiana and 74th Ohio, the six guns of Battery G, 1st Ohio Artillery, deployed. On the far left the three guns of Lieutenant Alban A. Ellswoth's Battery B, 1st Kentucky, dropped trail.[59]

The brigade had barely realigned before James Chalmers's Mississippians hammered the Kentucky battery and the left flank of the 21st Ohio. Ellsworth's gunners loaded double canister and fired as rapidly as possible. "The Rebs came up two or three columns deep, screeching and yalping like nigger hounds," wrote Private Liberty Warner of the 21st Ohio, but the Buckeyes "made them yell a different tune." Lieutenant Colonel James

Neibling admonished his men to "Give 'em hell by the acre boys." The Ohioans fixed bayonets, but by the time they charged the Mississippians were already reeling in disorder. "My God boys! We gave 'em hell, didn't we!" Neibling yelled, ignoring the buckshot that had nicked him in the shoulder. The 74th Ohio, commanded by former Methodist preacher Granville Moody, swung his regiment around to fire into the flanks of the Mississippians. "Now men, resume your praying, fight for God, your country, your kind, aim low and give 'em Hail Columbia," he exhorted. The 37th Indiana also swung about to get into the action, encouraged by Moody's words: "Come on, Christian brethern." Chalmers's men, attacking Cruft's and Hazen's positions head on (to be detailed in the next chapter), fled the field. Lieutenant William Curry boasted that they had "fought them like tigers."[60]

Although Miller's line held, with Sheridan's division to his right collapsing, his flank and right became exposed. An unidentified staff officer rode up and ordered the 78th Pennsylvania off its hill. Seeing the regiment withdraw, Miller countermanded the order, but by that time the Rebels had nearly gained the position. Negley sent an order for the entire brigade to retreat into the cedars. Stubbornly resisting the order to withdraw, Miller grabbed a flag from a color bearer and shouted: "Rally here, men! We will not be driven off! If we cannot whip them we can at least show them how men can die!" The effect proved electric, as men shouted: "There's John F.— there's John F!" Sergeant C. L. Riddle of Battery G, 1st Ohio, could see canister "sweep a space ten feet wide through their ranks, piling them up in winnows, but they would close up in a moment, and press steadily upon us." Despite the momentary rally, the inevitable retreat soon resumed. Battery G, due to the loss of horses, had to abandon three of its pieces, one cannoneer vainly attempting to get a gun off with only one horse, and Ellsworth left a single gun. Moody's horse fell dead, and the colonel, limping in pain, barely made it out. Samuel A. Linton of the 21st Ohio "found nothing in my way that I could not get over," his escape hastened by enemy shouts of "Halt, you damn Yankee son-of-a-bitch," and "Run Yank."[61]

Two hours of intense fighting had swept away Sheridan's and Negley's divisions from the Slaughter Pen. Sheridan had clearly emerged the hero, having done for Rosecrans's army in the cedar forest what Colonel Benjamin Prentiss did for Ulysses S. Grant's army in the Hornet's Nest at Shiloh—buy precious time. With McCown's and Cleburne's divisions hot on their heels, however, had it been enough?

8

WE MUST WIN THIS BATTLE

At 6:00 a.m. the muffled sound of gunfire could be heard from Rosecrans's position at Stones River. It appeared that McCook had become engaged, and the battle was progressing as planned. As Van Cleve prepared his division for an assault, he walked the line, shouting, "Boys, be careful, and don't get excited. Keep cool, keep your guns down, and be sure and shoot low." At 7:00, after hearing the army commander's stirring battle order read aloud, the troops gave a resounding cheer, piled knapsacks, and splashed into the frigid, knee-deep river at McFadden's Ford, with Sam Beatty's brigade and Battery B, Pennsylvania Artillery in the van. Samuel Price's brigade and the 3rd Wisconsin Artillery followed at 8:00, and once across deployed five hundred yards in advance of the river on Beatty's left. Rosecrans, with Crittenden accompanying, rode to Wood's division at the Upper Ford. "Move Harker in front, then Hascall, then Wagner," he told the Indiana general. Wood turned to Crittenden and said: "Good-bye general; we'll meet at the hatter's as one coon said to another when the dogs were after them."[1]

Returning to his headquarters on the Nashville Pike, Rosecrans, wearing his black felt hat and old blue overcoat buttoned to the chin, chomping a cigar, and mounted on his large gray horse "Boney," found everything in order and staff officers casually warming themselves. Garesche told of a report claiming that Rebel cavalry had gained McCook's rear, and that he had sent Captain Elmer Otis and his 4th U.S. Cavalry "to hunt them." It must have been around 7:30 when Rosecrans received his first dispatch from McCook, advising that he was being heavily pressed and needed assistance. McCook's failure to mention the rout of Kirk and Willich (hauntingly similar to his understated initial dispatches at Perryville) shrouded the true state of affairs. The army commander replied that McCook should "hold his ground obstinately." Additional information began to trickle in. Sill had been killed —"We cannot help it. Brave men must be killed," Rosecrans uttered grimly. Willich had been captured—"Never mind, we must win this battle."[2]

More intelligence began to arrive—shocking intelligence. "The right wing is being driven. It needs reserves," reported an aide. "So soon? Tell General McCook I will help him," the army commander answered, adding: "Never mind! We will make it right." As the sound of battle ominously magnified and began to curl around to the rear, it became evident even to the lowliest private that something had gone terribly wrong. Then, like swarming ants, stragglers began emerging from the woods by the hundreds. An officer cocked his pistol at one fleeing soldier and demanded to know what had happened. The breathless man replied: "The right wing is broken!" Another staff officer arrived, this one from Otis, declaring: "The right wing is broken, and the enemy is driving it back!"[3]

Though doubtless shaken, Rosecrans kept his composure; indeed, it would be his finest hour. Later images at Chickamauga of a stuttering and indecisive commander simply do not stand here. He worked feverishly to regain control, and his commanding presence and timely shifting of troops clearly saved the day. Indeed, the two allegations leveled at him, that he meddled and reduced himself to a brigade commander and that he recklessly exposed himself, though true, are problematic. Rosecrans had delegated authority to McCook; he could take no more such chances. Simply put, he had no other choice; proper chain of command would only have slowed matters. He did what he had to do and in the process re-energized Union morale with his presence.[4]

The roar of battle now became alarming, with the Rebels obviously attempting to wrestle control of the Nashville Pike. "The most terrible state of suspense prevailed the entire left, and it became more and more evident that the right was being driven rapidly upon us," Milo Hascall observed. To Captain Marcus Woodcock, in the ranks of the 9th Kentucky of Sam Beatty's brigade, the thunder of musketry became "terrible to hear," and it appeared to all that the right wing "seemed to be giving way." One of Wood's men wrote on January 11: "For two long hours we waited in fearful suspense expecting momentary orders to move but no orders came. Meanwhile the battle raged fiercely on the right." Rosecrans hurriedly directed Thomas to have Rousseau's reserve division moved into the cedars to shore up Sheridan's line. He then rode to Crittenden and suspended the movement of Van Cleve's and Wood's divisions and had them recalled to the west bank. He directed Sam Beatty's brigade up the Nashville Pike to buttress the right and Samuel Price's brigade to hold McFadden's Ford. The McFadden Farm, occupied by sixty-one-year-old Mollie McFadden and some of her children, was located in the vicinity of the ford that bore her family name, but the precise location has been lost to time. James Fyffe's brigade and the 7th Indiana Artillery had earlier been detached toward the Widow Burris House to protect the wagon train. Rosecrans frantically rode over to Wood's division and ordered Harker's and Hascall's brigades to the right. Colonel George Wagner's brigade would spread out to cover the Upper Ford.[5]

Rosecrans realized that it would be risky leaving only two brigades at the fords. A large force of the enemy (Breckinridge's division) remained on the east bank and might attack in a pincers movement. He rode to Price and asked who commanded the brigade. "I do, sir," came the response. "Colonel Price, will you hold this ford?" "General, I will try." Again the army commander queried, "Will you hold this ford?" "I will die right here." "General Price, look me in the eye and tell me, will you hold this ford?" Price merely answered, "General, I will," to which Rosecrans said: "That will do."[6]

Back on the Nashville Pike, as it crossed Overall Creek, Colonel John G. Parkhurst, commanding the 9th Michigan, serving as the provost guard of Thomas's corps, began to notice teamsters galloping on harnessed mules. Then came cavalry and still more mules cut from the harness, each one carrying two or three riders, followed by panic-stricken infantry. Parkhurst quickly collected two hundred to three hundred stragglers, but the magnitude of the disaster did not become evident until he glanced up in horror to see several thousand, the debris of McCook's corps, swarming toward him, many yelling, "We are all lost!" and threatening to trample his men. "Men were running with hats off, their arms thrown away, and their tongues out of their mouths panting for breath," the colonel related to his sister. Parkhurst had actually returned from a Rebel prison only a few days earlier, having been captured by Forrest back in July, and he doubtless wondered if he would be returning. He formed his regiment, ordered fixed bayonets, and stretched his flanks to the maximum to establish a straggler's line. "[In] a number of instances our men had to knock down some of them [fugitives] to keep them from pushing their way through," Thomas J. Conley wrote his sister. "There was about 5,000 of them running pell mell, as fast as their legs would carry them, a great many had thrown away their arms and they were the worst frightened sete of men that you ever heard of." To John C. Love of the 9th, it appeared to be "another Bull Run stampede." Within half an hour Parkhurst had collected most of Zahm's cavalry, seven guns, and two infantry regiments. The colonel disgustedly reported that he succeeded in netting a brigade commander (presumably Zahm, but left unnamed), and that a colonel had managed to escape and "passed on towards Nashville."[7]

Colonel Moses Walker's brigade and Battery D, 1st Michigan Artillery of Thomas's corps, slowly came up from the rear. Forty-three-year-old Ohio-born Walker, a Yale graduate and former Dayton attorney, had been ordered to proceed to Stewart's Creek to guard the army's wagon trains. There he encountered Colonel Joseph Burke's 10th Ohio in line of battle, having rounded up an estimated eleven hundred stragglers who had managed to slip past Parkhurst's line. Walker deployed in support, placing the Michigan battery on a hill to the left of the pike. At 9:00 Walker received an order to proceed to the front and attach his brigade to Rousseau's division. Stanley promised cavalry support on his right. At 10:00 the brigade arrived at Overall Creek, where Walker learned from Major George E. Flynt, a Thomas staff officer, that Rebel cavalry had been threatening the rear. The Ohio general immediately deployed his brigade in an old British square formation, with a section of guns at three corners. What came was not Rebel cavalry, however, but more stragglers and another Thomas staff officer, Andrew J. Mackey, with an order to gather them up. A desperately needed brigade could not be held in the rear indefinitely; with the morning virtually spent, Walker marched toward the scene of the fighting.[8]

. . . .

Rousseau's reserve division had been waiting in column of brigades in a large cottonfield south of the Nashville Pike. From their position the men could see the debris of McCook's shattered corps running to the rear. In a letter to his sister, Reuben Jones of the 19th United States recounted: "Rousseau viewed the crisis with tears in his eyes and he rode before his veterans & spoke with tears rolling down his cheek & we were warned by him of what was left for us to do to rescue that portion of the army from a ruinous disaster. We must turn the tide of battle." At 9:00 Thomas ordered the division into the thickets on Sheridan's right. "Old Rousseau is here and intends to stay!" the Kentuckian shouted as he rode the line. In truth, the division would only serve as a holding action; already Rosecrans was viewing a second defensive position along the Nashville Pike. The division (minus Starkweather's brigade guarding wagons) began clawing its way into the cedars, following a makeshift road previously cut by the Pioneers, with John Beatty's brigade in the lead, followed by Benjamin Scribner's brigade, and Lieutenant Colonel Oliver L. Shepherd's brigade of Regulars bringing up the van. The division marched and counter-marched for an hour before deploying, Beatty's brigade on the left of the pioneer road, Shepherd's Regulars to the right of it, and Scribner's brigade initially to the left of the road and a hundred yards to the rear in reserve.[9]

"I knew it was hell in there before I got it," Rousseau would later recall, "but I was convinced of it when I saw Phil Sheridan with hat in one hand and sword in the other, fighting as if he were the devil incarnate!" Hearing Sheridan swear, the Kentucky general warned: "Hold on Sheridan, omit the profanity. Remember, the first bullet may send you to eternity." "I can't help it, general," the Irishman answered. "We must hold this point and my men won't think I'm earnest unless I swear at them like hell."[10]

Leading the 1,566 Regulars was forty-seven-year-old New Yorker Oliver "Blackjack" Shepherd, a West Point graduate. After the battle he was canned and sent to a desk job, and in postwar years he would embezzle money raised to build a monument to the Regulars at Stones River. As the brigade thrashed through the thickets, the two units on the far right, Major John H. King's First Battalion, 15th United States, and Major Adam J. Slemmer's First Battalion, 16th United States, got in advance of the brigade line. As Shepherd struggled to form the 18th and 19th United States, he instructed King to take command of the two right battalions. Billy Carlin's retreating brigade passed through Shepherd's line in disorder, Carlin commenting that the Regulars appeared "cool as if nothing particular was going on."[11]

After placing his infantry, Rousseau shamelessly exited the cedars while he began personally placing his artillery along the Nashville Pike, a task that could have been left to Major Cyrus O. Loomis, the division artillery chief. Lieutenant Alfred Pirtle had posted his thirty-seven ordnance wagons (twenty-two with artillery ammunition and fifteen with cartridges) on a knoll east of the turnpike. (Visiting the battlefield years later, he would

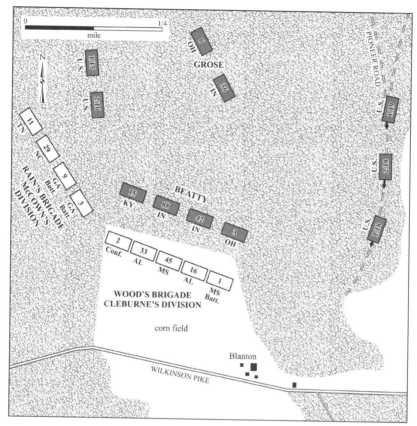

December 31, 9:45 a.m., Attack on Rousseau's Division

recall the precise location as being the highest elevation in the National Cemetery.) He galloped up to Rousseau, who was with Lieutenant George Van Pelt's Battery A, 1st Michigan, and asked: "General, shall I post the battery where my wagons are? It is the best position on the field." "Do it instantly. Tell Van Pelt I will get him infantry support," the Kentuckian answered. Pirtle moved his wagons to a hollow behind the knoll, huddling them as close together as possible. As Van Pelt unlimbered his guns, Lieutenant Frank L. Guenther's Battery H, 5th United States Artillery, deployed to his right, making twelve guns hub-to-hub ready to sweep the four-hundred-yard-wide cottonfield west of the pike.[12]

Meanwhile Major Frederick Townsend, commanding the companies of the 18th United States, received Shepherd's order to fall back to the support of Guenther's battery. Not knowing its location (it was in fact behind the Nashville Pike), Townsend surmised it to be on his right. He sent his adjutant, Frederick Phisterer, to hunt for it. Under a hail of bullets, Phisterer made his way to Slemmer's battalion. Slemmer revealed that he had seen nothing of the battery "nor anybody else except the enemy." Phisterer told Slemmer to immediately fall back, an order easier given than executed. Returning to Townsend, the adjutant assured the major that Guenther was nowhere to be found and must have passed to the rear. Towsend ordered the 18th to withdraw. For transmitting the order to Slemmer under extreme conditions, Phisterer would be awarded the Medal of Honor.[13]

Back at Shepherd's line, the 18th and 19th United States began withdrawing from the cedars. Two versions arose as to what occurred. Major Stephen D. Carpenter reported that insufficient room made it impossible for his men to deploy. In postwar years, however, Lieutenant William Lowe claimed that Lieutenant Harrison Millard of Rousseau's staff rode up to Carpenter and declared: "The General directs the brigade to fall back to the railroad and support the battery." Lowe adamantly wrote that he was within ten feet of Carpenter as the major protested. "Tell the General we cannot fall back until we have repulsed the attack." "The order is imperative, sir," Millard answered, and he then rode off.[14]

Colonel Benjamin F. Scribner's 1,583-man First Brigade entered the cedars behind John Beatty and Shepherd. His troops came under artillery fire—Darden's Mississippi Battery between the Gresham and Harding Houses overshooting Sheridan's line, it has been speculated. To avoid these incoming rounds, the thirty-seven-year-old former New Albany, Indiana, pharmacist ordered his brigade to the right. Without his knowledge, a Rousseau staff officer ordered his far-left regiments—the 2nd and 33rd Ohio—to the Nashville Pike in support of the new defensive line. Captain Ephraim J. Ellis, commanding the 33rd, asked: "By whose orders?" "By orders of Major General Rousseau, by God," Captain Cyrus O. Loomis barked. Ellis shouted: "By the left flank, march!" Left with only the 38th Indiana, 94th Ohio, and 10th Wisconsin, Scribner remained in position only ten minutes before being withdrawn, not having fired a shot.[15]

Scribner ordered his men back in broken formation so as not to present a compact target for enemy sharpshooters. Nonetheless, the sight of groups of soldiers straggling back in a leisurely fashion (a color bearer casually carried his flag over his shoulder) "looked badly to me," Lieutenant Pirtle remembered. Scribner feared it would look badly to Thomas as well, who watched near the Nashville Pike. The Indiana colonel rode up to him and explained that the men had dispersed under his orders. Pointing to the pike, he added: "And now General, you see they are re-forming. Have you any further orders?" "No, reform on the pike," Thomas replied.[16]

Scribner's brigade and most of Shepherd's Regulars thus cleared the woods, leaving behind only John Beatty's brigade and two battalions of Regulars on his right, but with a gap in between. Beatty, the thirty-four-year-old ex-banker, would boldly write in his after-action report that his troops had been "forgotten by the division commander," words that, although true, could not have settled well with Rousseau when he later read them. The Kentuckian had earlier admonished Beatty to hold "till hell freezes over," and then he rode to the left, where he said he would be with George Van Pelt's battery. Van Pelt, of course, had never entered the cedars. Beatty and the two battalions of Regulars thus stood isolated. Beatty's line, which had been on the division left, extended south toward the Wilkinson Pike, from left to right, the 3rd Ohio, 42nd Indiana, 88th Indiana, and 15th Kentucky. A flock of confused and frightened wild turkeys suddenly ran through the ranks of the 42nd. Gaps of from seventy-five to a hundred yards separated the regiments, and in the thickets the men could not even see the length of their own regiment. The Hoosiers of the 42nd began hurriedly constructing makeshift breastworks of logs and downed trees in anticipation of an attack certain to come. They did not have to wait long. S. A. M. Wood's brigade could be seen approaching in the open woods. The initial attack proved short-lived—an out-and-out repulse, according to Beatty, but a withdrawal to replenish ammunition by Wood's version.[17]

The action now turned to Beatty's far right, held by the 15th Kentucky, commanded by the "boy colonel," twenty-one-year-old Colonel James Forman. Just before going into the Slaughter Pen, Forman had been joined by several of Rousseau aides, Lieutenant Will McDowell among them. "Will, you have always wanted this horse; now it is my desire that after this battle you should have him. I will be killed in the fight, and I can call on you gentlemen to see that he gets it," Forman said. Attempting to joke off the gesture, McDowell quipped: "Jimmy, if you are going to be killed let me have him right now and [you] take my horse." Forman answered solemnly: "I am in earnest. I know what I am talking about and I want you to remember I will be killed, you will be wounded, and the horse will also be wounded, and I want Major Allen to see that the horse is cared for and given to you." Beatty's men, still not realizing their isolated position, braced for a second assault.[18]

. . . .

Eager to gain the Nashville Pike, Hardee ordered McCown's division forward. Rains's brigade had replenished ammunition at the Gresham House. Although not heavily engaged, a number of men had fallen behind due to sheer exhaustion. Nonetheless, Rains had probably 1,300 troops, which he now shifted from the division left to the division right. Rains also reshuffled his units, with the 11th Tennessee on the left, the 29th North Carolina and 9th Georgia Battalion in the center, and the 3rd Georgia Battalion on the right.[19]

In the thick cedars north of the Wilkinson Pike and northeast of the Blanton House, Rains's brigade became separated, with the 3rd Georgia Battalion and 9th Georgia Battalion veering off to the right. This put the Georgians on a direct collision course with Jimmy Forman's 15th Kentucky. "Orderly," the soldier/correspondent of the 3rd Georgia Battalion, reported to his readers: "Concealed by a slight valley and timber from view we moved ten steps further and drew their fire. We gave them one volley and then 'charged.' They could not stand, but like the Ohio troops, broke and fled before us like frightened antelopes." The Kentuckians left eighty dead and wounded behind, the slain colonel Forman among them.[20]

The left of Rains's brigade, the 11th Tennessee and 29th North Carolina, now barreled down on King's First Battalion, 15th United States, and Slemmer's First Battalion, 16th United States, together 597 men. At first the Regulars mistook Rains's skirmishers for Carlin's retreating troops. They were "dressed in our uniforms" and "moving leisurely down upon the left of our line laughing and holding their heads down and otherwise behaving mysteriously," a Regular observed. The truth soon became known, as the Confederates approached to within fifty yards and unleashed a volley, followed by perhaps 750 troops of the 11th Tennessee and 29th North Carolina surging from the woods. The initial Rebel volley, delivered at 150 yards, was "followed by a shout which made the woods ring," Colonel Vance boasted. The 11th overlapped the Federal right, causing both battalions to fall back in disarray. The Regulars fell back across a fence, where they made a brief stand, but they could not hold for long. "On they came pouring voley after voley into our ranks," bugler William J. Carsons of the 15th United States told his mother.[21]

The 6th Ohio and 36th Indiana of William Grose's brigade of Palmer's division, which had been sent in support of Rousseau's far right, had seen the Regulars file in front of them. As they tramped through the undergrowth, fallen logs, and protruding rocks, Colonel Nicholas Anderson's 6th Ohio suddenly encountered King's men "flying in wild disorder, and hotly pursued by the enemy." Corporal Ebenezor Hannaford of the 6th remembered that the Regulars came "toward us in utter confusion. Organization and discipline were forgotten; they were fleeing for their lives." Hannaford heard his lieutenant yell from atop a boulder: "Fire boys, fire! They are advancing!" The 36th Indiana had no warning, as they suddenly received a volley from the enemy that "riddled our ranks," reported Captain Pyrrhus Woodward. Both regiments fell back in confusion, with Anderson being wounded. Lieutenant Robert King of the 15th United States related a somewhat different story to his mother. "After we had fired two or three rounds, we were ordered to fall back, which we did in good order—until we reached the 6th Ohio Vols.—where we rallied our men, and made another stand, but were again obliged to fall back; and as the 6th Ohio broke, our men separated in confusion."[22]

A lull occurred during which a retreating Michigan regiment, unspecified by Beatty but probably the 21st Michigan of Sheridan's division, linked up from the south and was placed in line, presumably on the brigade left. The respite did not last long. Lucius Polk's brigade slammed headlong into Beatty's isolated line in an extended forty-five-minute assault, the first sortie of which was bloodily repulsed, claiming the life of Lieutenant Colonel Don McGregor of the 1st Arkansas. Rousseau and Van Pelt were nowhere to be found on the left, and on the right remained only the dead of the 15th Kentucky. For the first time Beatty grasped the gravity of his position. He ordered his regiments to make a fighting retreat, which they were in the process of doing anyway. "When we raised up [to retreat]," admitted William R. Stuckey of the 42nd Indiana, "the dam Devils was within a few rods of us. We run like hell." He briefly rallied the line, but when his horse tumbled dead, Beatty got to his feet to find his men "sweep in disorder to the rear."[23]

John Beatty's brigade and the battalions of the 15th and 16th U.S. exited the cedars and fell back in disorder across the large field between the cedars and the Nashville Pike. "We then came to a corn field. As we were crossing that, I tell you, they packed it to us," admitted Bugler Carson. Rousseau reformed his division behind the railroad, with Shepherd on the left, Beatty in the center, and Scribner on the right. Rosecrans rode up "in his everlasting old conical wool hat," face scratched up by bushes, with a two-inch cigar stump in one hand and looking "as cool as a cucumber." He rode up to Beatty, grasped his hand, and said: "Why, Colonel Beatty, how do you do, I thank God I see you here." He then turned to the troops and said: "Boys, I am glad to see you all, you have done nobly and I hope by the blessing of God we will today strike this infernal rebellion a crumbling blow." He then passed along the line, shouting: "I thank you, my boys."[24]

THE FIGHT AT THREE MILE MARKER

McCown, under orders from Hardee, gave Ector's and McNair's brigades little time to rest. The physical stress proved too much for McNair, who, sick and exhausted, could no longer keep up. Brigade command fell to twenty-nine-year-old Colonel Robert W. Harper, a former Little Rock attorney and plantation owner. The Texans and Arkansans pushed across the Wilkinson Pike at quick time, swinging right (northeast), with Harper to the right rear of Ector. McNair's division would soon crash into Rosecrans's last defensive line along the Nashville Pike.[25]

Morton's Pioneers lay seventy-five yards in advance of and parallel to the Nashville Pike at the Three Mile Marker, with the First Battalion on the left, the Third Battalion in the center, and the Second Battalion on the right. Due to a mishap, some companies had been issued only twenty rounds. Morton gave the order to "Fix bayonets!" prompting a lieutenant to mumble: "Confound it. That will interfere with their loading." Rosecrans personally positioned the Chicago Board-of-Trade Battery on a knoll between the First and Third Battalions (to the side of today's park headquarters). Battery B, Pennsylvania Artillery, unlimbered to the left of the Chicago battery, thus making a formidable line—sixteen hundred muskets and twelve guns. As Ector's Texans became visible in the woods, the artillerymen opened a horrific fire. The roar of the discharges caused all discipline to break down in the horses, as they began rearing and neighing uncontrollably. The dismounted riders, clutching their bridle bits, were tossed like rag dolls in the air, and extra men had to be detailed to keep the animals under control. Rosecrans told Captain James H. Stokes, a West Point graduate, that if he could hold the position for an hour the day would be won, and if not the entire right would be lost. The captain retorted that "he would hold it as long as there was a button on our 'coats.'"[26]

Sergeant Henry V. Freeman of the Pioneers heard the command: "Battalion, rise up!" but the fire of the artillery so demoralized the enemy, he noted, that they "did not stand long." "Men were dropping here and there, and others filled the vacant places. The rebel flag, seen dimly through the smoke and trees, wavered, started forward, and then surged back," one of Stokes's gunners related. "They came on with terrible yells and they got very near us. But we mowed them down like hay." Edward Wood, another cannoneer, explained to his brother: "At one time they got within 200 feet of us when the pioneers who were supporting us sprang to their feet and poured a volley of musketry which was too much for them. They broke and ran." The smoke became so thick that one of the ammunition boys came too close to the muzzle of a gun as it discharged, tossing him down and nearly killing him. He staggered to the rear, dazed and burned. "Our shot would cut clear through them, yet they moved on to within pistol shot when our support poured a well directed fire into their front, and they were again driven from the fields into the woods, with the loss of a Col. and other officers prisoners," Stokes remembered. When the smoke cleared, a group of Texans came in waving a white handkerchief to surrender. Said one: "I am tired of this damned foolishness and I want to see it stopped." One gunner claimed that a Rebel captain said that his Texans had pledged to take the battery or die trying. "And we did die. We never saw such firing before," the captain confessed. To the left of the Chicago battery, the Texans managed to get within fifteen to twenty yards of the muzzles of the Pennsylvania battery before being hurled back. The Texans left their dead in heaps—nineteen bodies in a single pile.[27]

The 14th and 15th Texas on Ector's left got separated and plunged into Samuel Beatty's brigade, which lay concealed in woods a hundred yards south of Asbury Road, forming an obtuse angle with the Pioneers on their right. There were actually two Colonel Beattys commanding brigades in the Army of the Cumberland—"Sam" and John. When forty-two-year-old Sam, a former sheriff, took furlough in April 1863 to get married, the

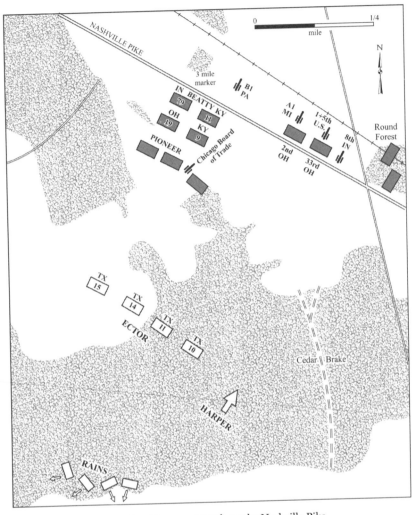

December 31, noon, Assault on the Nashville Pike

Ohio Journal mistakenly reported that it was John taking a new wife. A dismayed John noted that he might have to ask Sam to change his last name—"My reputation cannot stand many more such blows." Rosecrans personally positioned Sam's brigade, prompting Colonel Lyne Sterling of Crittenden's staff to throw up his hat and shout: "Here comes the gallant old 11th Brigade, I know we will whip the Rebels now." Rosecrans stirred emotions by adding, "Boys, you must drive them," although Crittenden sat expressionless.[28]

Beatty's fire easily checked the Texans, but they stubbornly held their ground for half an hour. "They stood fire like steel for about ten minutes," 19th Sergeant Alfred W. Stambaugh admitted. The near-sighted Major Charles F. Manderson of the 19th Ohio had his horse shot, and as he fell to the ground the major lost his glasses. Virtually helpless without them, he rushed his servant to his headquarters wagon to bring his backup pair. It became painfully obvious to Ector that he could not hold—"We had better give back," he conceded. In the din of battle no voices could be heard, but Colonel Julius Andrews of the 15th Texas could be seen running from tree to tree waving his men back. A Texas prisoner was later heard to say that the Yankees "fought more like demons than human beings." Beatty pursued Ector's fleeing men a quarter-mile over open and lightly wooded ground, but lacking artillery support, the colonel prudently called off the chase before entering the cedar swamp.[29]

ROSECRANS'S LAST LINE

To the left of the Pioneer Brigade, Rosecrans planted Rousseau's division behind the railroad. Between the pike and the railroad, Van Pelt's and Guenther's batteries unlimbered their twelve pieces, and to their left the 8th Indiana Battery (from Hascall's brigade but acting independently) came on line. Grose's brigade of Palmer's division had initially been in reserve. As the battle curled to the rear, he realigned some of his troops from southwest to west. This meant that the 84th Illinois, Parson's eight-gun Battery H/M, 4th United States Artillery, the 23rd Kentucky, and the 24th Ohio faced toward the cottonfield, where they could deliver enfilade fire. Twenty-six guns and a wall of infantry thus provided a crossfire—a virtual killing field. In this tense moment, as the troops braced for an assault certain to come, Rosecrans had several bands brought forward which played the "Star Spangled Banner." "The effect was as if by magic," noted a soldier.[30]

Lieutenant Pirtle glanced back at the edge of the woods from which Beatty's men debauched and saw a mass of gray coats and brown hats—McNair's and Rains's brigades. Loomis ordered Van Pelt to give them double canister "as hot as hell will let you!" Guenther strangely held his fire, causing Rousseau to nervously point to the enemy. "I see them, sir." Again he held his fire, saying to Rousseau's repeated order to open fire—"They are not near enough, sir." Meanwhile, the Union center began taking incoming rounds from an unidentified Confederate battery. Lieutenant Robert King of the 15th United States described: "As one of the rebel batteries had the exact range of the railroad, at the point we were, it was anything but pleasant, round shot and shell falling all around us, and in one instance a round shot struck and killed a man, who was lying on the ground not two yards beyond me, and the ball ricocheted over my head. Whenever we heard a shell or saw a round shot coming, every one of us, either made a very low bow, or fell flat to the ground."[31]

Martin Van Buren Coder of the 42nd Indiana, writing to his sister on January 21, told what happened next: "They came out of the woods when seeing the Battery [Van Pelt's] they concluded to capture it and a Georgia reg. made the charge the rest of the Brigade being held in reserve to support it but Captain Loomis of our Battery was ready for them and gave them a mass of grapes that they had no idea of. Still they came on till within 150 yards of the Battery when what few of them was left threw down their arms and surrendered." John Carroll, a former office boy in the *Cleveland Morning Leader*, now a gunner in Battery H, 5th United States, remarked: "After we had ceased firing not a rebel was to be seen, with the exception of a squad of eight or ten who rose from their hiding places with a white handkerchief and hollering 'don't fire.'" A member of the 40th Indiana observed that as many as four to six guns would be discharged simultaneously at no more than 200 yards, sweeping down entire companies "as grass to a reaper. They soon broke and ran back to the shelter of the woods." In describing Rains's assault, Captain Henry Hammon noted how the gray line stretched "from one side of the field to the other." He saw their battle flag (white ground with red cross) "shot down twice but still some bold spirit bore it aloft. A third time it fell and was not raised again but left upon the field."[32]

Although it was "little less than suicide to continue," acknowledged Captain William A. Cotter of the 30th Arkansas, still the Arkansas brigade plunged ahead to within three hundred yards before being checked. A handful of determined men refused to stop and actually came to within a hundred yards of the guns before running back. The 2nd Ohio claimed to have captured thirty men of the 30th. Harper called off the abortive assault, "being nearly decimated." According to Major J. A. Ross of the 4th Arkansas Battalion, "It was nearly impossible for men to withstand such a fire." The flag bearer of the 30th Arkansas was one of the few who made it to the Confederate high-water-mark, before he had his hand blown off and he dropped his banner. A Yankee later claimed it, and described it as being made of coarse bunting, a white cross on a blue field, with "30th Reg." along the top and "Ark. Inf." on the bottom. In 1905 the U.S. War Department returned the flag to the State of Arkansas, where it resides today in the Old State House Museum in Little Rock.[33]

By the time Rains made his ill-advised solo charge across the large field (today behind the park headquarters), his numbers had dwindled. The 29th North Carolina, after deducting casualties and 50 stragglers, was down to 250 men and the 9th Georgia Battalion to only 130. In the midst of the fire, color bearer James Lanning of the 29th North Carolina carried the flag presented by the ladies of Reems Creek; the banner was shredded by thirteen bullets. Brigadier General Rains fell from his horse, a bullet cutting the gauntlet on his right hand and passing through his chest. The word of his death spread "like wild fire along the whole line," Colonel Robert Vance noted. The Federals recovered Rains's body and buried it on the battlefield, but it was later reentered. Earlier in the spring he had received a battle flag at a formal ceremony at the Old City Hotel in Nashville. At that time he promised that "we will conquer before or fall beneath it"; his oath had been fulfilled. Also seriously wounded in the attack was twenty-six-year-old Colonel George Gordon of the 11th Tennessee, a graduate of the Western Military Institute of Nashville and in civilian life a civil engineer. At one point Gordon let his hair grow long, prompting Cheatham to jokingly send him a message to cut it. The rebellious colonel answered: "Tell General Cheatham I will carry out his military orders, but tell him it is none of his business how I wear my hair."[34]

As the Rebels withdrew, Rosecrans ordered a change front, with Shepherd's two right regiments swinging across the Nashville Pike and facing south. Scribner's 38th Indiana formed on their right, and the 94th Ohio on the right of the 38th. In this exposed position, Scribner's two regiments came under sniper fire from the cedars. "We were ordered to be down and it needed no second bidding," a private in the 94th notified his mother. "I will tell you we hugged the ground close. They could see us from the woods as we lay and they kept pecking away at us, most of the balls passing over us, but they struck in the mud all around us." In this position, Colonel Joseph W. Frizzell took a bullet in the shoulder. The regiments were drawn back to a less exposed position.[35]

THE FIGHT AT ASBURY ROAD

Fyffe's brigade, which had withdrawn from its earlier position in supporting the Federal cavalry, waited in position along a wooded ridge that roughly paralleled the Nashville Pike. Van Cleve now ordered it to move up and support Sam Beatty's right, the last having returned from its attack on Ector's brigade. Harker's brigade marched to a hill east of the Widow Burris House and five hundred yards from Fyffe's right. Fyffe, a thirty-four-year-old Ohioan, had served in the Mexican War, where he got into a duel with a captain over rank. In the subsequent exchange both parties missed and shook hands. His brigade moved beyond the woods in their front into an open field in a two-two formation, with the 59th Ohio and 44th Indiana in the front line, and the 13th Ohio and 86th Indiana on the second line. Worried about his flank, Fyffe sent three messages to Harker calling on him to close the gap between his right and Harker's left. Finally, Fyffe himself rode to Van Cleve and requested support for his endangered flank, which was in the air. The division commander ordered Sam Beatty to send two regiments to his assistance, but they never arrived.[36]

Thus far Van Cleve's two fresh brigades had easily driven back Ector's two under-strength Texas regiments. What occurred next, however, must have left them aghast. Emerging from the cedars was "Old Pat" Cleburne, with operational command of five brigades, at least 6,000 troops, even after deducting casualties and stragglers. Lucius Polk confronted Sam Beatty, Wood fronted Fyffe, and Johnson and Liddell approached Harker, with a three-quarters-of-a-mile gap between Liddell's right and Johnson's left. In the rear, Vaughn's Tennesseans were moving up. Initially marching diagonally to the right, Cleburne realigned to the left, so as to approach Van Cleve and Harker directly. Despite repeated calls, Harker had not yet closed the gap between his left and Fyffe's right, prompting one modern writer to flatly conclude: "Harker panicked." Perhaps, but Van Cleve could have partially closed the gap himself by extending his line northwest, using the five regiments in his second line. He chose to maintain a compact position, while Harker stretched *his* line. Harker chose the same in reverse.[37]

When Fyffe's troops arrived on Beatty's right, at the edge of the cedar forest, the front line crossed a high rail fence and advanced twenty yards into the woods, while the second line moved up to the fence. The front line soon became engaged. The 44th Indiana discovered that the enemy occupied the 150-yard woods that projected finger-like into the open field on their right. Fyffe directed Colonel George Dick of the 86th Indiana in the second line to move up and secure the right, but fighting commenced before the movement could be made. George Squires of the 44th Indiana wrote after the battle: "When within 80 rods of their lines we were ordered down, then to raise and fire. We had fired but three rounds when a great blunder was discovered. We were flanked on our right and in five minutes would have been prisoners." Hit in front and flank, Colonel William C. Williams ordered the 44th back, but the retreat quickly turned into a rout— "Oh! Heavens! Can it be?" the colonel cried. Squires described the scene as "a perfect stampede—men running for dear life, disengaging haversacks, cartridge boxes, canteens, overcoats, guns, everything that could impede their progress."

The panicked Hoosiers nearly trampled the 86th Indiana in their rear as they laid down at the fence. The 59th Ohio also fell back in confusion but managed to reform at the fence line, where they held until informed that the brigade right had buckled. Colonel Joseph G. Hawkins of the 13th Ohio encouraged his men to hold firm, but he fell mortally wounded. Both lines of the brigade now collapsed (they "ran like a flock of scared sheep," according to Corporal Thomas H. B. McCain of the 86th Indiana), falling back toward the left through Beatty's line. As he attempted to rally Fyffe's men, a bullet struck Van Cleve in his right leg, narrowly missing the artery. (He never mentioned the incident in his after-action report.) Hoosier Nelson Sowers believed that all of the old veterans would have preferred hours of fighting at Shiloh to the "fifteen or twenty minutes occupied in falling back across that open field."[38]

Fyffe's men had been hit by S. A. M. Wood's brigade and the left regiments of Lucius Polk's brigade—both reduced in numbers, but still carrying a lethal punch. The 45th Mississippi reported capturing seventy prisoners. After driving the bluecoats from the woods, Major J. F. Cameron of the 3rd Confederate noted that the enemy's line posted behind a fence. With the aide of fifty stragglers, the 3rd charged the fence, driving the enemy, capturing the colors of the 86th Indiana, and about thirty prisoners. The Yankees fled to the pike and protection of their guns. Cleburne lamented that Wood's men almost made it to the pike, but taking casualties in an open field, they were forced to retire. Cleburne advanced a hundred sharpshooters, but they were soon driven back.[39]

Fyffe's troops nearly trampled Beatty's men as they careened diagonally through their front line. "Our men kept firm, and we tried to rally them, but with no effect," Colonel Benjamin C. Grider of the 11th Kentucky reported. Viewing the action from the second line, Marcus Woodcock recalled: "They [Fyffe's men] had scarcely passed the front line when the pursuing rebels [Polk's brigade] came in view of my front line, and then was begun one of the most magnificent shooting scenes that was presented. . . . The 11th Ky. with their breech-loading five-shooters, and the 79th Ind. with their heavy [Enfield] Rifles poured volley after volley into the advancing rebels." As the enemy closed the distance, Beatty gave the order to withdraw three hundred yards to the pike, an order not received by Major Manderson of the 19th Ohio. Twice he sent word to Beatty of his exposed position, but to no avail. He ordered his regiment to lay down, while the regimental flag was placed in a new line in his right rear. As soon as he gave the order, the Buckeyes raced to the new position. Sensing a stampede, the Confederates moved in for the kill, but the 19th held and repulsed the attack. When the entire brigade had fallen back to the pike, it was scattered, in some instances by Rosecrans himself—the 19th Ohio on the left of the 2nd Pioneer Battalion and the right of Fyffe's brigade, the 79th Indiana also to the support of Fyffe, and the 9th and 11th Kentucky to the support of the Chicago Board of Trade Battery.[40]

S. A. M. Wood, crossing "a small dirt road" (Asbury Road) was fast approaching the Nashville Pike. He sent word back to Vaughn to hurry up his brigade to cover his right. Vaughn came under a severe fire on his right flank, however, and his Tennesseans fell back in disorder. He later blamed Lucius Polk for not keeping pace and thus exposing his flank. The attack ground to a halt. Their troops, exhausted and thinned, fell back south through the cedars to the Wilkinson Pike.[41]

Charles G. Harker, a twenty-five-year-old bachelor who had a penchant for drinking, had proven a natural-born leader. Though orphaned at an early age, he nonetheless graduated West Point and served two terms in the U.S. Congress. His brigade of Wood's division had moved by the right flank and crossed the Nashville Pike between the Three and Four Mile Marker, ultimately deploying north of the Asbury Road at the Widow Burris House—the 65th Ohio and 51st Indiana on the front line, 73rd Indiana and 64th Ohio behind them, and the 13th Michigan in reserve. As his flank came under artillery fire from Swett's Mississippi Battery, Harker

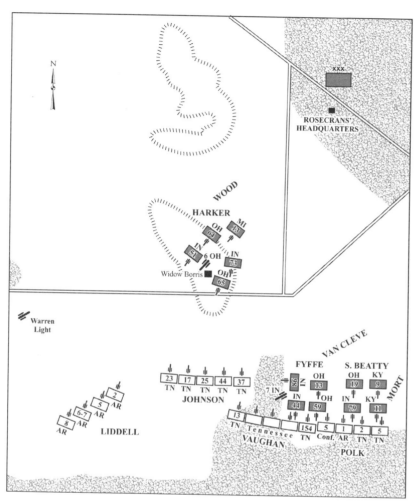

December 31, 1:00 p.m., Hardee's Repulse

shifted his five regiments right. Although the move secured his own flank, it further widened the gap between him and Fyffe. Captain Cullen Bradley's 6th Ohio Battery unlimbered near two small houses on the lane in support of Harker. "In front of the line was literally a blaze of fire while the dense smoke almost concealed the combatants from view," noted a member of the 65th Ohio. Bushrod Johnson's Tennessee brigade soon slammed into the 65th Ohio and Bradley's battery, the last rapidly blasting off 150 rounds of canister. Within twenty minutes the 65th broke under a raking crossfire, the troops overrunning the 73rd Indiana (a new regiment) in their rear. "I expected every minute to get a chuck in my side," John Sowash of the 65th Ohio admitted. The Buckeyes finally managed to rally at a fence. In a splendid performance, the 73rd held its ground, unleashed a dozen volleys, and reoccupied the former Ohio position. The 51st Indiana now fell back, leaving the 73rd alone on the ridge.[42]

At about noon Harker ordered Colonel Alexander McIlvain's 64th Ohio forward in support of the 73rd Indiana. "We moved up near the woods where the 73rd was being driven back by the rebs," Joe Coe of the 64th explained to his parents. "[O]ur brave Col. Harker commanded us to fix bayonets and relieve our fellow soldiers for I expect something from you Ohio boys today[.] [H]e gave the command forward & into it we went firing & loading as fast as we could & driving them back, the balls flying thick all around us & men dropping on our right & on our left. We drove them about a quarter-of-a-mile when we got ourselves to fall back—the order was unexpected to us for we was determined on doing something. But the brigade on our left [Fyffe's] was falling back & we had to[.] I was close by the colors & the color bearer being wounded I bore the colors off the field." Both regiments fell back toward the pike.[43]

Only the 65th Ohio remained at the fence, and it soon became isolated. "When we commenced firing from behind the fence the enemy were but 150 yards distant and our hearts almost sank within us as we saw the long dark line advancing bold and defiant flaunting their banners of treason," Lieutenant Wilbur W. Hinman of the 65th wrote his friends on January 11. "On came the hordes of rebels till their line was but 20 paces distant and the fire of both sides was most deadly and appalling." As Johnson's Tennesseans enveloped them, the Buckeyes fled for their lives. "Five minutes more and everyone who escaped the balls would have been a prisoner and the order 'Retreat' was give," Hinman wrote. "To execute this however seemed almost certain death for us soon as we rose up we would be exposed to a terrible fire without any protection whatever. Any delay however and we were doomed & rising to our feet we took a *double* double-quick while the rebels poured a terrific volley onto us. On this occasion . . . we made I believe the fastest time on record. Many lost overcoats, haversacks, canteens, etc. but almost without exception the guns were brought off. Many fell—one just at my side was struck by a ball and dropped upon the ground with a heart rendering groan."[44]

Bradley abandoned two of his guns as Harker's line fell back to the wooded ridge bordering the Nashville Pike. The 27th and 51st Illinois of Bradley's brigade, Sheridan's division, which had made its way out of the cedars and had been sent to the right, reinforced the 13th Michigan. Colonel Michael Shoemaker of the 13th ordered a charge that so stunned the enemy that Bradley's two guns were retaken, along with fifty-eight prisoners. The 51st Illinois joined in the charge, but to Shoemaker's chagrin stopped short and allowed the Michiganders to charge solo—"I think that there was not a gun fired from their ranks," Shoemaker wrote in disgust.[45]

Even before the charge of the 13th Michigan, Johnson's attack showed signs of sputtering out. Almost within view of the pike, the brigade right suddenly buckled. "The retreat was made without order. The lines were broken and men of different regiments, brigades, and divisions were scattered all over the fields," Johnson admitted. "The movement was totally unexpected and I have yet to learn that there existed a cause commensurate with the demoralization that ensued." Indeed, Johnson was "almost run over by our retreating troops." Lieutenant Colonel Watt W. Floyd claimed that his 17th Tennessee halted at the fence, "but no one seemed disposed to stop and support me." Colonel John A. Fulton could not see "any apparent cause" for the sudden reversal, although flags with a blue field and a red cross could be seen giving way on Johnson's right. An investigation subsequently revealed that Vaughn's brigade of Cheatham's division, on Johnson's right, had broken, thus spreading the panic. Vaughn would blame S. A. M. Wood's brigade, which had been repulsed by Fyffe, for not keeping pace and thus exposing his right to an enfilade fire.[46]

Liddell advanced his brigade on the Confederate far left. Dr. W. R. Kibler, a regimental surgeon, rode up to the brigadier and said: "General, I am ordered to come and look after you or your staff should any be shot." "You are too close up for a surgeon. I fear you will be shot," Liddell answered. "No, I think not—I am not afraid," said Kibler. Seeing a Yankee regiment appearing to crumble, the general raised his cap, spurred his horse, and rode forward firing his revolver. Just then he heard Kibler shout out: "My God, I am hit." "Where, Doctor?" "In the side." Before Liddell could catch him, Kibler slumped from his saddle.[47]

Momentarily, Liddell viewed the troops on his right hastily falling back. Astonished, he galloped over and attempted to head them off. "They were Johnson's men, and I soon met the General, in like haste looking for them.

He told me that my brigade had also fallen back." Liddell encountered his confused command at the edge of some woods. It appeared to him that a misunderstanding had precipitated the retreat since "no enemy was in sight, and none had pursued." At that point Cleburne and Hardee sent directions to halt and await further orders. The time was now 3:00; the Confederate advance on the far left had come to a grinding halt. Time yet remained to win the battle, but it would have to come on the right, in an area called the Round Forest.[48]

General Braxton Bragg in Montgomery, Alabama, in the summer of 1862. (Confederate Museum, New Orleans, La.)

Major General William S. Rosecrans usually had his photograph taken from the left in order to hide a disfiguring prewar scar on his right cheek. (United States Army Military History Institute, Carlisle Barrack, Pa.)

Union cabins on the grounds of the Rutherford County Courthouse.
(Albert Gore Research Center, Middle Tennessee State University.)

The Nashville Turnpike as seen in the 1880s.
(Stones River National Battlefield Park, Murfreesboro, Tenn.)

A 1928 image from the Widow Smith House facing towards Carlin's position in the woods. (Stones River National Battlefield Park, Murfreesboro, Tenn.)

Remains of the brick kiln at the Harding House.
(Stones River National Battlefield Park, Murfreesboro, Tenn.)

A 1928 image from the Wilkinson Pike facing toward the V between Sheridan and
Negley. (Stones River National Battlefield Park, Murfreesboro, Tenn.)

Assault of Samuel Beatty's brigade near the Nashville Turnpike.
(From Robert Underwood Johnson and Clarence Clough Buel, eds.,
*Battles and Leaders of the Civil War: Being for the Most Part Contributions by
Union and Confederate Officers* (New York: Century Co., 1887–88).

Rosecrans's Last Line. In the foreground are Loomis's and Guenther's
batteries at the sight of the present-day National Cemetery.
(From Johnson and Buel, eds., *Battles and Leaders of the Civil War*.)

A 1928 image from the position of the Cowan House showing the field over which Chalmers's brigade attacked. Cruft's brigade held the woods in the distance. (Stones River National Battlefield Park, Murfreesboro, Tenn.)

The artillery monument on McFadden's Hill as seen in 1928. (Stones River National Battlefield Park, Murfreesboro, Tenn.)

McFadden's Ford in the 1880s.
(From the Collections of Dayton History, Kern Collection.)

The charge of Negley's division across Stones River on January 3 as depicted by Alfred E. Matthews. (From Johnson and Buel, eds., *Battles and Leaders of the Civil War.*)

Henry Lovie's sketch of Negley's January 2 assault. (Stones River National Battlefield Park, Murfreesboro, Tenn.)

The advance of Moses Walker's brigade on the evening of January 2. (From Johnson and Buel, eds., *Battles and Leaders of the Civil War.*)

9

THE ROUND FOREST

Rosecrans's final defense line had thus far proven impenetrable. The center and right had hurled back repeated Confederate assaults along the Nashville Pike. Yet one sector remained untested—the Federal left held by Palmer's division. Cruft's brigade, with Grose's regiments in support, formed along McFadden's Lane, and to their left Hazen's brigade anchored the juncture of the pike and railroad at the Round Forest. George Wagner's brigade of Wood's division extended Hazen's left to the river. The question remained: would Bragg strike this sector or continue his swing around the Union right on the Nashville Pike? The Federals would soon have their answer.

• • • •

The far right of Withers's division, the brigade of thirty-one-year-old Brigadier General James Chalmers, a former Holly Springs attorney, was the pivot of Bragg's grand turning movement. For two days the 2,000 Mississippians huddled behind their slight log-and-rail breastworks in the cold and rain, yet Polk boasted "not a murmur of discontent" could be heard. At 10:00 the old "Pensacola Brigade," as the press referred to it, received the order to move out. The troops surged across an 800-yard-wide field south of the destroyed Cowan House.[1]

As the brigade approached the house, it split, the 7th, 41st, and 10th Mississippi and Garrity's Alabama Battery veering left, the last with a section on each flank. They would be tangling with Cruft's brigade, the 2nd Kentucky and 31st Indiana on the front line, supported by the six guns of Battery B, 1st Ohio Artillery, and the enfilade fire of Battery B, Kentucky

Artillery, 300 yards south of Cruft. Positioned in front of the cedar woods, the Federals quickly tore down the rails along McFadden's Lane and fashioned a stone wall from rocks. The 10th Mississippi took cover in the ruins and outhouses of the Cowan House and opened a long-distance fire. The 7th and 41st Mississippi drew such a blistering fire out in the open that the men broke to the rear. In attempting to rally the 7th, a bullet struck thirty-eight-year-old Yale law graduate Colonel William H. Bishop in the thigh. Chalmers was likewise struck in the head by a shell fragment, and carried senseless from the field. A forty-one-year-old Harvard law graduate, Colonel Thomas H. White, assumed command. The 41st Mississippi attempted a second sortie, approaching to within a hundred yards (sixty according to Confederate reports), before planting their colors and hitting the ground. By 10:30 they could take no more, and the graycoats staggered back in squads and companies. The Mississippians left a carpet of 376 casualties in their rear—nearly a quarter of their strength. Garrity's battery alone sustained 21 killed and wounded, and twenty horses lay dead. Chalmers had only three shredded regiments to show for his efforts.[2]

In the midst of the melee, Cruft ordered his second line, the 90th Ohio and 1st Kentucky, to replace his first line, now out of ammunition. The exchange went remarkably well under the circumstances, but then Cruft strangely directed the 1st Kentucky to attack. Exactly what he had in mind is not known; he owned up to it only in a second report, but even then he gave no explanation. Perhaps he wished to take advantage of Chalmers's disorganized state. Perhaps, as has been suggested, he wished to buy time for Negley's division on his right, which was about to break. The Kentuckians' brazen sortie came to within 40 to 50 yards of the section of Garrity's battery near the Cown House, when Colonel David A. Enyart, sporting a beard that stretched to his heart, glanced to his right and saw Rebel infantry sweeping past his flank. He immediately ordered his regiment back to the fence line along McFadden Lane.[3]

As the fighting raged, Daniel S. Donelson's Tennessee brigade came forward and occupied the log-and-rail breastworks vacated by Chalmers. At age sixty-two, Donelson, the former private secretary to Andrew Jackson, was the oldest brigadier in Bragg's army. The heavy thud of bullets could be heard everywhere—the overshooting of Cruft's troops. The men from the Volunteer State soon discovered that even stray bullets could have a deadly effect—the 8th Tennessee lost 15 to 20 men killed and wounded within twenty minutes, as they huddled behind their flimsy rails. At 11:00, as Chalmers's Mississippians fell back in disarray, Donelson waved his 1,400 troops forward over the same ground now strewn with hundreds of dead and wounded. Donelson had his horse shot from under him. It would not be a Yankee bullet that would kill him, however, but rather chronic diarrhea three and a half months later.[4]

Colonel John Chester reported that his 51st Tennessee took several casualties even before reaching the charred Cowan House; a single shell killed and wounded three of his color guard. As with Chalmers's brigade, the Tennesseans split at the house, the 8th and 38th Tennessee and seven companies of the 51st Tennessee, about a thousand men, angling left at the house toward Cruft's front line and the 6th Kentucky of Hazen's brigade. The gray infantry fixed bayonets and advanced "with a yell." To artilleryman Thomas L. Potter of Standart's Battery B, 1st Ohio Light Artillery, the Tennesseans appeared "maddened and half crazy by whiskey," despite the fact that canister "tore great gaps in their ranks." He continued: "Never did I see men face the music [like this]. When so close to our guns they pulled their hats over their eyes so that they could not see the flash of our pieces, and moved steadily as if they were on the parade ground." Sergeant William Buskey of the 1st Kentucky saw a half-dozen Rebel flags "fluttering above the corn stalks, the men pressing our front in four ranks as orderly as on dress parade, although we were mowing down scores of them at every volley." With Negley's division to his right being rolled back, Cruft had little choice but to retreat north through the cedars toward the Nashville Pike. He yelled to the 31st Indiana: "Now men, for God's sake remember you are from my own native state." In the fight and "wild retreat" that followed, Cruft lost a third of his infantry, including several hundred prisoners, although he managed to save four of Standart's guns. Donelson paid heavily for his momentary victory. Colonel W. L. Moore of the 8th Tennessee fell dead, a bullet to his heart, and his regiment lost a staggering 306 of 472 men, a hideous 65 percent loss.[5]

Noon found Negley's and Cruft's troops streaming in disorder through the cedars; with them went most of the last vestiges of Rosecrans's original battle line. In order to buy time to stabilize the left, the army commander rode over to the Regulars and said: "Shepherd, take your brigade in there," with Thomas adding, "and stop the Rebels." Shepherd hurriedly marched his infantry to McFadden's Lane and ordered the men to shed their cumbersome overcoats. The 16th U.S. formed the center, the 18th U.S. the left, and the 15th and 19th U.S. the right. With the brigade's distinctive blue-and-gold battle flag flapping in the winter wind, Shepherd advanced his battalion west of the lane and directly into the cedars. Jacob Vaan Zwaluwerburg of the 16th admitted: "I had rather been in mother's back yard just then to tell the truth."[6]

No sooner had the Regulars entered the woods than they encountered Negley's and Cruft's fleeing men. "We laid down as ordered and lay with our guns cocked and fingers on our triggers (our men fell back over us in confusion and the wounded with bloody cloths hobbled over us while others less able were shot & shot again & fell full of wounds lifeless)," Private Reuben Jones of the 16th U.S. wrote to his sister. A momentary lull occurred, but soon the sounds of the advancing Rebels could be heard—lots of them. Barreling down on them would be A. P. Stewart's brigade, three regiments of Donelson's brigade, John K. Jackson's small brigade which had recently crossed Stones River and came up on Stewart's right, and the 29th Mississippi of Patton Anderson's brigade, roughly 3,000 troops to confront 1,400. As the Rebels approached to within 80 yards, clearly expecting no organized opposition, the Regulars suddenly raised up and unleashed a volley that staggered them. A withering twenty-minute exchange ensued. Fearful that Shepherd would be overlapped, Rosecrans sent in the 18th Ohio to bolster their right; it proved too little, too late. The lines closed to within 100 yards—"We could see nothing but the blaze of their guns," Captain M. W. Halsey of the 18th U.S. recalled. Men dropped by the dozens.

Shepherd calmly ordered his men back, but other officers were more animated. Major Stephen D. Carpenter of the 19th U.S. shouted, "Scatter and run, boys!" and Captain Ansel Denton of the 18th U.S. screamed, "For God's sake men, get back to the railroad or we'll all be killed." The blue-coats now had to scramble back over the same cottonfield in which Rains's brigade had just been slaughtered. The Rebels came up to the wood line and fired directly into their backs. "How any of us got across that field alive I cannot imagine," Captain James Biddle of the 16th U.S. admitted. Many did not make it across, including Major S. D. Carpenter of the 19th U.S., who fell with six bullets; a private heroically retrieved his body. The Regulars had performed courageously in their questionable mission, but at a staggering cost. Within forty-five minutes, 600 of their 1,400 men had been killed, wounded, or captured. The grays had suffered similarly. John

Jackson had his horse shot from under him and lost 305 of his 777 infantry. It had been mutual annihilation.[7]

During the height of the fighting, "Old Straight" Stewart could be seen leisurely smoking a pipe and talking with his staff officers. An odd incident occurred when, in the midst of the assault, Colonel John A. Jaques of the 1st Louisiana Regulars rode up to Colonel Egbert E. Tansil of the 31st and 33rd Tennessee. Insisting that he was a member of Cheatham's staff, he ordered the regiment to break off the attack and fall back. Tansil obeyed, and soon the entire brigade followed suit. Jaques, as it turned out, had earlier deserted his own regiment. Whether or not he had a breakdown could not be determined, but for the time being he was placed under arrest. He would later be cashiered.[8]

HELL'S HALF ACRE

The lynchpin of the Federal defense on the left became a thinly wooded rise of ground "not exceeding two feet in height" east of the turnpike, opposite the toll-gate house, known to the locals as the Round Forest. To those who fought there, it would become "Hell's Half Acre." At this point the Federal line would no longer cave. Commanding in this crucial sector was thirty-one-year-old, Vermont-born but Ohio-raised West Pointer William B. Hazen. Tough to the point of tyrannical, and not universally popular (Palmer denounced him as a "vain and selfish man"), there could not have been a better selection. Back in November 1859 he had gotten a bullet lodged in his back while fighting Comanches. Surgeons had never been able to remove it. On this day, the eyes of the nation would be on William B. Hazen.[9]

Earlier in the morning, Hazen had deployed in the cottonfield south of the turnpike, with a 250-yard gap between his right and Cruft's left. When Palmer received word that Negley's division would be advancing, he directed Cruft and Hazen forward to cover the Pennsylvania's flank. The movement had barely commenced when the Federal right collapsed and Negley came under attack, prompting Palmer to cancel his order. Hazen, believing his position in the cottonfield utterly untenable, moved his two left regiments, the 41st Ohio and 110th Illinois, left to the Round Forest (referred to variously as a "slight crest" and a "slight elevation"), between the pike and the railroad.[10]

Chalmers launched his attack at 10:00, his right wing, comprised of the

9th Mississippi and Blythe's Mississippi, together only 518 men, advancing on either side of the pike toward Hazen. The 9th halted at the stockade fence blocking their path and commenced firing at fleeing Yankee skirmishers of the 6th Kentucky (U.S.). This left Blythe's Mississippi advancing against the 41st Ohio and 110th Illinois in the Round Forest and the six guns of Captain Daniel T. Cockerill's Battery F, 1st Ohio Artillery, east of McFadden's Lane. "I will never forget the splendid appearance of the rebel line of battle as it advanced to engage our brigade," Private James M. Kirkpatrick of the 41st Ohio intoned to his friends. C. P. Ball, also of that regiment, wrote more bluntly, stating that they "came at us with a yell, as if to gobble us up." Blythe's men, armed with such inferior muskets that rounds could hardly be rammed down, staggered to within 200 yards of the 41st Ohio, but they were too few to make more headway. When Lieutenant Colonel Aquila Wiley of the 41st related that he was running out of ammunition, Hazen calmly answered: "Rely on the bayonet." The Illinois boys to their left, who had no bayonets, were told to use their guns as clubs. The Mississippians finally pulled back, leaving behind 136 killed and wounded. This portion of the cottonfield would become known as the "Mississippi Half-Acre."[11]

Donelson's 11:00 attempt against the Round Forrest with his right wing also proved feeble, with only the 16th Tennessee and three companies of the 51st Tennessee participating. The small 39th North Carolina later moved up on the right, but the total attacking force probably did not exceed 800, and the 39th soon "gave way." The Rebels approached to within 100 yards before they could go no farther—"we lay shooting, they standing," according to Jim Wommack of the 16th. Forty-seven-year-old Colonel John Savage, commanding the 16th Tennessee, openly blurted that Donelson had placed them in a position where all of them would be killed; his brother, Lieutenant Colonel L. N. Savage, fell mortally wounded. Scores went down, 30 of them "left dead upon the spot where they halted dressed in perfect line of battle." The carnage would claim 207 of Savage's 400 men.[12]

At one point Palmer rode over to Hazen and yelled: "Hazen, you'll have to fall back." The colonel bluntly returned: "I'd like to know where in hell I'll fall back to." Hazen had his roan horse shot from under him; his orderly fell dead in retrieving the saddle. The 9th Indiana replaced the 41st Ohio when it exhausted its ammunition. The Buckeyes took shelter in a hollow in the rear, but according to James Kirkpatrick, "There was no safe place, and some were hit while in reserve." A few months after the battle, a detail from the brigade built a ten-foot-high limestone monument on the precise spot of the heaviest fighting in the Round Forest. It remains today, the oldest Civil War monument in the nation, with 45 Union graves around it. In postwar years, Lieutenant E. K. Crebbin of the 9th Indiana wrote that 113 of his regiment were killed or wounded at the site of the moment, grim testimony to the depressing body count.[13]

A Palmer aide, searching for reinforcements, found Brigadier General Milo Hascall of Wood's division and requested immediate assistance for Hazen. With the approval of his division commander, Hascall sent Colonel Samuel McKee's 3rd Kentucky (U.S.) It deployed in an open field south of the pike on the right of the 9th Indiana. As the men laid down and exchanged fire with some of Donelson's troops in front at the Cowan House, the balance of the Tennesseans, having driven Cruft's men through the cedars, swung right to within 200 yards, catching the Kentuckians in a deadly crossfire. Hascall watched as the 3rd Kentucky nearly vanished, including McKee, with a bullet just above his right eye. Still, the line held.[14]

Searching for reinforcements, Palmer spotted Grose's uncommitted brigade. The 24th Ohio and a portion of the 36th Indiana made double-quick to the right of the 41st Ohio which, with a fresh supply of ammunition, had come back into the fight. Parson's Batteries H/M, 4th U.S. Artillery, unlimbered to the right of the 24th Ohio. The young Parsons, who so effectively worked his guns against Donelson's Tennesseans, would in postwar years become an Episcopalian priest in Memphis, dying in the 1878 yellow fever epidemic. To his right the 84th Illinois came on line, with Battery B, Pennsylvania, to his rear. Facing toward the Cowan House, the line came under a savage crossfire from Donelson's men, who had pushed back Cruft and gained the cedars. The 24th Ohio fired across a cottonfield according to Buckeye J. H. Orton, who admitted (official reports to the contrary) that the regiment held only half an hour. By noon Grose's brigade, low on ammunition and having incurred serious losses, swung back toward the pike and railroad. Within twenty minutes in the new position, Colonel Fredrick C. Jones of the 24th Ohio fell dead. Orton also fell with a shot to his thigh that came out the other side just above the hip. "I have the bullet in my pocket," he boasted to his mother.[15]

· · · ·

By mid-morning the Confederate attacks on the left and center had ground to a halt. On the right, Polk began calling for reinforcements even before Chalmers and Donelson began their attack, on the assumption that more troops would be needed. Additional men could come from only one source, Breckinridge's 8,000-man division across the river, which had sat idle all morning. At 10:00 Bragg, still hoping to overlap Rosecrans's right on the Nashville Pike, dispatched a staff officer, Colonel Stoddard Johnston, with orders to Breckinridge to send one, and if possible two, brigades to reinforce Hardee. So far, so good. At 10:10, however, Breckinridge sent a startling dispatch, announcing that *he* would soon be attacked by a force advancing in two lines from the river ford. This was obviously Van Cleve's early morning crossing at McFadden's Ford, but the planned assault had long been aborted. At the same time, a dispatch arrived at army headquarters from Pegram, claiming that a "heavy force" of infantry was approaching Dr. Black's House south of the East Fork of Stones River on the Lebanon Pike, less than five miles from Breckinridge. Could it be the two Union divisions from Gallatin? For a fleeting moment, Bragg must have felt as though his worst nightmare had been realized.

Bragg acted quickly. He dispatched Colonel William Clare, followed shortly by Colonel Johnston, to Breckinridge with verbal orders to immediately attack the Stones River force. Breckinridge reluctantly and belatedly began a wheeling movement toward McFadden's Ford at 11:30, advancing a half-mile. He nonetheless warned Bragg that his present movement would "take me clear away from the Lebanon Pike, and expose my right and that road to a heavy force of the enemy from Black's." Pegram now sent a dispatch that there had never been any force on the Lebanon Pike and that only "a small body of skirmishers" stood in Breckinridge's front. This stunning reversal underscored the total collapse of intelligence that had occurred. Bragg's fury did not abate even after the battle. A staff officer, John A. Buckner, one of several aides riding back and forth that morning, arrived from army headquarters with orders that Breckinridge should fall back and immediately send at least one, if not two, brigades to Polk, not Hardee. Shortly thereafter the Kentuckian received an additional order to leave Hanson's brigade on the east bank and reinforce Polk with his other four brigades. The Bishop would throw "all the forces he could collect" against the Round Forest. Bragg hoped to either crush Hazen or force Rosecrans to weaken his right in order to strengthen his left, thus enabling Hardee to gain control of the Nashville Pike.

Time remained for yet one more blunder. Indecisiveness gripped the army commander; what if Breckinridge's 11:30 dispatch turned out to be true, and a threat remained on the Lebanon Pike? Bragg, the stress of battle beginning to take its toll, now countermanded the order to Breckinridge (although Jackson's brigade had crossed before noon), and ordered Polk to send two of *his* brigades to the east bank. At 12:50 the division commander suggested that the troops be held at the river ford until hard intelligence could be obtained. Within ten minutes it was confirmed that no enemy force had ever existed. Adams's brigade immediately went forth, followed by Preston's and Palmer's brigades. Pegram's misstep would be added with those of McCown's and Cheatham's to a growing list of battlefield gaffes.[16]

One modern writer has questioned whether Breckinridge fabricated the enemy force on the Lebanon Pike. Peter Cozzens concludes that the Kentuckian's lack of censure of Pegram's performance, and his desire to "forestall the probable mishandling [by Bragg] of his troops," suggest that this may have been the case. Cozzens goes so far as to add that Bragg's refusal to pardon the execution of Kentuckian Asa Lewis may have entered into Breckinridge's thinking. Such speculation seems highly implausible (Pegram would have to have participated in a conspiracy), but exactly how such wildly inaccurate information was transmitted will never be known.[17]

The stated assumption that faulty intelligence wasted three hours (10:00–1:00) may not be entirely accurate. Breckinridge did not receive Bragg's 10:00 dispatch until 10:30. He claims to have immediately started two brigades, and this may be true. It is known that Jackson's brigade crossed to the west bank, veered left of the Cowan House, and participated in the final Confederate assault (around noon) on Cruft and Negley. As for Adams's brigade, reports indicate it was on the west bank by 1:00, meaning that it had to have departed at least forty-five minutes to an hour prior to that time. Perhaps an hour and a half was squandered, but reinforcements were at last on the way.

· · · ·

Hardee would long argue that Bragg's best effort at this point should have been made against Rosecrans's right. The army commander insisted that it was too late to have troops make an exhausting trek following a winding route around the rear of the entire army. A second option would be to advance Breckinridge's division to attack the Yankee left at McFadden's Ford. It is possible, of course, that such an assault would have played out much as it did on January 2, when such a move was attempted. Operating on the defensive with interior lines and a superior force, Rosecrans could always rush reinforcements to a threatened portion of the line faster than Bragg. Despite limited options, Bragg's ultimate decision to continue hammering the Round Forest would prove disastrous.[18]

During the lull following Donelson's attack, the Federals significantly reinforced Hazen's position. Rosecrans ordered Schaefer's brigade of Sheridan's division, now re-supplied with ammunition, to the vicinity. At 1:30 the remains of the 2nd Missouri, 44th Illinois, and 75th Illinois formed on the north side of the railroad embankment in and to the southeast of the Round Forest. The 15th Missouri advanced as skirmishers at right angle to the 44th Illinois. Brigadier General Milo Hascall's brigade on the far left of Wood's division had earlier been withdrawn as a support to Hazen. Being the only general officer in the sector, Hascall took charge. He replaced the chewed-up 3rd Kentucky with the 58th Indiana, between the track and the pike. The brigadier then rushed the 100th Illinois into the Round Forest, where the 110th Illinois formed on its left. Hascall positioned the 97th Ohio and Lieutenant George Estep's 8th Indiana Battery on either side of Grose's 6th Ohio, which straddled the pike facing southeast. To the east of the Round Forest, the 15th and 57th Indiana regiments of Wagner's brigade and the 10th Indiana Battery slanted southwest to deliver an enfilade fire. Rosecrans arrived on the scene and personally approved the dispositions.[19]

· · · ·

Brigadier General Daniel W. Adams, a politically well-connected former New Orleans attorney, led his 1,400 infantry to the west bank of Stones River at 1:00. Twenty years earlier, Adams had killed in a duel a Vicksburg newspaper editor who had questioned the political views of his father, a federal judge. At Shiloh he was shot in the left eye and later left for dead upon the roadside, but he slowly recovered. Reporting directly to Polk, the brigadier was told: "Look at yonder battery," pointing to the 10th Indiana Battery, located on high ground 700–800 yards in advance of the ford and east of the Round Forest. "Take it and the day is ours." Rather than wait for Preston and Palmer to arrive, the Bishop foolishly committed the brigade piecemeal; it would prove disastrous.[20]

As Adams's troops crossed the river, a pale and emaciated Bragg rode up, pulled reign, took off his cap, and waved his hand as if to get silence. In a rare moment of inspiration he spoke: "Louisianans, the enemy's right wing has been routed and we are steadily driving it back. He still stands firm in the center. He must be defeated there. It remains for you to do this and the victory is ours. Remember the wrongs to your state, your insulted wives and mothers, your polluted shrines and desecrated homes. Be men and strike for vengeance and liberty." The troops broke into deafening cheers.[21]

Adams began forming his line at 1:00 in open ground near the intersection of the pike and railroad; the attack began at 2:00. Here and there enemy shells plowed up the ground, but still the brigade "moved up in splendid order through an open cotton field," although their "ranks were thinned at every step." Like Chalmers and Donelson before him, Adams was forced to split his regiments on either side of the Cowan House. Once past the house, thirty-six-year-old Lieutenant Colonel Henry "Harry" Maury, well known for his heavy drinking and eccentricities, formed his 32nd Alabama on the left of the pike while the 16th and 25th Louisiana (consolidated) straddled the road and the 13th and 20th Louisiana (consolidated) held the right. The 14th Louisiana Battalion marched up the pike as a reserve.

The 32nd Alabama came under a withering fire from Hazen's and Schaefer's troops, the last behind the railroad embankment. When the standard bearer of the 32nd fell, Colonel Maury, his horse now dead, grabbed the banner and proceeded only a few steps before he fell severely wounded. Adjutant John L. Chandler snatched the flag and rode forward. Gibson's front line entered a virtual killing zone. John W. Bell of the 32nd Alabama admitted that the enemy "mowed us down like straw." Lieutenant Clement S. Watson looked on in horror as a shell "took the heads, or the greater portion of the head, off of four of my men at one shot[,] wounding four more and covering me with dirt and splinters." Colonel Randal Gibson, a Yale graduate, saw the Yankees (the 15th and 57th Indiana of Wagner's brigade) sweeping around his right flank to get in his rear and another regiment (the 15th Missouri of Schaefer's brigade) edging forth in a skirmish line in the field in front. The Missourians, according to Captain John McGrath of the 13th and 20th Louisiana, "instantly raised up and poured a deadly volley into our surprised ranks. We were knocked into confusion, and fell back to a fence. . . . My gallant boys began falling pretty fast, so did all in the regiment." The savage fire sent the graycoats reeling back in confusion. The 15th Indiana charged and claimed 170 prisoners, but not without losing 130 casualties themselves. The 457-man 16th and 25th Louisiana (consolidated) sustained 217 casualties, the 32nd Alabama 126 casualties.[22]

John Ellis, a member of the 16th Louisiana, noted that at the crucial moment "the regiment on our right [13th and 20th Louisiana] began to waver. It was thrown into confusion and finally broke and ran is a disorderly retreat. The 32nd Alabama[,] though in much confusion[,] stood its ground. Nothing daunted, the regiment [16th and 25th Louisiana] with wild cheers swept forward. The battery was reached and two guns captured [abandoned between the lines by F, 1st Ohio]." Wagner's troops then began to edge around their flank. Colonel S. W. Fisk of the 16th and 25th Louisiana (consolidated), one of several Harvard law graduates in the army, fell mortally wounded (he lived only a few hours), and then two color bearers fell. Adams, slightly wounded in the left arm by an artillery projectile, ordered his men back while defiantly shouting: "Boys, we fall back, but damn it, we are *not* whipped."[23]

A Mobile correspondent described the action. "Adams marched his brigade under a galling fire to within 300 yards of their position but the storm of shot and shell was so terrible that they were compelled to fall back. The brigade immediately reformed, however, and charged again, with most intrepid courage, and succeeded in getting within fifty yards of their position." The withering fire proved so overwhelming, however, that the brigade was once again forced back. "It was here that the gallant Col. [S. W.] Fisk of the consolidated 16th & 25th Louisiana was killed; Lieut. Col. Maury of the 32nd Alabama was wounded while rallying his left wing and heroically bearing the colors of his regiment, the staff of which was shot into twice, and the flag pierced by fifteen balls, and Adams . . . was also shot through the arm. The consolidated 13th and 20th Louisiana, Col. [Randal] Gibson, also suffered severely." Adams admitted that it took a while for the troops to reform. A couple of weeks later, while recuperating in Marietta, Georgia, Adams confided his disgust to his wife. "How or why Genl. Polk

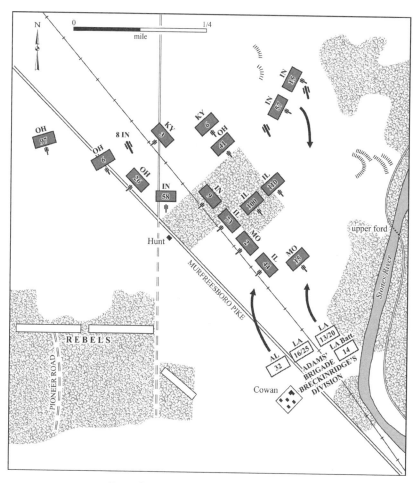

December 31, 2:00 p.m., the Round Forest

who gave the order or Gen. Bragg who was standing by when it was given expected me to take it [Round Forest], I cannot imagine. . . . I cannot help but regard the order as a very imprudent and unwise one."[24]

Leaving Hanson's brigade to hold Wayne's Hill, Breckinridge proceeded to the west bank of Stones River at the head of Palmer's and Preston's brigades. Sergeant Washington Ives of the 4th Florida, Preston's brigade, described to his sisters how the men discarded their blankets and waded through the crossing, "wetting us to the knees." As the troops crossed, they glanced at filled ambulances and walking wounded filing in the opposite direction. One soldier "walking with his arm shot off" inquired as to what regiment was marching by. "As our beautiful flag passed him being told 4th Fla. he said 'ya'll do it up right.'" One of the wounded had been hit four or five times—"his back I think was broken, but he bore it like a man, except as the wagon would jolt he'd groan." After crossing the river, Ives saw his first dead Confederate, "lying on his back with a cannon ball hole through his breast which I could stick my head in."[25]

Leading the brigades would be Brigadier Generals Joseph B. Palmer and William Preston, both former attorneys and politicians and both, at ages thirty-seven and forty-six respectively, sporting graying and receding hairlines. The highly popular but strongly anti-secessionist former mayor of Murfreesboro, the widower Palmer had only a seven-year-old son. As for the Harvard-educated Preston, his late sister had been the first wife to former army commander Albert Sidney Johnston. Preston served as an aide to his former brother-in-law at Shiloh and received a brigadier's commission shortly after the battle.[26]

By the time Breckinridge reported to Polk, Adams's Alabama and Louisiana troops were streaming back in disorder, with Colonel Gibson in command. They filed into Chalmers's old rifle pits, described by Breckinridge as a "low and very imperfect breastwork of earth and rails." Polk decided to hurl both brigades at the Round Forest, this time from the west. It was believed that at the point of contact the battles lines would be parallel, but the troops would actually be approaching the salient at an acute angle. At 4:00 "in fading light" the brigades moved out, Palmer on the left and Preston on the right, his right extending to the intersection of the railroad and pike. Lieutenant Frank Crosthwait of the 20th Tennessee turned to his friend Ralph J. Neal and confided his premonition of death. "Frank, I would not go into this charge feeling as you do. You will not be criticized, for we all know your courage, and you are too useful a soldier to be spared," Neal advised. Came the response: "I would rather die a soldier than to live a coward."[27]

A lull occurred since Adams's assault, and an "unearthly silence" prevailed. Shouts of "Forward!" rang out down Palmer's and Preston's lines, some 2,800 infantry, and they moved out across the open plain. Four guns of the Washington Artillery, a section of Semple's battery, and Byrne's Kentucky Battery, ten guns in all, offered cover fire on the west bank south of the pike, deploying in different positions to shoot at anything in range.

Unfortunately, the fourteen guns behind two earthworks on Wayne's Hill—Cobb's six, Lumsden's two, the Washington's Artillery's two, and Semple's six—provided little more than harassing fire from across the river.[28]

Several shots from one of the Wayne's Hill batteries (one historian has speculated Cobb's) nonetheless zeroed in on the general staff. Riding toward the tracks somewhat in advance of the Round Forest, a shell whizzed past Rosecrans and struck Garesche directly in the head, decapitating him and leaving only the lower jaw. His blood and brains splattered on the army commander's chest, and the headless body grisily rode on for another twenty paces before sliding off the horse. Minutes later, shells began exploding everywhere, leaving two aides and five of the escort either dead or wounded. Captain Frank Bond galloped up to the general and shouted: "Do you have the right to expose yourself so much?" Bond then related about the death of Garesche, prompting Rosecrans's response: "I am very sorry. We cannot help it, brave men die in battle. This battle must be won." Moments later Crittenden saw the army commander with stains of blood on his coat and asked: "Are you wounded?" "Oh no," came the answer. "Poor Garesche has just been killed." Despite the general's later comment that he "felt no sensation that day," he would later superstitiously explain the chief-of-staff's death as a Christ-like sacrifice to win the day.[29]

Sometime later, in front of the Committee on the Conduct of the War, Crittenden showed his anti-Rosecrans bias. Pertaining to Stones River, he testified: "I saw him [Rosecrans] galloping about the field in many directions. I have heard him censured by a great many officers for his impetuosity, for his great excitement during battle. I have heard him censured by commanders because they said they could not turn their backs on their commands without his ordering portions of them away." When specifically asked if a commanding general should expose himself in battle, the corps commander answered bluntly: "I do not think a commander who habitually exposes himself to a dangerous fire is qualified to command any large army."[30]

Good men were dying on the Confederate side as well. Yankee sharpshooters soon began to take a toll on Palmer's and Preston's men; the walk quickened to a run, and then the line dashed forward "with a yell." The ruins, outhouses, and fences of the Cowan House again had to be negotiated. As the 20th Tennessee on Palmer's right approached a fence, twenty-four-year-old Colonel Thomas B. Smith, a graduate of the Nashville Military Institute, shouted: "By the right flank, tear down that picket fence. March!"

causing an outburst of laughter in the ranks. In Preston's brigade, the 4th Florida crossed a picket fence and "in doing so we got our ranks broken and in forming [the] 60th N.C. crowded us so that we were all ordered out of place and the nine companies of the 60th turn and run like sheep," Ives wrote in disgust.[31]

At the Cowan House, the 20th Tennessee, on Preston's right, veered right and attempted a right swing around the Round Forest. They encountered Yankees (Wagner's men) among the trees and rocks of the eight-to-ten-foot-high river bluff. Colonel Smith ordered a charge, which successfully cleared out the river banks (taking twenty prisoners in the process), but the regiment sustained 67 killed and wounded, including the severely wounded Smith. With no support, the Tennesseans had no choice but to take their prisoners and withdraw. The bulk of Palmer's and Preston's men swung left of the house ("heaps of unburied dead lay in the cornfield," wrote Ives), in what turned out to be less of an attack and more of a run for the cover of the cedars. Once in the woods, Ives described limbs crashing down and the ground littered with Yankee dead. "We kept in the cedars and went on until we got to the edge of about 250 yards from where we entered, and then we could see the Yankee line of battle 1,000 yards north of us." In the feeble so-called final attack (a southern correspondent listed Adams's assault as the final true effort), Preston sustained 155 killed and wounded, mostly in the 20th Tennessee and the 60th North Carolina, the last losing 28 men; Palmer's Tennesseans lost a mere 23 in the entire brigade. Due to the lateness of the hour, and the fact that Polk had by now lost stomach for more blood letting, the attacks ceased, although the firing continued until dark.[32]

Only one serious attempt had been made directly upon the Round Forest, that of Adams's brigade. Indeed, of the 2,200 casualties inflicted upon Chalmers's, Donelson's, Adams's, Preston's, and Palmer's brigades, only half occurred in assaulting Hazen's position directly, and the other half in the attack upon Cruft's brigade and the Regulars along McFadden's Lane and in the cedars. Given the terrain fronting Hazen—the bend in Stones River and the wooded and rocky bluffs on the west bank—it is doubtful that a broader Confederate attack could have been attempted. Rosecrans needed an immovable anchor on his left, and he found it in William B. Hazen. The army commander would later say: "Hazen ought to be a major general."[33]

10

NEW YEAR'S DAY

I NEVER SUFFERED SO MUCH

With both armies utterly spent, a strange calm settled over the battlefield that night. Floridian Washington Ives admitted that "it was very little sleeping that any of us did for I like to have died of cold. My teeth chattered all night." The wounded, Confederate and Federal, were taken to the rear and placed in long rows, with fires built in between to keep the men from freezing. W. J. McMurray counted 22 dead Yankees within fifty feet of a tree. The Rebels openly pilfered the dead, James Mitchell of the 34th Alabama admitting, "Some of them [Yankees] left as naked as they were born." Several southern Good Samaritans were shot at as they attempted to help those wounded in no-man's land. Captain Fielder took a moment to write an entry in his diary. Although his 12th Tennessee had lost 18 killed and 137 wounded, he nonetheless gave "Thanks to God who gave us the victory and enabled us to drive the boasting foe before us in Wild confusion."[1]

James W. Ellis of the 4th Arkansas fell severely wounded early in the battle. Taken into Murfreesboro, he found himself in a sea of wounded. He overheard a surgeon say that his arm needed to come off. Ellis managed to sneak out and make his way to the train depot, where he boarded the first train south. To his good fortune, he had relatives who cared for him in Shelbyville. Dr. B. F. Duggan of nearby Unionville, Tennessee, came to Murfreesboro to offer assistance. In a church south of town, he came across a young wounded Confederate who begged him to cut a minie ball out of his hand—"It is nearly killing me," he pleaded. Duggan probed about and removed it.[2]

Dr. Quintard treated most of the wounded of the 1st Tennessee in the Methodist-affiliated Soule Female College. Among the wounded was a man by the name of Bryant House—"Shanty" to the boys. A surgeon had already pronounced his wound mortal, and House called for Quintard in his dual role of chaplain. Instead of giving a prayer, however, Quintard took out his surgical kit and dug around for the bullet. He successfully removed it, and Shanty lived until 1895, taking "great delight" in telling his story. There were far too many unhappy endings, however. As Hardee and Cheatham visited the Gresham House hospital, Rains's body was brought in on a stretcher, prompting Cheatham to openly weep.[3]

Scenes of life and death played out behind the Union lines as well. "I think I have never suffered so much with cold in my life, and to add to our suffering the horrible cries of the wounded could be distinctly heard over the field calling for help," on Ohioan explained to his mother. No fires were allowed; a lit pipe would bring a dozen bullets whizzing by. The rain began to come down in torrents, and the "cold wind roared through the tall cedars," described Captain J. H. M. Montgomery of the 33rd Ohio. Colonel Scribner recalled one poor wounded man who cried out in agony throughout the night: "Oh, God Almighty! God Almighty! God Almighty!"[4]

Henry M. Kendall rode over to a house that had been converted to a makeshift hospital. He found the front yard filled with wounded, and in one portion lay a grisly pile of amputated arms, legs, hands, and feet. When it came time for Ebenezer Hannaford of the 6th Ohio to finally see a surgeon, he was told bluntly: "A very narrow escape, young man. Hardly one in a hundred would ever have lived with such a wound as that." Asked if he would make it, the surgeon answered candidly: "If you were at home, I should not hesitate to say yes; but here in an army hospital, you know the case is different. It is more than I should like to promise." John McCabe of the 84th Illinois noted that at one hospital the wounded lay on the wet ground outside with nothing more than a blanket to cover them and a fire at their feet. He estimated that not one in ten had even seen a doctor.[5]

In the darkness, some men searched for fallen comrades or relatives—a dangerous mission. William Erb of the 19th Ohio found the precise location where his regiment had made a stand, marked by a long row of dead bodies. The corpses lay in different repose—some peacefully, as though sleeping, while others showed distorted expressions, as though grimacing in pain as they died. A Michigan artilleryman tried to save the life of a young Rebel, but it proved fruitless. "He lay with his little hands folded on his breast."[6]

Surgeons began taking preliminary tallies of the damage. Some regiments had lost three-fourths of their officers. Johnson had lost his two best brigade commanders; all three of Sheridan's lay dead. Wood hobbled around on a crutch, and Van Cleve returned to Nashville with wounds. Some 10 colonels, 10 lieutenant colonels, and 6 majors were dead or wounded. Sheridan alone had lost 72 officers. Best estimates placed Federal casualties on this day at 7,000. Large-scale assistance was on the way. Dr. Ebenezer Swift, the army's medical director, called down a reserve field hospital for 2,500 patients, with an additional twenty reserve ambulances. Swift established the hospital between the pike and the railroad, not far from army headquarters. At 7:00 p.m. a two-hundred-wagon train arrived with provisions and ammunition, under the escort of the 1st Middle Tennessee and 10th Michigan, 1,000 men. There would be sufficient ammunition for another day's fight. As the wagons were emptied, Rosecrans sent them back to Nashville under the same escort, stating that he could not afford to lose another two hundred wagons. Crittenden would later write that "all the wagons in the world wouldn't have made me send back a thousand fresh men."[7]

. . . .

At Union army headquarters at the Daniel cabin, a midnight council-of-war assembled to discuss options. Wood hobbled in on a crutch and, though offered a stool by the army commander, chose to sit on the floor with the others. Thomas found a board to lean on. Scribner walked and noticed the worn and anxious expression on Rosecrans's face. The mood appeared despondent—many of the troops had no subsistence. "We may all have to eat parched corn before we get out of this," Rosecrans uttered. He then put the question to his corps commanders: "Shall we fight it out here, or withdraw to an advantageous position covering our depots in Nashville?" The generals, as was the custom, answered by rank, beginning with the junior.[8]

Crittenden, according to Rosecrans, deferred and offered no opinion. Not surprisingly, Crittenden told a different story. He noted that his men would be "very discouraged" if they had to quit the field. He reminded the assembled company of the time when General Zachery Taylor faced a retreat at Buena Vista and said: "My wounded are behind me and I will not pass them alive." Bickham wrote that the corps commander boldly suggested that the offensive be resumed the next day, with his corps swinging into Murfreesboro. McCook spoke next. He expressed concern that the Army of the Cumberland was the only organized force that stood between the enemy and another invasion on Louisville or Cincinnati. He advised a retreat to Nashville and await reinforcements. Stanley concurred. Rosecrans mentioned that if he had to retire, he would make a stand on the high south bank of Overall Creek.[9]

It is Thomas's reaction that has proven the most controversial, because the accounts are so at variance. According to Rosecrans, Thomas refused to answer the question, and deferred to the army commander. One staff officer remembered that Thomas had fallen asleep, and had to be nudged to answer the question: "Will you protect the rear on a retreat to Overall's Creek?" The Virginian answered simply: "This army can't retreat," and went back to sleep. Whether or not this was a show of defiance or an assumption that communications with the rear had been severed is not certain. Yet another staff officer, Lieutenant John Yaryan, recalled that Thomas slowly arose and said: "General, I know of no better place to die than right here."[10]

Rosecrans thanked them for their advice and asked that they remain until he made a personal inspection of the rear with McCook and Stanley. Crittenden later related that Rosecrans's intent was to find a position beyond Overall Creek to which he could retire. Once at the creek, however, the party observed a line of men moving up and down with torches, prompting Rosecrans to utter: "They have got entirely in our rear and are forming a line of battle by torch light." The torches turned out to be troopers of the 4th U.S. Cavalry making a line of warming fires. Rosecrans determined to hold his position, call up provisions, and remain on the offensive. He returned to army headquarters and announced: "Well, gentlemen, we shall not retreat, but fight it out here and to the front." Yet another source quoted him as saying: "Gentlemen we have come out to fight and win this battle, and *we shall do it.* True, we have been a little mixed up today; but we won't mind that. . . . We will keep right on, and eat corn for a week, but we win this battle. *We can and we will do it!*" When asked privately by Stanley what he intended to do, Rosecrans answered: "By God's help, I am going to beat the enemy right here." Stones River, unlike Antietam, would have a second day.[11]

That evening Rosecrans readjusted his line. On the right, McCook's shattered corps formed a horseshoe-shaped line extending west from the pike. Starkweather's fresh brigade of Rousseau's division, newly arrived from Jefferson, constituted a reserve. Gruesel's brigade of Sheridan's division guarded the Overall Creek Bridge on the Nashville Pike, along with the cavalry. To McCook's left was the Pioneer brigade, and Thomas's corps on their left. At 3:00 a.m. Crittenden received orders to abandon the Round Forest for more favorable ground, and he withdrew 500–700 yards, his left extending to McFadden's Ford. Walker's fresh brigade replaced Van Cleve's division, which rejoined Crittenden's corps.[12]

The Army of the Cumberland began forming line of battle at 3:00 a.m. on January 1; there would be no more surprises. The army, though smaller in size, had a more compact line, and two fresh brigades made good some of the losses. Some of the troops received meager rations that morning, some not. One soldier noted the ration issue in his regiment—one-half pint of beans and two teaspoons of molasses. On Thursday morning of the first, the rain tapered off, and as the sun appeared through the mist, it gave a "red and bloody" appearance. The troops promptly went to work on breastworks of logs and stones. The chaplain of the 35th Indiana admonished his fellow Irishmen: "Boys . . . this is New Year; many of you will never live to see the sun go down today. . . . Your friends from home expect much from you—you must not disappoint them." The men looked all about and saw what appeared to be preparations for a retreat. "Thus we passed New Year's—not a happy one I assure you," William Mitchell wrote his family.[13]

In what would be the only significant tactical move of the day, Rosecrans ordered Sam Beatty's (Van Cleve's old) division to occupy the high ground east of McFadden's Ford. The army commander had seen in a day what Bragg had failed to see in six weeks—possession of the nameless ridge east of the river meant control of the entire east bank. At 5:00 a.m. Fyffe's brigade moved out, followed by Price, with Grider (Sam Beatty's old) brigade bringing up the rear at 10:00 a.m. The division deployed in the typical stacked formation of the Federals, with the right anchored on the river and extending north a half-mile to what some referred to as "rising ground." Grose's brigade of Palmer's division and the 3rd Wisconsin Artillery formed in support at the Hoover House, north of the ford.[14]

At some point an incident occurred, unsubstantiated but with enough details that it has a ring of truth, that a division commander, perhaps Davis, related to one of his brigade commanders that he planned to break out the next day. "This army is whipped; the rebels are between us and Nashville, and the only thing to do now is to cut our way through. Someone has to take the lead, and I want you to do it tomorrow; otherwise, we shall all be captured." The brigade commander protested and asked if the army commander had been broached on the subject. "No," the general answered, "but be ready tomorrow to cut your way through to Nashville." The brigade commander subsequently approached one of his peers, only to learn that the idea had been floated to him as well. "If he orders me to desert the balance of this army, and run away to Nashville, I'll arrest him as a traitor, and march him under guard to General Rosecrans' headquarters." When this information was related to the division commander, he dropped the proposal.[15]

GOD HAS GRANTED US A HAPPY NEW YEAR

Back at his Murfreesboro headquarters, Bragg sent a premature dispatch to Richmond hailing a great victory—"God has granted us a happy New Year." He boasted that the Yankees had been driven from every position except the far left, and that 4,000 prisoners and thirty-one guns had been taken. His losses had been great, that of the enemy greater. Before dawn Bushrod Johnson reported to Cleburne that he could distinctly hear the rumbling of wagons on the Nashville Pike, and he suggested that the division should press on. Cavalry intelligence indicated that the Nashville Pike was flooded with troops and wagons headed for Nashville. Bragg unquestionably expected a Federal retreat; indeed, he confidently wrote Johnston in Chattanooga that he would pursue. Governor Harris notified the press that the enemy was expected to withdraw.[16]

At dawn, as Bragg sent out skirmishers, he discovered the true state of affairs: the enemy remained in heavy force all along the front. Only the Federal angle in the Round Forest had been abandoned, which was quickly occupied by advancing Polk's right. Other than returning Palmer's brigade to the east bank at 1:00 a.m., he made no changes in his dispositions. Modern historians would later characterize him as confused and at a loss as to what to do. Perhaps, but no more so than Rosecrans. Liddell attempted to convince Hardee that by bringing up all reserves a final attempt could yet be made on the Nashville Pike, but the corps commander only muttered that "he was disgusted." Liddell later expressed his regrets at not personally going to Bragg's headquarters, but it would have done no good. There were no reserves to bring up.[17]

An incident occurred at 10:00 a.m., in and of itself insignificant, but having serious ramifications. A lone Federal battery on the east bank (the 3rd Wisconsin Artillery) fired a few rifled rounds at Palmer's position. In their after-action statements, Breckinridge staff officers Theodore O'Hara and John Buckner insisted that this was proof positive that the enemy had crossed in force to the east bank "while your command [save Hanson's brigade] was on the west bank." In other words, the fatal tactical decision of the day rested with Bragg, by not returning Breckinridge's division to the east bank during the night of December 31. This was only partially true. If Breckinridge had proof positive that the east bank had been occupied in force, it begs the question—why did he not immediately alert Bragg? Indeed, Breckinridge did not investigate his front until the morning of January 2. Statements of his staff to the contrary, it seems clear that the Kentuckian did not grasp that the Federals had crossed in force.[18]

While serious developments unfolded on the east bank, a rather farcical incident occurred on the west bank. Polk dispatched a staff officer, Lieutenant William B. Richmond, to Colonel Sidney S. Stanton of the 84th Tennessee, ordering him to proceed with his regiment to the Cowan House and tear down the fence that had so bedeviled the Confederates the day before. Some words were exchanged and, as bullets whizzed about them, the officers became embroiled in a fight, the colonel biting Richmond's thumb and the lieutenant gnawing away at Stanton's ear. Cooler heads finally prevailed, but Stanton was later relieved of command.[19]

At 2:00 Hardee, still hearing persistent rumors that the Federals had abandoned their lines, ordered Cleburne to advance a brigade and determine the matter. Liddell's Arkansans pushed beyond the Widow Burris House, but soon encountered stiff resistance. Liddell called for support on his right. Cleburne dispatched Wood's brigade, with Bushrod Johnson's skirmishers en echelon on Wood's right, in a move that was shaping up to be a reconnaissance-in-force. Wood advanced only to discover that Liddell had already withdrawn, thus leaving his left in the air, and under severe fire from Bradley's and Bernard Laiboldt's (Schaefer's old) brigades of Sheridan's division. Wood ordered his men toward a ravine near the Widow Burris House, with some troops of the 45th Mississippi fleeing to the safety of several outhouses. After twenty minutes of fighting, and with a Federal brigade (Gibson's) seen edging around to the left, Hardee ordered Wood and Johnson back. About 60 men of the 3rd Confederate and 45th Mississippi refused to leave the safety of their rocks and were taken prisoner. Wood lost 100 men in all; the Yankees had obviously gone nowhere.[20]

Most of the action on Thursday took place in the Federal rear. Initially believing the Yankees to be in retreat, Bragg ordered his cavalry chief to strike at Federal communications. Given the information as he understood it, the decision was of course a correct one. Starting at Wilkinson's Crossroads, Wheeler's, Buford's, and Wharton's brigades, indeed all of the cavalry with the army, save two regiments remaining with Pegram, proceeded to the Stewart's Creek Bridge of the Nashville Pike. Unfortunately, at the bridge the column encountered the 10th Ohio, four companies of the 4th Michigan Cavalry, and a section of Battery D, 1st Ohio Artillery—more than Wheeler wished to contend with. He bypassed the position and rode south around Stewart's Creek toward La Vergne, hoping to repeat his success of the thirtieth.[21]

At La Vergne the horsemen spotted a train of three hundred wagons headed for Nashville and stretching along the road for six miles. A delighted Wheeler must have thought that lighting was about to strike twice. He left Wharton to attack the rear of the train and the village, while he and Buford rode to cut off the head of the train. Wharton pounced on the rear, easily scattering the 2nd Tennessee Cavalry (U.S.) and, according to a wagoneer, "got up a panic & such running & crashing & smashing wagons upside down & teams scared off." Wharton claimed a hundred wagons (ten saved and the balance torched), three hundred mules, 150 prisoners, and a cannon. At 2:00 he made a dash upon the town, held by Colonel William P. Innes's 1st Michigan Engineers & Mechanics—391 strong. Innes had taken a position on the heights in the rear of town, and constructed a flimsy barricade of cedar brush. Wharton opened with White's two-gun section, blasting away for an hour at a range of 400 yards. A demand for surrender was rejected—"We don't surrender much," Innes defiantly answered. Repeated assaults by the 4th Tennessee Cavalry, 1st Confederate Cavalry, and 14th Alabama Cavalry Battalion failed to dislodge the engineers. To repeated demands for surrender, Innes barked "go to the devil" and warned that no more flags of truce would be received. At 5:00, having sustained "very considerable" losses while inflicting only 16, Wharton broke off the contest.[22]

Meanwhile, Wheeler struck the train north of the village. He overran a thirty-wagon section, bagging 95 members of the 22nd Indiana serving as train guards. Fightin' Joe then led his troopers west, hoping to overtake the balance of the lumbering column. Two miles from La Vergne he encountered Zahm's cavalry escort, comprised of the 3rd Ohio Cavalry and 15th Pennsylvania Cavalry. Zahm sent out flankers, but Wheeler broke off the affair, hoping to overtake the lead of the train. Two miles father, Wheeler again brushed with Zahm's horsemen; this time he was repulsed. The Federals lost only five wagons under Zahm's protection, all of the them broken down and abandoned. Zahm noted the shameful conduct of the 15th Pennsylvania Cavalry, which "scampered off" at each fray and proved utterly worthless. Wheeler later junctured with Wharton south of La Vergne, ending the day's activities.[23]

11

BRAGG ATTACKS

Friday, January 2, dawned gray and raw. Before sunrise White's (Chalmers's old) brigade occupied the woods bordering Stones River west of the railroad and fronting the Round Forest. At 2:00 a.m. Polk ordered up Cheatham's batteries in support, with William Carnes on the right directly confronting the Round Forest, Stanford in the center, and Turner on the left at the railroad. Scott positioned his guns between the railroad and the pike, and Robertson dropped trail at the Cowan House. Carnes, in postwar years, related that he had been assigned a particularly dangerous location because he had angered Cheatham by defending a battery commander's conduct on the first day's battle. "Well, I'll have you put your battery in the same place in the morning and see how long you stay there!" the division commander barked.[1]

At daylight Captain Osborne F. West's 9th Mississippi Battalion rushed the Round Forest, clearing it of snipers. They were in turn driven back as the Yankees attempted to wrestle control. At 8:00 a.m. Polk's guns opened fire, not only at the Round Forest, but also Bradley's 6th Ohio Battery and Estep's 8th Indiana Battery. "They had our range perfectly," admitted a Federal officer. Estep, many of his horses down, pulled out within three minutes, leaving behind two guns. Rounds burst among Harker's infantry, who "hugged old mother earth closer than we ever did before." Solid shot skidded up the Nashville Pike "like balls on a bowling alley." Oddly, Rosecrans rode up to Bradley during the thirty-minute exchange and admonished him: "Don't fire so damn fast." A rare friendly fire incident added to Bradley's woes. A false report had been received that the Rebels had rushed the line and captured a section of guns—apparently Estep's abandoned pieces. The Chicago Board of Trade Battery, about 300 yards in the rear, let loose several rounds into Bradley's gunners, wounding five men and several horses, before realizing the mistake.[2]

Over on the east bank, Breckinridge felt increasingly uneasy and belatedly ordered a reconnaissance in front of Hanson's brigade. Captain William P. Bramblett's Company B (the Flat Rock Grays) of the 4th Kentucky manned the picket line. "Peter" to his friends, the thirty-nine-year-old had only hours before he would fall mortally wounded. Bramblett, accompanied by two lieutenants, crawled along the riverbank and crept within 100 yards of the enemy. What they observed was Beatty's division, or at least the division picket line, which had come into position under the veil of darkness. The officers concluded, and thus reported, that Rosecrans was baiting a trap, hoping to draw Breckinridge into an attack that would bring him within killing range of the Yankee artillery on the west bank. Breckinridge next sent Captain Thomas Steele Jr. commanding Company E, 4th Kentucky, which had replaced Company B. Steele confirmed the earlier report.[3]

Despite the sighting of the Federal battery the day before, Breckinridge appeared to be genuinely startled by the intelligence. He determined to make his own reconnaissance. Accompanied by three staff officers, including his son, Lieutenant Cabell Breckinridge, the major general rode toward the river. On the way he encountered Hardee and Polk, the former alone and the last with only a single staff officer, Captain William D. Pickett. Together the cluster of officers continued, but a courier overtook Polk and informed him that he was needed. Hardee continued, but he too was recalled. Turning to Breckinridge he said: "I must return, but will leave Pickett here to represent me." Breckinridge and the remaining officers made their way through the woods to the 4th Kentucky picket post, a two-story frame farmhouse about 500 yards in front of Hanson's line. Fronting the farmhouse was a 500-yard-wide field, with woods toward the river. A slight rise, running at right angle to Hanson's line, blocked a clear view, but the appearance of a strong picket line made it clear that the enemy had crossed to the east bank in force.[4]

At about 10:00 a.m. Lieutenant Colonel John A. Buckner approached Breckinridge with a proposal to develop the enemy's line on their left, and in the process drive away the troublesome Yankee battery (3rd Wisconsin Battery) that had shelled Palmer's brigade the day before. The Kentuckian agreed, and at about 11:00 skirmishers from the 18th and 45th Tennessee pushed forward, followed by four 12-pounder Napoleon guns from the Washington Artillery that had come over from Wayne's Hill. The crack of gunfire could soon be heard. Enemy pickets had taken shelter in several houses (unmarked on maps, but apparently log cabins or shanties) a thousand yards from the river. The New Orleans gunners blasted them out, having "some fancy practice," according to one officer. As the Federals retired to their main line, the cannoneers opened an enfilade fire on the 3rd Wisconsin Battery. Beatty ordered it withdrawn, "to the astonishment of all," admitted Lieutenant Colonel James C. Evans of the 21st Kentucky (U.S.), who feared Price's brigade would be sacrificed, "in order to draw the enemy on." The Louisiana battery eventually retired, having exhausted its ammunition. Palmer lost 13 men in the fray; the Federals reported a half-dozen. The bluecoats indeed appeared to be in strength all along Breckinridge's front.[5]

At noon Bragg summoned Breckinridge to his headquarters, underneath a large sycamore tree at the ford below the Nashville Pike. During the morning he had sent out his own reconnaissance party—Colonel Brent and Captain Felix Robertson—to find an elevation for artillery to enfilade Crittenden's left. They, too, had spotted the enemy activity along the ridge. An alarmed Bragg immediately recognized that from this position Union artillery could enfilade Polk's right. Bragg had been outmaneuvered—pure and simple. Breckinridge's lack of vigilance, for which Bragg must also bear responsibility, would prove disastrous. The army commander's options were few: dislodge the Federals and regain the high ground or withdraw his army. Convinced he was on the verge of a great victory, he determined to attack. Bragg would choose Breckinridge's division for the assault, which had not been seriously damaged in the first day's fighting. Hearing the news, the Kentuckian protested, arguing that even if he gained the ridge, Union artillery on the west bank at McFadden's Ford had a higher elevation, subjecting him to a frontal and flank fire. He picked up a stick and sketched the relative positions in the ground, but Bragg, dismissive of the political general, remained adamant. "Sir," he said firmly, "my information is different. I have given the order to attack the enemy in your front and expect it to be obeyed."[6]

The attack plan, simple in its inception, would prove complicated in its implementation. The division would form in two lines and secure the heights occupied by Beatty. Palmer's brigade had re-crossed to the east bank at daylight. Gibson's (Adams's old) and Preston's brigades, in the cedar brakes two miles distant, would also be returned. Once the ridge had been gained, the artillery would come up and open fire, with the ten guns of Semple's and Robertson's batteries in support. Pegram's and Wharton's brigades, 2,000 troopers, located somewhere on the division right, would guard the flank and cooperate in the attack. Polk would support the assault with a barrage from the west bank. A single shot would signal the attack at 4:00. A furious but obedient Breckinridge departed army headquarters at 2:30.[7]

As the Kentuckian formed his troops, he could hardly contain his rage. He pulled Preston aside and confided: "General Preston, this attack is made against my judgment, and by the specific orders of General Bragg. Of course we must all try to do our duty, and fight the best we can. If it should result in disaster, and I be among the slain, I want you to do justice to my memory, and tell the people that I believed this attack to be very unwise, and tried to prevent it." None of the brigadiers supported the plan. The volatile Hanson denounced the order as "murderous" and threatened to go to army headquarters and "kill Bragg." Adding to Breckinridge's problems, Bragg at the last moment sent him Brigadier General Gideon J. Pillow to command Palmer's brigade. The worthless Tennessee brigadier, blamed by many for the loss at Fort Donelson, had recently arrived on the field and begged for a command. A remorseless pursuer of recognition, Pillow viewed superiors as rivals. Palmer rejoined his regiment.[8]

In an attempt to mask his formation, Breckinridge formed his first line, Hanson's and Pillow's brigades, in a skirt of woods, although he admitted that the enemy could observe nearly all his movements. The second line, Gibson's and Preston's brigades, deployed 200 yards in the rear—150 yards by Preston's estimate. The early phase of the attack would be made over ground covered with sassafras, brushwood, and briers. Once that had been cleared, 600–700 yards of open and gently rising ground had to be crossed—a virtual killing zone. Unknown to Breckinridge, he aligned Hanson's brigade too close to the river, meaning that Pillow would be overlapped on his right. The number of men available for the assault became a matter of contention—Breckinridge claimed 4,500, but Bragg accused him of underestimating by 1,500. A modern study estimates that, after deducting detachments, about 5,200 infantry and artillery formed in line.[9]

Confusion reigned. At 3:00 Major Graves placed the division artillery behind the second wave—the Washington Artillery on the left, Anderson's Georgia Battery in the center, and Wright's Tennessee Battery on the right.

When Robertson reported with his ad-hoc artillery command, a dispute rose with Breckinridge. The division commander desired to have the ten Napoleon guns advance between the two lines of infantry. The captain, who considered himself under Bragg's direct command, insisted that such an arrangement would crowd the field and cause confusion in the event of a reversal. Breckinridge relented and told Robertson to form his guns behind the second wave, along with the division artillery. Again Robertson refused, stating that he had positive orders to wait until the infantry had cleared the ridge before advancing. He would then place his battery on the summit and Semple's four guns to his right. Colonel Brent was an eyewitness to the conversation. The incident, never mentioned in Robertson's after-action report, was not documented until Bragg began gathering recriminating evidence against Breckinridge. Some historians have even questioned whether or not the exchange occurred. One postwar northern account claimed that Robertson later admitted that he lied at Bragg's suggestion.[10]

Problems also arose with the cavalry. Pegram's and Wharton's brigades were to form at the Hoover House (unknown to Bragg already occupied by the Yankees) and cover the right flank. Pegram clearly knew of his role, for he signed off on the order at 1:00 p.m. Breckinridge belatedly sent two staff officers to communicate with the cavalry, but they made no contact. Wharton would later write that he had "no intimation" of the assault. Pillow, likewise, insisted that he had never been told of any plan involving the cavalry. Breckinridge has been harshly criticized by historians for his failure to establish communications. In the post-battle acrimony that transpired, Bragg would pounce on this failure.[11]

WHO THE DEVIL WOULD NOT RUN

At noon Thomas and Crittenden arrived on a slight elevation and peered across Stones River to view Beatty's isolated position. The day before, Cruft's brigade, down to 801 men, had deployed to the left of Hazen's brigade and the right of McFadden's Hill, where they fashioned makeshift earthworks of rails and rocks. The Left Wing commander now called up Palmer's division, dispatching Grose's brigade to the east bank in support of Beatty's left flank, and Stanley's and Miller's brigades to be held in reserve in the rear of McFadden's Hill. With so much movement, "we knew something was up," an Illinois sergeant remarked. At 2:00 Rosecrans and

McCook joined Crittenden and Thomas. The army commander appeared cheerful, the others downcast and anxious. Rosecrans's supporters claimed that he planned to continue his original left-wing swing into Murfrees-boro, but no evidence exists to support this contention. Rosecrans never claimed such in his after-action report, and Crittenden openly stated that he received no plan for the day. Not until noon did Negley shift his position toward McFadden's Ford. Indeed, it was curious that Rosecrans did not cross Negley's entire division to the east bank, rather than a single brigade. Had he done so, Breckinridge's assault might have been beaten back from the start. Was Rosecrans baiting a trap, as some suspected? If so, he never stated as much. Based solely upon troop dispositions on the second, Rose-crans sought victory through the use of interior lines on the defensive.[12]

On the east-bank high ground, Sam Beatty maintained Fyffe's brigade on the left and Price's on the right. With a two-column formation, however, only five regiments held the front line. Colonel Benjamin Grider's (Beatty's old) brigade rested in reserve about 700 yards in the rear. The 11:00 skir-mish (Breckinridge's reconnaissance) had caused Beatty some concern. As a precaution, he called up Colonel Fred Knefler's 79th Indiana from the re-serve to the front line, between Price and Fyffe. The 3rd Wisconsin Battery, forced back by earlier artillery fire, withdrew to the vicinity of the Hoover House; it remained the only battery on the east bank. Beatty also worried about the west bank of Stones River. Crittenden had to secure the bank or snipers could cross over and enfilade Price's right. "We were all assured that this was attended to, and we rested on that assurance," Grider would report in a not-so-veiled criticism, belatedly tending to the matter. Throughout mid-afternoon, Federal skirmishers detected large-scale enemy movement 1,600 yards distant. At 2:30 an enemy battery could be seen moving on Beatty's right. At 3:00 Rebel skirmishers were detected throwing down fence rails, an obvious preparation for an attack. Yet, nothing happened. As 3:30 came and went, then 3:45, most of the officers conjectured that the attack would not come until the morning.[13]

A little before 4:00, Brigadier General Roger Hanson rode in front of his Kentucky brigade. Normally good-natured, the thirty-five-year-old portly former lawyer and Mexican War veteran could also be fiery and rancorous when agitated. A leg wound sustained in an 1848 duel had left him with a pronounced limp and the sobriquet "Old Bench Leg." "Colonel," he yelled to Colonel Joseph Lewis of the 6th Kentucky (C.S.), "the order is

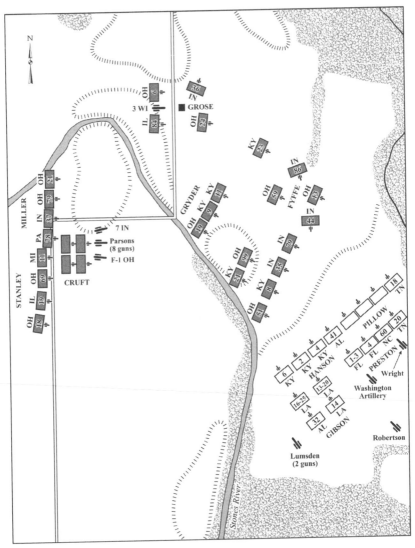

January 2, 4:00 p.m., Breckinridge Attacks

to load, fix bayonets and march through the brushwood. Then charge at double quick to within a hundred yards of the enemy, deliver fire, and go at them with the bayonet." Privately he confided to Breckinridge that he believed that he would be killed in the assault.[14]

At 4:00 a single gun boomed from Carnes's battery on the west bank—the signal for the attack. Then it happened. With banners waving, the line swept forward "in beautiful order." It appeared nothing short of spectacular, a scene rarely witnessed in the rugged terrain of the western theater. So smartly did Hanson's troops step out that Breckinridge exclaimed: "Look at old Hanson!" Even a viewing Ohio soldier in the distance had to grudgingly admit that "they came not as a mob, but in good order. They advanced so coolly and gracefully as if on parade. . . Thorough discipline was indicated in every step." A half mile away, one of Beatty's soldiers could "plainly and distinctly hear them giving commands—'Forward!' 'Guide Center!' 'March!'"[15]

Straight away, problems began to occur. In order to get more room to maneuver, the Kentucky brigade had to realign to the right, thus forcing the brigade into a three-regiment front, with the other two regiments squeezed into a second line. Further complicating matters, Pillow did not lead his brigade from the front; indeed, he did not lead it at all. Even as the second assault line moved out, Pillow cowered behind a tree and did not move until ordered to do so by Breckinridge. The incident, witnessed by three officers, resulted in charges of behavior unbecoming an officer, although they were later withdrawn. It mattered not; for all intents and purposes, his career was over.[16]

Back at the ford, as Beatty and Fyffe conferred with Rosecrans, a messenger galloped up, stating that the Rebels were massing for an attack. As the colonels rushed to their commands, an adjutant rode up and breathlessly announced that sixteen enemy flags had been counted! The Federal skirmish line began to rapidly fall back. "Boys, they are coming! The woods are full of them," one of Price's men shouted. Lieutenant Colonel Richard W. McClain of the 51st Ohio calmly walked along his line, saying: "Don't rise until you can see their hats as they come over the hill and then rise and fire."[17]

Some 600 yards into the advance, Breckinridge encountered more trouble. A staff officer brought word that the cavalry had not come up and that his right was in the air. He ordered Major Graves to hurriedly bring up a battery and cover the gap. As Wright's battery rumbled ahead, an artillery projectile struck the lead horse of a 6-pounder team, causing the animal to drop and the other horses to careen into it, thus disabling the gun. Wright unlimbered his remaining three pieces and opened fire at 300 yards on the 3rd Wisconsin Battery. Graves also spotted Semple's four Napoleon guns and dispatched them to Wright's location, thus making seven pieces.[18]

The gray line came under a punishing artillery fire. "Many officers and men fell before we closed with their infantry," Breckinridge admitted. In the midst of the shelling, Hanson's brigade ground to a halt. Breckinridge rode over to find that the Kentucky brigadier had been struck in the leg above the knee by a lead sabot from a shell, severing the femoral artery. In the midst of the shelling, Breckinridge knelt by his friend and attempted to slow the bleeding. An ambulance carried Hanson back into Murfreesboro to the home of J. C. Haynes, where Hanson's wife and Mrs. Breckinridge attended him. Seeing that he had lost so much blood, doctors determined not to amputate; he would die two days later. Colonel Robert Trabue, a thirty-eight-year-old former Mississippi attorney and Mexican War veteran, took command of the brigade.[19]

As the Orphan Brigade continued to stall, a part of the 2nd Kentucky crossed to the west bank (the very thing that Beatty had feared) and began sniping into Price's exposed right. About half of the 6th Kentucky (C.S.) made for the timber along the east bank in a flanking move. Trabue's line finally resumed its advance, closing to within 200 yards when the men "set up a hideous yell" and charged. The Rebels came "yelling like Blue Devils. . . . Jesus, Lord of Moses—but the bullets whistled all around us like hail," wrote a Federal. At less than 100 yards, Price's front line—the 35th Indiana, 8th Kentucky, and 51st Ohio—rose and unleashed a withering fire, initially staggering the Kentuckians. Gibson advanced his 355 or so men to the front line, while the 16th Louisiana, perhaps 125 men, joined the 6th Kentucky in their concealed flank movement in the timber along the east bank.[20]

The opposing lines blasted away in a death struggle. "My company was shot down around me until only 8 or 10 were left but still we stood our ground," Captain John McGrath of the 13th and 20th Louisiana told his wife. "The man on my right fell at my side, poor old [Matthew] Sheffield, and died as quietly as if he had gone to sleep. Poor [R.] Lowry fell at my left and grasp my leg with his dying grip saying, 'Oh! Captain.' I stooped down and unloosened his hand, when he looked beseechingly at me I said, 'My poor boy I can do nothing for you, and in a second may be with you.' The poor fellow's eyes sunk and he died while I was looking at him. Lieut. [James] Kerrigan fell along side him. I looked around and my poor gallant fellows covered the ground. How my heart bleeds for them."[21]

The 99th Ohio, in Price's supporting line, lay flat in the mud as the bullets "sung around us like bees." Twice calls went out for the 99th to come forward, but to no avail. Flanked on his right, Price's front line gave way.

As the troops rushed back, they collided with their second line; within minutes the entire brigade melted. "Who the devil would not run with ten thousand yelling, whooping, shouting, chargeing [*sic*] savages coming double quick against three thousand," 51st Ohio member Milton A. Roming explained to a relative. In a similar comment, an officer in the 99th Ohio admitted, "away we went like the Devil and Tom Walker." Another Buckeye conceded that the men ran for a quarter of a mile, "best man first. You may swear I done some tall running." Samuel Bolton of the 99th Ohio apologetically explained to his brother: "The 35th [Indiana] broke and the rebels after them, so we could do no better than run too. For we could not fire on account of our troops being in front of us. The truth of it is, we run like Turks." M. E. Thorn, color bearer of the 99th Ohio, was told to fall in with another regiment. "I'll be damned if I will. I will wave this flag over the Ninety-Ninth Ohio or I will wave it nowhere." With Beatty's right swept away, the 79th Indiana in the center also got caught in the melee.[22]

Beatty watched helplessly as his command disintegrated. He desperately called up Grider's brigade, in reserve at McFadden's Ford. The 19th Ohio, 9th Kentucky, and 11th Kentucky rushed up a gentle slope 200 yards, and suddenly collided with the enemy. After four or five volleys, the graycoats appeared on the verge of collapse. Grider pleaded that if he had artillery he could check the enemy. He spoke too soon; the Rebels swarmed around the 19th Ohio. "We are flanked on our right. We had better fall back and rally at the foot of the hill, if we can," Major Manderson advised. The three regiments joined in the cascade to the river. Captain Marcus Woodcock admitted: "We fell back down the hill and across the river in the greatest disorder, every man taking his own course and running at the top of his speed." Some of the Federals plunged into the river, a captain admitting that the water was "cold enough to make one catch his breath as it reached the hips."[23]

The loudly screaming southerners pursued with fury. Pillow's brigade, supported by Preston, surged forward on the division right. With Pillow's line overlapped by 300 yards, the Federals poured "a most deadly fire" into his right for several minutes. The 20th Tennessee, on the far right of Preston's line, made for a fence at the timber's edge and returned fire. His advance stalled, Pillow ordered his troops to lie down. Preston's approaching line, unable to advance, also laid down, both brigades forming a thick line four columns deep. With their flank finally secured, the juggernaut continued, the Tennesseans sending Fyffe's brigade fleeing "in utter confusion and disorder."[24]

Colonel James P. Fyffe, "Perry" to his friends, glanced toward Price's brigade to see the Confederates "sweeping them backward like fall leaves before a wintry wind." His front line broke, with Pillow's Tennesseans hot on their heels. "All over the field was one dense mass of confusion. Men running with all their might," confessed a Hoosier. The brigade made a fruitless attempt to rally at a fence. Colonel William C. Williams of the 44th Indiana fell captive, and Fyffe was thrown from his horse and dragged. The 44th Indiana, 86th Indiana, and 59th Ohio rallied at the Hoover House, while the 13th Ohio made an orderly retreat across the river.[25]

One brigade yet remained: Grose's of Palmer's division, braced behind rail barricades on Beatty's left. The front three regiments (23rd Kentucky, 24th Ohio, and 36th Indiana) formed a tiered defense, while the 6th Ohio and 84th Illinois deployed parallel to McFadden's Lane in the vicinity of the Hoover House. Grose expected the enemy from the east, the precise direction from which Pillow's and Preston's lines, described as "mingled into one," were fast approaching. With Beatty's troops flooding to the rear, however, Grose looked on in horror to see the Rebels "rushing wildly and madly" from the south. The colonel attempted a change front, but with cries of "we are surrounded," his advanced regiments fell back and rallied at the Hoover House. Everywhere the bluecoats broke for the rear, with the Rebels firing "death in their backs." Some 400 Yankees fell captive, including 100 taken at the river bank. The 29th Tennessee seized the riddled flag of the 9th Kentucky (U.S.). When the 20th Tennessee came upon a line that had been occupied by the Federals, Lieutenant William J. McMurray witnessed "the straightest and prettiest line of dead Yankees I ever saw."[26]

THE VERY FOREST SEEMED TO FALL

Tension mounted as the troops on the west bank braced for the inevitable tidal wave bearing down on them. "They were still not in our range of guns, but approaching very fast. We were holding ourselves in breathless suspense awaiting our turn—and such suspense," Lieutenant Colonel Milton Barnes described. "I looked around to the rear and I saw our re-enforcements coming up column after column with flags flying. I called out to my men to be of good cheer." As Negley rode the line of his two brigades at McFadden's Ford, his men greeted him with a cheer. "Boys, you will have an opportunity to pay them back for what they did on Wednesday," he shouted.[27]

Even before Breckinridge's assault began, Crittenden had amassed a formidable array of artillery on the west bank. Captain George Swallow's 7th Indiana Battery had been posted on the highest point of McFadden's Hill since the morning of January 1. During the late morning of the second, Captain John Mendenhall, Crittenden's artillery chief, moved Parson's Batteries H/M, 4th U.S. Artillery, and Norval Osborn's Battery F, 1st Ohio Artillery, a hundred yards to the right and rear of Swallow, south of the dogleg in McFadden's Lane. At noon, Negley formed Miller's and Stanley's brigades to the rear of McFadden's Hill. With them came the remains of three batteries (G, 1st Ohio Artillery, M, 1st Ohio Artillery, and B, Kentucky Battery, in all six guns), which unlimbered to the left (north) of Swallow. Some twenty-five pieces had thus been deployed before the 4:00 attack began.[28]

With Beatty's division collapsing, Crittenden turned to Mendenhall and said: "Now, Mendenhall, you must cover my men with your cannon." The artilleryman, without so much as an expression, immediately ordered Parson's guns forward a little. Parson's advanced Lieutenant Henry A. Huntington's four 3-inch rifles, holding in reserve Lieutenant Henry C. Cushing's four 12-pounder howitzers. He next approached the 8th Indiana Battery and ordered it to McFadden's Hill, where it unlimbered next to Osborn's battery. Continuing his ride, he encountered Captain Morton, who asked where he should deploy his Pioneer brigade. Mendenhall sent it to the rear of McFadden's Hill, behind Negley's division, directing Stokes's Chicago Board of Trade Battery to the right of Parson's guns. A Rosecrans staff officer subsequently ordered Osborn's guns to an open field to the right of Stokes. At the railroad, Mendenhall directed Battery B, Pennsylvania Artillery, to change front to the left and open a crossfire. Also in the vicinity were the six guns of Battery B, 1st Ohio Artillery. Mendenhall kept three guns in position and sent the other three to the far left of McFadden's Hill. Eventually the 3rd Wisconsin Battery crossed the river to the west bank and also unlimbered on the hill. This brought the total number of guns to fifty-eight, with twenty-one hub-to-hub pieces on the hill proper.[29]

MCFADDEN'S HILL (Left to right)	GUNS
B, 1st Ohio Artillery	3 "
M, 1st Ohio Artillery	3 "
B, Kentucky	1 "
G, 1st Ohio Artillery	2 "
7th Indiana Battery	6 "
3rd Wisconsin Battery	6 "

SOUTH OF MCFADDEN'S HILL	
H/M, 4th U.S. Artillery	8 "
Chicago Board of Trade Battery	6 "
F, 1st Ohio Artillery	5 "
8th Indiana Battery	6 "

RAILROAD	
B, Pennsylvania Battery	6 "
6th Ohio Battery	6 "

The scene was set for one of the most concentrated uses of artillery in the war in the west; the effect was stupefying. As Breckinridge's infantry seized Price's ridge, Mendenhall's guns unleashed a sheet of flame that literally shook the ground. Gunnery skill and northern industrial might dominated the scene. "As the mass of men swarmed down the slope they were mowed down by the score," a Union staff officer observed. So deafening was the musketry that Colonel B. F. Mullen of the 35th Indiana admitted that he "did not hear or know of a single piece of artillery [that] was giving us any aid until I reached the crest of the woods upon our right." Over and over again the redlegs sponged barrels, rammed home rounds, and jerked lanyards—a hundred rounds a minute estimated one officer. "It sounded like a constant thunder," a Buckeye described to his wife.[30]

The combination of massed artillery and musketry decimated the southern ranks. Everywhere men fell. Colonel Palmer received leg, head, and shoulder wounds, but he refused to relinquish command. Twenty-three-year-old Colonel Preston D. Cunningham of the 28th Tennessee fell dead. All of the color bearers of the 2nd Kentucky, 18th Tennessee, and 20th Tennessee were wiped out. Artillery fire killed Major Willis S. Roberts of the 4th Kentucky and Adjutant Henry M. Curd of the 9th Kentucky. Lieutenant Colonel Joseph P. Nuckols of the 4th Kentucky received a shoul-

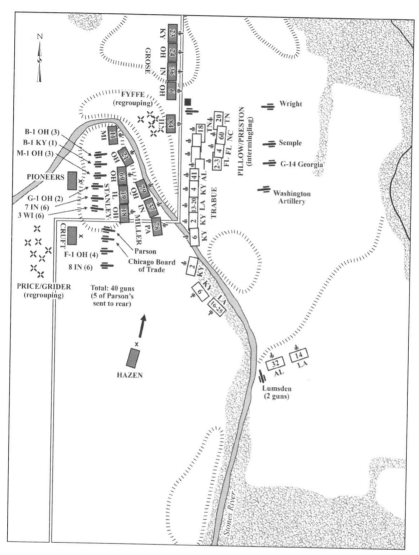

January 2, 4:45 p.m., Breckinridge Attacks

der wound. Henry Hall, a lad in the 4th Kentucky, died instantly when a cannon ball passed through his thighs, severing both his legs. A single shell exploded in the midst of one Kentucky company, hurling 18 dead and wounded men in every direction. After several unsuccessful attempts to rally his regiment, the flag bearer of the 6th Kentucky walked slowly away shouting: "Here is your 6th Kentucky." Colonel William Miller of the 1st and 3rd Florida fell wounded, but he remained on the field. On the division right, the Federal artillery proved more fatal to Preston's brigade than Pillow's. "A more terrific fire of artillery I have never been under," recalled a 20th Tennessee member.[31]

With the crest of the ridge gained, Major Graves advanced the Washington Artillery and Anderson's battery, in a desperate attempt to effect counter-battery fire. The cannoneers unlimbered under a fierce shelling. The gunners managed to disable one Union piece, but little else went their way. The New Orleans gunners expended all their rounds, only to discover that an unidentified officer had wrongly sent their caissons to the rear. While they waited for additional rounds, some of them manned one of Anderson's guns, the Georgians having hit the ground to avoid exposure. Now was the time for Robertson's command to come forward and unlimber, but he was nowhere to be found. Indeed, in his after-action report, Graves mentioned that he never even saw Robertson. Sensing that the infantry would be unable to hold the ridge, Robertson decided on his own to "altar the plan"; his guns never left the safety of the woods. To be sure, the presence of six additional guns would not have turned the tide; Breckinridge admitted as much.[32]

Rosecrans galloped up to Negley and blurted: "Sir, they have turned me back, and all depends on you. The day must be ours." "Let them come, my boys are ready," the Pennsylvanian answered. Stanley's and Miller's brigades remained behind McFadden's Hill, some 300 yards from the river. As the troops lay down in a cornfield, Sergeant Mike Rice of the 21st Ohio calmly walked down the line of his company, shouting: "We can check them and anyone who runs now is a damned coward. Get this, hug the ground harder and keep quiet." Beatty's routed soldiers soon streamed across the river. "We laid still till they ran over us and had to get out of the way," George T. Squires of the 21st Ohio related to his parents. Colonel William L. Stoughton of the 11th Michigan reported that one regiment in particular crossed in disorder, many of the men without arms, and rushing wildly through his ranks. An Ohioan in Fyffe's brigade clamored the twenty-foot-high west bank of the river, with bullets striking the rocks all about him. "My idea was that the army of the Cumberland was rapidly passing out of existence and that the Union cause was hopelessly lost. We then reached the top of the bluff. We found that General Negley's division was quietly massed in a column in a cornfield nearby ready to move into action."[33]

As the Rebels approached the east bank, Miller ordered his brigades to rise and fire. Lieutenant Colonel Jim Neibling of the 21st Ohio yelled: "Get up boys and give them thunder!" The brigade unleashed a thunderous volley: "the enemy halted and began to waver," reported Miller. The colonel advanced his men to the rail fence along the river bank, where both sides briefly traded blows. A few Rebels actually began crossing the river, but they were forced to hug the western bank and escaped only by re-crossing at the ford three-fourths of a mile upriver. Someone in the 78th Pennsylvania shouted: "They are retreating! They are retreating!" Miller rode over to his right to Colonel Joseph R. Scott of the 19th Illinois of Stanley's brigade. "Colonel, if we don't charge the rebels will charge us. Will you join me if I do?" "Certainly, I'll get my command ready," Scott answered. Without waiting for orders from Negley, Miller ordered his brigade and the 19th Illinois forward. Stanley yelled to the 11th Michigan: "Up my Michiganders and at 'em!" The 19th Illinois and 78th Pennsylvania were the first to plunge into the frigid water. Scott was one of the first to fall, with a bullet wound to his groin.[34]

The regiments became badly intermingled as they crossed, but Miller realigned them at a fence on a rise of ground. As the infantry waded across, a Palmer staff officer came up and ordered Miller back, stating that Miller's right flank would be endangered (apparently referring to the Kentucky and Louisiana troops along the east bank). A second staff officer arrived with the same message—withdraw. Miller turned to an orderly and bellowed: "Go find your horse and then hunt up General —— [Crittenden?], General Thomas, General Rosecrans, or any other —— general in reach. Tell him I can't stop these men, and I'm —— if I want to stop them!"[35]

Seeing Negley's division continue, Palmer dispatched Hazen's brigade in support. "Now, 6th Kentucky, you have work to do; stand up to them and you may steal for six months!" Palmer shouted. Once on the east bank, Hazen left three of his regiments in reserve and advanced the 41st Ohio along with Grose's troops, which he observed with some contempt were already charging ahead as a disorganized mob. Grider, his troops having escaped to the west bank, now got into the act. Grabbing the flag of the 9th Kentucky, he led his exhausted brigade back across the river. Negley, who should rightly have been at the head of his division, instead chose to remain on the west bank and forward troops. Riding to the brigade in his rear, he asked: "Whose command is this?" "Mine," answered St. Clair

Morton. "These are the Pioneers." "For God's sake, help my division on the left," he pleaded. By 4:45 no less than seven Federal brigades had crossed the river in a large, if not somewhat disjoined, counterattack. The enemy snipers who had infiltrated the western bank were also dealt with. Crittenden belatedly ordered the 31st Indiana and 90th Ohio into the woods fronting Cruft's brigade, while Palmer dispatched the 18th Ohio, part of the 37th Indiana, and part of the 78th Pennsylvania to clear the woods to the right of Negley's division.[36]

The Rebels fled in disorder according to Pillow; in truth, it was a terror-stricken rout. The graycoats now had to traverse the same blood-stained plain that had already cost them so dearly. Many, claiming to be conscripts, fell on their knees before the Yankees and begged for mercy. "We had to march back for half a mile through an open corn field and many were so exhausted that they could not go faster than a slow walk," 26th Tennessee member Hannibal Paine explained to his sister. William D. Rogers of the 1st Florida wrote that he never felt frightened "until we were ordered back and then I was badly scared[.] My back itched the whole time." The stars and bars flag of the 26th Tennessee of Pillow's brigade fell into the hands of the 26th Pennsylvania; this day it resides in the William Penn Memorial Museum in Harrisburg.[37]

Preston struggled to rally his troops. "Fresh & murderous vollies poured in from the other side of the river and the line recoiled wildly over the crest of the hill we had just won," he wrote. The men fled to the safety of the trees, where the brigadier "found and beat all fugitive men and officers over the head with my saber, till I got a handful of men around me, near the colors of the 45th Tennessee[,] one of Pillow's regiments. I called for its colonel, and he coming up Col. [Anderson] Searcy, I hand him the color & with [Colonel] O'Hara rallied them. My persuasions were not very affectual, but the blows were, and finally by an appearance of safety (a touch of stump speaking address) I got a good many together and left them to their Colonel."[38]

On the verge of collapse, Major Graves ordered his guns to the right—Wright's three and Semple's four—to limber up. As the enemy closed to within a hundred yards, however, he directed them to unlimber and fire one last salvo of canister. He later explained the suicidal order by claiming that he was buying time for the infantry, but Lieutenant John W. Philips, one of Wright's officers, could hardly restrain his anger at the major.

Wright was killed and Graves shot in the hand and knee. With 11 men and ten horses down, the Tennessee artillerymen abandoned two of their pieces, along with their disabled gun, and Semple left behind one of his prized Napoleons. As many as four enemy regiments claimed the trophies. Semple's detachment was nearly wiped out, losing 20 of 45 men within half an hour.[39]

Robertson unlimbered his six Napoleons in the woods where the attack began in a last-ditch effort to save the Confederate right. He claimed that his guns, supported by only 150 infantry in a nearby ravine, represented the only organized resistance preventing the Federals from marching into Murfreesboro. This appears to have been an exaggeration, for the Washington Artillery, resupplied with ammunition, also came on line, and Preston wrote that his brigade came on line in support. With night fast approaching, the Federal attack sputtered to a halt. The 41st Ohio took a final parting shot at a battery in the woods 400 yards distant. Robertson withdrew his guns in the darkness, admitting that he had to cock his revolver at several of his men who nearly deserted. In less than an hour it was over. The Confederate attack had utterly failed, and only night spared Breckinridge from destruction. "The Yankees three cheers sounded hatefully in my ears," Captain Clay admitted.[40]

They cavalry had made a pathetic showing—"they were mere spectators," Brent disgustedly wrote. Pegram, having earlier sent a regiment to both Wharton and Wheeler, was down to two regiments, the 1st Louisiana Cavalry and the 1st Georgia Cavalry. The troopers, perhaps no more than 600 after deducting the horse holders, formed a skirmish line and "loitered about" throughout the afternoon. Wharton later arrived with his escort company, two companies of the Texas Rangers, and, borrowing Pegram's two-gun mountain howitzer battery, moved into action. The small howitzers set up on a hill and at 500 yards fired into the heavy Federal column on their right. Palmer, fearing that the shells might hit his escaping men, ordered the companies and battery back to the last defense line forming in the woods. So much for the cavalry.[41]

The attack had effectively ended by 5:00, but Federal reinforcements continued to stream across the river. Davis, without orders, sent a brigade from the Right Wing, and then, under orders, crossed with his entire division. Rosecrans came galloping down the Nashville Pike, sweat pouring down his face, and ordered Carlin to report to him. The colonel found the army commander in a three-foot-high log pen, looking "very pale." According to Heg, Rosecrans pleaded: "I beg you for the sake of the country and for your own sake to go at them with all your might. Go at them with a whoop and a yell." Crittenden, not knowing of Davis's movement, sent to McCook for help, and within five minutes Gibson's brigade also moved out. As the brigade passed by Rosecrans, he admonished Gibson: "Give them the bayonet, that's what they need."[42]

Hearing of the disastrous turn of events, Bragg dispatched Patton Anderson's brigade across the river. Brent initially deployed the troops in the woods where the attack had begun, but Breckinridge arrived and ordered them 200–300 yards farther to the rear. It was 9:00 p.m. before Anderson got into his second position. A 9:45 reconnaissance discovered that he stood virtually alone, with the enemy directly in front of him. He had no troops on his right, and 800 yards separated his left from Hanson's brigade. A battery partially filled the gap, but it could obviously not cover nearly half a mile. About this time a staff officer summoned Anderson to a general's meeting in the drawing room of the Murfree House. Unable to leave his command at such a critical moment, Captain Edward T. Sykes, the brigade adjutant, went in the brigadier's place. Upon his arrival, Sykes reported Anderson's exposed position; Breckinridge accepted responsibility for the error. Later that night, Pillow's, Preston's, and Gibson's brigades arrived on the right, and before daylight Jackson's brigade filed in between Anderson's left and Hanson's right. Concerned that Rosecrans would resume the attack in the morning, Bragg, a little before 10:00, ordered Cleburne's and McCown's divisions to the east bank. At 11:00 p.m. Cleburne's skirmishers easily beat back a slight enemy reconnaissance. After midnight the divisions crossed the river in a cold rain, with Cleburne deploying behind Breckinridge and McCown, forming a reserve north of Murfreesboro near the Lebanon Pike. Ector's brigade, bringing up the rear, did not get into position until 10:00 a.m. on the third.[43]

That evening the Federals scoured the ridge for wounded. "Headless, armless, legless men, dead men torn to pieces by shells, wounded men lacerated beyond description," an officer described. A Buckeye grimly noted that "scores of rebels lay in every form." Private Noah Mills was aghast at the sight—"some [bodies] with their heads shot off and in short they were mangled in every way that you can imagine." James Jones expressed horror at bodies "torn to pieces and throwed in every direction one leg here and another there." For now, the murder was over.[44]

As the fighting on the east bank sputtered out, Colonel Moses Walker, on Rosecrans's right, reported that the enemy appeared to have withdrawn. Thomas ordered a reconnaissance to "test the fact." Supported by the 4th Michigan Battery and Starkweather's brigade, Walker's brigade leaped over their breastworks and silently advanced 300 yards through sparsely wooded country. They came under a peppering fire but continued another 80 yards as the enemy retreated to their works. Having ascertained that the Rebels had not withdrawn in that sector, Walker pulled back. At 7:30 Sheridan ordered another reconnaissance, with similar results.[45]

12

I FEAR THE CONSEQUENCES

Matters appeared grim during the late hours of January 2. Bragg had lost nearly a third of his army, specifically 1,294 killed, 7,945 wounded, and 1,027 missing, a total of 10,266. The exhausted troops had been in line of battle in severe cold and rain for five days. The baggage train had been sent four miles to the rear; rations remained scant. Stones River was rising dangerously high, threatening to divide his army. Bragg nonetheless determined to hold his ground and await developments. Fearing an attack upon Breckinridge, he ordered Cleburne's and McCown's divisions to the east bank, the first as a support for Breckinridge, the last as a reserve near the Lebanon Pike. Hardee assumed command in this sector. This left only Cheatham's and Withers's crippled divisions and Wharton's cavalry on the west bank to confront two corps. The army was stretched to the breaking point.[1]

At 2:00 a.m. on January 3, Lieutenant Richmond awakened Bragg with a dispatch from Cheatham and Withers. "We deem it our duty to say to you frankly that in our judgment this Army should promptly be put in retreat." Polk, through whose headquarters the dispatch had been channeled, endorsed it in pencil: "I greatly fear the consequences of another engagement at this place with the enemy's army. . . . We could now perhaps get off with some safety and with some credit, if the affair was well managed." Bragg would have none of it. Without even reading the entire note, he snapped to Richmond: "Say to the General [Polk] we shall maintain our position at every hazard." Perhaps regretting that he had not first gotten Hardee's backing, the Bishop notified him of the development. The Georgian would later state that this was the first he had heard of a possible retreat. Given Bragg's determination to remain on the field, however, nothing could be done.[2]

With daylight came an unrelenting rain and more bad news. Bragg summoned Polk and Hardee at 10:00 a.m. Recent intelligence had been received. The captured papers of Alexander McCook revealed his corps strength to be 18,000. Using this as a base, staff officers had devised an estimate, exaggerated as it turned out, that placed Rosecrans's army strength at 70,000, far larger than anticipated. Wheeler had also reported that the Yankees were receiving "heavy reinforcements," also an exaggeration, although two additional Federal brigades had arrived from Nashville and two more would arrive. Bragg's only reinforcement was the 37th Mississippi, which had arrived from Shelbyville after its small pox quarantine clearance. The generals were in agreement; a retreat was imperative. The orders were cut at noon and a partial evacuation begun, with half of the wagons taking the Manchester Pike and half the Shelbyville Pike.[3]

The battlefield remained generally quiet until dusk, when the Federals assaulted the Round Forest. Guenther's and Van Pelt's batteries opened a brisk ten-minute barrage, followed by an assault by two of John Beatty's regiments and James G. Spears's newly arrived brigade. In the midst of a bitterly cold rain, Coltart's and White's regiments were driven back, losing at least 49 prisoners. In the darkness, Spear's inexperienced East Tennesseans delivered a scattering fire in the backs of Beatty's veterans. After an hour of fighting, and having retaken the Round Forest, the Federals strangely retired. The Confederates promptly moved back and reoccupied their old works.[4]

At 7:00 p.m. Bragg called another general's meeting, with Hardee, Polk, Breckinridge, and Cleburne in attendance. A retreat was no longer in question, only whether or not it should be suspended twenty-four hours. This delay would allow Wheeler, then believed to be at La Vergne, time to close up, and to get more of the wounded evacuated. Only Cleburne voted to delay. He believed that a Federal attack could be beaten back, but even he equivocated by stating the obvious: "it might turn out otherwise." In the end, all agreed that the time for waiting had passed. The army would begin a formal retreat at 11:00. The pickets were withdrawn, and the infantry quietly slipped out of their works ("no one scarcely spoke above a whisper"), their places being taken by dismounted cavalry. The prisoners captured on the first day's battle had already been sent to Chattanooga, but the wounded and all supplies had to be evacuated. Earlier that evening, seven long trains, filled to overflowing with wounded, creaked passed the Nashville & Chattanooga depot, the last one not departing until the morning of the fourth. As Bragg feared, 1,423 wounded had to be left (640 would later die), along with 250 sick, and 200 surgeons and assistants to care for them. The decision proved a wrenching one for Bragg; in a rare moment, a surgeon saw him weeping.[5]

Seeking shelter from the rain, Liddell later entered the Murfree House and brazenly approached Bragg. The army commander explained that a retreat had been ordered because the Federals had been heavily reinforced. Liddell rejected the notion, stating that he had just come from the left and had seen no such signs. Bragg remained convinced: "It must be so. Wheeler seems assured of the fact." Liddell attempted to dissuade him in a last ditch effort, but it was no use. "No, it has become a matter of imperative necessity to withdraw. It must be done at once," Bragg insisted.[6]

During the early morning hours of January 4, the Army of Tennessee sullenly snaked south from Murfreesboro, with Polk's corps on the Shelbyville Pike, Wharton bringing up the rear, and Hardee's corps on the Manchester Pike, Wheeler serving as rear guard. The troops trudged through mud typically an inch thick, but at places much worse—"a perfect loblolly," John Jackman wrote. Rain fell throughout the night, intermittently at times and occasionally in torrents. Large-scale staggering characterized the retreat, with broken-down wagons strewn for miles. Polk's column, having slogged an exhausting twenty miles, stopped five miles short of Shelbyville shortly after sunrise. The clouds began to break at dawn, creating a rainbow in the eastern sky. Bragg, traveling in a carriage and accompanied by his wife, arrived in town at 7:30 a.m. At 3:00 p.m. the couple departed for Winchester.[7]

· · · ·

During the late hours of January 2, Rosecrans became increasingly alarmed about the rising level of Stones River. Considering it imprudent to remain on the east bank, he withdrew his brigades in the darkness, even as Bragg began his retreat. At 1:00 a.m. on the third, Colonel Daniel McCook's provisional brigade from the Nashville garrison arrived, escorting a ninety-five-vehicle wagon train of ammunition and medical supplies. At 7:00 a.m. word arrived at army headquarters that the Rebels had retreated in the rain and darkness. Rosecrans never gave any serious thought to a pursuit, claiming he had to first re-establish communications with Nashville. In conversation with Crittenden, the two officers also concluded that it would be unwise to provoke the Almighty with a Sunday march. In truth, Rosecrans had no stomach for it. A third of his army was out of commission, and he was more than willing to call it quits. The general, his staff, and friends began the morning of the fourth with mass in the Daniel Cabin. Throughout the day the dead were buried, rations distributed, and ammunition resupplied. That evening McCook, Crittenden, and Rousseau "imbibed freely," with Crittenden, the "merriest of the party," singing "Mary Had a Little Lamb."[8]

Thomas's corps and the Pioneer brigade moved down the Nashville Pike at 7:00 a.m. on the fifth, but the column was delayed until 9:00 until the bridge over Stones River had been repaired. Troops occupied the town in mid-morning without incident. Yankee cavalry rode around the town square with fingers on triggers, suspiciously glancing at windows, followed by an infantry column with a brass band playing martial music. Minty's brigade and the reserve cavalry probed east along the Manchester Pike, skirmishing with the enemy's rear guard five miles out, while Zahm's brigade edged cautiously four-and-a-half miles down the Shelbyville Pike, rounding up a few stragglers but encountering no serious opposition. The Stones River Campaign had come to a conclusion. Rosecrans, coming down with a touch of fever, established his headquarters in the two-story Keeble House, formerly owned by a lawyer and county clerk.[9]

The army commander telegraphed Stanton at 4:40 a.m. on the fifth. "God has crowned our arms with victory. The enemy are badly beaten and in full retreat." This victory, he boasted, had been won over a numerically superior Confederate army of 62,500. In truth, Rosecrans had barely held his own with an army for 40 percent smaller. His initial estimate of casualties—1,000 killed and 5,500 wounded—was also off the mark. The final tally would come in at a staggering 1,730 killed, 7,802 wounded, and 3,717 captured, totaling 13,249. Most of the medical supplies of the Right Wing had been destroyed, but fortunately a medical train arrived with bedding for 2,500 patients, along with twenty ambulances. Eleven other medical wagons reported, and the Left Wing had a reserved train of ten wagons. Twenty civilian surgeons arrived from Indiana.[10]

For the first time the Federals were able to view the full magnitude of the destruction. Colonel Beatty rode over the battlefield and for miles saw men "with their legs shot off, one with brains scooped out with a cannon ball, another with half a face gone, another with entrails protruding." Colonel Michael Shoemaker of the 13th Michigan prepared himself for the worst as he visited the tent hospital of his brigade, but he admitted being sickened at a "cord of amputated legs, arms, and feet, interspersed with slices of human flesh and lacerated by shells and cannon balls." Every few minutes a wounded man would be brought in and dumped "as if he were a log of wood." James Maxwell, a Confederate nurse attendant, wrote that the Federals gave him no problem, as he checked on his patients from one to six times a day, changing dressings. Pus flowed freely—"under each stump would be a puddle of it," and disinfectants proved scarce.[11]

Many of the Union dead had already been gathered in piles of three to thirty-five by Yankee prisoners. All of the bodies had been stripped of their clothing, and many had legs, arms, and heads missing. "My heart was sickened at the sight," remembered a Buckeye. Near the railroad, eleven shallow graves from the 74th Ohio and 45th Mississippi were dug. In a nearby area a small cemetery had been prepared and marked with a placard: "This patch of ground contains the bodies of 93 soldiers of the 15th, 16th, 18th, 19th U.S. Do not disturb these graves by additions or otherwise." Nearby were thirty-one graves—four men of the 19th Illinois and twenty-seven of the 41st Alabama. Some of the markers had names, most not.[12]

SOME SAY HE IS A FOOL

Morale in Richmond soared upon the arrival of Bragg's initial dispatches. John Jones in the War Department wrote that it "put us almost 'beside' ourselves with joy, and caused even enemies to pause and shake hands in the street." A civilian in North Carolina expressed jubilation over the victory: "That is the New Year's gift presented by our brave soldiers to the country." When the truth ultimately came out, Jones lamented in his diary: "We are all *down* again."[13]

The *Memphis Appeal, Augusta Constitutionalist,* and the Atlanta papers, all having reported the battle as a victory based upon Bragg's early reports, wondered why the retreat had occurred. "General Bragg has certainly retreated . . . from his victory at Murfreesboro, as he did last fall from his victory at Perryville," attested the *Richmond Examiner.* Captain Thomas Patton wrote frankly: "The more I think of it, the more shameful our recent retreat appears. I am anxious to see what the public and press think about it." A cavalryman, J. L. Hammer, declared bluntly: "Bragg is the laughing stock of the whole country. Many of the Tennessee troops will desert, and I can't say they are to blame." Tennessean Frank Carter informed his wife: "There is no doubt that Gen. Bragg has in a great degree lost the confidence of the army and many think there was no reason for the retreat." A major in Breckinridge's division confided: "Every Tennessean is bitter beyond expression; some swear he is a fool. I think myself he has been blessed with very little sense, and no genius."[14]

On the sixth, Bragg ordered the army to continue its retreat yet another twenty miles southeast to Tullahoma. The abandonment of the Duck River line brought consternation among the army staff, especially given that Wharton's scouts had reported Rosecrans as making only a tepid effort at pursuit. Bragg nervously destroyed the Duck River Bridge near Wartrace and dispatched an engineer officer to check the fords over Elk River. Brent believed that "the line of the Duck" should have been decided upon before leaving Murfreesboro. "The movement so far to the rear has had a bad effect on the troops & the public mind," he wrote, later adding: "Spirits bad. Matters look gloomy." Johnston, at Jackson, Mississippi, expressed shock at Bragg's "falling back so far." On Friday the ninth, the army commander regained his composure and ordered Polk's corps back to Shelbyville. Having to retrace their steps in the mud, the troops predictably groused. Hardee's corps remained at Tullahoma, where Bragg and his staff arrived on Saturday the tenth.[15]

Had Rosecrans moved quickly to secure Shelbyville during Bragg's week of indecision, it would have proven a logistical nightmare for the Confederates. The Duck River Valley was second only to the Murfreesboro region in agricultural production. Bragg's much ballyhooed (by modern writers) widespread defensive cordon, stretching seventy miles from Columbia on the left to McMinnville on the right, did not initially exist. Bragg only perfunctorily reclaimed the Duck River line. It was not until February that he dispatched the Arkansas brigade to Wartrace, eight miles east of Shelbyville, and the Kentucky brigade to Manchester, fifteen miles southeast of Wartrace. Only two small cavalry regiments protected Columbia. Pegram's cavalry was ordered back to East Tennessee on January 2, and on January 7 most of the remaining horsemen—Wheeler's and Wharton's brigades, soon to be joined by Forrest's returning brigade, in all over 6,000 troopers, were sent on a questionable raid into northwestern Tennessee, leaving the army, with the exception of Morgan's brigade, nearly blind through the end of January. Yet, Patton Anderson felt "confident" as he wrote his wife on January 11, believing that Rosecrans was so badly damaged that he could not possibly launch a second winter offensive.[16]

. . . .

For over a year and a half, Captain Theodore O'Hara had harbored a grudge against Bragg. Back at Pensacola, Florida, in 1861 the general had dismissed him as a "drunken loafer," a reputation that had dogged the captain ever since his army days on the Texas frontier in the 1850s. Frustrated by his inability to obtain regimental command, the forty-three-year-old Kentuckian settled in as Breckinridge's adjutant general. Following Stones River, he sought his revenge. O'Hara leaked a damaging account of the battle to a correspondent, Samuel C. Reid, that became the basis of an article that appeared in the *Mobile Register*. Although the pro-Bragg editor, John Forsyth, censored the article, damage had been done. Clearly suspecting O'Hara (perhaps with Breckinridge's tacit approval) as the source, Bragg wrote the division commanders that this "deluge of abuse . . . will destroy my usefulness and demoralize the army," pointedly adding that many of the accusations had originated from staff officers.[17]

The proverbial straw that broke the camel's back, however, came from an article in the anti-Bragg *Chattanooga Rebel*. It stated that Bragg had retreated from Murfreesboro against the advice of his generals and that he had lost the confidence of his army. On January 10, the general summoned his staff and read them the article. Only Brent left an account. Stoddard Johnston was apparently at Estill Springs at the time and, although he must have heard about the meeting upon his return, he made no record of it. Colonel David Urquhart remained silent in his postwar writings. According to Brent, Bragg stated that if they considered the accusations to be true, he would relinquish command. The staff caucused and, showing both candor and a degree of disloyalty, advised the general that he should step down.[18]

There was still time to mitigate the damage and drop the subject, but Bragg now considered his honor at stake. He had read newspaper accounts that Kirby Smith had reported to Richmond, apparently to replace him. (Smith would actually replace Theophilus H. Holmes in the trans-Mississippi.) Possibly believing that time was of the essence, on January 11 Bragg wrote his corps and division commanders a circular letter, asking them to admit that they had advised a retreat at Murfreesboro. Regarding the articles, he continued to believe that staff officers had leaked information. Again, had he stopped there the damage might have been mitigated, but obsessed with vindication, he imprudently (and against the pleadings of his staff) went on to ask a second question. Hardee and Polk, and their division and brigade commanders, should confer and candidly reply as to whether he had lost their confidence. If so, he would "retire without regret." It was a gamble, but in his mind not a desperate one; clearly he expected to be sustained. What Bragg had in fact done was to place his career in the hands of a jury of eighteen—two lieutenant generals, three major generals, six brigadiers, and seven colonels.[19]

Hardee pounced on the opportunity. In his response on the thirteenth he admitted that he had agreed with the decision to retreat. To the second question he wrote: "I feel that frankness compels me to say that the general officers, whose judgments you have invoked, are unanimous in the opinion that a change of command of this army is necessary. In this opinion I concur." He concluded that no information had been leaked by his staff officers. It was a lie; O'Hara had been in constant communication with Hardee's staff officers and with the general himself. O'Hara confided to Breckinridge: "Hardee has sent copies of *the correspondence* [memorandum] to the President—he told me so in confidence. I am delighted he did so. BB [Braxton Bragg] reminds me of the poetic simile of the 'scorpion begrit by fire.' If he bites himself he is sure to die of his own loathsome venon."[20]

Breckinridge followed suit. He conferred with his brigade commanders—Preston, Pillow, Gibson, and Trabue who unanimously agreed "that you do not possess the confidence of the army." Preston's vote came as no surprise. He denounced Bragg as tyrannical, impetuous, and narrow-minded, adding that he was "too weak to fight" and "too unpopular to run." He openly referred to the army commander as "Boomerang Bragg," and wrote that he had a "heart of ice and a head of wood." The animus between Gibson and Bragg dated back to Shiloh, where Bragg had unfairly branded him a coward; the two now detested one another. Interestingly, Trabue quickly backed off his vote, much to the chagrin of O'Hara. "Trabue has actually gone to Bragg & clingingly, basely, dirtily backed out from his previous expression of opinion," the captain wrote Breckinridge on January 24.[21]

Since Pillow later came to Bragg's defense, some modern writers have speculated that the Kentuckian may have taken liberties with his position. It has also been speculated that Pillow may have played both ends against the middle. At the time, Pillow knew that Breckinridge might press charges against him for cowardice in the late battle. (Breckinridge did not proceed, on the advice of Hardee.) Pillow may have considered his support for Bragg a quid pro quo against possible charges from Breckinridge. There may have been a second reason. Brigadier General John C. Brown, a known Bragg ally, returned to duty in mid-January, having partially recovered from his Perryville wound. Brown resumed command of his brigade, thus leaving Pillow in search of a command. Pillow may have changed his vote in support of Bragg in an effort to oust McCown, whose division he coveted.[22]

Modern writers have also concluded that, had Bragg simply waited for some of those generals friendly to him to recuperate from their sicknesses and wounds, he would have fared better. In Hardee's corps, the only one in which an actual vote took place, such may not have been the case. In Breckinridge's division, Bragg had attempted to place Brigadier General Marcus J. Wright, a supporter, in command of the Kentucky brigade, but the appointment was overturned by the War Department. In February, Richmond assigned Brigadier General Benjamin H. Helm, who had recovered from his hemorrhoids and horsing accident of the previous summer. Helms certainly would have fallen into the Kentucky bloc and supported Breckinridge. When Brigadier General Daniel Adams, a solid Bragg supporter, had recovered from his wound, he certainly would have supported Bragg, but he did not recuperate from his arm wound until May—far too late to help Bragg in the present crisis. Even so, he would not have altered the overall vote.[23]

Cleburne likewise consulted with his brigadiers—Lucius Polk, Liddell, Johnson, and Wood, all concurring "with regret" that Bragg had lost the confidence of the army. Strangely, Bragg overlooked Cleburne's rebuff. When the army commander subsequently placed charges against McCown, he placed Cleburne in charge of a court panel comprised of his solid supporters. Indeed, Cleburne was the only one from Hardee's corps.[24]

There is also some question about Liddell's "no" vote. Prior to the Battle of Stones River, he had resolved a rift with Bragg. "I felt we were friends again. We had been classmates, and it was right that I should uphold him in every good motive." Yet, the brigadier had been angered by the decision to retreat from Murfreesboro, which he considered to be the turning point of the war. Strangely, he never mentioned in his candid memoir that Cleburne, with whom he did not have good relations, asked his opinion in a vote of confidence on Bragg.[25]

Polk was on leave in Asheville, North Carolina, when the circular was forwarded to him. The Bishop returned to Shelbyville around January 20, but he did not respond until the thirtieth. He replied that some confusion existed on the part of his officers, Cheatham in particular, as to whether one or two questions had been posed; he requested clarification. Having been stung by the response of Hardee and his officers, Bragg now wrote that the letter had been "grossly and intentionally" misrepresented. He had intended only one question, which related to the issue of retreat. In truth, despite all of his back-stabbing, Polk was looking for a way out. Had he truthfully desired a showdown with Bragg, he would have supported Hardee and given his view regardless. He was more than content to let Hardee do the dirty work and take the fall. He then promptly sent a cowardly and shameful letter to Davis, expressing his negative views of the army commander. It was never Polk's style to confront face to face; he worked behind the scenes.[26]

It is difficult to predict how a vote in Polk's corps would have gone. The Bishop assured Davis that, had positions been made public, Cheatham and Withers would have united with him in voting no confidence. There is little doubt that Cheatham hated Bragg, but with potential drunkenness charges pending, he might have been reticent to speak with candor. Indeed, McCown railed at Cheatham's hypocrisy, stating that he "said one thing among the officers behind Bragg's back and wrote him a totally different thing." Cheatham's brigadiers appear to have been largely pro-Bragg.[27]

As for Withers, he defended Bragg in a January 18 article in the *Mobile Advertiser & Register*. Patton Anderson believed that Breckinridge had been drinking during the January 2 assault, and he probably would have supported the army commander. He nonetheless wrote privately to his wife: "Gen. Bragg is more unpopular with the army than ever[,] since he fell back from a victorious field. The victory was a much more decisive one than at Perryville, but I doubt if we reap any of the fruits beyond the artillery and other captured property we took away."[28]

Even before Polk returned to Tullahoma, Bragg's staff gossiped that the primary source of the discontent lay in Hardee's corps, with Breckinridge

as the catalyst. The Kentuckian "by some means seduced Hardee to participate." O'Hara sensed impending doom. Writing to Breckinridge (temporarily in Knoxville) on January 19, he warned: "Old Bragg is moving Heaven
and Earth to prepare to wage war against you[,] a war to the knife." Again
on January 23 he cautioned: "You got to prepare yourself to confront him
[Bragg] boldly on the issue [Stones River report]. . . . It would be better
if you could anticipate his onslaught upon you by convincing him of the
danger he is incurring—by cowing him—which I think you could do." He
concluded that if Breckinridge did not return "& give back bone to your
Co. (conspirators, I had like to say) Bragg will gain an important advantage
over you . . . 'give you Hell' in his report."[29]

O'Hara was right. Bragg assailed Breckinridge in his after-action report,
both for his failure to send timely reinforcements on December 31, and
for his mishandling of the January 2 assault. As evidence he produced two
"special reports," one from Captain Felix Robertson of the artillery and the
other from Colonel Brent. Robertson's initial report had not been critical
of the Kentuckian, so Bragg requested an addendum that would come
directly to his headquarters. Taking the cue, Robertson now ripped into
Breckinridge for his mishandling of the assault. A postwar second-hand
account claimed that Robertson later admitted that he lied to please Bragg.
Historians have judged the accusations as suspicious, if not an out-and-
out lie. Nonetheless, Bragg had his first exhibit. Pillow also submitted a
statement, claiming that he never knew that the cavalry was to play a role
in the attack. While Breckinridge gathered evidence from his own staff officers, he requested that the War Department conduct a court of inquiry.
No court was ever held, and the Bragg-Breckinridge feud dragged on until
May 1863, when the Kentuckian was transferred to Mississippi.[30]

Mystified that Bragg "invited judgment" upon himself, Davis notified
Johnston on January 22 to proceed to Tullahoma and investigate the state
of affairs. Although personally maintaining confidence in Bragg, the president feared "a disaster may result" if the army commander had indeed
lost the confidence of the generals. Should necessity require it, Johnston
was to take command himself. The theater commander, then in Mississippi, arrived at Tullahoma on February 3. Bragg acknowledged that a
problem had existed, but that it had been resolved. Hardee and Polk both
expressed concerns, but mostly about the Kentucky Campaign. Governor
Harris, who kept his hand on the pulse of the general staff, believed that

the tension had cooled. A review of the troops on the third and again on the twelfth revealed the men to be in high spirits. Indeed, returning absentees actually made the army stronger than before the battle. The theater commander sustained Bragg and shunned the suggestion that he personally take command. Refusing to order Johnston to take command, and ill in early February, Davis chose to do nothing. "The Prest is always loath to yield a General to the popular clamor. . . . He always hopes for better luck next time," William Preston Johnston confided to his wife on January 28. "But," he added, "Bragg is incompetent."[31]

But for Johnston's subsequent supportive report to Congress, a February 1863 resolution congratulating Bragg for the Battle of Stones River might never have cleared the House of Representatives. Congressman Foote voted in the affirmative, although the next day he went on the attack. He railed that he never considered Bragg capable of commanding a big army, had often said so, and "had not a word to take back." Texas Congressman F. B. Sexton wrote in his diary under the heading of February 26: "In the House thanks voted to Genl. Bragg for the Battle of Murfreesboro. I voted in affirmative with many misgivings. Did so solely because J. E. J. sent in orders that his [Bragg's] conduct was good & his generalship able. [George] Hodge made a strong appeal against him."[32]

Even while his private war with Breckinridge continued, Bragg, having now been sustained by the government, continued the purge of his generals. He next went after McCown, an officer whom he had always detested. Supported by Hardee, Bragg accused the division commander of delaying the attack on December 31, an accusation which was patently untrue. Unfortunately, McCown became his own worst enemy by his stunning lack of discretion. In front of Pillow, he went on a tear against Davis, Bragg, and Governor Harris, and denounced the Confederacy as a "damned stinking cotton oligarchy." He bellowed that he did not care if he was cashiered, as he had four acres of land in East Tennessee and he "could go there and make potatoes." The actual charge against the Tennessean proved petty; on several occasions he had breached protocol by assigning details of men to Charleston, South Carolina. On March 16 a court, which included Cleburne, Withers, and Anderson, found him guilty and suspended him for six months.[33]

Bragg also saw a chance to be rid of Cheatham. He accused the Tennessean of being tardy in the assault on December 31. Interestingly, Withers had been guilty of a similar offense, but being a Bragg ally he received praise. Eventually the issue of Cheatham's drunkenness came to the forefront. The army commander was taken aback when he heard that Polk had only given him a verbal reprimand, and in his after-action report he even praised Cheatham. Bragg thus took the issue directly to the War Department. Secretary of War James Seddon characterized the issue as "very unfortunate," and there was even talk of a court of inquiry. Cheatham had strong support within the Tennessee congressional delegation, and he maintained his command, much to Bragg's chagrin.[34]

The army upheaval took an accelerated turn when Bragg audaciously moved against Hardee and Polk. Unwilling to let the issue of the Kentucky Campaign die, he requested statements from both corps commanders. He came just short of accusing Polk of disobeying orders. Neither officer responded, with Hardee boasting that he could "tear Bragg to tatters" on the issue. The turmoil continued through April and May 1863, although no formal charges were forthcoming. Hardee would eventually be transferred to Mississippi. Bragg had seemingly won against the enemy within. In truth, Stones River had left the army's top command in shambles. In June, Bragg sustained a complete physical and mental breakdown, although he continued to maintain command.[35]

GOD HAS CROWNED OUR ARMS WITH VICTORY

With Bragg's career mired in acrimony, Rosecrans's star continued to ascend. At 4:30 a.m. on January 5, he wired Stanton: "God has crowned our arms with victory. The enemy are badly beaten and in full retreat. We shall press them as rapidly as our means of traveling and subsistence will permit." Never mind that the decision to advance from Nashville might never have come had it not been for the constant badgering of the War Department. Never mind that McCook's corps had been routed on the first day's battle, and the army commander had come dangerously close to having his communications severed. Never mind that the battle had ended in a tactical draw. Rosecrans possessed the battlefield; it was enough.[36]

It took several days for the North to realize that a great battle had been fought in Tennessee. A midwestern blizzard on January 4 brought dispatches to a standstill. On the sixth the news flashed across the Union— "Murfreesboro—Victory! The Enemy in Full and Disorderly Retreat. Their

Defeat a Complete One," hailed the *New York Times*. "Rosecrans Wins a Complete Victory: The Enemy in Full Retreat," echoed the *Chicago Tribune*. When complimented for his tenacity, Rosecrans quipped to a Chicago reporter: "Yes, you know Bragg is a good dog, but Hold Fast is better." While post-battle rifts occurred between Rosecrans and McCook, Rousseau, and Palmer, for most of the army "confidence with Rosecrans is boundless."[37]

Rosecrans became the darling of the nation. His career soared, surpassing even Grant's. Congratulatory dispatches arrived from all quarters. "God bless you, and all with you! Please tender to all, and accept for yourself, the nation's gratitude for your and their skill, endurance, and dauntless courage," Lincoln dispatched. Other communications followed from Congress and the state legislatures of Indiana and Ohio. Secretary of the Navy Gideon Welles logged in his journal on January 9: "Rosecrans has done himself and the country service."[38]

Beyond securing Middle Tennessee for the Union, the Battle of Stones River had far-reaching implications. The stock exchange and gold markets stabilized, and a "Tennessee argument" for British intervention no longer existed. Politically the battle countered the loss at Fredericksburg and undercut the growing antiwar movement. Rosecrans's cavalry chief wrote plainly: "The Battle of Stone's River saved the Northwest from falling under the domination of the peace or coward's party." The Emancipation Proclamation, which went into effect on January 1, 1863, was ushered in by the Stones River victory rather than the Fredericksburg debacle. Lincoln would later write to Rosecrans: "I can never forget, whilst I remember anything, that about the end of last year and the beginning of this, you gave us a hard-earned victory, which, had there been a defeat instead, the nation could scarcely have lived over." Although minimal territorial gains resulted, the battle proved to be the first step in a drive that would lead the Federal Army toward Tullahoma, Chickamauga, Chattanooga, and ultimately Atlanta. Stones River also helped answer the salient question: would this become a war of southern attrition or northern will? New Yorker George Templeton Strong knew the answer: "It [the battle] may have been indecisive, but our troops will stand the wear and tear of indecisive conflict longer than those of salvedom, and can soon be repaired." The South could not win such a war.[39]

APPENDIX A

The Opposing Forces at Stones River

ARMY OF THE CUMBERLAND

(Fourteenth Army Corps)
Major General William S. Rosecrans

RIGHT WING

Major General Alexander McD. McCook

. . . .

First Division
Brigadier General Jefferson C. Davis

First Brigade: Colonel Phillip Sidney Post
  59th Illinois
  74th Illinois
  75th Illinois
  22nd Indiana
  5th Wisconsin Battery

Second Brigade: Colonel William P. Carlin
  21st Illinois
  38th Illinois
  101st Ohio
  15th Wisconsin
  2nd Minnesota Battery

Third Brigade: Colonel William E. Woodruff
  25th Illinois
  35th Illinois

81st Indiana
8th Wisconsin Battery

. . . .

Second Division
Brigadier General Richard W. Johnson

First Brigade: Brigadier General August Willich (C), Colonel William Wallace, Colonel William H. Gibson
  89th Illinois
  32nd Indiana
  39th Indiana
  15th Ohio
  49th Ohio
  Battery A, 1st Ohio Light Artillery

Second Brigade: Brigadier General Edward N. Kirk (MW), Colonel Joseph P. Dodge
  34th Illinois
  79th Illinois
  29th Indiana
  30th Indiana
  77th Pennsylvania
  Battery E, 1st Ohio Light Artillery

Third Brigade: Colonel Philemon P. Baldwin
  6th Indiana
  5th Kentucky
  1st Ohio
  93rd Ohio
  5th Indiana Battery

Cavalry: 3rd Battalion, 3rd Indiana Cavalry (4 cos.): Major Robert Klein

. . . .

Third Division
Brigadier General Philip H. Sheridan

First Brigade: Brigadier General Joshua W. Sill (K), Colonel Nicholas Greusel, Jr.
  36th Illinois
  88th Illinois

21st Michigan
24th Wisconsin
4th Indiana Battery

Second Brigade: Colonel Frederick Schaefer (K), Lieutenant Colonel Bernard Laiboldt
44th Illinois
73rd Illinois
2nd Missouri
15th Missouri
G, 1st Missouri Light Artillery

Third Brigade: Colonel George W. Roberts (K), Colonel Luther P. Bradley
22nd Illinois
27th Illinois
51st Illinois
C, 1st Illinois Light Artillery

CENTER

Major General George H. Thomas
Provost Guard: 9th Michigan: Colonel John G. Parkhurst

. . . .

First Division
Major General Lovell H. Rousseau

First Brigade: Colonel Benjamin F. Scribner
38th Indiana
2nd Ohio
33rd Ohio
94th Ohio
10th Wisconsin

Second Brigade: Colonel John Beatty
42nd Indiana
88th Indiana
15th Kentucky
3rd Ohio
A, 1st Michigan Light Artillery

Third Brigade:[1] Colonel John C. Starkweather
  24th Illinois
  79th Pennsylvania
  1st Wisconsin
  21st Wisconsin
  A, Kentucky Artillery

Fourth Brigade: Lieutenant Colonel Oliver L. Shepherd
  1st Battalion, 15th U.S.
  1st Battalion and Company B, 2nd Battalion, 16th U.S.
  Companies A and D, 3rd Battalion, 18th U.S.
  2nd Battalion and Companies B, C, E, and F, 3rd Battalion, 18th U.S.
  1st Battalion, 19th U.S.
  Battery H, 5th U.S. Artillery

Cavalry: 2nd Kentucky Cavalry (six companies): Major Thomas P. Nicholas

. . . .

Second Division
Brigadier General James S. Negley

First Brigade:[2] Brigadier General James G. Spears
  1st East Tennessee
  2nd East Tennessee
  6th East Tennessee

Second Brigade: Colonel Timothy R. Stanley
  19th Illinois
  11th Michigan
  18th Ohio
  69th Ohio
  M, 1st Ohio Light Artillery

Third Brigade: Colonel John F. Miller
  37th Indiana
  21st Ohio
  74th Ohio
  78th Pennsylvania
  B, Kentucky Artillery
  G, 1st Ohio Light Artillery

First Brigade,[3] Fry's Third Division: Colonel Moses B. Walker
  82nd Indiana

17th Ohio
31st Ohio
D, 1st Michigan Artillery

LEFT WING

Major General Thomas L. Crittenden

. . . .

First Division
Brigadier General Thomas J. Wood
Brigadier General Milo S. Hascall

First Brigade: Brigadier General Milo S. Hascall, Colonel George P. Buell
100th Illinois
58th Indiana
3rd Kentucky
26th Ohio
8th Indiana Battery

Second Brigade: Colonel George D. Wagner
15th Indiana
40th Indiana
57th Indiana
97th Ohio
10th Indiana Battery

Third Brigade: Colonel Charles G. Harker
51st Indiana
73rd Indiana
13th Michigan
64th Ohio
65th Ohio
6th Ohio Battery

. . . .

Second Division
Brigadier General John M. Palmer

First Brigade: Brigadier General Charles Cruft
31st Indiana
1st Kentucky

2nd Kentucky
90th Ohio
B, 1st Ohio Light Artillery

Second Brigade: Colonel William B. Hazen
110th Illinois
9th Indiana
6th Kentucky
41st Ohio
F, 1st Ohio Light Artillery

Third Brigade: Colonel William Grose
84th Illinois
36th Indiana
23rd Kentucky
6th Ohio
24th Ohio

Division Artillery: Batteries H/M, 4th U.S. Artillery

. . . .

Third Division
Brigadier General Horatio P. Van Cleve
Colonel Samuel Beatty

First Brigade: Colonel Samuel Beatty, Colonel Benjamin C. Grider
79th Indiana
9th Kentucky
11th Kentucky
19th Ohio
B, Pennsylvania Artillery

Second Brigade: Colonel James P. Fyffe
44th Indiana
86th Indiana
13th Ohio
59th Ohio
7th Indiana Battery

Third Brigade: Colonel Samuel W. Price
35th Indiana
8th Kentucky
21st Kentucky

51st Ohio
99th Ohio
3rd Wisconsin Battery

CAVALRY

Brigadier General David S. Stanley

. . . .

Cavalry Division
Colonel John Kennett

First Brigade: Colonel Robert H. G. Minty
    2nd Indiana Cavalry
    3rd Kentucky Cavalry
    4th Michigan Cavalry
    7th Pennsylvania Cavalry

Second Brigade: Colonel Lewis Zahm
    1st Ohio Cavalry
    3rd Ohio Cavalry
    4th Ohio Cavalry

Artillery: D, 1st Ohio Light Artillery (section)

Reserve Cavalry:
    15th Pennsylvania Cavalry
    1st Middle (5th) East Tennessee Cavalry
    2nd East Tennessee Cavalry
    3rd Tennessee Cavalry[4]

Unattached:
    4th U.S. Cavalry

PIONEERS AND ENGINEERS

Pioneer Brigade: Captain James St. Clair Morton
    1st Battalion
    2nd Battalion
    3rd Battalion

Engineers: 1st Michigan Engineers and Mechanics[5]

PROVISIONAL BRIGADES

Spears's Provisional Brigade: Brigadier General James G. Spears[6]
  85th Illinois
  14th Michigan
  1st East Tennessee
  2nd East Tennessee
  3rd East Tennessee Cavalry
  10th Wisconsin Battery

McCook's Provisional Brigade: Colonel Daniel McCook[7]
  60th Illinois (8 cos.)
  10th Michigan (2 cos.)
  52nd Ohio (5 cos.)
  6th East Tennessee

ARMY OF TENNESSEE

General Braxton Bragg

POLK'S CORPS

Lieutenant General Leonidas Polk

. . . .

First Division
Major General Benjamin F. Cheatham

First Brigade: Brigadier General Daniel S. Donelson
  8th Tennessee
  16th Tennessee
  38th Tennessee
  51st Tennessee
  84th Tennessee
  39th North Carolina[8]
  Carnes's Tennessee Battery

Second Brigade: Brigadier General Alexander P. Stewart
  4th & 5th Tennessee
  19th Tennessee
  24th Tennessee

31st & 33rd Tennessee
Stanford's Mississippi Battery

Third Brigade: Brigadier General George Maney
1st & 27th Tennessee
4th Tennessee Provisional Army
6th & 9th Tennessee
Maney's Company, Tennessee Sharpshooters
Turner's Mississippi Battery

Fourth Brigade: Colonel Alfred J. Vaughn, Jr.
12th Tennessee
13th Tennessee
29th Tennessee
47th Tennessee
154th Tennessee
Allin's company, Tennessee Sharpshooters
9th Texas
Scott's Tennessee Battery

. . . .

Second Division
Major General Jones M. Withers

First Brigade: Colonel John Q. Loomis, Colonel John Q. Coltart
19th Alabama
22nd Alabama
25th Alabama
26th Alabama
39th Alabama
17th Alabama Battalion sharpshooters
1st Louisiana Regulars
Robertson's Alabama Battery

Second Brigade: Brigadier General James R. Chalmers, Colonel Thomas W. White
7th Mississippi
9th Mississippi
41st Mississippi
Blythe's Mississippi Regiment
9th Mississippi Battalion Sharpshooters
Garrity's Alabama Battery

Third Brigade: Brigadier General James P. Anderson
    24th Mississippi
    27th Mississippi
    29th Mississippi
    30th Mississippi
    37th Mississippi[9]
    45th Alabama
    39th North Carolina
    Barret's Missouri Battery

Fourth Brigade: Colonel Arthur M. Manigault
    24th Alabama
    34th Alabama
    10th South Carolina
    19th South Carolina
    Waters's Alabama Battery

HARDEE'S CORPS

Lieutenant General William J. Hardee

. . . .

First Division
Major General John C. Breckinridge

First Brigade: Brigadier General Daniel W. Adams
    13th & 20th Louisiana
    16th & 25th Louisiana
    14th Louisiana Battalion
    32nd Alabama
    Washington Artillery (Fifth Company)

Second Brigade: Colonel Joseph B. Palmer, Brigadier General Gideon J. Pillow
    18th Tennessee
    26th Tennessee
    28th Tennessee
    32nd Tennessee[10]
    45th Tennessee
    Anderson's Georgia Battery

Third Brigade: Brigadier General William Preston
  1st & 3rd Florida
  4th Florida
  60th North Carolina
  20th Tennessee
  Wright's Tennessee Battery

Fourth Brigade: Brigadier General Roger W. Hanson
  2nd Kentucky
  4th Kentucky
  6th Kentucky
  9th Kentucky
  41st Alabama
  Cobb's Kentucky Battery

Jackson's Independent Brigade: Brigadier General John K. Jackson[11]
  5th Georgia
  2nd Georgia Battalion Sharpshooters
  5th Mississippi
  8th Mississippi
  Lumsden's Alabama Battery
  Pritchard's Georgia Battery

. . . .

Second Division
Major General R. Cleburne

First Brigade: Brigadier General Lucius E. Polk
  1st Arkansas
  13th & 15th Arkansas
  5th Confederate
  2nd Tennessee
  5th Tennessee
  Helena (Arkansas) Artillery

Second Brigade: Brigadier General St. John R. Liddell
  2nd Arkansas
  5th Arkansas
  6th & 7th Arkansas
  8th Arkansas
  Warren (Mississippi) Light Artillery

Third Brigade: Brigadier General Bushrod R. Johnson
   17th Tennessee
   23rd Tennessee
   25th Tennessee
   37th Tennessee
   44th Tennessee
   Jefferson (Mississippi) Artillery

Fourth Brigade: Brigadier General Sterling A. M. Wood
   16th Alabama
   33rd Alabama
   3rd Confederate
   45th Mississippi
   15th Mississippi Battalion Sharpshooters
   Semple's Alabama Battery

MCCOWN'S DIVISION[12]

Major General John P. McCown

First Brigade: Brigadier General Matthew D. Ector
   10th Texas Cavalry (Dismounted)
   11th Texas Cavalry (Dismounted)
   14th Texas Cavalry (Dismounted)
   15th Texas Cavalry (Dismounted)
   Douglas Texas Battery

Second Brigade: Brigadier General James E. Rains, Colonel Robert B. Vance
   3rd Georgia Battalion
   9th Georgia Battalion
   29th North Carolina
   11th Tennessee
   Eufaula (Alabama) Artillery

Third Brigade: Brigadier General Evander McNair, Colonel Robert W. Harper
   1st Arkansas Mounted Rifles (Dismounted)
   2nd Arkansas Mounted Rifles (Dismounted)
   30th Arkansas
   4th Arkansas
   1st Arkansas Light Artillery

CAVALRY

Brigadier General Joseph Wheeler

Wheeler's Brigade: Brigadier General Joseph Wheeler
1st Alabama Cavalry
3rd Alabama Cavalry
51st Alabama Partisan Rangers
8th Confederate Cavalry
Holman's Tennessee Battalion Partisan Rangers
2nd Kentucky Cavalry Battalion (Detachment)
McCann's Tennessee Cavalry (Detachment)
Wiggins's Arkansas Battery

Buford's Brigade: Brigadier General Abraham Buford
3rd Kentucky Cavalry
5th & 6th Kentucky Cavalry

Pegram's Brigade: Brigadier General John Pegram
1st Tennessee Cavalry
2nd Tennessee Cavalry
1st Georgia Cavalry
12th Tennessee Battalion[13]
Robinson's Mountain Howitzer Battery (2 Guns)

Wharton's Brigade: Brigadier General John A. Wharton
14th Alabama Cavalry Battalion
1st Confederate Cavalry
3rd Confederate Cavalry
2nd Georgia Cavalry
3rd Georgia Cavalry (Detachment)
4th Tennessee Cavalry
Davis's Tennessee Cavalry Battalion
8th Texas Cavalry (Texas Rangers)
Murray's Tennessee Cavalry Regiment
White's Tennessee Battery

NOTES

1. Arrived January.
2. Arrived January 3.

3. Walker's brigade was the only unit from the Third Division engaged at Stones River.

4. Assigned to Nashville garrison, but on January 2 accompanied Spears's Provisional Brigade as a wagon train escort.

5. Engaged with Wheeler's cavalry at La Vergne on January 1.

6. Arrived January 3 from the Nashville garrison.

7. Arrived January 4 from the Nashville garrison.

8. Recently arrived from the Department of East Tennessee. On January 2 ordered to Manigault's brigade.

9. Arrived January 2 from Shelbyville, Tennessee.

10. On detached service at Wartrace.

11. Bridge guard at Stevenson, Alabama, but temporarily assigned to Breckinridge.

12. Of Smith's corps, but temporarily attached to Hardee's corps.

13. Arrived January 3.

APPENDIX B
The Transfer of Stevenson's Division

Modern criticism notwithstanding, Jefferson Davis's decision to transfer Carter Stevenson's division to East Tennessee proved correct. Deducting garrisons and 2,000 Indians, Theophilus Holmes had only 16,000 scattered troops in the entire state, facing, according to best Confederate estimates, 30,000 Yankees at Springfield, Missouri, and 12,000–15,000 at Helena, Arkansas. At the time the request for reinforcements would have been made, the Federals were moving on Van Buren and Fort Smith, Arkansas. Holmes never considered sending anything other than Benjamin McCulloch's 6,000-man Arkansas division, and there was no guarantee that the troops would not desert en masse rather than cross the Mississippi River (as a Texas division did in 1864). Even if he had been willing to evacuate the state, as Joseph E. Johnston advised, it would take McCulloch's division as long to get to Vicksburg as Stevenson's. Davis held limited control over Holmes (as his repeatedly ignored orders indicated), and Holmes even less over troublesome subordinates, such as Major General Thomas Hindman.

The transfer of Stevenson's division has been criticized for two reasons. Confederates secured a victory at the Battle of Chickasaw Bayou on December 29 largely with troops already within the department. The reinforcements, as predicted, had served neither John Pemberton nor Bragg. Such a position is argued in hindsight. The advance elements of Stevenson's division arrived in time for the battle (contrary to Johnston's prediction), and were available in case of an enemy breakthrough. Second, historians have argued that the loss of Stevenson's division robbed Bragg of a victory at Stones River. Had Stevenson not left, however, there might not have been a battle. There is no assurance that the release of N. B. Forrest's and John Hunt Morgan's cavalry brigades alone would have prompted Rosecrans to advance. He did so because he wrongly thought Kirby Smith's "army" was moving toward Kentucky. (He found out the real destination only at the last moment.) If Rosecrans had not launched a winter campaign and the Confederates had subsequently lost Vicksburg due to a lack of timely reinforcements, Davis surely would have been castigated for not doing enough! Davis, not having hindsight, had to base his decision upon what *might* occur.

While concentrating Holmes's troops might have made sounder strategic sense, the political and morale effects of surrendering Arkansas, which would have resulted, would have had far-reaching implications. Arkansas troops in Bragg's army were already clamoring to go home. Losing about thirty miles of Middle Tennessee, even though it was a vital commissary area, proved a better option than losing the entire state of Arkansas. The counter-argument is that the destruction of William Rosecrans's army (with the aid of Stevenson's division) would have changed the dynamics of the war in the West. I simply do not believe that the annihilation of the Army of the Cumberland would have occurred at Stones River. In a disaster, Rosecrans would simply have fallen back to Nashville. There he would have been reinforced by the 15,000 troops from Kentucky, which subsequently arrived after the battle.

One more issue is worth mentioning. To win the Battle of Stones River with Stevenson's division meant that Bragg would have had to apply it at precisely the exact moment. Such may not have been the case. He probably would have hurled it in piecemeal fashion into the Round Forrest as he did other units, and with similar results. Bragg could have won the battle without Stevenson's division by not obsessing with the Lebanon Pike and doing one of two things. First, he could have placed most of Breckinridge's division on Withers's right in the vicinity of McFadden's Hill and attacked with his right, thus driving the Federals *away* from the Nashville Pike and not toward it. Second, he could have placed most of Breckinridge's division on McCown's left and stuck with the original plan. The east bank and Lebanon Pike could have been held (as it subsequently was on the afternoon of December 31) by Hanson's brigade and Pegram's cavalry and, I contend, Wheeler's cavalry. The last was needed more on the battlefield than burning Federal wagons, which could be easily replaced, in the rear. Had these options been exercised, Bragg might have won the battle. With the Confederates winning at both Chickasaw Bayou *and* Stones River, modern historians would doubtless have hailed Davis's decision to send Stevenson's division as correct.

NOTES

ABBREVIATIONS

ADAH	Alabama Department of Archives and History, Montgomery
BGSU	Bowling Green State University, Bowling Green, Ohio
CHS	Chicago Historical Society, Chicago
CCNBP	Chattanooga-Chickamauga National Battlefield Park, Chickamauga, Ga.
CINHS	Cincinnati Historical Society, Cincinnati
DU	Duke University, Durham, N.C.
EU	Emory University, Atlanta
FC	Filson Club, Louisville, Ky.
ILSHS	Illinois State Historical Society, Springfield
INHS	Indiana Historical Society, Indianapolis
KC	Knox College, Galesburg, Ill.
LC	Library of Congress, Washington, D.C.
LSU	Louisiana State University, Baton Rouge
MOLLUS	*Military Order of the Loyal Legion of the United States*
MDAH	Mississippi Department of Archives and History, Jackson
NA	National Archives, Washington, D.C.
NYHS	New York Historical Society, New York
OHS	Ohio Historical Society, Columbus
OR	U.S. War Department, *War of the Rebellion: A Compilation of the Official Records of the Union and Confederate Armies,* 128 vols. (Washington, D.C.: 1880–1902). All citations in Series I unless otherwise indicated.
RBHPL	Rutherford B. Hayes Presidential Library, Fremont, Ohio
SHC	Southern Historical Collection, University of North Carolina, Chapel Hill
SHSW	State Historical Society of Wisconsin, Madison
SOR	Janet B. Hewitt et al., eds., *Supplement to the Official Records of the Union and Confederate Armies.* 94 vols., Wilmington, N.C.: Broadfoot Publishing Co., 1994. All citations in Series I unless otherwise indicated.
SRNBP	Stones River National Battlefield Park, Murfreesboro, Tenn.
TSLA	Tennessee State Library and Archives, Nashville
TU	Tulane University, New Orleans

USAMHI   United State Army Military History Institute, Carlisle Barrack, Pa.
UM   University of Michigan, Ann Arbor
UMISS   University of Mississippi, Oxford
UT-Arlington University of Texas, Arlington
WKU   Western Kentucky University, Bowling Green
WRHS   Western Reserve Historical Society, Cleveland, Ohio
WTHS   West Tennessee Historical Society, University of Memphis, Memphis

PREFACE

1. Gary W. Gallagher, "The War Was Won in the East," *Civil War Times Illustrated*, February 2011, 19–21.

2. Donald Stoker, *The Grand Design: Strategy and the U.S. Civil War* (New York: Oxford University Press, 2010), 229.

3. Herman Hattaway and Archer Jones, *How the North Won: A Military History of the Civil War* (Urbana: University of Illinois Press, 1983), 322; Archer Jones, *Civil War Command and Strategy: The Process of Victory and Defeat* (New York: Free Press, 1992), 106–7.

CHAPTER ONE

1. *Charleston Mercury*, October 25, November 18, 1862; J. Cutler Andrews, *The South Reports the Civil War* (Pittsburgh: University of Pittsburgh Press, 1985), 253; Grady McWhiney, *Braxton Bragg and Confederate Defeat* (Tuscaloosa: University of Alabama Press, 1969), 325 (press reaction); Don Carlos Seitz, *Braxton Bragg, General of the Confederacy* (Columbia, S.C.: State Co., 1924), 206 ("dogs of detraction").

2. *OR* 16, pt. 2: 976; Edward Younger, ed., *Inside the Confederate Government: The Diary of Robert Garlick Hill Keen* (New York: Oxford University Press, 1957), 30; Thomas Bragg Diary, October 27, 1862, SHC; William Preston Johnston to wife, October 27, 1862, William Preston Johnston Papers, Mason Barret Collection, TU; J. B. Jones, *A Rebel War Clerk's Diary at the Confederate States Capital* (2 vols., Philadelphia: J. P. Lippincott & Co., 1866), vol. 1: 176.

3. George Hodge to W. P. Johnston, November 17, 1862, Johnston Papers, Mason Barret Papers, TU (Hodge's opposition); McWhiney, *Braxton Bragg and Confederate Defeat*, 324, 326 (Henry, Orr, Yancey opposition); Steven E. Woodworth, *Jefferson Davis and His Generals: The Failure of Confederate Command in the West* (Lawrence: University Press of Kansas, 1990), 162 (Davis-Bragg prewar conflict); William C. Davis, ed., *The Confederate Memoirs of Robert Barnwell Rhett* (Columbia: University of South Carolina Press, 2000), xiii, 67 ("egregious failure"); Eric H. Walther, *William Lowndes Yancey: The Coming of the Civil War* (Chapel Hill: University of North Carolina Press, 2006), 335, 345, 353–53; David J. Eicher, *Dixie Betrayed: How the South Really Lost the Civil War* (New York: Little, Brown and Co., 2006), 141 (Orr opposition); "Proceedings of Congress," *Southern Historical Society Papers* 46 (January 1928): 61, 113–19; George C. Rable, *The Confederate Republic: A Revolution Against Politics* (Chapel Hill: University of North Carolina Press, 1994), 170.

4. Earl J. Hess, *Banners to the Breeze: The Kentucky Campaign, Corinth, and Stones River* (Lincoln: University of Nebraska Press, 2000), 1-3; William C. Davis, *Jefferson Davis: The Man and His Hour* (New York: Harper Collins, 1991), 413 (fears for Vicksburg); Eicher, *Dixie Betrayed* (Rector).

5. Thomas L. Connelly, *Army of the Heartland: The Army of Tennessee, 1861-1862* (Baton Rouge: Louisiana State University Press, 1967), 205; Thomas L. Connelly, *Autumn of Glory: The Army of Tennessee, 1862-1865* (Baton Rouge: Louisiana State University Press, 1971), 70-71; Jack D. Welsh, *Medical Histories of Confederate Generals* (Kent, Ohio: Kent State University Press, 1967), 23; McWhiney, *Braxton Bragg and Confederate Defeat*, 28-29; James I. Robertson Jr., "Braxton Bragg: The Lonely Patriot," in Gary W. Gallagher and Joseph T. Glatthaar, ed., *Leaders of the Lost Cause: New Perspectives on the Confederate High Command* (Mechanicsburg, Pa.: Stackpole Books, 2004), 72, 73.

6. S. H. Lockett, "The Defense of Vicksburg," *Battles and Leaders of the Civil War* (4 vols., 1911; rpt. New York: Thomas Yoseloff, 1956), vol. 3: 482 (New Orleans garrison). James M. McPherson, *Battle Cry of Freedom: The Civil War Era* (New York: Oxford University Press, 1988), 432. William Drennan to wife, May 30, 1863, in William Drennan Papers, MDAH (conscript regiments). *OR* 17, pt. 1: 441, 449 (exchangees); 24, pt. 3: 624 (conscript regiments); 16, pt. 2: 888-89. Peter Cozzens, *The Darkest Days of the War: The Battles of Iuka and Corinth* (Chapel Hill: University of North Carolina Press, 1997), 139-40, 305-6.

7. Davis, *Jefferson Davis*, 156-59; Kenneth W. Noe, *Perryville: This Grand Havoc of Battle* (Frankfort: University Press of Kentucky, 2001), 157-58.

8. Jones, *Civil War Command and Strategy*, 92-93; McWhiney, *Braxton Bragg and Confederate Defeat*, 322 (2,000 recruits); *OR* 16, pt. 1: 932, 933, 1097; Larry J. Daniel, *Days of Glory: the Army of the Cumberland, 1861-1865* (Baton Rouge: Louisiana State University Press, 2004), 157, 167. Casualty totals are from the three major battles of the campaign—Richmond, Munfordville, and Perrville—and adding Bragg's losses on the retreat.

9. Howard Jones, *Union in Peril: the Crisis Over British Intervention in the Civil War* (Chapel Hill: University of North Carolina Press, 1992), 171; James M. McPherson, *This Mighty Scourge: Perspectives on the Civil War* (New York: Oxford University Press, 1992), 74-75; Gary W. Gallagher, *Lee and His Army in Confederate History* (Chapel Hill: University of North Carolina Press, 2001), 22-23 (double standard).

10. Davis, *Jefferson Davis*, 472; Woodworth, *Jefferson Davis and His Generals*, 166; McWhiney, *Braxton Bragg and Confederate Defeat*, 327-28; Eicher, *Dixie Betrayed*, 142 (Beauregard congressional support); Jones, *Rebel War Clerk's Diary* 1: 189 ("standing idle").

11. *Charleston Mercury*, November 4, 5, 1862; William K. Scarborough, ed., *The Diary of Edmund Ruffin* (2 vols., Baton Rouge: Louisiana State University Press, 1976), vol. 2: 478. Upon his return, Bragg announced to his staff that "his conduct in Kentucky had been approved by the President," and that Davis had "expressed his delight at the safe return of the Army." George W. Brent Diary, October 30, 1862, Braxton Bragg Papers, William Palmer Collection, WRHS.

12. Jones, *Civil War Command and Strategy*, 92; McWhiney, *Braxton Bragg and Confederate Defeat*, 328.

13. Joseph H. Parks, *General Edmund Kirby Smith, C.S.A.* (Baton Rouge: Louisiana State University Press, 1954), 42, 69, 76, 98, 117–19, 139–56; Woodworth, *Jefferson Davis and His Generals*, 126; Joseph T. Glatthaar, "Edmund Kirby Smith," in Gallagher and Glatthaar, eds., *Leaders of the Lost Cause*, 219–21.

14. Woodworth, *Jefferson Davis and His Generals*, 159; Davis, *Jefferson Davis*, 467 (lack of cooperation); Davis to Smith, October 29, 1862, Kirby Smith Papers, SHC; Smith to Davis, November 1, 1862, Jefferson Davis Papers, War Department Collection of Confederate Collections, NA; Parks, *General Edmund Kirby Smith*, 245.

15. Davis, *Jefferson Davis*, 28–29 (West Point friendship); Woodworth, *Jefferson Davis and His Generals*, 28–30; Grady McWhiney, "A Bishop as General," in *Confederate Crackers and Cavaliers* (Abilene, Texas: McWhiney Foundation Press, 2002), 209–19; Russell S. Bonds, "Leonidas Polk: Southern Civil War General," *Civil War Times Illustrated* 45 (May 2006): 52–54; Sam Davis Elliott, ed., *Doctor Quintard, Chaplain C.S.A. and Second Bishop of Tennessee: The Memoir and Civil War Diary of Charles Todd Quintard* (Baton Rouge: Louisiana State University Press, 2003), 56. Robertson wrote of Polk: "As a bishop, Polk knew how to lead, but as a soldier he never learned how to follow ("Braxton Bragg," 81, 82).

16. *OR* 20, pt. 2: 388, 393; Joseph H. Parks, *General Leonidas Polk, C.S.A.: The Fighting Bishop* (Baton Rouge: Louisiana State University Press, 1962), 280–81; Woodworth, *Jefferson Davis and his Generals*, 162, 167. Concluded Woodworth: "Davis simply could not be objective about Leonidas Polk. He would keep both Polk and Bragg if he could, but he would keep Polk in any event."

17. Nathaniel C. Hughes Jr., *General William J. Hardee: Old Reliable* (1965; rpt. Wilmington, N.C.: Broadfoot Publishing Co., 1987), 40, 41, 186–87; Woodworth, *Jefferson Davis and His Generals*, 165; Davis, *Jefferson Davis*, 473; Wilmer L. Jones, *Generals in Gray: Davis's Generals* (Mechanicsburg, Pa.: Stackpole Books, 2004), 315 (reading to Davis); Arthur James L. Fremantle, *Three Months in the Southern States, April–June 1863* (New York: J. Bradburn, 1864), 139 (women); Nathaniel C. Hughes, ed., *Liddell's Record: St. John Liddell, Brigadier General, C.S.A. Staff Officer and Brigade Commander Army of Tennessee* (Dayton, Ohio: Morningside, 1985), 122 ("running with women"); "A Gossiping Letter," in John Fitch, *Annals of the Army of the Cumberland* (1864; rpt. Mechanicsburg, Pa.: Stackpole Books, 2003), 576 (Hardee and the ladies). Woodworth (*Jefferson Davis and His Generals*, 167) considered Hardee "the most dangerous enemy in the army," surpassing even the troublesome Polk.

18. Jennifer L. Weber, *Copperheads: The Rise and Fall of Lincoln's Opponents in the North* (New York: Oxford University Press, 2006), 8–9, 50–51, 57.

19. Weber, *Copperheads*, 59–60; D. K. Newhouse to wife, December 25, 1862, D. K. Newhouse Letters, 101st Ohio File, SRNBP; Hillory Shifflett to wife, December 22, 1862, www .geocities.com/~jcrosswell/War/cw/hillory.htm; Theodore C. Pease and James G. Randal, eds., *Diary of Orville Browning* (2 vols., Springfield: Illinois State Historical Society, 1925–32), vol. 1: 588–89.

20. *OR* 16, pt. 2: 634 ("The butchery"), 623–27; *Indianapolis Daily Journal*, October 11, 1862 (Morton to Washington); T. Harry Williams, *Lincoln and the Radicals* (Madison: University of Wisconsin Press, 1936), 194; Hess, *Banners to the Breeze*, 179 ("dissatisfied and discouraged"); Stephen D. Engle, *Don Carlos Buell: Most Promising of All* (Chapel Hill: University

of North Carolina Press, 1999), 313–14, 318; David Donald, ed., *Inside Lincoln's Cabinet: The Civil War Diaries of Salmon P. Chase* (4 vols., 1954; rpt. Kent, Ohio: Kent State University Press, 1993–97), vol. 3: 285; LeRoy P. Graf, Ralph W. Haskins, and Paul W. Bergeron, eds., *The Papers of Andrew Johnson* (13 vols., Knoxville: University of Tennessee Press, 1979), vol. 6: 4–6.

21. David H. Donald, *Lincoln* (New York: Touchstone Books, 1996), 389; Daniel, *Days of Glory*, 97, 100; John Niven, ed., *The Salmon P. Chase Papers* (4 vols., Kent, Ohio: Kent State University Press, 1993–97), vol. 3: 305; *Chicago Tribune*, October 21, 1862.

22. Christopher J. Einolf, *George Thomas: Virginian for the Union* (Norman: University of Oklahoma Press, 2007), 87–88 (family rejection), 155–57 (enigma), 183 (humor); Francis F. McKinney, *Education in Violence: The Life of General George H. Thomas and the History of the Army of the Cumberland* (Detroit: Wayne State University Press, 1961), 82–83, 89–90; Freeman Cleaves, *Rock of Chickamauga: The Life of General George H. Thomas* (Norman: University of Oklahoma Press, 1948), 8, 21, 28–31, 45, 50–51, 59–61, 64, 71; *Chicago Tribune*, October 24, 1862; O. O. Howard, "Sketch of the Life of General George H. Thomas," *Military Order of the Loyal Union of the United States, New York* (1891; rpt. Wilmington, N.C.: Broadfoot Publishing Co., 1993), vol. 1: 287, 301; Daniel, *Days of Glory*, 135 (opposes Buell); Engle, *Don Carlos Buell*, 302 (argument with Buell); John Beatty, *The Citizen Soldier* (Cincinnati: Wilstach, Baldwin, 1879), 236.

23. Tyler Dennet, ed., *Lincoln and the Civil War: In the Diaries and Letters of John Hay* (1939; rpt. New York: Da Capo, 1988), 51–52; Cleaves, *Rock of Chickamauga*, 117–18; Leslie J. Gordon, "'I Could Not Make Him Do As I Wished': The Failed Relationship of William S. Rosecrans and Grant," in Steven E. Woodworth, ed., *Grant's Lieutenants: From Cairo to Vicksburg* (Lawrence: University of Kansas Press, 2001), 114 (Stanton's conflict); McKinney, *Education in Violence*, 167 ("Well, you have"), 169–70.

24. William M. Lamers, *The Edge of Glory: A Biography of General William S. Rosecrans, U.S.A.* (New York: Harcourt, Brace and World, 1961), 13, 16–18, 25–33, 54–55, 79–80, 154, 182; Whitelaw Reid, *Ohio in the War: Her Statesmen, Generals, and Soldiers* (2 vols., Columbus, Ohio: Electric, 1893), vol. 1: 312–17; Jack D. Welsh, *Medical Histories of Union Generals* (Kent, Ohio: Kent State University Press, 1996), 283; Hess, *Banners to the Breeze*, 119 (nervous breakdown); Gordon, "'I Could Not Make Him,'" 114–15; Albert Castel, "Victorious Loser: William S. Rosecrans," *Timeline*, July–August 2003, 32–33, 37.

25. Winfield Scott Miller to parents, March 23, 1863, Winfield Scott Miller Letters, INHS; Kenneth Noe, ed., *A Southern Boy in Blue: The Memoir of Marcus Woodcock 9th Kentucky Infantry (U.S.A.)* (Knoxville: University of Tennessee Press, 1996), 115; A. Stanley Camp to Hetta, November 14, 1862, A. Stanley Camp Letters, 18th Ohio File, SRNBP; Elizabeth E. P. Bascom, ed., *"Dear Lizzie"* (n.p., n.d.), 87; Frederick D. Williams, ed., *The Wild Life of the Army: Civil War Letters of James A. Garfield* (East Lansing: Michigan State University Press, 1964), 226–27; Theodore C. Blegen, ed., *The Civil War Letters of Colonel Hans Christian Heg* (Northfield: Minnesota-Norwegian American Historical Association, 1936), 152; Beatty, *Citizen Soldier*, 189; Liberty Warner to "Dear Friends," November 30, 1862, Liberty Warner Papers, BGSU.

26. Gordon, "'I Could Not Make Him,'" 115; William Shanks, *Personal Recollections of Distinguished Generals* (New York: Harper, 1866), 260–61; William Bickham, *Rosecrans' Campaign with the Fourteenth Army Corps, or the Army of the Cumberland: A Narrative of*

Personal Observations . . . with Official Reports of the Battle of Stones River (Cincinnati: Moore, Wilstach, Keys, 1863), 144 (stammer); Milo Hascall, "Personal Recollections and Experiences Concerning Battle of Stones River," *Military Order of the Loyal Legion of the United States, Illinois* (1907; rpt. Wilmington, N.C.: Broadfoot Publishing Co., 1992), vol. 4: 151–52 ("completely turned" and "a crank"); Beatty, *Citizen Soldier*, 256–57, 260–63 (temper); George T. Palmer, *A Conscientious Turncoat: The Story of John M. Palmer, 1817–1900* (New Haven, Conn.: Yale University Press, 1941), 104 ("Another weakness"), 105 (profanity); Lyman S. Widney to mother, February 20, 1863, Lyman S. Widney, 34th Illinois File, SRNBP; Louis M. Starr, *Bohemian Brigade: Newsmen in Action* (Madison: University of Wisconsin Press, 1987), 183 (Catholicism); Fitch, *Annals of the Army of the Cumberland*, 35.

27. *The Army Reunion: Reports of the Meetings of the Society of the Army of the Cumberland, 1887 Reunion* (Cincinnati: Robert Clarke, 1888), 48; "Old Rosy," *National Tribune*, May 26, 1887; Thomas B. Van Horne, *The Life of Major General George H. Thomas* (New York: Charles Scribner's Sons, 1882), 88; Benson Bobrick, *Master of War: The Life of General George H. Thomas* (New York: Simon & Schuster, 2009), 135 (insubordination).

28. Charles and Barbara Whalen, *The Fighting McCooks: America's Fighting Family* (Bethesda, Md.: Westmoreland Press, 2006), 69–78, 170; Daniel, *Days of Glory*, 18, 174; Beatty, *Citizen Soldier*, 235; Henry Richards, *Letters of Captain Henry Richards of the Ninety-Third Ohio Infantry* (Cincinnati: Wrightson, 1883), 14; Sam Starling to daughter, November 15, 1862, in Lewis-Starling Collection, WKU.

29. Damon R. Eubank, *In the Shadow of the Patriarch: The John J. Crittenden Family in War and Peace* (Macon, Ga.: Mercer University Press, 2009), 19, 20, 105; Welsh, *Medical Histories of Union Generals*, 82; Beatty, *Citizen Soldier*, 235 (cursing and drinking); Emerson Opdycke to wife, October 14, 1863, folder 9, box 2, Emerson Opdycke Papers, OHS ("has just enough"); Palmer, *Conscientious Turncoat*, 105; Daniel, *Days of Glory*, 131.

30. Fitch, *Annals of the Army of the Cumberland*, 246–48; Louis Garesche, *Biography of Lieut. Col. Julius P. Garesche* (Philadelphia: J. P. Lippincott, 1887), 35, 37, 388–89, 402, 411, 415.

31. Ezra J. Warner, *Generals in Blue: Lives of the Union Commanders* (Baton Rouge: Louisiana State University Press, 1964), 470; *OR* 16, pt. 2: 655; 30, pt. 1: 220 (drinking); 31, pt. 2: 63 (drinking). Palmer, *Conscientious Turncoat*, 100 (Catholic prejudice).

CHAPTER TWO

1. Connelly, *Autumn of Glory*, 13–15, 23 (offensive); *OR* 16, pt. 2: 974; John P. Dyer, *"Fightin' Joe" Wheeler* (Baton Rouge: Louisiana State University Press, 1941), 56. Bragg and Forrest would later exchange sharp words. "Look at Forrest. . . . The man is ignorant, and he does not know anything of cooperation. He is nothing more than a good raider," Bragg openly stated, as quoted in James Lee McDonough, *Chattanooga—A Death Grip on the Confederacy* (Knoxville: University of Tennessee Press, 1984), 32.

2. *OR* 16, pt. 2: 858, 888; 20, pt. 2: 988 (Federal strength); Thomas L. Sneed, "With Price East of the Mississippi," in Robert C. Johnson and Clarence C. Buel, eds., *Battles and Leaders of the Civil War* (4 vols., 1911; rpt. New York: Thomas Yoseloff, 1956), vol. 3: 728.

3. *OR* 16, pt. 2: 997, 1000, 1001.

4. C . C. Henderson, *The Story of Murfreesboro* (Murfreesboro, Tenn.: n.p., 1929), 1–3, 5, 6; Beatty, *Citizen Soldier,* 122; Washington Ives to sister, October 20, 1862, in Jim R. Cabaniss, comp., *Civil War Journal and Letters of Washington Ives 4th Fla. C.S.A.* (n.p.: by author, 1987), 30; William C. Davis, ed., *Diary of a Confederate Soldier: John S. Jackman of the Orphan Brigade* (Columbia: University of South Carolina Press, 1990), 64; *OR* 20, pt. 2: 402; Larry J. Daniel, *Cannoneers in Gray: The Field Artillery of the Army of Tennessee* (rev. ed., Tuscaloosa: University of Alabama Press, 2005), 53.

5. *OR* 20, pt. 2: 1002, 416 (abandons offensive); Bruce S. Allardice, *Confederate Colonels: A Biographical Register* (Columbia: University of Missouri Press, 2008), 74; Connelly, *Autumn of Glory,* 14–16; George Brent Diary, November 4, 6, 1862, Braxton Brag Papers, WRHS.

6. *OR* 16, pt. 2: 385–86; 20, pt. 2: 392–93, 417 ("large accessions"). Brent Diary, November 6, 1862, Bragg Papers, WRHS. About this time, John Jackman of the 9th Kentucky mentioned two "fresh companies" joining his regiment—probably comprised of some of the emigrants Bragg had drafted. Davis, ed., *Diary of a Confederate Soldier,* 64.

7. Christopher Losson, *Tennessee's Forgotten Warriors: Frank Cheatham and His Confederate Division* (Knoxville: University of Tennessee Press, 1989), 21–23, 25, 28, 30, 55–56, 58, 253–54; Ezra J. Warner, *Generals in Gray: Lives of the Confederate Commanders* (Baton Rouge: Louisiana State University Press, 1959), 342; McWhiney, *Braxton Bragg and Confederate Defeat,* 203 ("self-willed"); Welsh, *Medical Histories of Confederate Generals,* 238–39; R. Lockwood Tower, ed., *A Carolinian Goes to War: The Civil War Narrative of Arthur M. Manigault, Brigadier General, C.S.A.* (Columbia: University of South Carolina Press, 1983), 15 (training under Bragg); William C. Davis, *Breckinridge: Statesman, Soldier, Symbol* (Baton Rouge: Louisiana State University Press, 1974), 56–57. 167–70, 228–33, 244–45, 283, 325–28; Woodworth, *Jefferson Davis and His Generals,* 117, 119–20.

8. Craig L. Symonds, *Stonewall Jackson of the West: Patrick Cleburne and the Civil War* (Lawrence: University Press of Kansas, 1997), 52–53, 104–5; Woodworth, *Jefferson Davis and His Generals,* 144; Welsh, *Medical Histories of Confederate Generals,* 40–41; Connelly, *Autumn of Glory,* 31–32; Woodworth, *Jefferson Davis and His Generals,* 130, 196; *OR* 20, pt. 2: 422 (11,000).

9. *OR* 20, pt. 2: 420 (cavalry strength), 446 (Pegram's strength); pt. 1: 970 (Buford's strength).

10. Edward A. Longacre, *A Soldier to the Last: Maj. Gen. Joseph Wheeler in the Blue and Gray* (Washington, D.C.: Potomac Books, Inc., 2007), 2–3, 7, 125–26; Connelly, *Autumn of Glory,* 27.

11. *OR* 20, pt. 2: 421; Frank A. Dennis, ed., *Kemper County Rebel: The Civil War Diary of Robert Masten Holmes, C.S.A.* (Jackson: University and College Press of Mississippi, 1973), 17–18; Ray Mathis, ed., *In the Land of the Living: Wartime Letters by Confederates from the Chattahoochee Valley of Alabama and Georgia* (Troy, Ala.: Troy State University Press, 1981), 39–41; Brent Diary, November 14–17, 1862, Bragg Papers, WRHS; Connelly, *Army of the Heartland,* 47, 49, 112. Oaklands is located at 900 N. Maney Ave. in Murfreesboro and is open to the public.

12. Craig L. Symonds, *Joseph E. Johnston: A Civil War Biography* (New York: W. W. Norton & Co., 1992), 183–84, 187–88; Woodworth, *Jefferson Davis and His Generals*, 176, 180–81.

13. Thomas B. Van Horne, *History of the Army of the Cumberland: Its Organization, Campaigns, and Battles* (2 vols., 1875; rpt. Wilmington, N.C.: Broadfoot Publishing Co., 1988), vol. 1: 207; Henry M. Cist, *The Army of the Cumberland* (1882; rpt. Wilmington, N.C.: Broadfoot Publishing Co., 1989), 77.

14. Nathaniel C. Hughes Jr. and Gordon D. Whitney, *Jefferson Davis in Blue: The Life of Sherman's Relentless Warrior* (Baton Rouge: Louisiana State University Press, 2002), 3, 6–12, 108–10; Daniel, *Days of Glory*, 253–54; Fitch, *Annals of the Army of the Cumberland*, 146, 152–53; Roy Morris Jr., *Sheridan: The Life and Wars of Phil Sheridan* (1992; rpt. New York: Vintage Books, 1993), 97–98.

15. Warner, *Generals in Blue*, 412–13, 100 (Negley); William F. G. Shanks, "Recollections of General Rousseau," *Harper's Magazine* 30 (November 1865): 765, 767; Beatty, *Citizen Soldier*, 235; *Chicago Tribune*, November 10, 1862; Daniel, *Days of Glory*, 192; Palmer, *Conscientious Turncoat*, 100 (Negley's Catholicism).

16. Warner, *Generals in Blue*, 569; Beatty, *Citizen Soldier*, 235 (Wood characterization); John M. Palmer, *Personal Recollections of John M. Palmer: The Story of an Ernest Life* (Cincinnati: Robert Clarke Co., 1901), 140–41; Palmer to wife, March 9, 1862, John Palmer Papers, ILHS (hatred of West Pointers); Albert Castel, *Decision in the West: The Atlanta Campaign of 1864* (Lawrence: University of Kansas Press, 1992), 98; Fitch, *Annals of the Army of the Cumberland*, 174; Welsh, *Medical Histories of Union Generals*, 349–50.

17. Fitch, *Annals of the Army of the Cumberland*, 298–99; *OR* 20, pt. 1: 237–40.

18. Philip L. Shinman, "Engineering and Command: The Case of General William S. Rosecrans 1862–1863," in Steven E. Woodworth, ed., *The Art of Command in the Civil War* (Lincoln: University of Nebraska Press, 1998), 89–93.

19. *OR* 20, pt. 1: 200, 372; pt. 2: 213. *Bucyrus Journal*, January 9, 1863. See also *Daily Commercial Register* (Sandusky), January 7, 1863. My estimate of Union strength is: Right Wing: 18,411, Center, 13,395, Left Wing, 18,412, Pioneers, 1,700, and cavalry, 3,209, for a total of 55,127.

20. Lamers, *Edge of Glory*, 186–87, 189, 192; Hess, *Banners to the Breeze*, 120; *OR* 20, pt. 2: 59.

21. Lamers, *Edge of Glory*, 189–90; *OR* 20, pt. 2: 12 ("they cannot live"), 19, 25 ("visit their friends"), 35 ("will press them"), 35, 49, 53–54, 56, 59, 61, 64, 77, 93; *OR* 20, pt. 2: 135; Chandler to Jenkins, November 4, 1862, Telegrams Sent and Received, October 1862–January 1865, Department of the Cumberland, Entry 916, RG 393.

22. *OR* 20, pt. 2: 59 102; Lamers, *Edge of Glory*, 197 ("The Administration").

23. Rosecrans to brother, November 1, 1862, and Rosecrans to wife, November 24, 1862, as quoted in Francis Philip Varney, "The Men Grant Didn't Trust: Memoir, Memory, and the American Civil War," Ph.D. diss., Cornell University, 2007, 157. In 1865 Rosecrans testified before Congress: "Every mile those rebels traveled toward us . . . was to us an advantage and to them a disadvantage."

24. A. Stanley Camp to wife, December 7, 1862, A. Stanley Camp Letters, 18th Ohio File, SRNBP.

25. Brent Diary, November 28; December 1, 2, 1862, Bragg Papers, WRHS.

26. *Mobile Advertiser & Register* as reported in the *Memphis Appeal*, December 15, 19 (Bragg to Mississippi), 1862; Brent Diary, December 5, 1862, Bragg Papers, WRHS; Dennis, ed., *Kemper County Rebel*, 28–29. On December 9, Mississippian Robert Holmes told his diary: "Late in the evening Gens. Bragg and Johns[t]on and their staffs with them rode through the camps looking over and seeing how the troops are fixed up. It is surposed that he Gen. Johns[t]on will take command of the army now under Gen. Bragg."

27. *OR* 20, pt. 1: 63; pt. 2: 438. Knox to Cellie, December 7, 1862, in Richard M. McMurry, ed., *An Uncompromising Secessionist: The Civil War of George Knox Miller, Eighth (Wade's) Confederate Cavalry* (Tuscaloosa: University of Alabama Press, 2007), 101; James A. Ramage, *Rebel Raider: The Life of General John Hunt Morgan* (Lexington: University Press of Kentucky, 1986), 130–31; George Winchester Diary, December 8, 1862, TSLA; Mathis, ed., *In the Land of the Living*, 41.

28. *Chattanooga Daily Rebel*, December 17, 1862; *Memphis Appeal*, December 13, 18, 1862; *Mobile Advertiser & Register*, December 18, 1862; James Lee McDonough, *Stones River: Bloody Winter in Tennessee* (Knoxville: University of Tennessee Press, 1980), 36; Lynda L. Christ, ed., *The Papers of Jefferson Davis* (12 vols., Baton Rouge: Louisiana State University Press, 1974–2008), vol. 8: 548; Davis, *Jefferson Davis*, 481–83; Davis, ed., *Diary of a Confederate Soldier*, 65; Reuben Searcy to father, December 12, 1862, Reuben Searcy Letters, December 12, 1862, ADAH; James A. Hall to sister, December 14, 1862, James A. Hall Letters, Walter K. Hoover Collection, ADAH; William Mecklinburg Polk, *Leonidas Polk: Bishop and General* (2 vols., New York: Longmans, Green and Co., 1893), vol. 2: 169; Thomas Warrick to wife, December 15, 1862, Thomas Warrick Letters, ADAH; Tower, ed., *A Carolinian Goes to War*, 53; *Daily Rebel Banner*, December 13, 15, 1862, as quoted in McDonough, *Stones River*, 37. See also James Robert Maxwell, *Autobiography of James Robert Maxwell of Tuscaloosa, Alabama* (New York: Greenburg, 1926), 157; Brent Diary, December 12, 14, 16, 19, 1862, Bragg Papers, WRHS; *OR* 20, pt. 2: 447; Connelly, *Autumn of Glory*, 32.

29. Hess, *Banners to the Breeze*, 186 (dinner). *OR* 13: 918–19, 927–28; 20; 13, pt. 2: 412–13, 435, 441, 436, 444, 462, 450; 22, pt. 2: 753, 757, 783–84, 787, 793, 800, 810, 832–33; 52, pt. 2: 398. Archer Jones, *Confederate Strategy from Shiloh to Vicksburg* (1961; rpt. Baton Rouge: Louisiana State University Press, 1991), 116–17, 124; Symonds, *Joseph E. Johnston*, 191–92. See Appendix B.

30. *Atlanta Intelligencer* as quoted in *Charleston Mercury*, October 25, 1862; *Mobile Advertiser & Register* as quoted in *Memphis Appeal*, December 23, 1862; *Huntsville Confederate* as quoted in *Charleston Mercury*, December 30, 1862; *Memphis Appeal*, December 26, 1862; *OR* 20, pt. 2: 448, 457, 458, 462; Brent Diary, December 18, 1862, Bragg Papers, WRHS; Robert Bunting to Editor, December 9, 1862, Robert Bunting Papers, 8th Texas Cavalry File, SRNBP.

31. Ramage, *Rebel Raider*, 134–35.

32. Ibid., 135–37; *OR* 20, pt. 2: 462; *Chicago Tribune*, December 17, 1862.

33. Hall to father, December 22, 1862, James A. Hall Letters, Walter K. Hoover Collection, ADAH; Davis, ed., *Diary of a Confederate Soldier*, 147–50; *Daily Rebel Banner*, December 27,

1862; Cabaniss, comp., *Civil War Journal and Letters of Washington Ives*, 32; *Savannah Republican*, January 10, 1863; E. P. Norman to wife, December 25, 1862, E. P. Norman Letter, 28th Alabama File, SRNBP.

34. *OR* 20, pt. 1: 674; pt. 2: 446. These figures represent "present for duty" strength. One of Pegram's regiments by this time had been assigned to Wharton, and there is evidence that a battalion in the brigade was on detached service, thus reducing the number in that command. The sudden drop in Wheeler's cavalry is unexplained, but perhaps relates to cavalry recuperating horses in the rear. The traditionally accepted number at Stones River is 37,712 versus 43,400. I contend the more accurate number is 37,992 versus 55,127.

35. *OR* 20, pt. 1: 117–18; Bickham, *Rosecrans' Campaign*, 120.

36. *OR* 20, pt. 2: 123–24; Niven, ed., *Salmon P. Chase Papers* 3: 331–32; Rosecrans to Sylvester, December 15, 1862, as quoted in Varney, "The Men Grant Didn't Trust," 157.

37. Fitch, *Annals of the Army of the Cumberland*, 647 (low gauge), 382. *OR* 20, pt. 1: 34; pt. 2: 141 (convoys). M. S. Bright to uncle, December 11, 1862, in Aida C. Truxall, ed., *"Respects to All": Letters of Two Pennsylvania Boys in the War of the Rebellion* (Pittsburgh: University of Pittsburgh Press, 1962), 84.

38. Beatty, *Citizen Soldier*, 193–94; Robert Caldwell to father, December 19, 1862, Robert Caldwell Letters, RBHPL.

39. *OR* 20, pt. 2: 200, 201, 202, 208, 216–18, 236 (Reynolds's strength), 240, 241, 272, 281, 283, 287 (30,000 troops); Daniel, *Days of Glory*, 226–27; Stoker, *The Grand Design*, 240.

40. *OR* 20, pt. 2: 144, 145, 155, 156, 170, 173, 201, 231–32, 233, 234.

41. *Mobile Advertiser & Register* as quoted in *Nashville Dispatch*, December 31, 1862; *Savannah Republican*, January 10, 1863; Spencer B. Talley Memoir, Acc. No. 99078, TSLA.

42. Helm Bush Diary, December 25, 1862, FC; William Rogers Diary, December 25, 1862, SHC ("Captains, Lieutenants"); Reuben Searcy to mother, December 26, 1862, Reuben Searcy Letters, ADAH; Dennis, ed., *Kemper County Rebel*, 35; Leonidas Polk to wife, December 25, 1862, Leonidas Polk Papers, University of the South; Patrick B. O'Neal, "The General's Son: William Joseph Hardee, Jr.," *Confederate Veteran*, March–April 2007, 16–22.

43. Lewis to parents, December 25, 1862, in William D. Dillon, ed., "The Civil War Letters of Enos Barret Lewis, 101st Ohio Volunteer Infantry—Part 1," *Northwestern Ohio Quarterly* 57 (Spring 1985): 57; "G.B.R." to Editor, December 25, 1862, in *Daily Commercial Register*, January 7, 1863; G. Allen Wright to wife, December 25, 1862, in "A Part of Leonard Family History," April 1995, in 49th Ohio File, SRNBP; L. G. Bennett and William M. Haigh, *History of the Thirty-Sixth Regiment Illinois Volunteers, During the War of the Rebellion* (Aurora, Ill.: Knickerbocker and Hodder, 1876), 316–17; A. S. Bloomfield to sister, December 25, 1862, A. S. Bloomfield Letters, A, 1st Ohio Artillery File, SRNBP.

44. Fitch, *Annals of the Army of the Cumberland*, 686, 692; Cist, *The Army of the Cumberland*, 87; *OR* 20, pt. 1: 219–20, 221; Robert King to mother, December 25, 1862, Robert King Letters, 1st Battalion, 15th U.S. File, SRNBP.

45. Bickham, *Rosecrans' Campaign*, 135–39; Fitch, *Annals of the Army of the Cumberland*, 382; David Stephenson, *Indiana's Roll of Honor* (2 vols., Indianapolis: A. D. Streight, 1864), vol. 1: 574.

CHAPTER THREE

1. *OR* 20, pt. 1: 253, 262, 269, 295, 328, 334, 347; pt. 2: 240, 241. Fitch, *Annals of the Army of the Cumberland*, 383–84 (Sheridan and Johnson on direct road). Hughes and Whitney, *Jefferson Davis in Blue*, 131. Bennett and Haigh, *History of the Thirty-Sixth Regiment Illinois*, 318 (black guide).

2. Henry V. Freeman, "Some Battle Recollections of Stone's River," Illinois, *MOLLUS* (1899; rpt. Wilmington, N.C.: Broadfoot Publishing Co., 1992), vol. 3: 230 ("Fairly poured"); William J. K. Beaudot, *The 24th Wisconsin in the Civil War: The Biography of a Regiment* (Mechanicsville, Pa.: Stackpole Books, 2003), 142–43; Benson Bobrick, *Testament: A Soldier's Story of the Civil War* (New York: Simon & Schuster, 2003), 124 ("three days rations"). See also Lars O. Dokken Diary, January 10, 1863, 15th Wisconsin File, SRNBP; Bennett and Haigh, *History of the Thirty-Sixth Regiment Illinois*, 317 (refused tents).

3. *OR* 20, pt. 1: 253 (two miles out), 262, 269; Bobrick, *Testament*, 124 (rain breaks); David Gould and James B. Kennedy, eds., *Memoirs of a Dutch Mudsill: The War Memoirs of John Henry Otto, Captain, Company D, 21st Regiment Wisconsin Volunteer Infantry* (Kent, Ohio: Kent State University Press, 2004), 78 ("a miserable poor village"); "Letter from the Ninety-Fourth," January 26, 1863, *Springfield Republic*, February 4, 1863. Larry K. Smith, *Stone's River Campaign: 26 December 1862–5 January 1863* (2 vols., n.p.: by author, 2008 and 2010), vol. 1: 12, surmises that McCook took multiple routes "to lessen the congestion and confusion." According to Smith (*Stone's River Campaign* 1: 27), Wharton's four guns comprised two from White's Tennessee Battery and two 6-pounders from King's battery, 14th Georgia Artillery Battalion.

4. *OR* 20, pt. 1: 262 (Davis deploys division), 266 (Pinney shells town), 269 (enemy moves on flank), 273 (59th Illinois), 274, 278 (22nd Indiana); Alexander C. Cooper, "Memoirs of the Civil War," 59th Illinois File, SRNBP; Arnold Gates, ed., *The Rough Side of the War: The Civil War Journal of Chesley A. Mosman, 1st Lieutenant, Company D, 59th Illinois Volunteer Infantry Regiment* (Garden City, N.Y.: Basin, 1987), 34 (shots from houses); Bickham, *Rosecrans' Campaign*, 150–51; William E. Patterson Memoir, 38th Illinois File, SRNBP; "From the 101st," in *Bucyrus Journal*, January 30, 1863.

5. *OR* 20, pt. 1: 253 (enemy makes stand), 262 (Hotchkiss and Pinney), 263 (Post carries Heights), 347 (Sheridan moves up); pt. 2: 246–47 (Negley moves up); Robert I. Girardi Jr. and Nathaniel C. Hughes Jr., eds., *The Memoirs of Brigadier General William Passmore Carlin U.S.A.* (Kent, Ohio: Kent State University Press, 1999), 72.

6. Girardi and Hughes, eds., *Memoirs of Brigadier General William Passmore Carlin*, 73 ("each man"); *OR* 20, pt. 1: 252, 262, 263, 284; Lewis W. Day, *A Story of the One Hundred and First Infantry: A Memorial Volume* (Cleveland: W. M. Bayne, 1894), 75–76 ("not a beautiful"); Colonel Heg's report is not in *OR* but may be found in *Wisconsin State Journal*, January 17 1863; J. A. Stewart, "Stone's River," *National Tribune*, August 27, 1885 (6-pounder previously captured); Blegen, ed., *Civil War Letters of Colonel Hans Christian Heg*, 160–61; Bickham, *Rosecrans' Campaign*, 150–52; Dokken Diary, January 10, 1863, and Rollin Olson Letter, December 28, 1862, both in 15th Wisconsin File, SRNBP. According to a Texas Ranger, the

gun captured was from King's battery of the 14th Georgia Artillery Battalion, not White's regularly attached battery. Bunting to Editor, January 6, 1863, in Robert Bunting Papers, 8th Texas Cavalry File, SRNBP. King's battery was later consolidated.

7. *OR* 20, pt. 1: 295, 347; Philip H. Sheridan, *The Personal Memoirs of P. H. Sheridan* (2 vols., 1888; rpt. New York: Da Capo Press, 1992), vol. 1: 115–16; Fitch, *Annals of the Army of the Cumberland*, 384 (casualties).

8. Bickham, *Rosecrans' Campaign*, 156–62; Alexis Cope, *The Fifteenth Ohio Volunteers and Its Campaigns 1861-1865* (Columbus, Ohio: by author, 1916), 229 (tents); *OR* 20, pt. 1: 843 (Wood's brigade). See also *Cincinnati Daily Commercial*, January 5, 1863.

9. Van Horne, *History of the Army of the Cumberland* 1: 221; Bickham, *Rosecrans' Campaign*, 149; Will Carson to parents, January 7, 1863, Will Carson Letters, CWTI Collection, USAMHI ("consistency of"); John R. Woodworth Papers, in James Barnett Papers, WRHS, as quoted in Smith, *Stone's River Campaign* 1: 18.

10. *OR* 20, pt. 1: 633 (attempts to find Thomas), 635 (ten captured), 641 (re-crossed); W. L. Curry, *Four Years in the Saddle: History of the First Regiment Ohio Volunteer Cavalry* (1898; rpt. Jonesboro, Ga.: Freedom Hill Press, Inc., 1984), 83 (one wagon to a regiment); "Letter From Murfreesboro," *Toledo Blade*, January 23, 1863 (arrived 4:00 p.m.).

11. Dr. F. C. Sessions to Editor, *Ohio State Journal*, January 8, 1863 ("miserable little village"); *OR* 20, pt. 1: 221 (four hour estimate), 457 (Wood advances); Noe, ed., *Southern Boy in Blue*, 118 ("should happen"); Palmer, *Personal Recollections*, 142 (mix-up in march); Ebenezer Hannaford, "In the Ranks at Stones River," in Peter Cozzens, ed., *Battles and Leaders of the Civil War* (6 vols., Urbana: University of Illinois Press, 2004), vol. 6: 173 ("only stand").

12. *OR* 20, pt. 1: 622 (four rounds), 627, 631.

13. Ibid., 958, 962, 733–34 (Maney's report); Miller to Cellie, January 10, 1863, in McMurry, ed., *An Uncompromising Secessionist*, 113–14.

14. *OR* 20, pt. 1: 454, 520 (B, 1st Ohio engaged), 623 (half-hour duel), 526 (bayonet charge), 532–33 ("rushed forward"), 543, 446 (casualties); "The Seventh Pennsylvania Cavalry in the Battle of Murfreesboro," *Pottsville Miner's Journal*, January 24, 1863 ("we commenced"); Gilbert C. Kniffen, "Army of the Cumberland and the Battle of Stone's River," District of Columbia, *MOLLUS* (1907; rpt. Wilmington, N.C.: Broadfoot Publishing Co., 1993), vol. 3: 422 (Robert Crittenden); Palmer, *Personals Recollections*, 142–43.

15. Miller to Cellie, January 10, 1863, in McMurry, ed., *An Uncompromising Secessionist*, 114.

16. Wheeler to Brent, December 27, 1862 (Stewart Creek–Nolensville Road connections); Wheeler to Brent, 2:00 p.m., December 26, 1862, "Allen" to Murfreesboro, December 26, 1862, all in folder #6, Brent Diary, December 26, 1862, in Bragg Papers, WRHS. Peter Cozzens, *No Better Place to Die: The Battle of Stones River* (Urbana: University of Illinois Press, 1990), 55, is critical of Wheeler's slow and incomplete reports. Seven hours between dispatches does appear dilatory, even allowing an hour's ride from the Hurricane Creek skirmish line to the Stewart's Creek operator. The sparseness of the information (the dispatches revealed no more information than the men in the ranks had surmised by listening to the cannon fire) leads me to concur with Cozzens that Wheeler "had been unable to develop fully the nature of the Federal advance during the day."

17. *OR* 20, pt. 1: 633.

18. Connelly, *Autumn of Glory*, 45, 47 (multiple approaches); *OR* 20, pt. 1: 896, 900–901; pt. 2: 464 (39th North Carolina). Connelly's claim that Bragg had a fifty-mile front is based upon the extreme cavalry flanks, thus making an admittedly overdrawn line appear even worse. Daniel W. Adams's brigade of Breckinridge's division was temporarily assigned to Cleburne's division at College Grove, referred to as "Harpeth" on some Civil War maps.

19. *OR* 20, pt. 2: 462 (Polk's orders); pt. 1: 911. "The Third Georgia Battalion and the Battle of Murfreesboro," *Columbus Daily Sun*, January 7, 1863 (1:00 a.m.). Longacre, *A Soldier to the Last*, 73. John W. Dubose, *General Joseph Wheeler and the Army of Tennessee* (New York: Neale Publishing Co., 1912), 120. William C. Dodson, *Campaigns of Wheeler and His Cavalry, 1862–1865* (Atlanta: Hudgins Publishing Co., 1899), 50.

20. *OR* 20, pt. 1: 772, 843, 896; William T. Charles, *Recollections of a Christmas During the War* (n.p.: Florence Burch Charles Hall, 1959), 7–8; W. D. Pickett, "Reminiscences of Murfreesboro," *Confederate Veteran* 16 (September 1908): 450; Hardee to Brent, December 27, 1862, 4:00 a.m. dispatch, Bragg Papers, WRHS.

21. *OR* 20, pt. 1: 190.

22. Ibid., pt. 2: 242; Bickham, *Rosecrans' Campaign*, 163.

23. Bickham, *Rosecrans' Campaign*, 179.

24. *OR* 20, pt. 1: 253, 617, 646, 252 (fifty yards); Susan C. Wilson, ed., *Column South: With the Fifteenth Pennsylvania Cavalry* (Flagstaff, Ariz.: J. F. Colton, 1960), 38; J. A. Bedford, *Leaves from a Trooper's Diary* (Philadelphia: by author, 1868), 36, 37.

25. *OR* 20, pt. 1: 254, 295 (4:00 p.m.), 299 (E, 1st Ohio), 302, 319, 325, 328, 345, 843 (Cleburne ordered to withdraw), 897 (sleet); Dodge, "What I Saw at Stone River," 30th Indiana File, SRNBP; Smith, *Stones River Campaign* 1: 26–27; Edwin C. Bearss, "Cavalry Operations in the Battle of Stones Rover," *Tennessee Historical Quarterly* 19 (March 1960): 37.

26. *OR* 20, pt. 1: 254 (bridge destroyed), 647, 896, 901 ("fleeing in confusion"); Cope, *Fifteenth Ohio*, 230 (town ransacked).

27. Bearss, "Cavalry Operations," 38; *OR* 20, pt. 1: 633, 641; David C. Shotts Diary, December 28, 1862, 18th Ohio File, SRNBP.

28. *OR* 20, pt. 1: 190, 242, 247, 372; pt. 2: 249, 257, 272. Smith, *Stone's River Campaign* 1: 34; George H. Puntunney, *History of the Thirty-Seventh Regiment of Indiana Infantry Volunteers* (Rushville, Ind.: Jacksonian Book and Job Department, 1896), 72; Beatty, *Citizen Soldier*, 198–99 (11:00); Mead Holmes, *A Soldier of the Army of the Cumberland: Memoir of Mead Holmes, Jr., Sergeant of Company K, 21st Regiment Wisconsin Volunteers* (Boston: American Tract Society, 1864), 128.

29. Hascall, "Personal Recollections," 156; Hannaford, "In the Ranks," 475; *Nashville Daily Union*, October 2, 1862, and January 9, 1863; Smith, *Stones River Campaign* 1: 36; Wheeler to Brent, December 27, 1862, 2:00 telegram, Bragg Papers, WRHS; *OR* 20, pt. 1: 458.

30. Hascall, "Personal Recollections," 157; *OR* 20, pt. 1: 190 (bridge saved), 458, 459, 464, 465 (Rebel battery), 466 (Alabama Partisan Rangers), 475 (8th Indiana Battery) , 483, 487, 488, 490.

31. *OR* 20, pt. 1: 447, 542–43, 630, 962; Robert L. Kimberly and Ephraim S. Holloway, *The Forty-First Ohio Veteran Volunteer Infantry in the War of the Rebellion* (Cleveland: W. R.

Smellie, 1897), 39 (three Confederate officers); Henry Potter to parents, January 18, 1863, Henry Potter Letters, 4th Michigan Cavalry File, SRNBP. "Allen," Bragg's telegraph operator, had moved his position to Smyrna. In a telegram sent Saturday afternoon, he stated: "Our cavalry report enemy cavalry on north side of railroad. It is probable they are making for this place. It is raining hard here." Allen to Brent, December 27, 1862, Bragg Papers, WRHS.

32. *OR* 20, pt. 2: 247, 249; Smith, *Stone's River Campaign* 1: 43.

33. *OR* 20, pt. 1: 843, 894, 897, 903; Brent Diary, December 27, 1862, Bragg Papers, WRHS; Magee Diary, December 27, 1862, DU.

34. *OR* 20, pt. 1: 762 (fog); pt. 2: 464 (7:30 a.m.). Tower, ed., *A Carolinian Goes to War*, 54–55.

35. *OR* 20, pt. 1: 772 (terrain description), 663 (macadamized road); *The Goodspeed Histories of Maury, Williamson, Rutherford, Bedford & Marshall Counties of Tennessee* (1886; rpt. Columbia: Tenn.: Woodward & Stinson Printing Co., 1971), 811 (Uriah Stone), 816 (N&C Railroad), 817 (Nashville Pike); Sean M. Styles, "Stones River National Battlefield Historic Research Study" (February 2004), 26, 28, SRNBP.

36. *OR* 20, pt. 1: 672–73 (dispositions), 763 (breastworks), 768 (Barret), 762 (Chalmers), 754 (Robertson), 705 (Cheatham); William J. Bass, "A Short Sketch of My Life in the Confederate Army From August 28 A.D. 1861 to May 14, 1863," 12–13, MDAH; Tower, ed., *A Carolinian Goes to War*, 55 ("I do not"); Matt Spruill and Lee Spruill, *Winter Lighting: A Guide to the Battle of Stones River* (Knoxville: University of Tennessee Press, 2007), 25. Modern criticism that Bragg did not entrench is technically true. The decision was apparently made by individual brigade commanders. See McWhiney, *Braxton Bragg and Confederate Defeat*, 348. Colonel Brent wrote: "Bragg has never had much confidence in them [breastworks]—Murfreesboro for example."

37. Bearss, "Cavalry Operations," 25, 52; *Atlas to Accompany the Official Records of the Union and Confederate Armies* (Washington, D.C.: U.S. Government Printing Office, 1891–95), plate 30.2. Pegram's strength was listed in the latest return as 1,800, but the 6th Tennessee Battalion was not present during the battle. I have thus lowered the number to an estimated 1,500.

38. *Mobile Daily Advertiser & Register*, January 4, 1863; Jackman Diary, December 28, 1862, in Davis, ed., *Diary of a Confederate Soldier*, 66 ("a city").

39. *OR* 20, pt. 1: 781 (Breckinridge's disposition), 782 (Wright's battery), 825 (Wayne's Hill occupied). The position of Hanson's brigade in Cozzens's map *(No Better Place*, 75) as being in advance of Breckinridge's line and parallel to Stones River is at variance with both the A. F. Stevenson and Ed Bearss maps, both of which show the brigade on line with the balance of the division. The Stones River Country Club now sits atop Wayne's Hill.

40. I have taken some liberty with the use of "McFadden's Hill," which was not technically named thus.

41. In battle one cannot be strong everywhere, so the question is where can one be weak. Until confirmation of an actual threat on the Lebanon Pike could be confirmed, I contend the place to be weak was on the east bank. Bragg had been in Murfreesboro for six weeks, yet the indication is that he either did not thoroughly examine the terrain or, if so, failed to appreciate prominent features.

42. Bickham, *Rosecrans' Campaign*, 172; Hannaford, "In the Ranks," 175; Joseph W. De-Wees, ed., *Joshua DeWees: His Civil War Diary, Co. D, 97th O.V.I., IV Army Corps, Army of the Cumberland* (Nashville, Ind.: Brown County Printing, 1991), 11; *Philadelphia Weekly Times*, April 12, 1884 ("Does your mother"); McMurry, ed., *An Uncompromising Secessionist*, 116; Thomas J. Wright, *History of the Eighth Regiment Kentucky Vol. Inf.* (St. Joseph, Mo.: Joseph Steam Printing, 1880), 122–23; *OR* 20, pt. 1: 190, 509; Noe, ed., *Southern Boy in Blue*, 119; Smith, *Stone's River Campaign* 1: 51.

43. *OR* 20, pt. 1: 253 (Hazen), 248 (contraband), 246 ("to hear more").

44. Ibid., 303 (forty-one prisoners); pt. 2: 254 (Willich dispatches); Cecil H. Fisher, ed., *A Staff Officer's Story: The Personal Experiences of Colonel Horace Newton Fisher in the Civil War* (Boston: Todd, 1960), 51–52.

45. *OR* 20, pt. 2: 255, 256, 258; Beatty, *Citizen Soldier*, 198–99; Henry Hall to father, December 28, 1862, Henry Ware Hall Papers, 1851–1876, Massachusetts Historical Society ("the boys"); Luther L. Bradley Journal, December 28, 1862, in vol. 3, 51st Illinois Volunteer Infantry, Records of the Adjutant General's Office, 1780s–1917, RG 94, NA.

46. Ann Y. Franklin, comp., *The Civil War Diaries of Capt. Alfred Tyler Fielder 12th Tennessee Regiment Infantry, Company B 1861–1865* (Louisville, Ky.: by author, 1996), 97.

47. Alexander F. Stevenson, *The Battle of Stone's River near Murfreesboro Tenn. December 30, 1862, to January 3, 1863.* (1884; rpt. Dayton, Ohio: Morningside, 1983), 25–26; Mamie Yeary, *Reminiscences of the Boys in Gray, 1861–1865* (Dallas: Smith & Lamar Publishing House, 1912), 361 (Polk and Cheatham).

48. *OR* 20, pt. 1: 710, 720–21; *Philadelphia Weekly Times*, August 9, 1885. I am basing the strength of the 84th Tennessee upon the "Present for Duty Return," March 1863, Palmer Collection, WRHS, which is the earliest number available. The regiment sustained only two wounded during the battle, so this is fairly accurate.

49. Bickham, *Rosecrans' Campaign*, 176 (Bridge's House). *OR* 20, pt. 1: 190, 373, 516 (Parson's), 523, 560 (waist deep); pt. 2: 261, 262, 516, 523–24. Wheeler to Brent, December 29, 1862, 1:30 p.m., Bragg Papers, WRHS.

50. *OR* 20, pt. 1: 448, 459 (Negley seven miles), 501 (Harker), pt. 2: 263 ("in full view").

51. Ibid., 190 ("the enemy"); pt. 2: 264 ("Occupy Murfreesboro"). Palmer, *Personal Recollections*, 143–44.

52. Palmer, *Personal Recollections*, 144. *OR* 20, pt. 1: 448; pt. 2: 264.

53. Palmer, *Conscientious Turncoat*, 104.

54. *OR* 20, pt. 1: 501, 506, 507 ("to seize"), 509–10, 511; Alfred B. Wade, "Hoosier Journal": The Civil War Journal of Alfred B. Wade," in *History of the Seventy-Third Indiana in the War of 1861–1865* (Washington, D.C.: Caqrnahan Press, 1909), 116–17; William R. Hartpence, *History of the Fifty-First Indiana Volunteer Infantry* (Cincinnati: Robert Clarke, 1894), 104–6.

55. Patricia L. Faust, ed., *Historical Times Illustrated Encyclopedia of the Civil War* (New York: Harper and Row, 1986), 726; *OR* 20, pt. 1: 782, 825, 837; Davis, ed., *Diary of a Confederate Soldier*, 67; Rice Graves Report, January 25, 1863, John C. Breckinridge Papers, NYHS.

56. *OR* 20, pt. 1: 191 (Crittenden apologizes), 448 (Harker recalled), 464 (10:00), 501 (casualties); Bickham, *Rosecrans' Campaign*, 179 (log cabin).

57. Dennis, ed., *Kemper County Rebel*, 37; Leigh article in *Memphis Appeal*, January 22, 1863.

58. *Murfreesboro Post*, www.Murfreesboropost.com/news.php?viewStory=4069; Davis, ed., *Diary of a Confederate Soldier*, 67; John L. Spence, *A Diary of the Civil War* (Murfreesboro, Tenn.: Rutherford County Historical Association, 1993), 57; Report of Lieutenant Colonel Samuel K. McSpadden, 19th Alabama, Bragg Papers, WRHS. The National Park Service unsuccessfully attempted to purchase the Cowan property in the 1990s. The land is today owned by the New Haven Baptist Church. The house stood in the present-day baseball diamond. See also J.N.'s article in *Toledo Blade*, January 23, 1863.

59. *Philadelphia Weekly Times*, April 12, 1884.

60. *OR* 20, pt. 1: 254, 263, 347 (Wilkinson's Pike); pt. 2: 255 (Davis at Lane's Store), 266 (three stragglers). Beaudot, *24th Wisconsin*, 145 ("one of the").

61. *OR* 20, pt. 2: 346, 52; pt. 1: 327-29. Joshua C. Ruff, "Fifteenth Pennsylvania (Anderson) Cavalry at Stone River," 84; Allen D. Frankenberry, "The Halt at Overall's Creek," 101; John G. Marshall, "What I Saw of Stone River," 108-9; William W. Blackmar, "The Charge on Infantry at Stone River," 112, 113; William McGee, "With Rosengarten's Battalion at Stone River," 118-19; Simeon Lord Jr., "Major Rosengarten's Last Order to Major Ward," 145; George F. Mish, "From Stone River to Libby," 148-49; Charles H. Kirk, "My Charge at Stone River," 173, all in Allen D. Frankenberry, ed., *History of the Fifteenth Pennsylvania Volunteer Cavalry Known as the Anderson Cavalry in the Rebellion of 1861-1865* (Philadelphia: n.p., 1906). Tower, ed., *A Carolinian Goes to War*, 55-56. C. I. Walker, *Rolls and Historical Sketch of the Tenth Regiment So. Ca. Volunteers in the Confederate States* (1881; rpt. Alexandria, Va.: Stonewall House, 1985), 89-90.

62. *OR* 20, pt. 1: 635, 644 (ambush), 268 ("Prisoners and negroes"); pt. 2: 269. "Third Ohio Cavalry," *Toledo Blade*, January 23, 1863. Bearss, "Cavalry Operations," 46 (Begsley Lane Church).

63. *OR* 20, pt. 1: 254 (dispositions), 269 (5:30), 270 (10:20); Beaudot, *24th Wisconsin*, 145 (rain); Cozzens, *No Better Place*, 68. Cozzens writes that a lack of reliable intelligence kept Bragg from exploiting the gap between Thomas and McCook. Yet, if Bragg did not know about the gap on the night of December 29, he had no one to thank but himself; his line far overlapped Palmer's division.

64. *OR* 20, pt. 1: 663.

65. Ibid., 254. Bickham, *Rosecrans' Campaign*, 182-83. Cozzens (*No Better Place*, 70) characterizes this meeting as being between an "exasperated" Rosecrans and a "chastised McCook," but there is no evidence to suggest that McCook was dressed down.

CHAPTER FOUR

1. *OR* 20, pt. 1: 454, 478, 502, 803, 826, 837, 842; Rice Graves, John C. Breckinridge Papers. NYHS; Cobb to W. F. Thompson, May 17, 1899, as quoted in Smith, *Stone's River Campaign* 1: 80; Hardee to Breckinridge, 9:20, December 30, 1862, John C. Breckinridge Papers, CHS.

2. Bickham, *Rosecrans' Campaign*, 183; *OR* 20, pt. 1: 218-19.

3. *OR* 20, pt. 1: 254 (McCook's report), 238, 352, 360 (all stating 7:00 a.m.); Otis Moody Memoirs, 51illinois.org/moody_st_river.html.

4. *OR* 20, pt. 1: 360, 347, 369, 763; Sheridan, *Personal Memoirs*, 116; Stevenson, *Battle of Stone's River*, 14–15; Moody Memoirs. Roberts sustained forty-two casualties in the day's skirmishing, Patton Anderson thirty-five.

5. *OR* 20, pt. 1: 348, 352, 355 (two hour duel), 356 (3:00 p.m.), 358, 360, 362 (3:00), 363; Stevenson, *Battle of Stone's River* 1: 15–16 (noon at Harding House); Greene letter quoted in Beautot, *24th Wisconsin*, 146.

6. *OR* 20, pt. 1: 724, "Leigh" article in *Memphis Appeal*, January 22, 1863; Magee Diary, December 28, 1862, DU; Charles Roberts to wife, January 7, 1863, Charles Roberts Letters, UMISS (nature of Hardin's wound); Tower, ed., *A Carolinian Goes to War*, 56.

7. *OR* 20, pt. 1: 263 (2:00), 268, 279, 286–87; Hughes and Whitney, *Jefferson Davis in Blue*, 133–34; Stevenson, *Battle of Stone's River*, 18–19; John Russell to sister, January 14, 1863, John Russell Letters, Civil War Times Illustrated Collection, USAMHI; Allen M. Patton to "Dear Friend," January 10, 1863, in Kim C. Cox, comp., *Colonel Grant's Regiment: the 21st Illinois Volunteers from Muster to Stones River in the Letters of Private Allen M. Patton* (San Diego: by author, 1997), 85–86; "Memoir of Charles Barney Dennis, 101st O. V. I.," RBHPL; Nils J. Gilbert to brother, January 4, 1863, in Waldemar Agers, *Colonel Heg and His Boys: A Norwegian Regiment in the American Civil War* (Northfield, Minn.: Norwegian Historical Association, 2000), 72.

8. *OR* 20, pt. 1: 280, 705, 706 (seventy-five casualties), 748, 925, 943; Street to wife, January 3, 1863, J. K. Street Letters, SHC; Blegen, ed., *Civil War Letters of Colonel Hans Christian Heg*, 163; Daniel, *Cannoneers in Gray*, 12.

9. "Volunteer" Letter, January 8, 1863, in *Atlanta Southern Confederacy*, January 13, 1863.

10. David Urquhart, "Bragg's Advance and Retreat," *Battles and Leaders of the Civil War* (4 vols., 1911; rpt. New York: Thomas Yoseloff, 1956), vol. 3: 665 (Bragg on the field). *OR* 20, pt. 1: 665; pt. 2: 469 (initial intelligence reports). W. A. Garner Letter, June 1, 1897, as quoted in David R. Logsdon, *Eyewitnesses at the Battle of Stones River* (n.p.: by author, 2002), 14 (crossing Stones River).

11. *OR* 20, pt. 1: 773, 774, 912, 918–19, 922, 950 (150 yards), 844 (fording), 853, 875, 898, 903; E. J. Wall letter, www.mqamericana.com/Stones_River_2nd_AR_CSA.html.

12. Urquhart, "Bragg's Advance and Retreat," 665 (night council of war); Brent Diary, Bragg Papers, WRHS; Thomas Roy to Breckinridge, 3:30 p.m., December 30, 1862, Breckinridge Papers, CHS; *OR* 20, pt. 2: 469 (1:50 order). Colonel Urquhart is the only direct source of a night council of war. Yet, McCown wrote that he positioned McNair's brigade around sunset of December 30, "before I left for General Bragg's headquarters." *OR* 20, pt. 1: 921. This appears to be a reference to the council of war. If so, it would have occurred in the early evening.

13. McWhiney, *Braxton Bragg and Confederate Defeat*, 363–64 ("like a snowball"); Stanley F. Horn, *Army of Tennessee* (1941; rpt. Norman: University of Oklahoma Press, 1953), 280 ("easy prey"). See also Andrew Haughton, *Training, Tactics, and Leadership in the Confederate Army of Tennessee* (London: Frank Cass, 2000), 109; Cozzens, *No Better Place*, 76; Hess, *Banners to the Breeze*, 194.

14. *OR* 20, pt. 1: 255, 262–63, 295, 309, 319.

15. Ibid., 191–92, 255; Bickham, *Rosecrans' Campaign*, 188 ("Tell General McCook").

16. *OR* 20, pt. 1: 192; pt. 2: 382–83.

17. Ibid., 192.

18. Richard W. Johnson, *A Soldier's Reminiscences* (Philadelphia: J. P. Lippincott, 1886), 210; Richard W. Johnson, "Losing a Division at Stones River," in Cozzens, ed., *Battles and Leaders of the Civil War* 6: 297–98 (meeting with division commanders); Daniel, *Days of Glory*, 205–6.

19. James H. Woodward, "Gen. A. McD. McCook at Stone River," *Military Order of the Loyal Legion of the United States, California/Oregon* (rpt. Wilmington, N.C.: Broadfoot Publishing Co., 1993), vol. 1: 154–55; Sheridan, *Personal Memoirs*, 120; Stevenson, *Battle of Stone's River*, 30–31 (failure to go to front); David S. Stanley, *Personal Memoirs of Major-General D. S. Stanley U.S.A.* (Cambridge, Mass.: Harvard University Press, 1917), 124–25.

20. Samuel J. Seay, "A Private at Stone River," *Southern Bivouac* 4 (August 1885): 156; Worsham, *Nineteenth Regiment*, 68–69; Squire H. Bush Diary, December 30, 1862, FC.

21. Wallace to wife, January 9, 1862, in *Belmont Chronicle*, January 29, 1863; Woodward, "Gen. A. McD McCook," 155.

22. *OR* 20, pt. 1: 664, 958 (1st Tennessee Cavalry), 963, 965 (two guns); Miller to Cellie, January 10, 1863, in McMurry, ed., *An Uncompromising Secessionist*, 118; Wheeler to Brent, December 30, 1862, 4:00 a.m. dispatch, Bragg Papers, WRHS (1,600 men).

23. Miller to Cellie, January 12, 1863, McMurry, ed., *An Uncompromising Secessionist*, 118; Wheeler to Brent, December 30, 1863, 4:00 a.m. dispatch, Bragg Papers, WRHS.

24. *OR* 20, pt. 1: 392, 958, 960, 965; Michael H. Fitch, *Echoes of the Civil War: John Henry Otto, War Memories* (Kent, Ohio: Kent State University Press, 1994), 91–96; Smith, *Stone's River Campaign*, 100 (Espey Church); Wheeler After Action Report, December 31, 1862, Bragg Papers, WRHS.

25. Miller to Cellie, January 12, 1863, in McMurry, ed., *An Uncompromising Secessionist*, 116; *OR* 20, pt. 1: 960; Wheeler's "Near Prestonburg" Report, December 31, 1862, Bragg Papers, WRHS (200 wagons); G. C. Kniffen, "The Battle of Stone's River," in Johnson and Buel, eds., *Battles and Leaders of the Civil War* 3: 614; Bearss, "Cavalry Operations," 114 n13; John D. Innsbrook Diary, December 30, 1862, OHS.

26. McMurry, ed., *An Uncompromising Secessionist*, 118; Wheeler's "Near Prestonburg" Report, December 31, 1862, Bragg Papers, WRHS.

CHAPTER FIVE

1. *OR* 20, pt. 1: 304, 334 (4:00); Wallace to wife, January 9, 1863, in *Belmont Chronicle*, January 29, 1863; Sean M. Syles, "Stones River National Battlefield Historic Resource Study," February 2004, 51, SRNBP. (Gresham House). The Gresham House stood until 1947. A portion of Gresham Lane exists today, but not entirely in the same location.

2. Dodge, "What I Saw at Stone River; *OR* 20, pt. 1: 319 (dispositions), 332, 334 (cedar descriptions), 320 (200 yards). Cozzens (*No Better Place*, 82) concluded that Kirk "continued to display a singular lack of concern for preparedness, and the brigade remained as it had been." All distance estimates are based upon the Stevenson map.

3. *OR* 20 pt. 1: 304; R. B. Stewart, "The Battle of Stones River," in 30th Indiana File, SRNBP; Cope, *Fifteenth Ohio*, 249.

4. *OR* 20, pt. 1: 300 (horses to rear); Woodward, "Gen. A. McD. McCook," 13; Wallace to wife, January 9, 1863, in *Belmont Chronicle*, January 29, 1863; Solon Marks, "Experiences at the Battle of Stones River," Wisconsin *MOLLUS* (1896; rpt. Wilmington, N.C.: Broadfoot Publishing Co., 1993), vol. 2: 390–91; G. H. Stacey to father, January 4, 1863, *Cleveland Plain Dealer*, January 15, 1863 (Johnson rides to Baldwin).

5. Warner, *Generals in Blue*, 271, 565; George Sinclair to wife, May 28, 1863, George Sinclair Letters, 89th Illinois File, SRNBP ("illegitimate son"); Charles D. Stewart, "A Bachelor General," *Wisconsin Magazine of History* 17 (1933): 131–45.

6. *New York Herald*, January 9, 1863.

7. *OR* 20, pt. 1: 948 (150 yards in rear), 934 (4:00 a.m.), 950 (formed line); *SOR* 3: 650 (29th North Carolina); Welsh, *Medical Histories of Confederate Generals*, 250 (Rains sick); Washington L. Gammage, *The Camp, the Bivouac, and the Battlefield; Being a History of the Fourth Arkansas Regiment, from Its Organization Down to the Present Date* (Little Rock: Arkansas Southern Press, 1958), 63 (silence); P. R. Jones, "Recollections of the Battle of Murfreesboro," *Confederate Veteran* 31 (September 1923): 341–42 (rail breastwork and whiskey); David V. Stroud, *Ector's Texas Brigade and the Army of Tennessee 1861–1865* (Longview, Texas: Ranger Publishing, 2004), 76–77.

8. Warner, *Generals in Gray*, 81, 205, 250.

9. *OR* 20, pt. 1: 912, 934, 951 (600–800 yards), 926, 950 (6:00 a.m.), 933, 953 (quick time), 944 ("most terrific fire"), 927, 934, 955 (charge); Henry Watson to parents, January 23, 1863, Henry Watson Letters, 10th Texas Cavalry (dismounted) File, SRNBP; Stroud, *Ector's Texas Brigade*, 78 (Melton).

10. Widney Diary, December 31, 1862, 34th Illinois File, SRNBP; Edwin W. Payne, *History of the Thirty-Fourth Regiment of Illinois Volunteer Infantry* (Clinton, Iowa: Allen, 1902), 43–45 (wounded pickets).

11. William Sumner Dodge, *History of the Old Second Division Army of the Cumberland* (Chicago: Church and Goodman, 1864), 453 (Dodge); Dodge, "What I Saw At Stone River; *OR* 20, pt. 1: 325 (Dysart); *SOR* 3: 626–27; W. H. Carman to father, January 5, 1863, *Cleveland Morning Leader*, January 15, 1863.

12. *OR* 20, pt. 1: 203 (Edgarton censured), 325 (Dysart advances); *SOR* 3: 626–27 (34th ordered to advance), Widney Diary, December 31, 1862, 34th Illinois File, SRNBP.

13. Watson to parents, January 22, 1863, Watson Letters, 10th Texas Cavalry (dismounted) File, SRNBP; Payne, *History of the Thirty-Fourth Regiment*, 44 (fight for flag); Lon Payne to brother, January 31, 1863, Lon Payne Letters, ILSHL; *SOR* 3: 627 (Kirk seeks help).

14. *OR* 20, pt. 1: 927 (11th Texas), 931 (10th Texas), 242 (seven rounds), 301; Dodge, *History of the Old Second Division*, 409 (Edgarton); A. H. Heiner, "The Battle of Murfreesboro Again," *Confederate Veteran* 12 (March 1904): 118 (Burk's death); J. T. Tunnel, "Texans in the Battle at Murfreesboro," *Confederate Veteran* 16 (November 188): 574 (caisson lodged); Bloomfield to parents, January 16, 1863, A. S. Bloomfield Letters, A, 1st Ohio Artillery File, SRNBP (professor of elocution); Carman to father, January 5, 1863, *Cleveland Morning*

Letter, January 15, 1863 ("the front rank"); Alfred King, "Edgarton's Veteran Battery," in James Barnett Papers, WRHS; G. H. Stacy to father, January 4, 1863, in *Cleveland Plain Dealer,* January 15, 1863.

15. Welsh, *Medical Histories of Confederate Generals,* 196; *SOR* 3: 628; *Chicago Tribune,* July 23, 1863.

16. Ted R. Worley, ed., *The War Memories of Captain John W. Lavender C.S.A. They Never Came Back; the Story of Co. F Fourth Arks. Infantry, C.S.A.* (Pine Bluff, Ark.: W. M. Hackett and D. R. Perdue, 1956), 39 ("knocked it"); *OR* 20, pt. 1: 950 (fence), 755 (flag), 953 (30th Arkansas); J. A. Williamson to "Miss Muldrow," January 16, 1863, J. A. Williamson Letters, 2nd Arkansas Mounted Rifles, SRNBP; Worley, ed., *The War Memories of Captain John W. Lavender,* 38–40 (coffee pots).

17. *OR* 20, pt. 1: 329–30 (29th Indiana), 332 (30th Indiana); Dodge, "What I Saw at Stone River," 30; Stevenson, *Battle of Stone's River,* 39 (northwest exodus). See also John A. Templeton to parents, January 9, 1863, "War Time Letters of the Sixties," *Confederate Veteran* 12 (January 1904): 24.

18. *OR* 20, pt. 1: 323, 334, 912, 929; Stevenson, *Battle of Stone's River,* 40; Douglas to Sallie, January 29, 1863; Lucia R. Douglas, ed., *Douglas' Texas Battery, C.S.A.* (Waco, Texas: Smith County Historical Society, 1966), 57. Templeton to parents, January 9, 1863, "War Time Letters," 24. Although the Federal report claims to have recaptured Edgarton's guns, Douglas's letter disputes this. He concluded that the Pennsylvanians ran "in indiscriminate flight." Shortly after the battle, Rosecrans visited the site.

19. Francis A. Kiene Diary, December 31, 1863, in Ralph E. Kiene Jr., ed., *A Civil War Diary: The Journal of Francis A. Kiene, 1862–1865* (n.p.: privately published, 1974),149; George Sinclair to wife, January 6, 1863, George Sinclair Letters, ILSHS; Joseph Buckley to wife, January 8, 1863, Joseph Buckley Letters, 89th Illinois File, SRNBP; Frederick W. Goddard Diary, December 31, 1863, 89th Illinois File. SRNBP; J. S. Rea to Editor, *Madison Daily Courier,* January 27, 1863.

20. *OR* 20, pt. 1: 304 (dispositions), 312 (32nd Indiana), 313–15 (39th Indiana), Smith, *Stone's River Campaign* 1: 134 (Hickey House); "Z" to "Worthy Friend," January 7, 1863, in Joseph E. Reinhart, *August Willich's Gallant Dutchmen: Civil War Letters from the 32d Indiana Infantry* (Kent, Ohio: Kent State University Press, 2006), 130, 134; James M. Cole to "Friend James," January 19, 1863, James M. Cole Letters, ILSHS; Cope, *Fifteenth Ohio,* 234. Exactly what house Fielder referred to is unknown; perhaps a log cabin. His map in the *OR*s makes it clear that it could not have been the Smith House.

21. *OR* 20, pt. 1: 310; George Barry to wife, January 12, 1863, George Barry Letters, 89th Illinois File, SRNBP; Theodore Winfrey to family, January 8, 1863, Theodore Winfrey Letters, 89th Illinois File, SRNBP.

22. Johnson, *A Soldier's Reminiscences,* 213–14 (rides to Baldwin); Reinhart, *August Willich's Gallant Dutchmen,* 142; Dodge, *History of the Old Second Division,* 490 (Gibson); Woodward, "Gen. A. McD. McCook," 156; Kunkler Letter, in Kunkler Papers, Navarro College, Corsicana, Texas. Surgeon Kunkler was with Willich when he was captured and also gives an account. A statue of Gibson stands in front of the Seneca County Courthouse in Tiffin, Ohio.

23. Stewart, "The Battle of Stones River"; Samuel S. Petit to "Friend Brunner," January 20, 1863, in *Wyandot Pioneer*, February 6, 1863; Cope, *Fifteenth Ohio*, 235, 246, 249 (command blunders); Wallace to wife, January 9, 1863, *Belmont Chronicle*, January 29, 1863.

24. Petit to "Friend Brunner," January 20, 1863, *Wyandot Pioneer*, February 6, 1863; Marks, "Experiences at the Battle of Stones River," 391–92.

25. Cope, *Fifteenth Ohio*, 234, 235, 236 (fence); Stewart, "The Battle of Stones River," 13; OR 20, pt. 1: 316 (fence), 317-18 (court-martial).

26. *New York Herald*, January 9, 1863.

27. Henry M. Davidson, *History of Battery A, 1st Ohio Volunteer Light Artillery* (Milwaukee: Daily Wisconsin Steam Printing House, 1865), 61–63; Bloomfield to parents, January 16, 1863, Bloomfield Letters, SRNBP; Stevenson, *Battle of Stone's River*, 39. Captain Goodspeed had been placed under arrest by Willich on December 16, and technically Lieutenant Belding commanded the battery. Goodspeed's postwar conversation with Stevenson makes it clear that he was not present.

28. OR 20, pt. 1: 938–39, 941, 200 (Union strength and casualties); SOR 3: 650; Hess, *Banners to the Breeze*, 200; Hubbard Butler Watson, comp., *Letters Home: Jay Caldwell Butler* (n.p.: privately published, 1930), 57 (blame on Johnson); *New York Times*, January 9, 1863; Stevenson, *Battle of Stone's River*, 44; Anonymous to Editor, January 30, 1863, in *Ohio State Journal*, February 11, 1863 (on Johnson). The "sold again" expression was not a reference to Shiloh, as some have supposed, but the Battle of Perryville, where many soldiers believe that Buell sold them out.

29. *Savannah Morning News*, January 29, 1863.

30. OR 20, pt. 1: 857 (after sunrise), 852 (6,000 veterans), 889 (oblique), 857 (re-alignment), 844, 853 (Loomis fails to advance).

31. Ibid., 875, 889, 893, 853 ("I did not"), 844 ("unaccountably"). The McCulloch House stood near I-24 south of Old Fort Parkway until 2006.

32. Peter Cozzens, "Forgotten Hero: Philip Sheridan Post," *Illinois Historical Journal* 84 (Summer 1991): 75–100; Marsh to wife, January 5, 1863, *Rockford Register*, January 17, 1863; OR 20, pt. 1: 274 (350 yards), 264 (Davis orders withdrawal), 270 (second position), 267 (Pinney), 337 (77th Pennsylvania), 330 (29th Indiana); Stevenson Map (475 yards). Davis claims that he ordered Post's brigade withdrawn from its first position, but Post seems to imply that he gave the order. Post never mentioned the 77th Pennsylvania; he may not have been aware of its presence.

33. Logsdon, *Eyewitnesses at the Battle*, 30.

34. OR 20, pt. 1: 875 (900 strong); "Souvenir of First Reunion of the Fifth Wisconsin Battery," 7, 10-11, 5th Wisconsin Battery File, SRNBP.

35. OR 20, pt. 1: 875, 876, 894 (Darden), 278 ("on and on"), 236 (Pinney wounded), 267 (Pinney withdraws), 271, 273 (guns pulled to safety), 877 ("Boys, do you see"), 882 (Marks wounded), 877 (twenty officers); Smith, *Stone's River Campaign* 1: 179 (one gun disabled); "The 17th Tennessee," *Chattanooga Daily Rebel*, January 27, 1863 (Fitzpatrick); Logsdon, *Eyewitnesses at the Battle*, 30-31; Sidney Post Diary, December 31, 1862, Knox College; David Lathrop, *The History of the Fifty-ninth Regiment Illinois Volunteers* (Indianapolis: Hall

and Hutchison, 1865), 199; George W. Herr, *Episodes of the Civil War in Nine States* (San Francisco: Bancroft, 1890), 125–26.

36. *OR* 20, pt. 1: 275, 892 (twenty minutes), 890–91 (25th Tennessee), 892 (37th Tennessee), 892 (44th Tennessee), 877 (officers lost); Logsden, *Eyewitnesses,* 31; William Sumner Dodge, *A Waif of the War or, the History of the Seventy-Fifth Illinois Infantry* (Chicago: Church and Goodman, 1866), 64–65; *Society of the Seventy-Fourth Illinois Volunteer Infantry: Reunion Proceedings and History of the Regiment* (Rockford, Ill.: W. P. Lamb, 1903), 12–14.

37. Smith, *Stone's River Campaign* 1: 151 (Baldwin); Levi Wagner Reminiscences, Civil War Times Illustrated Collection, USAMHI ("great confusion"); Whalen, *The Fighting Mc-Cooks,* 181 (McCook shaving).

38. *OR* 20, pt. 1: 337 (initial position), 343, 345 (second deployment). Cozzens (*No Better Place,* 95) places the time at 7:00.

39. *OR* 20, pt. 1: 337, 341, 343, 314, 326 (79th Illinois); Dodge, "What I Saw at Stone River," 30th Indiana File, SRNBP (79th Illinois arrives).

40. *OR* 20, pt. 1: 859 (1,700 Arkansans), 857, 912, 944, 945; Hughes, ed., *Liddell's Record,* 180; Welsh, *Medical Histories of Confederate Generals,* 140; John M. Barry, "Reminiscences from Missouri," *Confederate Veteran* 7 (1900): 73 (cursing prisoners); *Rockbridge Register,* January 24, 1863 ("He gave me"). Cozzens (*No Better Place,* 94) asserts that a "passionate argument arose" between McNair and Liddell over deployment, but this appears questionable.

41. *OR* 20, pt. 1: 860, 865 (shelling), 867 (200 yards), 857, 871, 868 (Warren Artillery), 341 (5th Kentucky casualties); "The First Ohio at the Battle of Murfreesboro," *Dayton Journal,* February 2, 1863; Barry, "Reminiscences from Missouri," 73.

42. Dodge, "What I Saw at Stone River."

43. S. P. Simmons to parents, January 9, 1863, *Scioto Gazette,* January 27, 1863; *OR* 20, pt. 1: 341 ("utter amazement"), 343 ("entangled"), 339 (6th Indiana); Matthew Askew Memoir, Askew Family Papers, MS 1380, BGSU; Jermone P. Holcombe to sister and brother, Jermone P. Holcolmb Letters, 6th Indiana File, SRNBP; Charles Briant, *History of the Sixth Regiment Indiana Volunteer Infantry: Of Both the Three Months' and Three Years' Services* (Indianapolis: W. B. Burford, 1891), 194 ("My God").

44. Samuel Hughes to Editor, January 5, 1863, *Dayton Journal,* January 17, 1863; *OR* 20, pt. 1: 337, 346 ("in slow time"); "The First Ohio in the Battle of Murfreesboro," *Dayton Journal,* January 17, 1863; Richards, *Letters,* 11.

45. *OR* 20, pt. 1: 862–63, 865, 877–79, 883–85, 887–88.

46. Warner, *Generals in Gray,* 243–44, 344; Welsh, *Medical Histories of Confederate Generals,* 175, 239; Wood to Hardee, December 26, 1862, S. A. M. Wood Papers, ADAH; *OR* 20, pt. 1: 853 (orderly wounded), 898 (1,100 men), 901 (16th Alabama), 906 (45th Mississippi).

47. Girardi and Hughes, ed., *Memoirs of Brigadier General William Passmore Carlin,* xi, 13–26, 70–71, 75, 138, 250 n34.

48. Ibid., 76; *OR* 20, pt. 1: 280 (Carlin), 284 (101st Ohio), 898 ("Several minutes"), 901, 903 (33rd Alabama).

49. *OR* 20, pt. 1: 280–81, 284; W. H. Williams to James Moore, January 11, 183, *Bucyrus Journal,* February 6, 1863; Girardi and Hughes, eds., *Memoirs of Brigadier General William*

Passmore Carlin, 77; Stevenson, *Battle of Stone's River,* 48; *Bucyrus Journal,* January 16, 30, February 13, 1863; "From the 101st Reg't.," *Tiffin Weekly Tribune,* January 23, 1863.

50. *OR* 20, pt. 1: 281, 282 (101st reduced), 284, 237 (2nd Minnesota Battery), 855 (Key's battery); Day, *Story of the One Hundred and First Ohio Infantry,* 84–87; Dillon, ed., "Civil War Letters of Enos Barret Lewis," 60; Watson, comp., *Letters Home,* 52; Lyman Parcher to "Dear Friends," January 8, 1863, *Bucyrus Journal,* January 30, 1863; Wirt A. Cate, ed., *Two Soldiers: The Campaign Diaries of Thomas J. Key C.S.A. and Robert J. Campbell U.S.A.* (Chapel Hill: University of North Carolina Press, 1938), 3–4; Daniel E. Sutherland, *Reminiscences of a Private: William E. Bevins of the First Arkansas Infantry, C.S.A.* (Fayetteville: University of Arkansas Press, 1992), 113; "From the 101st Regiment," January 23, 1863 ("Stand by") and Jessie Shriver to wife, January 9, 1863, both in *Tiffin Weekly Tribune,* January 23, 1863. I cannot be certain that Key's battery engaged the 2nd Minnesota Battery, but it appears logical. Key claims to have killed the battery captain, which is not true. Captain Pinney, in the nearby 5th Wisconsin Battery, was killed by small-arms fire.

51. *OR* 20, pt. 1: 281 (38th Indiana holds); Stevenson, *Battle of Stone's River,* 53 (captain remains); Blegen, ed., *The Civil War Letters of Colonel Hans Christian Heg,* 165–66; Dokken to parents, Lars O. Dooken Letters, 15th Wisconsin File, SRNBP.

52. Girardi and Hughes, eds., *Memoirs of Brigadier General William Passmore Carlin,* 79.

53. Haughton, *Training, Tactics, and Leadership,* 107; Symonds, *Stonewall of the West,* 110; Grady McWhiney and Perry D. Jamison, *Attack and Die: Civil War Military Tactics and the Southern Heritage* (University: University of Alabama Press, 1982), 85. Concluded Woodworth (*Jefferson Davis and His Generals,* 188): "His [Cleburne's] resourcefulness kept the Confederate drive from stalling at the very outset, but his division, which should have been saved for striking a decisive blow at the climatic moment of the battle, was now fully committed and would not be available to serve as Bragg's 'knockout punch.'"

CHAPTER SIX

1. Cope, *Fifteenth Ohio,* 236; *OR* 20, pt. 1: 305, 310, 312.

2. Cope, *Fifteenth Ohio,* 237.

3. Smith, *Stone's River Campaign* 2: 40; Warner, *Generals in Gray,* 331; Welsh, *Medical Histories of Confederate Generals,* 231–32; Haratio to wife, April 11, 1862, 22nd Alabama File, ADAH ("Certainly a"); *OR* 20, pt. 1: 966 (gallop).

4. *Society of the Army of the Cumberland, 22d Reunion, 1891* (Cincinnati: Robert Clarke, 1892), 170 (Zahm); "Third Ohio Cavalry," *Toledo Blade,* January 23, 1863 ("Never mind boys"); *OR* 20, pt. 1: 636 ("pretty lively"); Martin Buck to "Friend," January 30, 1863, *Highland Weekly News,* February 12, 1863 (Moore's death); "1st Ohio Cavalry," *Norwalk Reflector,* February 17, 1863 (Zahm's fall).

5. *OR* 20, pt. 1: 242, 306, 312, 636, 966; Bearss, "Cavalry Operations," 119. The 39th Indiana had only 200 men at this point, and Gibson's other regiments only a few companies each. Wharton mentions capturing the 75th Illinois in this fight, but it is doubtful that this occurred in this particular action. The 75th was in Post's brigade and counted only 59 miss-

ing (*OR* 20, pt. 1: 207). It is impossible to determine exactly which guns Wharton captured. Davidson (*History of Battery A*, 65) admits losing three guns to the Confederate cavalry, but claims to have recaptured two of them.

6. Gates P. Thruston, "Personal Recollections of the Battle in the Rear at Stone's River, Tennessee," *Military Order of the Loyal Union of the United States* Ohio (1908; rpt. Wilmington, N.C.: Broadfoot Publishing Co., 1993), vol. 6: 225. Modern-day Asbury Lane takes a forty-five-degree turn. There is a small road that continues north at the turn, but soon dead-ends. It was on this small road that Asbury Church was located. I have kept the modern-day name designations. White's grandfather owned the house and in 1948 bloodstains could still be plainly seen in the unpainted upstairs. See Howard W. White, "The Bloodstains," home. carolina.rr.com/civilwarcauses/bloodstains2.htm.

7. Thruston, "Personal Recollections," 227 (Zahm promised); *OR* 20, pt. 1: 637 ("broke and ran"), 640 (cornfield), 641 ("at all hazards"); Curry, *Four Years in the Saddle*, 269.

8. Thruston, "Personal Recollections," 227–28; "From the Battle at Murfreesboro," *Daily Commercial Register*, January 17, 1863; Friend, "The Rout of Rosecrans," *Philadelphia Weekly Times*, August 9, 1885 ("the poorest horsemen").

9. Amandus Silsby to father, February 8, 1863, in Amandus Silsby Letters, 24th Wisconsin File, SRNBP.

10. *Philadelphia Weekly Times*, April 12, 1884.

11. Smith, *Stone's River Campaign* 1: 420–21; 2: 440. *OR* 20, pt. 1: 637, 640, 619 (casualty returns), 597 (Fyffe arrives) 621. Bunting to Editor, January 6, 1863, Bunting Letters, 8th Texas Cavalry Files, SRNBP. Albert G. Hart, "The Surgeon and the Hospital in the Civil War," *Papers of the Military Historical Society of Massachusetts* (Boston: The Society, 1902), vol. 12: 276. Curry, *Four Years in the Saddle*, 83–85, 269. "The First Ohio Cavalry at Murfreesboro," *Perrysburg Journal*, January 21, 1863. B. F. Batchelor to wife, January 10, 1863, in H. J. H. Rugeley, ed., *Batchelor-Turner Letters, 1861–1864: Written by Two of Terry's Texas Rangers* (Austin: University of Texas Press, 1961), 42. "The Seventh Pennsylvania Cavalry in the Battle of Murfreesboro." Claims of thirty-one killed and wounded and a hundred prisoners by the historian of the 1st Ohio Cavalry cannot be substantiated in casualty returns. Wharton stated that the 2nd Tennessee Cavalry was the unit assaulted by the 1st Ohio Cavalry, but the Rangers emphatically claimed the 2nd Georgia Cavalry.

12. *OR* 20, pt. 1: 649 (4th U.S. Cavalry), 627 (3rd Kentucky Cavalry), 967; Bearss, "Cavalry Operations," 120; *Philadelphia Weekly Times*, April 12, 1884; Silsby to father, February 8, 1863, Silsby Letters, 24th Wisconsin File, SRNBP.

13. Thruston, "Personal Recollections," 229; Fitch, *Annals of the Army of the Cumberland*, 210–13 (Long); *OR* 20, pt. 1: 627 (recaptured 250), 649 (hundred prisoners), 967, 853 (five wagons).

14. Thruston, "Personal Recollections," 231.

15. *OR* 20, pt. 1: 968, 958–59, 970.

16. Ibid., 618; Stanley, *Personal Memoirs*, 125. Cozzens (*No Better Place*, 107) criticizes both Stanley and Rosecrans for the incident.

17. *OR* 20, pt. 1: 624, 632.

18. Bearss, "Cavalry Operations," 127–28; Smith, *Stone's River Campaign* 2: 457; OR 20, pt. 1: 618, 624–25, 959–60.

19. Connelly, *Autumn of Glory*, 57–58. Edward G. Longacre, *Cavalry of the Heartland: The Mounted Forces of the Army of Tennessee* (Yardley, Pa.: Westholme, 2009), 183, blames the apparent lack of cavalry coordination on Bragg, who issued no order for cooperation.

CHAPTER SEVEN

1. Losson, *Tennessee's Forgotten Warriors*, 90–91, 96; Hughes, ed., *Liddell's Record*, 119. After the battle, Liddell was talking to Chaplain Charles Quintard about officers under the influence of alcohol. Liddell had heard that Cheatham "was high on his horse." "Yes, I am sorry to say, he was on his low horse, too," the chaplain answered. When asked what he meant, Quintard answered: "Why, he fell, he went under."

2. Connelly (*Autumn of Glory*, 55) believed Polk's last-minute tinkering to be "an unwieldy system," and Woodworth (*Jefferson Davis and His Generals*, 188) called it "ill-advised"; *Savannah Morning News*, January 29, 1863 (Bragg passes).

3. M.H.S. to "Dear Editor," January 2, 1863, in *Daily Register* (Selma, Alabama), January 10, 1863 (2,400); Stevenson, *Battle of Stone's River*, 48–49 (line of advance); John G. Coltart's After Action Report, January 5, 1863, Bragg Papers, WRHS (enemy held opposite); "From a Conversation with Mr. John W. James," Civil War Soldier's Letters, LPR 78, ADAH. Loomis is buried in the Wetumpka, Alabama, city cemetery.

4. OR 20, pt. 1: 288; Warner, *Generals in Blue*, 448–49; Reid, *Ohio in the War* 1: 919–20.

5. Wier to mother, January 8, 1863, James K. Wier Letters, 25th Illinois File, SRNBP; OR 20, pt. 1: 288 ("mowed down"), 292 (150 yards), 268 (Carpenter killed); "M.H.S." to "Dear Editor," January 2, 10, 1863, in *Selma Daily Reporter*, January 10, 1863 (Loomis injured); 1860 Alabama Census, U.S. Census Bureau, microfilm reel M653–15, p. 214 (Coltart & Son); Ambrose Doss to wife, January 19, 1863, 19th Alabama File, SRNBP; Stevenson, *Battle of Stone's River*, 50 ("We will plant").

6. 26th Alabama After Action Report, Bragg Papers, WRHS; A. F. Flewellen, "Battle of Murfreesboro," undated article in *Columbus Daily Sun*, Newspaper File, SRNBP. Apparently mistaking the Federal counter-attack as fresh troops, Coltart wrote: "The enemy now advanced with reinforcements and the brigade fell back in some confusion." See Coltart After Action Report, Bragg Papers, WRHS.

7. OR 20, pt. 1: 324 (7:15), 364; Robert Chivas Letter, January 5, 1863, in Alexander Mitchell Papers, SHSW; Beaudot, *24th Wisconsin Infantry*, 150–56 (flag bearer).

8. *Portrait and Biographical Album of Henry County, Iowa* (Chicago: Acme Publishing Co., 1888), 279–81.

9. OR 20, pt. 1: 348 (simultaneous with Woodruff), 350 (fifty yards); Sheridan, *Personal Memoirs* 1: 121; Stevenson, *Battle of Stone's River*, 49–50. Coltart reported that, after his repulse, the Alabamians made a second sortie, but someone in the 19th Alabama, it was never determined exactly who, gave the order to fall back, thus foiling the attempt. See Coltart After Action Report, Bragg Papers, WRHS.

10. Ed Abbott Reminiscences, 4th Indiana Battery File, SRNBP; John Mitchell to mother, January 8, 1863, John Mitchell Letters in Alexandra Mitchell Papers, SHSW; Beaudot, *24th Wisconsin*, 158; John Mitchell, *In Memoriam: Twenty-Fourth Wisconsin Infantry* (Milwaukee: n.p., 1906), 27; *OR* 20, pt. 1: 857, 888 (argued over body). General Hardee expressed outrage that his soldiers had stolen Sill's boots and pants. (*Rockbridge Register*, January 24, 1863).

11. Major John Marrast, 22nd Alabama After Action Report, Bragg Papers, WRHS; "T" to "Dear Editor," January 28, 1863, in *Mobile Advertiser & Register*, February 14, 1863 (Austin).

12. *OR* 20, pt. 1: 709 (1,773 infantry); John Henry King Memoir in Ben K. Green Papers, AR 326, UT-Arlington (Smith's wife); Warner, *Generals in Gray*, 315; Seay, "A Private at Stone River,"158 ("You'll soon"); Thomas R. Ford to Ruth, December 28, 1920, 12th Tennessee File, SRNBP.

13. *OR* 20, pt. 1: 687 (every horse), 706, 746, 747, 748; "Private M'Dearman at Murfreesboro," *Confederate Veteran* 9 (1901): 306; Van Horne, *History of the Army of the Cumberland* 1: 233 (casualties); Hiram Clark Moorman, *The Moorman Memorandum* (Somerville, Tenn.: The Society, 1959), vol. 3. See also A. J. Vaughn, *Personal Record of the Thirteenth Regiment, Tennessee Infantry* (Memphis: S. C. Toof & Co., 1897), 24–25. Cozzens (*No Better Place*, 113–14) states that the 25th Illinois and 81st Indiana launched a second counter-attack that drove the Confederates back. Perhaps, but for me the record is inconclusive.

14. Losson, *Tennessee's Forgotten Warriors*, 82.

15. Tower, ed., *A Carolinian Goes to War*, ii, ix–x, 58 (2,200 men); Welsh, *Medical Histories of Confederate Generals*, 153 (wounds); Warner, *Generals in Gray*, 210–11.

16. Allardice, *Confederate Colonels*, 275; Charles, *Recollections of a Christmas During the War*, 24.

17. *OR* 20, pt. 1: 706 (8:00), 355 (4th Indiana Battery), 359 ("fresh brigade"); C. Knight Aldrich, ed., *Quest for a Star: The Civil War Letters and Diaries of Colonel Francis T. Sherman of the 88th Illinois* (Knoxville: University of Tennessee Press, 1999), 27–33, 56. Major George W. Chandler of the 88th Illinois happened to be riding in front of Houghtaling's and Hescock's batteries when one of the guns was depressed too low and accidentally fired a cannonball through his mount. Stevenson, *Battle of Stone's River*, 54.

18. Aldrich, ed., *Quest for a Star*, 22; William McGregor to Friend, February 9, 1863, William McGregor Letters, Pearce Collection, Navarro College, Corsicana, Texas.

19. Stevenson, *Battle of Stone's River*, 54 (Manigault admitted); W. B. Dennett After Action Report, 24th Alabama, January 11, 1863, Bragg Papers, WRHS.

20. *OR* 20, pt. 1: 744, 746, 747 ("Having rested"); Fielder Diary, December 31, 1863, in Franklin, comp., *Civil War Diaries of Capt. Alfred Tyler Fielder*, 98. Carlin's report clearly stated that Woodruff's brigade departed first, thus exposing his left flank. Both Davis and Woodruff claim just the opposite. I believe that Carlin withdrew first. Polk (*OR* 20, pt. 1: 687) wrote that Vaughn attacked "in conjunction with Colonel Coltart," but brigade and regimental reports mention no such coordination.

21. *OR* 20, pt. 1: 743, 744, 749; Warner, *Generals in Gray*, 348–49; John Henry King Memoir in Ben K. Green Papers, AR 326, UT-Arlington).

22. *OR* 20, pt. 1: 289, 292, 293 ("fresh troops").

23. *OR* 20, pt. 1: 292, 348, 366; Stevenson, *Battle of Stone's River*, 52 (Miller). Lieutenant Colonel John Weber of the 15th Missouri claimed that his Missourians got as far as Woodruff's original position, based upon the fact that he recaptured a 10-pounder Parrott rifle from Carpenter's battery. He did not know, however, that the 25th Illinois had previously pulled the gun from the front line and abandoned it in the woods. See *OR* 20, pt. 1: 292.

24. *OR* 20, pt. 1: 362; Azra Bartholomew to Frank, January 5, 1863, Azra Bartholomew Letters, 21st Michigan File, SRNBP.

25. Tower, ed., *A Carolinian Goes to War*, 57; *OR* 20, pt. 1: 734, 737 (8:00).

26. T. M. Eddy, *Patriotism of Illinois* (2 vols., Chicago: Clarke, 1865), vol. 2: 382; Fitch, *Annals of the Army of the Cumberland*, 250; *OR* 20, pt. 1: 348, 370; Stevenson, *Battle of Stone's River*, 55–57; Dwight A. Lincoln letter in Lydia M. Post, ed., *Soldiers' Letters from Camps, Battlefield and Prison. U.S. Sanitary Commission* (U.S. Sanitary Commission, 1865), 88th Illinois File, SRNBP; Thomas J. Maxwell to Uncle, January 19, 1863, *Delaware Gazette*, February 6, 1863.

27. Dennett After Action Report, Bragg Papers, WRHS; *OR* 20, pt. 1: 348, 370, 770 (Waters); Stevenson, *Battle of Stone's River*, 57 (fired too high).

28. Sheridan, *Personal Memoirs* 1: 122; Stevenson, *Battle of Stone's River*, 55; *OR* 20, pt. 1: 348, 364. The ridge used by Sheridan's artillery still survives, but is on private property. By driving on modern-day Wilkinson Pike, turning south on Van Cleve, and then turning right onto Harding Place, it may be seen by driving to the dead end and looking south. Spruill's map (*Winter Lightning*, 96) shows Davis's division supporting Sheridan's second line, with Woodruff to the right of Greusel, Carlin supporting Woodruff, and Post on Gresham Lane. While thousands of troops were in motion, this may leave a somewhat false impression. All division and brigade reports make it clear that Davis did not stop and support Sheridan in his second position. See *OR* 20, pt. 1: 264, 271, 289.

29. Bennett and Haigh, *History of the Thirty-Sixth Regiment Illinois*, 330–31; "The Harding House," *Rutherford County Historical Society* (Summer 1984): 1–2, 4, 6. The piano became a spectacle to visiting northern veterans in postwar years. It was photographed, made into a postcard, and billed as the "wounded piano."

30. *OR* 20, pt. 1: 706 (Manigault repulsed), 734, 736. Seay, "A Private at Stone River," 158. Cozzens (*No Better Place*, 118) suggests that the two batteries in question were Houghtaling's and Bush's, the last at Sheridan's second defensive position at the Harding House. I believe that Bush fell back to Hescock's position on the ridge, but may not have been engaged there. All Confederate reports speak of only two batteries.

31. Seay, "A Private at Stone River," 159; Sam R. Watkins, *"Co. Aytch": A Side Show of the Big War* (1962; rpt. New York: Touchstone Book, 1990). 61–62; Stevenson, *Battle of Stone's River*, 60–61 (Roberts).

32. *OR* 20, pt. 1: 735, 737–38, 740; Seay, "A Private at Stone River," 159; Stevenson, *Battle of Stone's River*, 62 (Hooker). The James House survives to this day, although it was badly damaged by fire in 2003.

33. *OR* 20, pt. 1: 706, 742 (two hundred rounds); Stevenson, *Battle of Stone's River*, 64 (42nd Illinois); Thomas H. Malone, *Memoir of Thomas H. Malone* (Nashville: Baird-Ward,

1928), 146–47; Magee Diary, December 31, 1862, DU. Even a Federal report made mention of the Rebel battery at the kiln. See *OR* 20, pt. 1: 370.

34. Stevenson, *Battle of Stone's River*, 60; Watkins, *Co. Aytch*, 62.

35. Andrew Galliford, "Van Cleve Lane: Recovering a Trace of History," Middle Tennessee State University Study, April 23, 1991 (Wilkinson Pike); Wilson Vance, "A Man and a Boy at Stone River," *Blue & Gray* 1 (1893), copy in 21st Ohio File, SRNBP; William H. Newlin, *A History of the Seventy-third Illinois Infantry Volunteers, and in Many Battles of the War, 1861–1865* (Springfield: n.p., 1890), 129–30, 171–72; Bennett and Haigh, *History of the Thirty-Sixth Regiment Illinois*, 344; Sutherland, ed., *Reminiscences of a Private*, 115; Sheridan, *Personal Memoirs* 1: 122–23 ("no matter what"); Stevenson, *Battle of Stone's River*, 55; *OR* 20, pt. 1: 349.

36. Sheridan, *Personal Memoirs* 1: 113 (Schaefer); S. F. Hoskinson, "Stone's River," *National Tribune*, November 27, 1884 (suspected murder of Schaefer); Newlin, *A History of the Seventy-third Illinois*, 126 (Pressman's speech); *OR* 20, pt. 1: 366, 357 (Greusel on Schaefer's right), 361, 362 (21st Michigan), 364, 359 (36th Illinois withdraws), 289 (Woodruff withdraws), 292, 293; Stevenson, *Battle of Stone's River*, 58–59.

37. *OR* 20, pt. 1: 348, 353, 354, 370. Sheridan's batteries were placed roughly along modern-day Van Cleve. Roberts's two regiments stretched diagonally between Van Cleve and the Wilkinson Pike, all of which was heavily wooded at the time of the battle.

38. *OR* 20, pt. 1: 353, 354 (artillery positions), 370 (27th Illinois).

39. Ibid., 846 (Darden and Helena Artillery), 898, 901 (11:00), 904–6 (seventy-five yards), 895 (Darden); Stevenson, *Battle of Stone's River*, 59–60. Some Confederate reports mention Sheridan's artillery as being "on an eminance." This seems to imply that his batteries were still on the ridge northwest of the Harding House. It seems questionable, however, that the infantry would have moved to the third position and left the batteries without support. Perhaps the attack took place *during* Sheridan's withdrawal. Other information implies that the artillery had already withdrawn from the ridge. The truth will never be known. The location of the Blanton House today is at the northeast corner of Wilkinson Pike and Blanton's Point, on the edge of the SRNBP.

40. *OR* 20, pt. 1: 775, 846, 853 (Polk).

41. Ibid., 878 (garden fence and McReynolds), 879, 884, 889, 891 (second assault), 892 (37th Tennessee routed), 892–93 (prisoners).

42. Ibid., 856, 878, 895, 926 (Humphreys); Stevenson, *Battle of Stone's River*, 62.

43. James S. Jackson Deposition, January 1888, and Harley S. Sherwood Deposition, 1888, both in Battery C, 1st Illinois Artillery File, SRNBP.

44. *OR* 20, pt. 1: 689, 764; Warner, *Generals in Gray*, 7; Patton Anderson to wife, January 8, 11, 1863, in Margaret A. Uhler, ed., "Civil War Letters of Major General James Patton Anderson," *Florida Historical Quarterly* 56 (October 1977): 156, 159.

45. *OR* 20, pt. 1: 763; C. I. Walker to wife, January 15, 1863, C. I. Walker Letters, 10th South Carolina File, SRNBP.

46. Stevenson, *Battle of Stone's River*, 64.

47. Walker to wife, January 15, 1863, Walker Letters, 10th South Carolina File, SRNBP. 10th South Carolina After Action Report, January 12, 1863; 24th Mississippi After Action

Report, January 16, 1863; and 45th Alabama After Action Report, January 16, 1863, all in Bragg Papers, WRHS.

48. Tower, ed., *A Carolinian Goes to War*, 56–57; Dennett After Action Report, Bragg Papers, WRHS (Hugar); *OR* 20, pt. 1: 706 (second sortie); Malone, *Memoir*, 138–40 (duel).

49. William E. Garlock to "Dear Abe," January 7, 1863, William E. Garlock Letters, 42nd Illinois File, SRNBP; Stevenson, *Battle of Stone's River*, 65.

50. 30th Mississippi After Action Report, January 16, 1863, Bragg Papers, WRHS; J. E. Robuck, *My Own Personal Experiences and Observation as a Soldier in the Confederate Army During the Civil War, 1861–1865* (1911; rpt. Memphis: Burke's Book Store, 1970), 44–45; *OR* 20, pt. 1: 764; John T. Gibson, *History of the 78th Pennsylvania Volunteer Infantry* (Pittsburgh: Pittsburgh Print Co., 1905), 180. The James L. Autry Papers are located in the Andrew Forest Muir Papers, Fondren Library, Rice University. The field over which the 27th and 29th Mississippi met such a bloody repulse is within the SRNBP at the northwest corner of Thompson Lane and Wilkinson Pike. Thompson Lane did not exist at the time of the battle, and the field extended past the road. At this writing, it is the plan of park officials to eventually have Hescock's and Bush's knoll position and the field in its front as one of the interpretive stops. Robuck, in his postwar writings, wrongly declared that the regiments making the charge were the 29th and 30th Mississippi.

51. *OR* 20, pt. 1: 709 (1,635), 724 (Stewart advances), 727–28 (six wounded); Sam Davis Elliott, *Soldier of Tennessee: General Alexander P. Stewart and the Civil War in the West* (Baton Rouge: Louisiana State University Press, 1999), 9–11, 27, 14–16, 286–87.

52. *OR.*, 20, pt. 1: 732, 768. The position would today be south of Medical Center Parkway, in the field east of Wilkinson Pike.

53. Stevenson, *Battle of Stone's River*, 67–70; *OR* 20, pt. 1: 349, 370; Sheridan, *Personal Memoirs*, 124; James M. McCarty to brother, February 7, 1863, James S. McCarty Letters, 27th Illinois File, SRNBP.

54. *OR* 20, pt. 1: 242 (3,436 rounds), 349 (Taliaferro killed), 354 (guns abandoned), 357, 366, 368 (ammunition exhausted); Matt and Lee Spruill, *Winter Lightning: A Guide to the Battle of Stones River* (Knoxville: University of Tennessee Press, 2007), 98, 100 (dispositions), 103 ("we would all"); S. Emmanuel, "An Historical Sketch of the Georgetown Rifle Guards," in Walker, *Rolls and Historical Sketch*, 17–18; *Jacksonville Journal*, January 29, February 12, 1863; Moody Memoirs. Two of the abandoned guns may be seen today at the Stones River National Military Park.

55. *OR* 20, pt. 1: 727–30; 24th Mississippi After Action Report, January 15, 1863, Bragg Papers, WRHS; Dennis, ed., *Kemper County Rebel*, 38.

56. Anderson to wife, January 8, 1863, Uhler, ed., "Civil War Letters of Major General James Patton Anderson," 156–57.

57. Welsh, *Medical Histories of Confederate Generals*, 33–34; *Jacksonville Journal*, January 29, February 12, 1863.

58. *OR* 20, pt. 1: 407, 423 (1,800-man), 426 (11th Michigan), 428, 353 (Hescock), 355 (Bush); Tower, ed., *A Carolinian Goes to War*, 57; "Palmetto" article in *Columbia Daily Guardian*, January 28, 1863 ("that was rightly"); Daniel B. Weber, ed., *From Michigan to Murfreesboro: The Diary of Ira Gillaspie of the Eleventh Michigan Infantry* (Mt. Pleasant: Central

Michigan University Press, 1965), 43; J. W. Slater, "Narrow Escapes: Interesting War Experiences No. 28," *Ironton Register*, May 26, 1887; James H. Haynie, *The Nineteenth Illinois: A Memoir of a Regiment of Volunteer Infantry* (Chicago: Donahoe and Co., 1912), 187–88.

59. Warner, *Generals in Blue*, 324; *OR* 20, pt. 1: 431–32.

60. *OR* 20, pt. 1: 431–32, 411; Theodore W. Blackburn, *Letters From the Front: A Union Preacher's Regiment (74th Ohio) in the Civil War* (n.d.; rpt. Dayton, Ohio: Morningside Bookshop, 1981), 29; John H. Bolton Journal, December 31, 1863, BGSU; Warner to "Dear Friends," February 10, 1863, Liberty Warner Letters, BGSU; Robert H. Caldwell to father, January 3, 1863, Robert H. Caldwell Letters, BGSU; Jacob Adams, *Diary of Jacob Adams, Private in Company F, 21st OVI* (Columbus, Ohio: F. J. Heer, 1930), 19; "Letter from the 21st Ohio Regiment," *Perryville Miner's Journal*, February 4, 1863 ("fought them"); John C. Leanard to E. K. Kleckner, January 6, 1863, John C. Leanard Letters, 21st Ohio File, SRNBP (Neibling's wound); Silas S. Canfield, *History of the 21st Regiment Ohio Volunteer Infantry In the War of the Rebellion* (Toledo, Ohio: Vrooman, Anderson, and Bateman, 1893), 74 ("My God boys").

61. *OR* 20, pt. 1: 432, 433, 437–38, 439, 411–12 (Ellsworth); Gibson, *History of the 78th Pennsylvania*, 53; Vance, "A Man and a Boy at Stone River," copy in 21st Ohio File, SRNBP ("Rally here"); Samuel A. Linton Memoir, BGSU; George T. Squire to parents, January 9, 1863, George T. Squire Letters, 21st Ohio File, SRNBP; *Jeffersonian Democrat*, January 23, 1863.

CHAPTER EIGHT

1. M. B. Butler, *My Story of the Civil War and the Under-ground Railroad* (Huntington, Ind.: United Brethren Publishing Establishment, 1914), 264 ("Boys, be careful"); *OR* 20, pt. 1: 460 (distant firing heard), 574 (7:00), 583, 592 (8:00 a.m.), 607 (Price crosses); *Fort Wayne Weekly Sentinel*, January 31, 1863 (Rousseau addresses troops); Lamers, *Edge of Glory*, 217–18 ("Goodbye, General"); Captain Oscar Mills to father, *Western Reserve Chronicle*, January 21, 1863; Noe, ed., *Southern Boy in Blue*, 121. Bickham incorrectly stated that, when Rosecrans met Wood, the division commander had a bandaged foot and crutches strapped to his saddle. Wood was not wounded until 10:00 a.m.

2. *OR* 20, pt. 1: 193; John Lee Yaryan, "Stone River," *Military Order of the Loyal Legion of the United States. Indiana* (1898; rpt. Wilmington, N.C.: Broadfoot Publishing Co., 1991), 169 (Rosecrans description); Bickham, *Rosecrans' Campaign*, 210 (Boney); Daniel, *Days of Glory*, 152, 154–55 (McCook at Perryville).

3. Yaryan, "Stone River," 168; Bickham, *Rosecrans' Campaign*, 209.

4. Hess, *Banners to the Breeze*, 212–13. For criticism of Rosecrans see Cozzens, *No Better Place*, 129–30. While conceding that Rosecrans helped restore Union morale, Cozzens concluded that "his frenzy completely overcame his better judgment," and that his actions were "the groping to do something, anything, of a man too stunned to seize control of events." For contemporary criticism of Rosecrans's overexposure and meddling see *OR* 16, pt. 1: 578.

5. *OR* 20, pt. 1: 193 (Rosecrans's order), 460 (Wood's movement suspended), 467 ("The most terrible"), 502 (Rosecrans orders Harker), 574 (Van Cleve recalled), 583 (Beatty recalled), 597 (Fyffe recalled), 607 (Price assigned to ford); Wilbur F. Hinman to "Dear Friends," January

11, 1863, Wilbur F. Hinman Letters, WRHS ("For two long"); Noe, ed., *Southern Boy in Blue*, 121; "Stones River National Battlefield History Research Study," 48, SRNBP (McFadden House).

6. "Mack" to "Friend Allen," *Ohio State Journal*, January 17, 1863. For a slightly different version of the exchange, see Kniffen, "The Battle of Stone's River," 623. I have used the "Mack" version because of its earlier date.

7. *OR* 20, pt. 1: 652. J. G. Parkhurst, "Recollections of Stone's River," *Military Order of the Loyal Legion of the United States, Michigan* (1890; rpt. Wilmington, N.C.: Broadfoot Publishing Co., 1991), vol. 1: 302–3 (two or three riders); John G. Parkhurst to sister, January 7, 1863, John G. Parkhurst Letters; Thomas J. Conley to sister, January 3, 1863, Thomas J. Conley Letters; John C. Love to parents, January 7, 1863, John C. Love Letters, all in Bentley Historical Library, UMI. McDonough, *Stones River*, 112 (Parkhurst previously captured). John H. Carpenter Diary, December 31, 1862, 9th Michigan File, SRNBP. Charles Bennett, *Historical Sketches of the Ninth Michigan Infantry* Coldwater, Mich.: Daily Courier, 1913), 28.

8. Walker bio, www.tshaonline.org/handbook/online/articlesWW/fwa21.html; *OR* 20, pt. 1: 442 (Walker), 654 (Burke).

9. Mark W. Johnson, *That Body of Brave Men: The U.S. Regular Infantry and the Civil War in the West* (New York: Da Capo, 2003), 272, 274–75; Reuben Jones to sister, January 9, 1863, Reuben Jones Letters, 19th U.S. File, SRNBP; Luke Lyman Letter, January 8, 1863, Luke Lyman Letters, 18th U.S. File, CCNBP; *OR* 20, pt. 1: 377–78, 379 (Starkweather), 386 (marching an hour), 388 (counter-marching).

10. Lamers, *Edge of Glory*, 227.

11. Daniel, *Days of Glory*, 189, 240 (Shepherd); *OR* 20, pt. 1: 200 (1,566), 394 (Sutherland), 399–401; Girardi and Hughes, eds., *Memoirs of Brigadier General William Passmore Carlin*, 80; "R.G.H." to Editor, January 4, 1863, January 26, 1863, *Cleveland Plain Dealer;* William J. Carson to mother, January 7, 1863, William J. Carson Letters, 15th U.S. File, SRNBP; Frederick Phisterer, *Association of Survivors, Regular Brigade, Fourteenth Army Corps, Army of the Cumberland* (n.p., n.d.), 6.

12. *OR* 20, pt. 1: 378; Alfred Pirtle, "Stone's River Sketch," *Military Order of the Loyal Union of the United States, Ohio* (1908; rpt. Wilmington, N.C.: Broadfoot Publishing Co., 1991), vol. 6: 98–99.

13. Johnson, *That Brave Body of Men*, 279–80.

14. *OR* 20, pt. 1: 375, 405; Hosea, "Regular Brigade," 341.

15. *OR* 20, pt. 1: 200 (1,583), 383, 387, 388; Daniel F. Griffith to wife, January 9, 1863, Daniel F. Griffith Letters, 38th Indiana File, SRNBP.

16. Pirtle, "Stone's River Sketches," 99; B. F. Scribner, *How Soldiers Were Made; or the War As I Saw It* (1887; rpt. Huntington, W.Va.: Blue Acorn Press, 1995), 79.

17. Welsh, *Medical Histories of Union Generals*, 24; Beatty, *Citizen Soldier*, 201; Francis M. Carlisle Autobiography, 42nd Indiana File, CCNBP (wild turkeys); Spillard Horrall, *History of the 42nd Indiana Volunteer Infantry* (Chicago: Horrall, 1892), 167.

18. Kirk C. Jenkins, *The Battle Rages Higher: The Union's Fifteenth Kentucky Infantry* (Lexington: University of Kentucky Press, 2003), 250.

19. *OR* 20, pt. 1: 913, 938, 939, 941–43; *Official Records Supplement* 3: 650.

20. *OR* 20, pt. 1: 938, 941, 942; William P. McDowell, "The Fifteenth Kentucky," *Southern Bivouac* 5 (1886): 250; Horrall, *History of the Forty-Second Indiana*, 167; "The Third Georgia Battalion and the Battle of Murfreesboro," *Columbus Daily Sun*, January 14, 1863.

21. *OR* 20, pt. 1: 189, 240, 913, 938, 939, 941–43; "R.G.H." to Editor, January 4, 1863, January 26, 1863, *Cleveland Plain Dealer*; William J. Carson to mother, January 7, 1863, William Carson Letters, 15th U.S. File, SRNBP. The field mentioned by Carson is very possibly Tour Stop 3 at the SRNBP. Park officials, who identify it as a cottonfield, believe it was the one through which Rains's brigade advanced, but they privately concede they are not certain.

22. *OR* 20, pt. 1: 560, 567, 570; Hannaford, "In the Ranks," 181–82; C. C. Bowman, "Stone's River: How Grose's Brigade Helped Stay the Onset of the Rebels," *National Tribune*, November 6, 1884; Robert King to mother, January 8, 1863, Robert King Letters, 15th U.S. File, SRNBP.

23. *OR* 20, pt. 1: 854; William R. Stuckey to wife, January 20, 18633, in Jeanne Mc-Cracken Everett, *The McCracken Family Honor Roll of Civil War Soldiers* (South Bend: by author, 1986), 57; Beatty, *Citizen Soldier*, 202–3. Smith (*Stone's River Campaign* 1: 240) surmises that the Michigan regiment in question could only have been the 11th or 21st, and he states that the evidence points to the 21st. Polk only briefly mentions the attack, and other regimental reports are silent.

24. Carson to mother, January 7, 1863, William Carson Letters, 15th U.S. File, SRNBP; H. Breidenthal to Editor, January 8, 1863, *Ohio State Journal*, January 24, 1863.

25. *OR* 20, pt. 1: 913, 927, 933 (quick time); Allardice, *Confederate Colonels*, 182–83.

26. *OR* 20, pt. 1: 243, 245, 247, 249; Freeman, "Some Battle Recollections of Stone's River," 235; Silas C. Stevens Account, Chicago Board of Trade Battery, SRNBP (horse neighing); Edward Wood to Will, January 12, 1863, Edward Wood Letters, Lewis Leigh Collection, USAMHI.

27. *OR* 20, pt. 1: 246, 248, 580; Freeman, "Some Battle Recollections of Stones River," 235; "T" to Editor, in *Norfolk Reflector*, February 10, 1863; Wood to Will, January 12, 1863, Edward Wood Letters, Lewis Leigh Collection, USAMHI; Stevens Account, Chicago Board of Trade Battery File, SRNBP; Stokes Manuscript, Chicago Board of Trade Battery File, CHS; C. V. Lamberson to brother, January 9, 1863, C. V. Lamberson Letters, Pioneer Brigade File, SRNBP (nineteen dead in a pile).

28. Warner, *Generals in Blue*, 28; Beatty, *Citizen Soldier*, 254–55; *OR* 20, pt. 1: 584; Stevenson (*Battle of Stone's River*, 94) mentions Beatty's brigade as being "west of the cemetery." This could possibly be a reference to Evergreen Cemetery on Highway 41, which has prewar graves. This site should not be confused with the large city cemetery also named Evergreen, near Middle Tennessee State University.

29. *OR* 20, pt. 1: 584, 585, 592, 928, 935, 947; Tunnel "Texans in the Battle at Murfreesboro," 574; Stroud, *Ector's Texas Brigade*, 82–83; Noe, ed., *Southern Boy in Blue*, 123–24; Charles F. Manderson, *The Twin Seven-Shooters* (New York: F. Tennyson Neely, 1902), 16; James Dodson, *A Historical Sketch of Company K of the 79th Regiment Indiana Volunteers* (Plainfield, Ind.: Progress, 1894), 6–8; Thomas L. Sexton to Editor, *Mahoning Register*, January 22, 1863; Alfred W. Stambaugh to father, January 1863, *Ohio Repository*, January 28, 1863.

30. *OR* 20, pt. 1: 383, 387, 476, 524, 560, 565, 569, 572; John H. Bolton Diary, December 31, 1863, BGSU.

31. Pirtle, "Stones River Sketches," 101; Henry M. Mitzner, "The Fourteenth Michigan Infantry, the Battle of Murfreesboro, Tennessee, the Battle of Jonesboro, Georgia, and Incidents of My Life," Bentley Historical Library, UM; King to mother, January 8, 1863, Robert L. King Letters, 15th U.S. File, SRNBP; Johnson, *That Body of Brave Men*, 281.

32. Pirtle, "Stone River Sketches," 101; Martin Van Buren Coder to sister, January 21, 1863, Martin Van Buren Coder Letters, ILSHS; John Carroll to Editor, *Cleveland Morning Leader*, January 16, 1863; S. R. Haymond to mother, January 7, 1863, S. R. Haymond Letters, Battery H, 5th U.S. Artillery File, SRNBP; Catherine Merrill, *The Soldiers of Indiana in the War for the Union* (Indianapolis: Merrill & Co., 1889), vol. 2: 159–62; Henry Hammond to mother, January 7, 1863, 18th U.S. File, SRNBP.

33. *OR* 20, pt. 1: 949 ("being nearly"), 950, 952, 954 ("little less than"), 387 (thirty men); *Steubenville Weekly Herald*, January 28, 1863 (flag description); Howard M. Madaus and Robert D. Needham, *The Battle Flags of the Confederate Army of Tennessee* (Milwaukee: Friends of the Museum, Inc., 1976), 28.

34. *OR* 20, pt. 1: 938–39, 942, 943 (Gordon wounded); *SOR* 3: 650–51 ("In the midst"); Welsh, *Medical Histories of Confederate Generals*, 179; L. J. Watkins, "Address of Brig. Gen. James E. Rains," *Confederate Veteran* 16 (May 1908): 209–10; "Record of Gen. George W. Gordon," *Confederate Veteran* 20 (September 1912): 427–28. It should be noted that the total casualties for the brigade that day was only 199, perhaps two-thirds of them during this charge, thus making for a low total even in the midst of a severe barrage. *OR* 20, pt. 1: 681.

35. *OR* 20, pt. 1: 383, 386, 387, 388; Alex to mother, January 11, 1863, *Troy Times*, February 12, 1863; Smith, *Stone's River Campaign* 1: 265.

36. *A History and Biographical Cyclopedia of Butler County, Ohio* (Cincinnati: Western Biographical Publishing Co., 1882), 200–203 (Fyffe); *OR* 20, pt. 1: 597.

37. Cozzens, *No Better Place*, 148; Smith, *Stone's River Campaign* 2: 435.

38. *OR* 20, pt. 1: 601 (44th Indiana flanked), 602 (86th Indiana), 603 (twenty yards), 605 (59th Ohio); Stevenson, *Battle of Stone's River*, 95–96; John Rerick, *The Forty-Fourth Indiana Volunteer Infantry: History of Its Services in the War of the Rebellion* (LaGrange, Ind.: by author, 1880), 79–80; James A. Barnes, James R. Carnahan, and Thomas H. B. McCain, *The Eighty-Sixth Regiment, Indiana Volunteer Infantry: A Narrative of Its Service in the Civil War of 1861–1865* (Crawfordsville, Ind.: Journal Co., 1895), 102, 104; Julie A. Boyle, John D. Smith, and Richard M. McMurry, eds., *The Civil War Letters of George W. Squire, Hoosier Volunteer* (Knoxville: University of Tennessee Press, 1998), 36; Thomas H. B. McCain, *In Song and Sorrow: The Daily Journal of Thomas H. B. McCain, 86th Indiana Volunteer Infantry* (Carmel, Ind.: Guild Press of Indiana, 1998), 103–4; Nelson A. Sowers to Editor, January 9, 1863, *Fort Wayne Weekly Sentinel*, January 31, 1863. The fight between Fyffe and Wood took place south of Asbury Road, on either side of modern-day Gazebo Park Drive.

39. *OR* 20, pt. 1: 848 (almost on turnpike), 602 (86th Indiana flag), 899 (sharpshooters advanced), 904, 905 ("The enemy's"), 906 (45th Mississippi); Stevenson, *Battle of Stone's River*, 96.

40. *OR* 20, pt. 1: 584, 586, 592, 594; Fred Knefler to Lew Wallace, March 28, 1863, Fred Knefler Letters, INHS; Noe, ed., *Southern Boy in Blue*, 124; Stevenson, *Battle of Stone's River*, 97–98.

41. *OR* 744–45, 848, 854, 855, 898, 906. The fire on Vaughn's right presumably came from Rosecrans's artillery on the Nashville Pike, but with intervening woods it is difficult to see how that could happen.

42. Warner, *Generals in Blue,* 207; Beatty, *Citizen Soldier,* 278 (drinking); *OR* 20, pt. 1: 479 (150 rounds), 502 (Fyffe's collapse), 510 (65th Ohio gives way), 514 (raking crossfire); Hinman to "Dear Friends," January 11, 1863, Hinman Letters, WRHS; Wilbur F. Hinman, *The Story of the Sherman Brigade* (Alliance, Ohio: privately published, 1897; John Sowash to Friends, January 26, 1863, *Holmes County Farmer,* February 12, 1863; Alfred B. Wade Journal, INHS; Hartpence, *History of the Fifty-First Indiana,* 106.

43. John Coe to parents, January 5, 1863, historicpreservation.org/64th_Ohio. Fixing precise times is a tricky matter; modern writers disagree. I think the Spruills' estimate of noon is nearly accurate. Smith guesses late morning and Cozzens 1:00.

44. Hinman to friends, January 11, 1863, Hinman Letters, WRHS.

45. *OR* 20, pt. 1: 503, 511.

46. Ibid., 879 ("The retreat"), 884 ("but no way"), 891, 893 ("without any apparent"), 848 (Vaughn's brigade breaks), 744.

47. Hughes, ed., *Liddell's Record,* 112.

48. Ibid., 112–13.

CHAPTER NINE

1. Warner, *Generals in Gray,* 46; *OR* 20, pt. 1: 689 ("not a murmur").

2. Allardice, *Confederate Colonels,* 63, 393; Reports of Colonel James M. Walker, 10th Mississippi, Lieutenant Colonel Benjamin F. Johns, 7th Mississippi, and Captain Lewis Ball, 41st Mississippi, all in Bragg Papers, WRHS; *OR* 20, pt. 1: 527, 533, 537, 674 (Confederate casualties), 711, 714 (squads and companies); Eben P. Sturges Diary, December 30, 31, 1862, Battery B, 1st Ohio File, SRNBP; John Thomas Smith, *A History of the Thirty-First Regiment of Indiana Volunteer Infantry in the War of the Rebellion* (Cincinnati: Western Methodist Book, 1900), 40. Smith (*Stone's River Campaign* 1: 362) surmises that the second charge mentioned in Federal reports was that of the 41st Mississippi. I accept this interpretation (the unpublished reports make it clear that the Confederate assault was fragmented), but precisely what happened is not totally clear.

3. *OR* 20, pt. 1: 527 (charge of 1st Kentucky), 528, 533, 534, 536, 538 (exchange of lines), 540; Captain James Garrity Report, Garrity's Alabama Battery, Bragg Papers, WRHS (40 to 50 yards); Smith, *Stone's River Campaign* 1: 363 (buy time for Negley); F. E. Coffee, "The First Kentucky at Stone River," *National Tribune,* August 23, 1883; Smith, *History of the Thirty-First Regiment of Indiana Volunteer Infantry,* 40–41.

4. *OR* 20, pt. 1: 713 (1,400 men), 714, 715; Welsh, *Medical Histories of Confederate Generals,* 55.

5. *OR* 20, pt. 1: 528 ("wild retreat"), 536, 540, 707, 709 (1,000 men), 711, 714 ("with a yell"), 719; "Pvt. Thomas L. Potter, Standart's Battery B, 1st Ohio Light Artillery Vividly Describes the Battle of Stones River," *Blue & Gray* (December 2004): 24–25 ("maddened and half crazy"); William H. Buskey Account, *Springfield Republic,* January 21, 1863; Eben P. Sturgis Diary,

December 31, 1863, B, 1st Ohio Artillery File, SRNBP; Henry O. Harden, *History of the 90th Ohio Volunteer Infantry in the War of the Great Rebellion of the United States 1861-1865* (Stoutsville, Ohio: Press of Fairfield Pickaway News, 1902), 69; Smith, *History of the Thirty-First Regiment of Indiana Volunteer Infantry*, 40–41. A small portion of the 41st Mississippi attached itself to the 8th Tennessee.

6. Johnson, *That Body of Brave Men*, 283–84; *OR* 20, pt. 1: 395; Phisterer, "The Regular Brigade," 7.

7. Johnson, *That Body of Brave Men*, 284–96. Smith, *Stone's River Campaign* 1: 258–64 (3,000 estimate). *OR* 20, pt. 1: 395, 398 (casualties), 401, 403, 404, 405, 407, 724 (29th Mississippi), 725 (Jackson's brigade on Stewart's right), 726, 729, 838. M. W. Halsey, "Stone River: Brief Notes of the Great Battle," *Pomoroy Leader*, September 12, 1907. Frederick Phisterer, "Association of Survivors, Regular Brigade, Fourteenth Corps, Army of the Cumberland" (n.d., n.p.), 9–11. Hammond to mother, January 7, 1863, Hammond Letters, 18th U.S. File; King to mother, January 8, 1863, 15th U.S. File; Jones to sister, January 9, 1863, 19th U.S. File; and James Biffle Diary, December 31, 1862, 16th U.S. File, all in SRNBP. Hosea, "The Regular Brigade"; *Military Order of the Loyal Legion of the United States, Ohio* (1903; rpt. Wilmington, N.C.: Broadfoot Publishing Co., 1991), vol. 5: 341–42. Edmund Ritter, "The Regulars at Stone's River," *National Tribune*, September 6, 1883. H. K. Young, "Stone's River," *National Tribune*, November 27, 1884. See also E. R. Kellogg (16th U.S.) to brother, January 6, 1863, *Norwalk Reflector*, January 27, 1863; Stevenson, *Battle of Stone's River*, 182–83 (Jackson's casualties); Jackson to wife, January 1, 1863, in *Papers of the Military Historical Society of Massachusetts: Campaigns in Kentucky and Tennessee Including the Battle of Chickamauga 1862-1864* (Boston: Military Historical Society of Massachusetts, 1908), vol. 7: 318 (Jackson's horse killed).

8. Chattanooga *Daily Rebel*, June 11, July 8, 1863; Elliott, *Soldier of Tennessee*, 71; *OR* 20, pt. 1: 725; Allardice, *Confederate Colonels*, 212.

9. *OR* 20, pt. 1: 547; Daniel, *Days of Glory*, 58; Fitch, *Annals of the Army of the Cumberland*, 219–20; Welsh, *Medical Histories of Union Generals*, 165; Palmer, *Personal Recollections*, 140–41. For a historical review of how the Round Forest appeared at the time of the battle, see the National Park Service study by John George, "The Round Forest in the Historical Record," 1–3, SRNBP.

10. *OR* 20, pt. 1: 516–17, 522, 544, 551 555, 558; Kimberly and Holloway, *Forty-First Ohio*, 40.

11. *OR* 20, pt. 1: 555 (6th Indiana), 558 (41st Ohio), 677 (Mississippi casualties); Thomas W. White Report, Bragg Papers, WRHS ("Mississippi Half-Acre"); Kimberly and Holloway, *Forty-First Ohio*, 40; C. P. Ball to "Friend Converse," *Jeffersonian Democrat*, January 23, 1863; W. B. Hazen, *A Narrative of Military Service* (Boston: Ticknor and Co., 1885), 80 ("Rely on the bayonet"); Smith, *Stone's River Campaign* 2: 630, 636.

12. *OR* 20, pt. 1: 715, 717, 719; Bob Womack, *Call Forth the Mighty Men* (Bessemer, Ala.: Colonial Press, 1985), 208; J. J. Wommack, *The Civil War Diary of J. J. Wommack, Company E, Sixteenth Tennessee Volunteer Infantry* (McMinnville, Tenn.: Womack, 1961), 71; John B. Lindsley, ed., *Military Annals of Tennessee: Confederate* (2 vols., Nashville: J. M. Lindsley & Co., 1886), vol. 1: 391 ("gave way"). Alfred Pirtle, "Donelson's Charge at Stone River," *Southern Bivouac* 6 (May 1887): 768–70, despite its title, only vaguely mentions Donelson's attack.

13. Hazen, *Narrative*, 80, 81, 82; *OR* 20, pt. 1: 552, 544, 553; James M. Kirkpatrick to "Dear Friends," January 15, 1863, *Mahoning Register* (Ohio), February 12, 1863.

14. *OR* 20, pt. 1: 467, 488, 489. The reports place this action at 10:30–11:00, but I am convinced the Kentuckians faced Donelson's brigade as it swung past McFadden's Lane, not Chalmers's.

15. *OR* 20, pt. 1: 517, 524, 572, 580, 581; Joseph L. Freeman, "The Twenty-fourth Ohio V. I. at Stone River," *National Tribune*, July 19, 1883; *Troy Times* (Ohio), September 8, 1878 (Parson's obituary); J. H. Orton to mother, January 10, 1863, *Daily Commercial Register* (Sandusky), January 20, 1863; John Sparrer to "Dear Friend," January 5, 1863, *Cleveland Plain Dealer*, January 15, 1863 (Jones's death).

16. *OR* 20, pt. 1: 665, 666, 694, 782–83, 789–90, 841 (Jackson crossed before noon); Connelly, *Autumn of Glory*, 58; Davis, *Breckinridge*, 336–37; McWhiney, *Braxton Bragg and Confederate Defeat*, 358–60; Nathaniel Cheairs Hughes Jr. and Thomas Clayton Ware, *Theodore O'Hara: Poet-Soldier of the Old South* (Knoxville: University of Tennessee, 1998), 121–22. Connelly argues that Bragg should have requested reinforcements from Breckinridge before 10:00 a.m.

Two reports apparently came from Pegram. The 10:00 dispatch read: "Col. Harper [?] sends word that his pickets near Hoover's ford over West Fork of Stones River have retired a short distance before a pretty strong force of the enemy which has just crossed there. I shall at once go in that direction. I will report from time to time." Hoover's was not far from McFadden's Ford. The other dispatch claiming the enemy to be at Black's House on the Lebanon Pike is either missing or was verbally transmitted. Adding to the mystery, in postwar years Captain H. B. Clay of Pegram's cavalry related an interesting story. On the day in question, he insisted that a Bragg staff officer, Colonel St. Leger Grenfil, rode up and, with Pegram and his staff being absent, ordered him to immediately take the brigade to Black's Crossroads, as the enemy had been sighted on the Lebanon Pike. Up to that time, he knew nothing of such a sighting. H. B. Clay, "On the Right at Murfreesboro," *Confederate Veteran* 21 (December 1913): 588.

17. Cozzens, *No Better Place*, 161.

18. *OR* 20, pt. 1: 777 (Hardee); McDonough, *Stones River*, 148, 150; Hattaway and Jones, *How the North Won*, 321–22.

19. *OR* 20, pt. 1: 350, 366, 368, 468,469, 484, 489, 545, 557.

20. Faust, ed., *Historical Times Illustrated Encyclopedia*, 2; Welsh, *Medical Histories of Confederate Generals*, 1; *OR* 20, pt. 1: 793 (reported to Polk), 799 (1,400 infantry), 801; Stevenson, *Battle of Stone's River*, 111 ("Look at yonder"). While the decision to commit to a piecemeal attack was Polk's, there is little doubt that, had Bragg been on the spot, and he must have been nearby, he would have affirmed the decision. It would be the Hornet's Nest at Shiloh repeated.

Traditionally historians have placed John Jackson's assault after Donelson's and before Adams's. In reading Jackson's report, however, I am convinced that he never attacked the Round Forest directly, but veered left of the Cowan House and followed Donelson's brigade into the cedars, thus incurring most of his brigade's 305 casualties in the fight with the Regulars. See *OR* 20, pt. 1: 838.

21. John Ellis Memoirs, LSU.

22. *OR* 20, pt. 1: 366, 493, 759, 793, 799. Smith, *Stone's River Campaign* 1: 390–92; 2: 348 (32nd Alabama casualties). "M.H.S." to "Dear Editor," *Selma Morning Reporter*, January 27, 1863 ("moved up in"). Stevenson, *Battle of Stone's River*, 111–13. *Montgomery Weekly Advertiser*, January 17, 1863 (Maury grabs flag). Allardice, *Confederate Colonels*, 25. Clement S. Watson to wife, January 19, 1863, Clement S. Watson Family Papers, Louisiana Historical Association, TU. John McGrath to wife, January 13, 1863, John McGrath Letters, LSU. The claim of 170 prisoners seems exaggerated; Gibson counted only 146 missing in the entire brigade.

23. Ellis Memoirs, LSU; Welsh, *Medical Histories of Confederate Generals*, 1; Allardice, *Confederate Colonels*, 146.

24. Report from "ORA" of the *Mobile Advertiser & Register* as quoted in *Columbus (Ga.) Daily Sun*, January 10, 1863; Adams to wife, January 19, 1863, Daniel Adams Papers, LHA, TU.

25. *OR* 20, pt. 1: 690, 804, 811; Washington Ives to "Dear Sisters and Fannie," January 14, 1863, Cabaniss, comp., *Civil War Journal and Letters of Washington Ives*, 33.

26. Robert O. Neff, *Tennessee's Battered Brigadier: The Life of General Joseph B. Palmer CSA* (Franklin, Tenn.: Hillsboro Press, 2000), 18, 20–21, 24; Faust, ed., *Historical Times Illustrated Encyclopedia*, 601–2.

27. *OR* 20, pt. 1: 783 ("low and very"), 784 (acute angle), 811 (Preston's right); Ralf J. Neal, "Ralf J. Neal Letter," *Confederate Veteran* 7 (February 1899): 70; Spencer Talley Memoirs, TSLA ("in fading light").

28. *OR* 20, pt. 1: 460, 783–84, 908–9; Nathaniel C. Hughes Jr., *Pride of the Confederate Artillery: The Washington Artillery in the Army of Tennessee* (Baton Rouge: Louisiana State University Press, 1997), 85–86; Stevenson, *Battle of Stone's River*, 115–16.

29. *OR* 220, pt. 1: 219; Bickham, *Rosecrans's Campaign*, 277–79; Fitch, *Annals of the Army of the Cumberland*, 248–49; Thomas L. Crittenden, "The Union Left at Stone's River," *Battle and Leaders of the Civil War* (1911; rpt. New York: Thomas Yoseloff, 1956), vol. 3: 633; Starr, *Bohemian Brigade*, 183–84.

30. *OR* 16, pt. 1: 578.

31. James L. Cooper, "Service With the Twentieth Tennessee Regiment," *Confederate Veteran* 33 (February 1925): 57; W. J. McMurray, *History of the Twentieth Tennessee Regiment Volunteer Infantry, C.S.A.* (Nashville: Publication Committee, 1904), 233, 393–94 (Thomas B. Smith); Ives to sister, January 14, 1863, Cabaniss, comp., *Civil War Journal and Letters of Washington Ives*, 34–35.

32. *OR* 20, pt. 1: 784 (20th Tennessee veers), 821 (20 captured), 822 (67 lost in charge), 812 (run for the cedars); McMurray, *History of the Twentieth Tennessee*, 234–35 (bluffs six to ten feet); Ives to sister, January 14, 1863, Cabaniss, comp., *Civil War Journal and Letters of Washington Ives*, 35.

33. Stevenson, *Battle of Stone's River*, 172, 175–76; *OR* 20, pt. 1: 675; Bickham, *Rosecrans's Campaign*, 334.

CHAPTER TEN

1. Ives to sisters, January 14, 1863, Cabaniss, comp., *Civil War Journal and Letters of Washington Ives*, 35; Magee Diary, December 31, 1862, DU; Jill K. Garrett, ed., *Confederate*

Diary of Robert D. Smith (Columbia, Tenn.: United Daughters of the Confederacy, 1975), 44; McMurray, *History of the Twentieth Tennessee*, 235–36; James B. Mitchell to wife, January 13, 1863, James B. Mitchell Letters, LC; Fielder Diary, December 31, 1863, Franklin, comp., *Civil War Diaries of Capt. Alfred Tyler Fielder*, 98; *OR* 20, pt. 1: 880 (Good Samaritans).

2. James W. Ellis, "Gratitude of Veterans," *Confederate Veteran* 17 (December 1909): 581; G. B. Moon, "A Boy's Experience in Seeing a Battle," *Confederate Veteran* 7 (March 1899): 119.

3. Elliott, *Doctor Quintard*, 60; Bennett and Haigh, *History of the Thirty-Sixth Regiment Illinois*, 348.

4. Alex to mother, January 11, 1863, *Troy Times*, February 12, 1863; J. H. M. Montgomery to editor, January 5, 1863, *Gillopolis Dispatch*, January 28, 1863; Scribner, *How Soldiers Were Made*, 80.

5. Henry M. Kendall, "The Third Day at Stone's River," *Military Order of the Loyal Legion of the United States District of Columbia* (1903; rpt. Wilmington, N.C.: Broadfoot Publishing Co., 1993), vol. 3: 441; Logsdon, *Eyewitnesses at the Battle*, 63–64; Hannaford, "In the Ranks," 185–86; John McCabe to wife, January 5, 1863, *Rushville (Ill.) Daily Citizen*, December 31, 1907, copy in 84th Illinois File, SRNBP.

6. William Erb, *The Valley of Death, the Battle of Stones River: Extract from the Battles of the Nineteenth Ohio* (Washington, D.C.: Judd and Detweiler, 1893), 24–26; Newlin, *A History of the Seventy-third Illinois*, 143–44; James C. Geneco, ed., *To the Sound of Musketry and Tap of the Drum* (Detroit: Detroit Book Press, 1990), 74.

7. Bickham, *Rosecrans' Campaign*, 290–91, 286, 294; Smith, *Stone's River Campaign* 1: 120, 433; Crittenden, "The Union Left," 633.

8. Bickham, *Rosecrans' Campaign*, 289–90; Bobrick, *Master of War*, 154 (Thomas leans on board); Lamers, *Edge of Glory*, 235; Scribner, *How Soldiers Were Made*, 81. Lamers gives Rosecrans's verbatim account as found in the general's papers at the Huntington Library.

9. Lamers, *Edge of Glory*, 235; Crittenden, "The Union Left," 633; Bickham, *Rosecrans' Campaign*, 290.

10. Lamers, *Edge of Glory*, 235; McKinney, *Education in Violence*, 195; John Lee Yaryan, "Stone River,"173, 175, 178. Despite the title of his book, even Cozzens admits that the Yaryan version is probably apocryphal.

11. Lamers, *Edge of Glory* 235; Crittenden, "The Union Left," 633–34; *OR* 20, pt. 1: 94–95; Sheridan, *Personal Memoirs* 1: 128; Fitch, *Annals of the Army of the Cumberland*, 676–77 ("Gentlemen we have"); Stanley, *Personal Memoirs*, 127. Sheridan insisted that the issue of torches was resolved and that it had no effect upon Rosecrans's decision to remain on the battlefield.

12. *OR* 20, pt. 1: 194, 271, 450; Van Horne, *History of the Army of the Cumberland* 1: 245; Stevenson, *Battle of Stone's River*, 122–23.

13. *OR* 20, pt. 1: 371 (3:00 a.m.); Dodge, "The War As I Saw It," 30th Indiana File, SRNBP; Logsdon, *Eyewitnesses at the Battle*, 73; Clarence O. Pecoy Diary, January 1, 1863, 36th Illinois File, SRNBP; Stephenson, *Indiana's Roll of Honor* 1: 577 ("Boys"); C. T. DeVellin, *History of the Seventeenth Regiment, First Brigade, 3rd Division, 14th Corps, Army of the Cumberland* (Zanesville, Ohio: E. R. Sullivan, 1889), 71; Mitchell to family, January 4, 1863, William Mitchell Letters, 1st Wisconsin File, SRNBP.

14. *OR* 20, pt. 1: 450, 575, 576, 598; Noe, ed., *Southern Boy in Blue*, 129 (10:00 a.m.); Smith, *Stone's River Campaign* 1: 478.

15. Stevenson, *Battle of Stone's River*, 125–26. Stevenson was in Roberts's brigade of Sheridan's division. On January 1, his brigade was positioned next to one of Davis's brigades, leading me to believe that he heard the story by word of mouth.

16. Urquhart, "Bragg's Advance and Retreat," 607; OR 20, pt. 1: 662, 805; Kniffen, "Battle of Stone's River," 630; Connelly, *Autumn of Glory*, 61; Clay, "On the Right at Murfreesboro," 588; *Chattanooga Daily Rebel*, January 3, 1863.

17. *OR* 20, pt. 1: 784, 805 (1:00 a.m.); Connelly, *Autumn of Glory*, 61–62; Woodworth, *Jefferson Davis and His Generals*, 193; Hughes, ed., *Liddell's Record*, 113; McWhiney, *Braxton Bragg and Confederate Defeat*, 362.

18. *OR* 20, pt. 1: 582, 790; John A. Buckner Report and Theodore O'Hara Report, John C. Breckinridge Papers, NYHS.

19. Mercer W. N. Otey, "Organizing a Signal Corps," *Confederate Veteran* 7 (1899): 554; *OR* 20, pt. 1: 712, 721.

20. *OR* 20, pt. 1: 849 (rumors), 899 (2:00), 904 (twenty minutes), 350, 371.

21. Longacre, *A Soldier to the Last*, 80; OR 20, pt. 1: 959–60, 968–69, 654–55.

22. *OR* 20, pt. 1: 651, 959–60, 968–69; William A. Moore to father, January 18, 1863, William A. Moore Letters, 73rd Illinois File, SRNBP; Bickham, *Rosecrans' Campaign*, 300–301; Mark Hoffman, *"My Favorite Mechanics": The First Michigan Engineers and their Civil War* (Detroit: Wayne State University Press, 2007), 124–32.

23. *OR* 20, pt. 1: 634, 637–38, 642, 959; Bearss, "Cavalry Operations," 132–34.

CHAPTER ELEVEN

1. *OR* 20, pt. 1: 722, 742, 751; William D. Carnes Memoirs, 88–89, private collection; Lindsley, ed., *Military Annals of Tennessee* 2: 817.

2. *OR* 20, pt. 1: 455, 471, 476, 504, 722, 733, 742, 751; Stevenson, *Battle of Stone's River*, 127–28; Orlow Smith to Editor, *Ashland (Ohio) Times*, January 28, 1863; Elias Cole to Editor, January 29, 1863, *Delaware Gazette*, February 13, 1863; "From the 6th Ohio Battery," *Summit County Beacon*, January 22, 1863; Hinman, *Story of the Sherman Brigade*, 535; Beatty, *Citizen Soldier*, 206.

3. Bickham, *Rosecrans' Campaign*, 306 (weather); Davis, *Breckinridge*, 330–31, 338; Lot D. Young, *Reminiscences of a Soldier of the Orphan Brigade* (Louisville: Courier-Journal Printing Co., 1918), 47; "Identifying Bramblett/Bramlett Soldiers in the Civil War, www.bramblett. com/info/civilwar.htm; A. K. Kirwan, *Johnny Green of the Orphan Brigade: The Journal of a Confederate Soldier* (Lexington: University of Kentucky Press, 1956), 67. Davis asserts that Breckinridge's scouts "failed him" by not directly watching McFadden's Ford.

4. Pickett, "Reminiscences of Murfreesboro," 452; OR 20, pt. 1: 785.

5. *OR* 20, pt. 1: 785, 803, 805, 605, 608 (Union casualties), 776, 582; Rice E. Graves Report, John C. Breckinridge Papers, NYHS; J. A. Chalaron, "Memories of Rice Graves, C.S.A.," *Daviess County Historical Quarterly* 3 (1985): 7; Hughes, *Pride of the Confederate Artillery*,

87–88. Originally two guns of Byrnes's battery were supposed to be used, but they lacked the proper ammunition.

6. *OR* 20, pt. 1: 667, 759, 785; Stevenson, *Battle of Stone's River*, 131; Davis, *Breckinridge*, 341.

7. *OR* 20, pt. 1: 668, 785, 790.

8. Stevenson, *Battle of Stone's River*, 132; Davis, *Breckinridge*, 341–42; Nathaniel C. Hughes and Roy P. Stonesifer Jr., *The Life and Wars of Gideon J. Pillow* (Chapel Hill: University of North Carolina Press, 1993), 253, 325.

9. *OR* 20, pt. 1: 785, 786 (no cover), 785; Ed Porter Thompson, *History of the Orphan Brigade* (Louisville, Ky.: L. N. Thompson, 1898), 178; Smith, *Stone's River Campaign* 2: 525, 528. Davis (*Breckinridge*, 375) estimated division strength between 5,000 and 5,300. The 9th Kentucky, Cobb's battery, and a section of Semple's battery remained on Wayne's Hill. Additionally, the 14th Louisiana Battalion and 32nd Alabama were retained as a reserve. The division sustained losses of 730 on December 31. The "5,200" number does not include Robertson's battery, which was not a part of the division.

10. *OR* 20, pt. 1: 758, 759, 760; Stevenson, *Battle of Stone's River*, 143 n1; Connelly (*Autumn of Glory*, 63–64) questions whether the conversation between Breckinridge and Robertson ever took place. Davis (*Breckinridge*, 343 n19) totally dismisses Robertson's report as perjured. Cozzens (*No Better Place*, 182–83) and Smith (*Stone's River Campaign* 2: 526–27) accepted the incident at face value.

11. *OR* 20, pt. 1: 667, 785, 790, 810, 969. For criticism of Breckinridge's failure to establish communications with the cavalry see Davis, *Breckinridge*, 356, and Smith, *Stone's River Campaign* 2: 528. Exactly why Pegram did not contact Breckinridge is unknown.

12. Gilbert McWhirk to father, January 6, 1863, in *Ohio State Journal*, January 16, 1863 (Rosecrans cheerful); Bickham, *Rosecrans' Campaign*, 307 (left-wing offensive); *OR* 20, pt. 1: 528 (Cruft), 531 (801 men), 518, 195, 450; William H. Baskey to Editor, *Springfield (Ohio) Republic*, January 21, 1863 ("We knew something").

13. *OR* 20, pt. 1: 195, 576 (2:30), 582, 589–90, 561, 576, 587, 577 (3:00); *History of the Services of the Third Battery, Wisconsin Light Artillery in the Civil War of the United States, 1861–1865* (Berlin, Wis.: Convant Press, 1902), 7; Stevenson, *Battle of Stone's River*, 130; Samuel Welch, "A Sketch of the Movements of the Fifty-first Ohio Volunteer Infantry" (1908 reprint), 108, in 51st Ohio File, SRNBP.

14. Robert J. Girardi, "Brig. Gen. Roger Weightman Hanson," in Allardice and Hewitt, eds., *Kentuckians in Blue*, 124–29; Thompson, *History of the Orphan Brigade*, 179.

15. *OR* 20, pt. 1: 732–33, 786, 808 (Pillow); Stevenson, *Battle of Stone's River*, 132; William Brown Reminiscences, Stanford's Mississippi Battery File, SRNBP; Davis, *Breckinridge*, 343 ("Look at old Hanson"); Thomas C. Honnell Letter, in *Lima Gazette*, February 4, 1863 ("they came not"); Samuel Bolton to brother, in *Church Advocate*, February 5, 1863. A few sources refer to a volley from Carnes's battery, but most refer to "the signal gun." See for example *OR* 20, pt. 1: 786. Polk's supporting barrage is poorly reported; what damage was done is not known.

16. *OR* 20, pt. 1: 833; Smith, *Stone's River Campaign* 1: 535 (three regiment front); Charges and Specifications of Charges Against Brig. Gen. G. J. Pillow, undated, John C. Breckinridge Papers, CHS; Hughes and Stonesifer (*Life and Wars of Gideon J. Pillow*, 254–55)

question whether the incident actually occurred, but given that it was documented the very next day, and that specific details were put forth, it has a ring of truth.

17. *OR* 20, pt. 1: 195, 598–99; Welch, "Sketch of the Movements of the Fifty-first Ohio," 108.

18. *OR* 20, pt. 1: 786, 808–9, 823, 850; Rice Graves Report, John C. Breckinridge Papers, NYHS.

19. *OR* 20, pt. 1: 786 ("Many officers"); Pickett, "Reminiscences," 453–54; Thompson, *History of the Orphan Brigade*, 200; Girardi, "Brig. Gen. Roger Weightman Hanson," 129; Welsh, *Medical Histories of Confederate Generals*, 92–93; Allardice, *Confederate Colonels*, 375.

20. *OR* 20, pt. 1: 609, 610–11 (Trabue's line staggered), 165 ("{set up a hideous yell"), 613, 797 (Gibson moves up); Wright, *History of the Eighth Regiment Kentucky*, 128–29; Honnell to Benjamin C. Epler, January 5, 1863, Honnell Letters, OHS.

21. John McGrath to wife, January 13, 1863, John McGrath Papers, Louisiana and Lower Mississippi Valley Collection, LSU.

22. *OR* 20, pt. 1: 609, 615 (51st Ohio outflanked), 611 (appeals to 99th Ohio), 590 (79th Indiana); Milton A. Roming to cousin, January 7, 1863, Milton A. Roming Letters, 51st Ohio File, SRNBP; Honnell to Epler, January 5, 1863, Honnell Letters, OHS; *Lima Gazette*, February 4, 1863 (M. E. Thorn); Samuel Bolton to brother, in *Church Advocate*, February 5, 1863 ("The 35th broke"); Samuel Mullet Letter, reprinted in *Newcomestown News*, December 13, 1972; Jacob Early to wife, January 7, 1863, in Robert A. and Gloria S. Driver, *Letters Home: The Personal Side of the American Civil War by Jacob Early* (Roseburg, Ore.: by author, 1992), 6–7; Kevin B. McCray, *A Shouting of Orders: A History of the Ninety-ninth Ohio Volunteer Infantry* (n.d.), 66–67 ("Away we went").

23. *OR* 20, pt. 1: 587 ("Colonel we have them"), 588 (19th Ohio flanked), 591 (four or five volleys), 595 (advanced 200 yards); Noe, ed., *Southern Boy in Blue*, 133; Wright, *History of the Eighth Regiment Kentucky*, 5.

24. *OR* 20, pt. 1: 786 (Wright's battery), 806 ("A most deadly"), 809 (advance suspended), 810 (four ranks deep); McMurray, *History of the Twentieth Tennessee*, 239. Pillow incorrectly identified the battery as Anderson's.

25. James P. Fyffe to mother, January 10, 1863, as quoted in James L. McDonough, "The Last Day at Stones River—Experiences of a Yankee and a Reb," *Tennessee Historical Quarterly* 40 (Spring 1981): 8; *OR* 20, pt. 1: 577, 599 (Fyffe thrown), 601, 603, 604, 606; Julie A. Doyle, John David Smith, and Richard M. McMurry, eds., *This Wilderness of War: The Civil War Letters of George W. Squier, Hoosier Volunteer* (Knoxville: University of Tennessee Press, 1998), 82–83 ("All over the field").

26. *OR* 20, pt. 1: 561 (tiered deployment), 562 (changed front), 567 (attacked on right), 569 ("We are surrounded"), 572 (barricades), 573 ("rushing wildly"), 786 ("mingled into one"), 806 ("death in their backs"), 786 (400 prisoners), 834 (hundred taken at river bend), 809 (flag); McMurray, *History of the Twentieth Tennessee*, 132.

27. Milton Barnes to wife, January 10, 1863, Milton Barnes Letters, 93rd Ohio File, SRNBP, Logsdon, *Eyewitnesses at the Battle*, 85.

28. *OR* 20, pt. 1: 455, 528, 579, 412, 415, 433, 524, 525.

29. Ibid., 451 ("Now Mendenhall"), 456, 477, 521, 523, 581. Traditionally the 3rd Wisconsin Battery, after it crossed to the west bank, has been placed on modern maps on the far right of

McFadden's Hill, but this cannot be completely verified, as the unit took several unspecified positions.

30. Crittenden, "The Union Left," 633; Kniffen, "Battle of Stone's River," 630–31; Noe, ed., *Southern Boy in Blue*, 134; Early to wife, January 7, 1863, in Driver, *Letters Home*, n.n.; James Jones to parents, January 8, 1863, James Jones Letters, 57th Indiana File, SRNBP.

31. *OR* 20, pt. 1: 808–9 (Palmer wounded), 813 (William Miller), 822, 831, 827–28, 836, 786 (fatal to Preston's brigade), 761 (6th Kentucky flag bearer); Neff, *Tennessee's Battered Brigadier*, 75; John S. Bransford, "Gallant Preston D. Cunningham," *Confederate Veteran* 10 (June 1902): 268; Allardice, *Confederate Colonels*, 119; John P. Murray, "Tribute to P. D. Cunningham," *Confederate Veteran* 1 (November 1894): 333; J.A.C., "Colonel P. D. Cunningham," *Confederate Veteran* 12 (May 1904): 240; Young, *Reminiscences*, 49–50 (eighteen to twenty); H. F. Nuckols to Mrs. Hall, February 9, 1863, H. F. Nuckols, 4th Kentucky File, SRNBP; McMurray, *History of the Twentieth Tennessee*, 239–40.

32. *OR* 20, pt. 1: 803, 759 ("altar the plan"); Rice Graves Report, John C. Breckinridge Papers, NYHS; Chalaron, "Memories of Rice Graves," 9.

33. George T. Squires to parents, January 9, 1863, George T. Squires Letters, 21st Ohio File, SRNBP; Samuel Linton Diary, January 2, 863, RBHPL; *OR* 20, pt. 1: 427, 430 (300 yards); Welch, "Sketch of the Movements of the Fifty-first Ohio," 110; Wayne C. Mann, "The Road to Murfreesboro: The Eleventh Michigan from Organization Through Its First Battle," 118, M.A. thesis, Western Michigan University, 1963 ("Sir, they have").

34. *OR* 20, pt. 1: 434 ("the enemy halted"), 430, 422 (Rosecrans and Negley), 786–87; Squire to parents, January 9, 1863, George Squire Letters, 21st Ohio File, SRNBP; Gibson, *History of the 78th Pennsylvania*, 62–63; D. D. Rose, "Stone's River," *National Tribune*, November 13, 1884. One version has Negley riding up to Colonel Scott and asking: "Who'll lead the way? Who'll save the Left?" Scott answered: "The Nineteenth Illinois!" "The Nineteenth Illinois it is them!" Negley replied (Haynie, *Nineteenth Illinois*, 207).

35. *OR* 20, pt. 1: 427, 429–30, 434; Vance, "A Man and a Boy at Stone River," 358.

36. *OR* 20, pt. 1: 547 (Hazen), 548 (41st Ohio), 588 (Grider takes flag), 595–96, 518–19, 434; Palmer, *Personal Recollections*, 148; Noe, ed., *Southern Boy in Blue*, 135; *Western Reserve Chronicle*, January 21, 1863 (Grider grabs colors); Kimberly and Holloway, *Forty-First Ohio*, 42; Stevenson, *Battle of Stone's River*, 141 (Pioneers).

37. *OR* 20, pt. 1: 808, 813, 204, 374, 408, 437; Joseph S. Johnston to mother, January 14, 1863, Joseph S. Johnston Letters, CHS; Hannibal Paine Letter, January 10, 1863, Hannibal Paine Letters, 26th Tennessee File, SRNBP; William D. Rogers to [?], January 22, 1863, William D. Rogers Letters, 1st Florida File, SRNBP; Madaus and Needham, *Battle Flags*, 23, 129, 131 n12.

38. Preston to William Preston Johnston, January 26, 1863, William Preston Johnston Papers, Mason Barret Collection, TU.

39. *OR* 20, pt. 1: 823, 824, 850, 909, 910; Rice Graves Report, John C. Breckinridge Papers, NYHS; Chalaron, "Memories of Rice Graves," 8–9; Charles, *Recollections of a Christmas During the War*, 28–29. The Federal regiments claiming the three guns included the 78th Pennsylvania, 19th Illinois, 19th Ohio, and 9th Kentucky.

40. *OR* 20, pt. 1: 760, 761, 813, 969, 548, 559; Clay, "On the Right at Murfreesboro," 589.

41. Brent Diary, January 2, 1863, Bragg Papers, WRHS; Clay, "On the Right at Murfreesboro," 588; *OR* 20, pt. 1: 969.

42. *OR* 20, pt. 1: 451; Heg to wife, January 4, 1863, Blegen, ed., *Civil War Letters of Colonel Hans Christian Heg*, 167; Girardi and Hughes, eds., *Memoirs of Brigadier General William Passmore Carlin*, 82–83; John H. Bolton to brother, January 9, 1863, in *Church Advocate*, February 12, 1863.

43. *OR* 20, pt. 1: 765–66; pt. 2: 477, 778, 850 (11:00 p.m. skirmish), 881, 914, 929, 932, 936, 937. E. T. Sykes, "A Cursory Sketch of General Bragg's Campaigns," *Southern Historical Society Papers* 11 (1883): 472–74.

44. Cummings to wife, January 9, 1863, in McCray, *A Shouting of Orders*, 72 ("Headless, armless"); *Bucyrus Journal*, January 16, 1863 ("scores of rebels"); Noah Mills to wife, January 9, 1863, Noah Mills Letters, 18th Ohio File, SRNBP; James Jones to parents, January 8, 1863, James Jones Letters, 57th Indiana File, SRNBP.

45. *OR* 20, pt. 1: 443–44.

CHAPTER TWELVE

1. *OR* 20, pt. 1: 669.

2. Ibid., 683, 700–701.

3. Ibid., 669, 683.

4. Ibid., 195, 374, 379, 416–18; Beatty, *Citizen Soldier*, 209–10; Thomas H. White and John C. Coltart After-Action Reports, Bragg Papers, WRHS.

5. *OR* 20, pt. 1: 669, 683, 684; *McArthur Democrat*, April 26, 1863; Street to wife, January 4, 1863, J. K. Street Letters, SHC; "The Battle of Murfreesboro—An Intercepted Letter Written by One of Bragg's Officers," January 10, 1863, in *New York Times*, February 5, 1863; Sam L. Clark and H. D. Riley, eds., "Outline of the Organization of the Medical Department of the Confederate Army and Department of Tennessee by Samuel H. Stout," *Tennessee Historical Quarterly* 16 (Spring 1957): 67; Pickett, "Reminiscences of Murfreesboro," 255; Glenna R. Schroeder-Lein, *Confederate Hospitals on the Move: Samuel H. Stout and the Army of Tennessee* (Columbia: University of South Carolina Press, 1994), 162–63 (Bragg weeping). The abandoned wounded had already been counted in the casualty returns and did not raise the total figure.

6. Hughes, ed., *Liddell's Record*, 114–15.

7. Fielder Diary, January 4, 1863, Franklin, comp., *Civil War Diaries of Capt. Alfred Tyler Fielder*, 101 (inch thick mud); Jackman Diary, January 4, 1863, Davis, ed., *Jackman Diary*, 71; Thomas Patton to mother, January 10, 1863, Thomas Patton Letters, SHC (debris); Holmes Diary, January 4, 1863, Dennis, ed., *Kemper County Rebel*, 31; J. Stoddard Johnson Diary, January 4, 1863, Bragg Papers, WRHS (Bragg and wife).

8. Bickman, *Rosecrans' Campaign*, 322; Lamers, *Edge of Glory*, 241; Fitch, *Annals of the Army of the Cumberland*, 329–30 (mass); Beatty, *Citizen Soldier*, 211–12; *OR* 20, pt. 1: 185–86.

9. *OR* 20, pt. 1: 409, 618, 638, 642; pt. 2: 301. Logsdon, *Eyewitnesses at the Battle*, 107. Fitch, *Annals of the Army of the Cumberland*, 258.

10. Surgeon General's Office, *The Medical and Surgical History of the War of the Rebellion, 1861–1863* (3 vols. in 6 parts, Washington, D.C.: U.S. Government Printing Office, 1870–88), vol. 1, pt. 2: 257, 259, 265; *Nashville Daily Union*, January 8, 1863 (Indiana surgeons).

11. Beatty, *Citizen Soldier*, 210–11; Shoemaker as quoted in Smith, *Stone's River Campaign* 1: 583; James R. Maxwell to wife, January 9, 1863, James R. Maxwell Letters, Civil War Soldier's Letters, LPR78, ADAH.

12. *McArthur Democrat*, April 26, 1863; *Nashville Daily Union*, February 15, 1863.

13. As quoted in Hess, *Banners to the Breeze*, 228–29.

14. *Memphis Appeal*, January 1, 1863; *Richmond Examiner*, January 6, 1863; Patton to mother, January 13, 1863, Thomas Patton Letters, SHC; J. L. Hammer to wife, January 5, 1863, J. L. Hammer Letters, WRHS; Frank Carter to wife, January 6, 1863, Frank Carter Letters, DU; *Nashville Daily Courier*, January 30, 1863. See also Ralph A. Wooster, ed., "With the Confederate Cavalry in the West: The Civil War Experiences of Isaac Dunbar Affleck," *Southwestern Historical Quarterly* 83 (July 1979): 8.

15. *OR* 20, pt. 1: 483, 485, 486, 487 ("falling back too fast"); Brent Diary, January 7–8, 1863, Bragg Papers, WRHS; Holmes Diary, January 9, 1863, Dennis, ed., *Kemper County Rebel*, 42 (retrace steps).

16. *OR* 23, pt. 2: 625, 760, 628; 20; pt. 1: 503 (6,000 troopers). Anderson to wife, January 11, 1863, Uhler, ed., "Civil War Letters of Major General James Patton Anderson," 159. Rosecrans never considered an offensive in January; indeed he considered himself on the defensive.

17. Hughes and Ware, *Theodore O'Hara*, 91, 109, 116, 127–28; Davis, *Breckinridge*, 350; *OR* 20, pt. 1: 697. On January 21, O'Hara tipped Reid that Bragg intended to arrest him the next day; the correspondent departed Tullahoma in the middle of the night. Andrews, *South Reports the Civil War*, 337.

18. Brent Diary, January 10, 1863, Bragg Papers, WRHS; Johnston Diary, January 10 and subsequent entries, 1863, Bragg Papers, WRHS; Urquhart, "Bragg's Advance and Retreat," 608.

19. *OR* 20, pt. 1: 699; Brent Diary, January 11, 1863, Bragg Papers, WRHS; McWhiney (*Braxton Bragg and Confederate Defeat*, 378) concluded that Bragg's circular was a "pathetic plea for love and understanding." See also Woodworth, *Jefferson Davis and His Generals*, 195.

20. *OR* 20, pt. 1: 683; O'Hara quoted in Hughes and Ware, *Theodore O'Hara*, 128.

21. *OR* 20, pt. 1: 682; Peter J. Ehlinger, *Kentucky's Last Cavalier: General William Preston, 1816–1887* (Lexington: Kentucky Historical Society, 2004), 146, 147, 155; Randal Gibson to "Dear Will," March 1, 9, 1863, William Preston Johnston Papers, Barret Collection, TU; O'Hara to Breckinridge, January 24, 1863, as quoted in Hughes and Ware, *Theodore O'Hara*, 129; Davis, ed., *Diary of a Confederate Soldier*, 164–65.

22. Welsh, *Medical Histories of Confederate Generals*, 29; Urquhart, "Bragg's Advance and Retreat," 609 (Urquhart places Brown on a list of Bragg supporters); Hughes and Stonesifer, *Life and Wars of Gideon J. Pillow*, 259–60.

23. McWhiney, *Braxton Bragg and Confederate Defeat*, 377 n10 (Adams listed as Bragg supporter). Woodworth, *Jefferson Davis and His Generals*, 195. *OR* 20, pt. 2: 497 (Wright given command); 23; pt. 1: 620 (Helm replaces Wright). Welsh, *Medical Histories of Confederate Generals*, 98.

24. *OR* 20, pt. 1: 684; pt. 2: 722. Symonds (*Stonewall of the West,* 121) asserts that Cleburne was "not prone to asserting his opinion." Yet his candor on the Bragg issue and his later controversial document on the arming of slaves leads me to a different conclusion. Liddell also documented the incident in which the Irishman indiscreetly spoke about Hardee's "running with women."

25. Hughes, ed., *Liddell's Record,* 115–16. 117, 151, 161.

26. *OR* 20, pt. 1: 698, 701.

27. Ibid., 698; Losson, *Tennessee's Forgotten Warriors,* 94; Pillow to Clare, March 9, 1863, Bragg Papers, WRHS (McCown on Cheatham). For a list of Bragg supporters see McWhiney, *Braxton Bragg and Confederate Defeat,* 331 n72 (Stewart), 377 n10 (Wright), 381 (Smith). A July 1864 letter from Wheeler to Bragg places A. P. Stewart on the list of supporters. Wheeler to Bragg, July [?], 1864, Braxton Bragg Papers, DU. Maney's position has never been documented.

28. Uhler, ed., "Civil War Letters of Major General James Patton Anderson," 154–55, 157.

29. Brent Diary, January 12, 1863, Bragg Papers, WRHS; O'Hara as quoted in Hughes and Ware, *Theodore O'Hara,* 128–29.

30. Connelly, *Autumn of Glory,* 82–84; Davis, *Breckinridge,* 359–62.

31. *OR* 23, pt. 2: 613, 624, 632–33, 640, 658, 729–30; Davis, *Jefferson Davis,* 494; Symonds, *Joseph E. Johnston,* 196–99.

32. "Proceedings of First Congress, Third Session, January 29-March 19, 1863," *Southern Historical Society Papers* 48 (1941; rpt. Wilmington: Broadfoot Publishing Co., 1992), 209–10; Mary S. Estill, ed., "Diary of a Confederate Congressman, 1862–1863," *Southwestern Historical Quarterly* (April 1935): 299.

33. Pillow to William Clare, March 9, 1863, H. W. Walter to John P. McCown, June 5, 1863, Bragg Papers, WRHS; *OR* 23, pt. 2: 653–54; Hughes and Stonesifer, *Life and Wars of Gideon J. Pillow,* 260; Connelly, *Autumn of Glory,* 81.

34. Losson, *Tennessee's Forgotten Warriors,* 95–96; Connelly, *Autumn of Glory,* 84–85.

35. Connelly, *Autumn of Glory,* 71, 146.

36. *OR* 20, pt. 1: 185.

37. Andrews, *North Reports the Civil War,* 312–13; *New York Times,* January 6, 1863; *Chicago Tribune,* January 6, 1863; Daniel, *Days of Glory,* 246–48.

38. *OR* 20, pt. 1: 186–88; Hess, *Banners to the Breeze,* 229.

39. Roy B. Basler, ed., *The Collected Works of Abraham Lincoln* (8 vols., New Brunswick, N.J.: Rutgers University Press, 1953), vol. 6: 424. Lamers, *Edge of Glory,* 246–47. *OR* 20, pt. 2: 123–24, pt. 1: 187–88. Templeton as quoted in Hess, *Banners to the Breeze,* 229.

BIBLIOGRAPHY

PRIMARY SOURCES

Manuscripts

Alabama Department of Archives and History, Montgomery (ADAH)
  "From a Conversation with Mr. John W. James," Civil War Soldiers' Letters.
  James A. Hall Letters, Walter K. Hoover Collection.
  Horatio Letter, 22nd Alabama File.
  James R. Maxwell Letters, Civil War Soldiers' Letters.
  Reuben Searcy Letters.
  Thomas Warrick Letters.
  S. A. M. Woods Papers.
Bowling Green State University, Bowling Green, Ohio (BGSU)
  Matthew Askew Memoir, Matthew Askew Papers.
  John H. Bolton Journal.
  Robert H. Caldwell Letters.
  Samuel A. Linton Memoir.
  Liberty Warner Letters.
Chicago Historical Society, Chicago (CHS)
  John C. Breckinridge Papers.
  Joseph F. Johnson Letters.
  J. H. Stokes Manuscript, Chicago Board of Trade Battery Folder.
Chickamauga-Chattanooga National Battlefield Park (CCNBP)
  Francis M. Carlisle Autobiography (42nd Indiana File).
  Lake Lyman Letters (1st U.S. File).
Cincinnati Historical Society, Cincinnati (CINHS)
  Stanley Matthews Letters.
Duke University, Durham, North Carolina (DU)
  Frank Carter Letters.
  John Magee Diary.

Emory University, Atlanta (EU)
    Benjamin P. Weaver Letters, Confederate Miscellany.
Illinois State Historical Society, Springfield (ILSHS)
    Martin Van Buren Coder Letters.
    James M. Cole Letters.
    John Palmer Papers.
    Lon Payne Letters.
    George Sinclair Letters.
Indiana Historical Society, Indianapolis (INHS)
    Frederick Knefler Letters.
    Winfield Scott Miller Letters.
    Alfred B. Wade Journal.
Knox College, Galesburg, Illinois (KC)
    Sidney Post Diary.
Library of Congress, Washington (LC)
    James B. Mitchell Letters (34th Alabama).
Louisiana State University, Baton Rouge (LSU)
    John Ellis Memoir.
    John McGrath Letters (Louisiana and Lower Mississippi Valley Collection).
Massachusetts Historical Society, Boston
    Henry Ware Hall Papers.
Mississippi Department of Archives and History, Jackson (MDAH)
    William J. Bass, "A Short Sketch of my Life in the Confederate Army from August 28
        AD 1861 to May 14, 1863.
    William Drennan Papers.
National Archives, Washington, D.C. (NA)
    Jefferson Davis Papers.
    Records of the Adjutant General's Office, 1780's–1917, Vol. 3, RG 94.
    Telegrams Sent and Received, October 1862–January 1865, Department of the
        Cumberland, Entry 916, RG 393.
Navarro College, Corsicana, Texas
    William McGregor Letters, Pearce Collection.
    Kunkler Letter.
New York Historical Society, New York (NYHS)
    John C. Breckinridge Papers.
Ohio Historical Society, Columbus (OHS)
    John D. Innsbrook Diary.
    Emerson Opdycke Papers.
    "The Journal of 1st Lieutenant John H. Bolton, Company F, 21st Ohio Volunteer
        Infantry."

Rutherford B. Hayes Presidential Library, Fremont, Ohio (RBHPL)

Robert Caldwell Letters.

"Memoir of Charles Barney Dennis, 101st O.V.I.

Southern Historical Collection, University of North Carolina, Chapel Hill (SHC)

Thomas Bragg Diary.

Irving Buck Letters.

Thomas Patton Letters (60th North Carolina).

William Rogers Diary (1st Florida).

Kirby Smith Paper.

J. K. Street Letters (9th Texas).

State Historical Society of Wisconsin, Madison (SHSW)

Robert Chivas Letters, in Alexander Mitchell Papers.

John Mitchell Letters.

Stones River National Battlefield Park, Murfreesboro (SRNBP)

Ed Abbott Reminiscences (4th Indiana Battery File).

George Barry Letters (89th Illinois).

Arza Bartholomew Letters (21st Michigan File).

A . S. Bloomfield Letters (A, 1st Ohio Light Artillery File).

William Brown Journal (Stanford's Mississippi Battery File).

Joseph Buckley Letters (89th Illinois File).

Robert Bunting Letters (8th Texas Cavalry File).

A. Stanley Camp Letters. (18th Ohio File).

John H. Carpenter Diary (9th Michigan).

William J. Carson Letters (15th U.S. File).

Alexander C. Cooper, "Memoirs of the Civil War" (59th Illinois File).

Joseph B. Dodge, "What I Saw at Stone River" (30th Indiana File).

Lars O. Dokken Diary (15th Wisconsin File).

Ambrose Doss Letters (19th Alabama File).

Thomas R. Ford Letters (12th Tennessee File).

William E. Garlock Letters (42nd Illinois File).

Frederick W. Goddard Diary (89th Illinois File).

D. S. Griffith Letters (38th Indiana).

Henry Hammond Letters (18th U.S. File).

S. R. Haymond Letters (5th U.S. Artillery File).

Jerome P. Holcolmb Letters (6th Indiana File).

James H. Jackson Deposition, January 1888 (C, 1st Illinois Artillery File).

James Jones Letters (57th Indiana File).

Reuben Jones Letters (19th U.S.).

Robert King Letters (15th United States File).

B . V. Lambersom Letters (Pioneer Brigade File).

"A Part of Leonard Family History" (49th Ohio File).

John K. Leonard Letters (21st Ohio File).

Dwight A. Lincoln Letter (88th Illinois File).

Luke Lyman Letters (18th U.S. File).

James S. McCarty Letters (73rd Illinois File).

William A. Moore Letters (73rd Illinois File).

D . K. Newhouse Letters (101st Ohio File).

D . P. Norman Letters (28th Alabama File).

H. F. Nuckols Letter (4th Kentucky C. S. File).

Hannibal Paine (26th Tennessee File).

Walter A. Patterson Memoir (38th Illinois File).

Clarence O. Pecoy Diary (36th Illinois File).

Henry Potter Letters (4th Michigan Cavalry File).

William D. Rogers Letters (1st Florida File).

Harley H. Sherwood Deposition, 1888 (C, 1st Illinois Artillery File).

David C. Shotts Diary (18th Ohio File).

Amandus Silsby Letters (24th Wisconsin File).

George Sinclair Letters (89th Illinois File).

Silas T. Stevens Account (Chicago Board of Trade Battery File).

"Souvenir of the First Reunion of the Fifth Wisconsin Battery (5th Wisconsin
    Battery File).

Eben P. Sturgis Diary (B, 1st Ohio Artillery File).

George T. Squire Letters (21st Ohio File).

C. I. Walker Letters (10th South Carolina File).

Henry Watson Letters (10th Texas Cavalry Dismounted).

Samuel Welch, "A Sketch of the Movements of the Fifty-first Ohio" (51st Ohio File).

Lyman S. Widney (34th Illinois File).

James K. Wier Letters (25th Illinois File).

J. A. Williamson Letters (2nd Arkansas Mounted Rifles).

Tennessee State Library and Archives, Nashville (TSLA)

George Winchester Diary.

Spencer B. Talley Memoirs.

Tulane University, New Orleans (TU)

William Preston Papers, Mason Barret Collection.

Clement S. Watson Papers, Louisiana Historical Association Collection.

United States Army Military History Institute, Carlisle Barracks, Pa. (USAMHI)

Will Carson Letters, Civil War Times Collection.

John Russell Letters, civil War Times Collection.

Edward Wood Letters, Lewis Leigh Collection.

University of Michigan, Bentley Historical Library (UM)

Thomas J. Conley Letters.

John C. Love Letters.

Henry M. Mitzner, "The Fourteenth Michigan Infantry, the Battle of Murfreesboro, Tennessee, the Battle of Jonesboro, Georgia, and Incidents of My Life."

John G. Parkhurst Letters.

University of Mississippi, Oxford (UMISS)
Charles Roberts Letters.

University of the South, Sewanee, Tennessee
Leonidas Polk Papers.

University of Texas, Arlington
John Henry King Memoir, Ben K. Green Papers, AR 326.

West Tennessee Historical Society, University of Memphis (WTHS)
J. L. Hammers Letters.

Western Kentucky University, Bowling Green (WKU)
Sam Starling Letters in Lewis-Starling Collection.

Western Reserve Historical Society, Cleveland (WRHS)
Braxton Bragg Papers, William Palmer Collection.
James Barnett Papers.
Wilbur F. Hinman Letters.
John R. Woodworth Papers.

Newspapers

NORTHERN

Belmont Chronicle (Ohio).
Bucyrus Journal (Ohio).
Chicago Tribune.
Church Advocate (Ohio).
Cincinnati Daily Commercial.
Cleveland Morning Leader.
Daily Commercial Register (Sandusky, Ohio).
Dayton Journal.
Delaware Gazette (Ohio).
Fort Wayne Weekly Sentinel.
Gillopolis Dispatch (Ohio).
Highland Weekly News (Ohio).
Holmes County Farmer (Ohio).
Indianapolis Daily Journal.
Ironton Register (Ohio).
Jacksonville Journal (Illinois).
Jeffersonian Democrat (Ohio).
Lima Gazette.
McArthur Democrat (Ohio).

Madison Daily Courier (Ohio).
Mahoning Register (Ohio).
Nashville Daily Union and American.
Nashville Dispatch.
Newcomestown News (Ohio).
New York Herald.
New York Times.
Norwalk Reflector (Ohio).
Ohio Repository.
Ohio State Journal.
Perryville Miner's Journal (Pennsylvania).
Philadelphia Weekly Times.
Pomoroy Leader (Ohio).
Pottsville Miners Journal (Pennsylvania).
Rockbridge Register (Illinois).
Scioto Register (Ohio).
Springfield Republic (Ohio).
Steubenville Weekly Herald.
Summit County Beacon (Ohio).
Tiffin Weekly Tribune.
Toledo Blade.
Troy Times (Ohio).
Western Reserve Chronicle (Ohio).
Wyandot Pioneer (Ohio).

SOUTHERN

Atlanta Intelligencer.
Charleston Mercury.
Chattanooga Daily Rebel.
Columbia Daily Guardian.
Columbus Daily Sun (Georgia).
Daily Rebel Banner (Murfreesboro).
Daily Register (Selma, Alabama).
Huntsville Confederate (Alabama).
Memphis Appeal.
Mobile Advertiser & Register.
Montgomery Weekly Advertiser.
Savannah Morning News.
Savannah Republican.
Selma Morning Reporter (Alabama).

Official Documents

Atlas to Accompany the Official Records of the Union and Confederate Armies. Washington, D.C.: U.S. Government Printing Office, 1891–95.

Hewitt, Janet, B., et al., eds. *Supplement to the Official Records of the Union and Confederate Armies.* 94 Vols. Wilmington: Broadfoot Publishing Co., 1994–1999.

U.S. War Department. *The War of the Rebellion; A Compilation of the Official Records of the Union and Confederate Armies.* 128 vols. Washington, D. C., 1880–1902.

Dissertations and Studies

Galliford, Andrew. "Van Cleve Lane: Recovering a Trace of History." Middle Tennessee State University Study. April 23, 1991.

Mann, Wayne. "The Road to Murfreesboro: The Eleventh Michigan Volunteer Infantry from Organization Through its First Battle." M.A. thesis, Western Michigan University, 1963.

"Stones River National Battlefield Historical Research Study." SRNBP.

Syles, Sean M. "Stones River National Battlefield Historic Resource Study." February 2004, SRNBP.

Varney, Francis Philip. "The Men Grant Didn't Trust: Memoir, Memory, and the American Civil War." Ph.D. diss., Cornell University, 2007.

Published Primary Sources

Adams, Jacob. *Diary of Jacob Adams, Private in Company F, 21st OVI.* Columbus, Ohio: F. J. Heer, 1930.

Aldrich, C. Knight, ed. *Quest for a Star: The Civil War Letters and Diaries of Francis T. Sherman of the 88th Illinois.* Knoxville: University of Tennessee Press, 1999.

The Annual Reunion: Reports of the Meetings of the Society of the Army of the Cumberland, 1887 Reunion. Cincinnati: Robert Clarke, 1888.

Barnes, James A., James R. Carnahan, and Thomas H. B. McCain. *The Eighty-Sixth Regiment, Indiana Volunteer Infantry: A Narrative of its Services in the Civil War of 1861–1865.* Crawfordsville, Ind.: Journal Co., 1895.

Barry, John M. "Reminiscences from Missouri." *Confederate Veteran* 7 (1900), 93.

Bascom, Elizabeth E. P., ed. *"Dear Lizzie."* (n.p., n.d.).

Basler, Roy B., ed. *The Collected Works of Abraham Lincoln.* 8 vols. New Brunswick, N.J.: Rutgers University Press, 1953.

Beatty, John. *The Citizen Soldier.* Cincinnati: Wilstach, Baldwin, 1879.

Bedford, J. A. *Leaves From a Trooper's Diary.* Philadelphia: by author, 1868.

Bennett, Charles. *Historical Sketches of the Ninth Michigan Infantry (General Thomas Headquarters Guards) with an Account of the Battle of Murfreesboro, Tennessee. Sunday, July 13, 1863.* Coldwater, Mich.: Daily Courier, 1913.

Bennett, L. G., and William M. Haight. *History of the Thirty-Sixth Regiment Illinois Volunteers, During the War of the Rebellion.* Aurora, Ill.: Knickerbocker and Holder, 1876.

Bickham, William. *Rosecrans' Campaign with the Fourteenth Corps, or Army of the Cumberland: A Narrative of Personal Observations . . . with Official Reports of the Battle of Stones River.* Cincinnati: Moore, Wilstach, Keys, 1863.

Blackburn, Theodore W. *Letters From the Front: A Union Preacher's Regiment (74th Ohio) in the Civil War.* N.d. Rpt. Dayton: Morningside Bookshop, 1981.

Blegen, Theodore C., ed. *The Civil War Letters of Hans Christian Heg.* Northfield: Minnesota-Norwegian American Historical Association, 1936.

Bowman, C. C. "Stone's River: How Grose's Brigade Helped Stay the Onset of the Rebels." *National Tribune,* November 6, 1884.

Boyle, Julie A., John D. Smith, and Richard M. McMurry, eds. *The Civil War Letters of George W. Squire, Hoosier Volunteer.* Knoxville: University of Tennessee Press, 1998.

Bransford, John S. "Gallant Preston D. Cunningham." *Confederate Veteran* 10 (June 1902): 268.

Briant, Charles. *History of the Sixth Regiment Indiana Volunteer Infantry: Of Both the Three Months' and Three Years' Services.* Indianapolis: W. B. Burford, 1891.

Butler, Jay. *Letters Home.* Binghampton, N.Y.: n.p., 1930.

Butler, M. B. *My Story of the Civil War and the Under-ground Railroad* (Huntington, Ind.: United Brethren Publishing Establishment, 1914.

Cabaniss, Jim R., comp. *Civil War Journal and Letters of Washington Ives 4th Fla. C.S.A.* N.p.: by author, 1987.

Canfield, Silas S. *History of the 21st Regiment Ohio Volunteer Infantry in the War of the Rebellion.* Toledo, Ohio: Vrooman, Anderson, and Bateman, 1893.

Carman, Henry J., ed. "The Diary of Amos Glover." *Ohio Historical Quarterly* 44 (1935).

Cate, Wirt A., ed. *Two Soldiers: The Campaign Diaries of Thomas J. Key C.S.A. and Robert J. Campbell U.S.A.* Chapel Hill: University of North Carolina Press, 1938.

Chalaron, J. A. "Memories of Rice Graves, C.S.A." *Daviess County Historical Quarterly* 3 (1985): 3–13.

Charles, William T. *Recollections of a Christmas During the War.* N.p., 1959.

Christ, Lynda L, ed. *The Papers of Jefferson Davis.* 12 vols. Baton Rouge: Louisiana State University Press, 1971–2008.

"The Civil War Letters of Henry Clay Reynolds Concerning Battles in Middle Tennessee January–July 1863." *Rutherford County Historical Society* 29.

Clark, Sam L., and H. D. Riley, eds. "Outline of the Organization of the Medical Department of the Confederate Army and Department of Tennessee by S. H. Stout." *Tennessee Historical Quarterly* 16 (Spring 1957): 55–82.

Clay, H. B. "On the Right at Murfreesboro." *Confederate Veteran* 21 (December 1913): 588–89.

Coffee, F. E. "The First Kentucky at Stone River." *National Tribune,* August 23, 1883.

Cooper, James L. "Service With the Twentieth Tennessee Regiment." *Confederate Veteran* 33 (February 1925): 57.

Cope, Alexis. *The Fifteenth Ohio Volunteers and Its Campaigns 1861–1865.* Columbus, Ohio: by author 1916.

Cox, Kim C, comp. *Colonel Grant's Regiment: the 21st Illinois Volunteers from Muster to Stones River in the Letters of Private Allen M. Patton.* San Diego: by author, 1997.

Crittenden, Thomas L. "The Union Left at Stone's River." *Battles and Leaders of the Civil War* 4 vols. 1911. Rpt. New York: Thomas Yoseloff, 1956. Vol. 3: 632–34.

Curry, W. L. *Four Years in the Saddle: History of the First Regiment Ohio Volunteer Cavalry* 1898. Rpt. Jonesboro, Ga.: Freedom Hill Press, Inc., 1984.

Day, Lewis W. *A Story of the One Hundred and First Infantry: A Memorial Volume.* Cleveland: W. M. Bayne, 1894.

Davidson, Henry M. *History of Battery A, 1st Ohio Volunteer Light Artillery.* Milwaukee: Daily Wisconsin Steam Printing House, 1865.

Davis, William C., ed. *The Confederate Memoirs Robert Barnwell Rhett.* Columbia: University of South Carolina Press, 2000.

———, ed. *Diary of a Confederate Soldier: John S. Jackman of the Orphan Brigade.* Columbia: University of South Carolina Press, 1990.

Dennet, Tyler, ed. *Lincoln and the Civil War: In the Diaries and Letters of John Hay.* 1939. Rpt. New York: Da Capo, 1988.

Dennis, Frank A., ed. *Kemper County Rebel: The Civil War Diary of Robert Masten Holmes, C.S.A.* Jackson: University and College Press of Mississippi, 1973.

DeVellin, C. T. *History of the Seventeenth Regiment, First Brigade, 3d Division, 14th Army Corps, Army of the Cumberland, War of the Rebellion.* Zanesville, Ohio: F. R. Sullivan, 1889.

DeWees, Joseph W., ed. *Joshua DeWees: His Civil War Diary, Co. D, 97th O.V.I., IV Army Corps, Army of the Cumberland.* Nashville, Ind.: Brown County Printing, 1991.

Dillon, William D. "The Civil War Letters of Enos Barret Lewis, 101st Ohio Volunteer Infantry—Pt. 1." *Northwestern Ohio Quarterly* 57 (Spring 1985).

Dobson, James. *A Historical Sketch of Company K of the 79th Regiment Indiana Volunteers.* Plainfield, Ind.: Progress Print, 1894.

Dodge, William Sumner. *History of the Old Second Division Army of the Cumberland.* Chicago: Church and Goodman, 1864.

———. *A Waif of the War or, the History of the Seventy-Fifth Illinois Infantry* Chicago: Church and Goodman, 1866.

Donald, David, ed. *Inside Lincoln's Cabinet: The Civil War Diaries of Salmon P. Chase.* 4 vols. 1954. Rpt. Kent, Ohio: Kent State University Press, 1993–97.

Douglas, Lucia R., ed. *Douglas' Texas Battery, C.S.A.* Waco, Texas: Smith County Historical Society, 1966.

Doyle, Julie A., John David Smith, and Richard M. McMurry, eds. *This Wilderness of War: The Civil War Letters of George W. Squier, Hoosier Volunteer.* Knoxville: University of Tennessee Press, 1998.

Driver, Robert A., and Gloria S. *Letters Home: The Personal Side of the American Civil War by Jacob Early.* Roseburg, Ore.: by author, 1992.

Elliott, Sam Davis, ed. *Doctor Quintard, Chaplain C.S.A. and Second Bishop of Tennessee: The Memoir and Diary of Charles Todd Quintard.* Baton Rouge, Louisiana State University Press, 2003.

Ellis, James W. "Gratitude of Veterans." *Confederate Veteran* 17 (December 1909): 581.

Erb, William. *The Valley of Death, the Battle of Stone's River: Extract from the Battles of the Nineteenth Ohio.* Washington, D.C.: Judd and Detweiler, 1893.

Fisher, Cecil H., ed., *A Staff Officer's Story: The Personal Experiences of Colonel Horace Newton Fisher in the Civil War.* Boston: Todd, 1960.

Fitch, John. *Annals of the Army of the Cumberland.* 1864. Rpt. Mechanicsburg, Pa.: Stackpole Books, 2003.

Fitch, Michael H. *Echoes of the Civil War: John Henry Otto, War Memoirs.* Kent, Ohio: Kent State University Press, 1994.

Frankenberry, Allen D., ed. *History of the Fifteenth Pennsylvania Volunteer Cavalry Known as the Anderson Cavalry in the Rebellion of 1861–1865.* Philadelphia: n.p., 1906.

Franklin, Ann Y., comp. *The Civil War Diaries of Capt. Alfred Tyler Fielder 12th Tennessee Regiment Infantry, Company B 1861–1865.* Louisville, Ky.: by author, 1996.

Freeman, Henry V. "Some Battle Recollections of Stone's River." *Military Order of the Loyal Legion of the United States, Illinois.* 1899. Rpt. Wilmington, N.C.: Broadfoot Publishing Co., 1992. Vol. 3: 227–46.

Freeman, Joseph L. "The Twenty-fourth Ohio V. I. at Stone River." *National Tribune,* July 19, 1883.

Fremantle, Arthur James L. *Three Months in the Southern States, April–June 1863.* New York: J. Bradburn, 1864.

Gammage, Washington L. *The Camp, the Bivouac, and the Battlefield, Being a History of the Fourth Arkansas Regiment, from Its Organization Down to the Present Date: Its Campaigns and Its Battles, with an Occasional Reference to the Current Events of the Times, Including Biographical Sketches of Its Field Officers and Others of the "Old Brigade." The Whole Interspersed Here and There with Descriptions of Scenery, Incidents of Camp Life, Etc.* Little Rock: Arkansas Southern Press, 1958.

Gates, Arnold, ed. *The Rough Side of the War: The Civil War Journal of Chesley A. Mosman, 1st Lieutenant, Company D, 59th Illinois Volunteer Infantry Regiment.* Garden City, N.Y.: Basin, 1987.

Geneco, James C., ed. *To the Sound of Musketry and Tap of the Drum: A History of Michigan's Battery D Through the Letters of Artificer Harold J. Bartlett 1861-1864.* Detroit: Detroit Book Press, 1990.

Gibson, John T. *History of the 78th Pennsylvania Volunteer Infantry.* Pittsburgh: Pittsburgh Print Co., 1905.

Girardi, Robert I., Jr. and Nathaniel C. Hughes Jr., eds. *The Memoirs of Brigadier General William Passmore Carlin U.S.A.* Lincoln: University of Nebraska Press, 1999.

Gould, David, and James B. Kennedy, eds. *Memoirs of a Dutch Mudsill: The War Memoirs of John Henry Otto, Captain, Company D, 21st Regiment Wisconsin Volunteer Infantry.* Kent, Ohio: Kent State University Press, 2004.

Graf, LeRoy P., Ralph W. Haskins, and Paul W. Bergeron, eds. *The Papers of Andrew Johnson.* 13 vols. Knoxville: University of Tennessee Press, 1966–2000.

Hallock, Judith Lee, ed. *The Civil War Letters of Joshua K. Callaway.* Athens: University of Georgia Press, 1997.

Hannaford, Ebenezer. "In the Ranks at Stones River." In Cozzens, ed., *Battles and Leaders of the Civil War* 6: 172–95.

Harden, Henry O. *History of the 90th Ohio Volunteer Infantry in the War of the Great Rebellion of the United States 1861-1865.* Stoutsville, Ohio: Press of Fairfield Pickaway News, 1902.

Hart, Albert G. "The Surgeon and the Hospital in the Civil War." *Papers of the Military Historical Society of Massachusetts.* Boston: The Society, 1902). Vol. 12.

Hartpence, William R. *History of the Fifty-First Indiana Volunteer Infantry.* Cincinnati: Robert Clarke, 1894.

Hay, Thomas R., ed. *Cleburne and His Command by Irving A. Buck.* Jackson, Tenn.: McCowat-Mercer Press, 1957.

Haynie, James Henry. *The Nineteenth Illinois: A Memoir of a Regiment of Volunteer Infantry Famous in the Civil War of fifty Years Ago for its Drill, Bravery, and Distinguished Services.* Chicago: Donohoe & Co., 1912.

Hascall, Milo. "Personal Recollections and Experiences Concerning Battle of Stones River." *Military Order of the Loyal Legion of the United States, Illinois.* 1892. Rpt. Wilmington, N.C.: Broadfoot Publishing Co., 1992. Vol. 4: 148–70.

Hazen, William B. *A Narrative of Military Service.* Boston: Ticknor and Co., 1885.

Heiner, A. H. "The Battle of Murfreesboro Again." *Confederate Veteran* 12 (March 1904): 118.

Herr, George W. *Episodes of the Civil War in Nine States: Fremont in Missouri—Curtis in Missouri and Arkansas—Halleck's Siege of Corinth—Buell in Kentucky—Rosecrans in Kentucky and Tennessee—Grant at the Battle of Chattanooga—Sherman From Chattanooga to Atlanta—Thomas in Tennessee and North Carolina—Stanley in Texas. In Which Comprised the History of the Fifty-ninth Regiment Illinois Volunteer Infantry.* San Francisco: Bancroft, 1890.

Hinman, Wilbur F. *The Story of the Sherman Brigade: The Camp, the Bivouac, the Battles and How 'The Boys' Lived and Died During the Four Years of Active Field Service.* Alliance: Ohio: Privately published, 1897.

History of the Services of the Third Battery, Wisconsin Light Artillery in the Civil War of the United States, 1861–1865. Berlin, Wis.: Convant Press, 1902.

Holmes, Mead, Jr. *A Soldier of the Army of the Cumberland: Memoir of Mead Holmes, Jr. Sergeant of Company K, 21st Regiment Wisconsin Volunteers.* Boston: American Tract Society, 1864.

Horrall, Spillard. *History of the Forty-Second Indiana Volunteer Infantry.* Chicago: Horrall, 1892.

Hoskinson, S. F. "Stone's River." *National Tribune,* November 27, 1884.

Howard, O. O. "Sketch of the Life of General George H. Thomas." *Military Order of the Loyal Order of the United States, New York.* 1891. Rpt. Wilmington, N.C.: Broadfoot Publishing Co., 1993.Vol. 1: 285–302.

Hughes, Nathaniel C., ed. *Liddell's Record: St. John Liddell, Brigadier General, C.S.A. Staff Officer and Brigade Commander Army of Tennessee.* Dayton, Ohio: Morningside, 1985.

J.A.C. "Colonel P. D. Cunningham." *Confederate Veteran* 12 (May 1904): 240.

Johnson, Robert J., and Clarence C. Buel, eds. *Battles and Leaders of the Civil War.* 4 vols. 1911. Rpt. New York: Thomas Yoseloff, 1956.

Johnson, Richard W. *A Soldier's Reminiscences.* Philadelphia: J. P. Lippincott, 1886.

——. "Losing a Division at Stones River." In Peter Cozzens, ed., *Battle and Leaders of the Civil War.* Vol. 6: 297–301.

Jones, J. B. *A Rebel War Clerk's Diary at the Confederate States Capital.* 2 vols. Philadelphia: J. P Lippincott & Co., 1866.

Jones, P. R. "Recollections of the Battle of Murfreesboro." *Confederate Veteran* 31 (September 1923): 341–42.

Kendall, Henry M. "The Third Day at Stone's River." *Military Order of the Loyal Legion of the United States, District of Columbia.* 1903. Rpt. Wilmington, N.C.: Broadfoot Publishing Co., 1993. Vol. 3: 3–14.

Kerwood, Asbury L. *Annals of the Fifty-Seventh Indiana Volunteers, Marches, Battles, and Incidents of Army Life, by a Member of the Regiment.* Dayton: W. J. Shuey, 1868), 116.

Kiene, Ralph E., Jr., ed. *A Civil War Diary: The Journal of Francis A. Kiene, 1862–1865.* Privately published, 1974.

Kimberly, Robert L., and Ephraim S. Holloway. *The Forty-First Ohio Veteran Volunteer Infantry in the War of the Rebellion.* Cleveland: W. R. Smellie, 1897.

Kirk, Charles H., ed. *History of the Fifteenth Pennsylvania Cavalry: Which Was Recruited and Known as the Anderson Troops in the Rebellion of 1861–1865.* Philadelphia: Privately Published, 1906.

Kirwan, A. K. *Johnny Green of the Orphan Brigade: The Journal of a Confederate Soldier.* Lexington: University of Kentucky Press, 1956.

Kniffen, Gilbert C. "Army of the Cumberland and the Battle of Stone's River." *Military Order of the Loyal Legion of the United States, District of Columbia.* 1907. Rpt. Wilmington, N.C.: Broadfoot Publishing Co., 1993. Vol. 3: 411–54.

———. "The Battle of Stones River." In Johnson and Buel, eds., *Battles and Leaders of the Civil War* 3: 616–32.

Lathrop, David. *The History of the Fifty-ninth Regiment Illinois Volunteers.* Indianapolis: Hall and Hutchison, 1865.

Lindsley, John B., ed. *Military Annals of Tennessee. Confederate.* 2 vols. Nashville: J. M. Lindsey & Co., 1886.

Lockett, S. H. "The Defense of Vicksburg." In Johnson and Buel, eds., *Battles and Leaders of the Civil War* 3: 482–92.

Malone, Thomas H. *Memoir of Thomas H. Malone.* Nashville: Baird-Ward, 1928.

Manderson, Charles F. *The Twin Seven-Shooters.* New York: F. Tennyson Neely, 1902.

Marks, Solon. "Experiences at the Battle of Stone's River." *Military Order of the Loyal Legion of the United States, Wisconsin.* 1896. Rpt. Wilmington, N.C.: Broadfoot Publishing Co., 1993. Vol. 2: 385–98.

Mathis, Ray, ed. *In the Land of the Living: Wartime Letters by Confederates from the Chattahoochee Valley of Alabama and Georgia.* Troy, Ala.: Troy State University Press, 1981.

Maxwell, James Robert. *Autobiography of James Robert Maxwell of Tuscaloosa, Alabama.* New York: Greenburg, 1926.

McCain, Thomas H. B. *In Song and Sorrow: The Daily Journal of Thomas H. B. McCain. 86th Indiana Volunteer Infantry.* Carmel, Ind.: Guild Press of Indiana, 1998.

McDowell, William P. "The Fifteenth Kentucky." *Southern Bivouac* 5 (1886): 246-58.

McMurray, W. J. *History of the Twentieth Tennessee Regiment Volunteer Infantry, C.S.A.* Nashville: Publication Committee, 1904.

McMurry, Richard M., ed. *An Uncompromising Secessionist: The Civil War of George Knox Miller, Eighth (Wade's) Confederate Cavalry.* Tuscaloosa: University of Alabama Press, 2007.

Moon, G. B. "A Boy's Experience in Seeing a Battle." *Confederate Veteran* 7 (March 1899): 119.

Moorman, Hiram Clark. *The Moorman Memorandum.* Somerville, Tenn.: The Society, 1959.

Murray, John P. "Tribute to P. D. Cunningham." *Confederate Veteran* 1 (November 1894): 33.

Neal, Ralf J. "Ralf J. Neal Letter." *Confederate Veteran* 7 (February 1899): 70-71.

Newlin, William H. *A History of the Seventy-third Illinois Infantry Volunteers, and in Many of the War, 1861-1865.* Springfield: n.p., 1890.

Niven, John, ed. *The Salmon P. Chase Papers.* 4 vols. Kent, Ohio: Kent State University Press, 1993–97.

Noe, Kenneth, ed. *A Southern Boy in Blue: The Memoir of Marcus Woodcock 9th Kentucky Infantry (U.S.A.).* Knoxville: University of Tennessee Press., 1996.

"Old Rosey." *National Tribune,* May 26, 1887.

Palmer, John M. *Personal Recollections of John M. Palmer: The Story of an Earnest Life.* Cincinnati: Robert Clarke Co., 1901.

Parkhurst, "Recollections of Stone's River." *Military Order of the Loyal Legion of the United States, Michigan.* 1890. Rpt. Wilmington, N.C.: Broadfoot Publishing Co., 1993. Vol. 1: 299–311.

Payne, Edwin W. *History of the Thirty-Fourth Regiment of Illinois Volunteer Infantry.* Clinton, Iowa: Allen, 1902.

Pease, Theodore C. and James G. Randal, eds. *Diary of Orville Browning.* 2 vols. Springfield: Illinois State Historical Society, 1925–32.

Phisterer, Frederick. *Association of Survivors, Regular Brigade, Fourteenth Army Corps, Army of the Cumberland.* N.p., n.d.

Pickett, W. D. "Reminiscences of Murfreesboro." *Confederate Veteran* 16 (September 1908): 450–52

Pirtle, Alfred. "Donelson's Charge at Stone River." *Southern Bivouac* 6 (May 1887): 768–70.

———. "Stone River Sketches." *Military Order of the Loyal Legion of the United States, Ohio.* 1908. Rpt. Wilmington, N.C.: Broadfoot, Publishing Co., 1991. Vol. 6: 95–110.

"Private M'Dearman at Murfreesboro." *Confederate Veteran* 9 (1901): 306.

"Pvt. Thomas L. Potter, Standart's Battery B, 1st Ohio Light Artillery Vividly Describes the Battle of Stones River." *Blue & Gray* (December 2004): 24–25.

"Proceedings of Congress." *Southern Historical Society Papers* 46 (January 1928): 1–256.

Puntunney, George H. *History of the Thirty-Seventh Regiment of Indiana Infantry Volunteers.* Rushville, Ind.: Jacksonian Book and Job Department, 1896.

"Record of Gen. George W. Gordon." *Confederate Veteran* 20 (September 1912): 427–28.

Reinhart, Joseph E. *August Willich's Gallant Dutchmen: Civil War Letters from the 32nd Indiana Infantry.* Kent, Ohio: Kent State University Press, 2006.

Rerick, John. *The Forty-Fourth Indiana Volunteer Infantry: History of Its Services in the War of the Rebellion and a Personal Record of Its Members.* LaGrange, Ind.: by author, 1880.

Richards, Henry. *Letters of Captain Henry Richards of the Ninety-Third Ohio Infantry.* Cincinnati: Wrightson, 1883.

Ritter, Edmund. "The Regulars at Stone River." *National Tribune,* September 6, 1883.

Robuck, J. E. *My Own Personal Experiences and Observation as a Soldier in the Confederate Army During the Civil War.* 1911. Rpt. Memphis: Burke's Book Store, 1970.

Rose, D. D. "Stone's River." *National Tribune,* November 13, 1884.

Rugeley, H. J. H., ed. *Batchelor-Turner Letters, 1861–1864: Written by Two of Terry's Texas Rangers.* Austin: University of Texas Press, 1961.

Scarborough, William K., ed. *The Diary of Edmund Ruffin.* 2 vols. Baton Rouge: Louisiana State University Press, 1976.

Scribner, Benjamin F. *How Soldiers Were Made; or the War As I Saw It.* 1887. Rpt. Huntington, W.Va.: Blue Acorn Press, 1995.

Seay, Samuel. "A Private at Stone River." *Southern Bivouac* 4 (August 1885).

Shanks, William F. G. *Personal Recollections of Distinguished Generals.* New York: Harper, 1866.

———. "Recollections of General Rousseau." *Harper's Magazine* 30 (November 1865): 762–68.

Sheridan, Philip H. *The Personal Memoirs of P. H. Sheridan.* 2 vols. 1888. Rpt. New York: Da Capo Press, 1992.

Smith, John Thomas. *A History of the Thirty-First Regiment of Indiana Volunteer Infantry in the War of the Rebellion.* Cincinnati: Western Methodist Book, 1900.

Sneed, Thomas L. "With Price East of the Mississippi." In Robert C. Johnson and Clarence C. Buel, eds., *Battle and Leaders of the Civil War.* 4 vols. 1911. Rpt. New York: Thomas Yoseloff, 1956. Vol. 2: 717–34.

Society of the Army of the Cumberland, 22d Reunion, 1891. Cincinnati: Robert Clarke, 1892.

Society of the Seventy-Fourth Illinois Volunteer Infantry: Reunion Proceedings and the History of the Regiment. Rockford, Ill.: W. P. Lamb, 1903.

Spence, John L. *A Diary of the Civil War.* Murfreesboro, Tenn.: Rutherford County Historical Association, 1993.

Stanley, David S. *Personal Memoirs of Major-General D. S. Stanley U.S.A.* Cambridge, Mass.: Harvard University Press, 1917.

Stevenson, Alexander F. *The Battle of Stone's River near Murfreesboro Tenn. December 30, 1862, to January 3, 1863.* 1884. Rpt. Dayton, Ohio: Morningside, 1983.

Stewart, J. A. "The Battle of Stone's River, As Seen by One Who Was There." *Blue & Gray* 5 (January 1895).

———. "Stone's River." *National Tribune,* August 27, 1885.

Sutherland, Daniel E., ed. *Reminiscences of a Private: William E. Bevins of the First Arkansas Infantry, C.S.A.* Fayetteville: University of Arkansas Press, 1992.

Thompson, Ed Porter. *History of the Orphan Brigade.* Louisville, Ky.: L. N. Thompson, 1898.

Thruston, Gates P. "Personal Recollections of the Battle in the Rear at Stone's River." *Military Order of the Loyal Legion of the United States, Ohio.* 1908. Rpt. Wilmington, N.C.: Broadfoot Publishing Co., 1993. Vol. 6.

Tower, R. Lockwood, ed. *A Carolinian Goes to War: The Civil War Narrative of Arthur Middleton Manigault. Brigadier General, C.S.A.* Columbia: University of South Carolina, 1983.

Truxall, Aida C., ed. *"Respects to All"*: *Letters of Two Pennsylvania Boys in the War of the Rebellion*. Pittsburgh: University of Pittsburgh Press, 1962.

Tunnel, J. T. "Texans in the Battle at Murfreesboro." *Confederate Veteran* 16 (November 1889): 574.

Uhler, Margaret A., ed. "Civil War Letters of Major General James Patton Anderson." *Florida Historical Quarterly* 56 (October 1977): 154–66.

Urquhart, David. "Bragg's Advance and Retreat." In Johnson and Buel, eds., *Battles and Leaders of the Civil War* 3: 600–609.

Vale, Joseph G. *Minty and the Cavalry: A History of the Cavalry Campaigns in the Western Armies*. Harrisburg, Pa.: Edwin K. Meyers, 1886.

Vaughn, A. J. *Personal Record of the Thirteenth Regiment, Tennessee Infantry*. Memphis: S. C. Toof & Co., 1897.

Wade, Alfred B. "'Hoosier Journal': The Civil War Journal of Alfred B. Wade." *History of the Seventy-Third Indiana in the War of 1861–1865*. Washington, D.C.: Caqrnahan Press, 1909.

Walker, C. I. *Rolls and Historical Sketch of the Tenth Regiment So. Ca. Volunteers in the Confederates States*. 1881. Rpt. Alexandria, Va.: Stonewall House, 1985.

"War Time Letters of the Sixties." *Confederate Veteran* 12 (January 1904): 24.

Watkins, L. J. "Address of Brig. Gen. James E. Rains." *Confederate Veteran* 16 (May 1908): 209–10.

Watkins, Sam R. *"Co. Aytch": A Side Show of the Big War*. 1962. Rpt. New York: Touchstone, 1990.

Watson, Hubbard Butler, comp. *Letters Home: Jay Caldwell Butler*. N.p.: privately published, 1930.

Weber, Daniel B., ed. *From Michigan to Murfreesboro: The Diary of Ira Gillaspie of the Eleventh Michigan Infantry*. Mount Pleasant: Central Michigan University Press, 1965.

Williams, Frederick D., ed. *The Wild Life of the Army: Civil War Letters of James A. Garfield*. East Lansing: Michigan State University Press, 1964.

Wilson, Susan C., ed. *Column South: With the Fifteenth Pennsylvania Cavalry*. Flagstaff, Ariz.: J. F. Colton, 1960.

Wommack, J. J. *The Civil War J. J. Wommack, Company E, Sixteenth Tennessee Volunteer Infantry*. McMinnville, Tenn.: Womack, 1961.

Woodward, James H. "Gen. A. McD. McCook at Stone River." *Military Order of the Loyal Legion of the United States, California/Oregon*. 1905. Rpt. Wilmington, N.C.: Broadfoot Publishing Co., 1991. Vol. 1: 154–58.

Wooster, Ralph, ed. "With the Confederate Cavalry in the West: The Civil War Experiences of Isaac Dunbar Affleck." *Southwestern Historical Quarterly* 83 (July 1979): 1–28.

Worley, Ted R., ed. *The War Memories of Captain John W. Lavender C.S.A. They Never Came Back; the Story of Co. F Fourth Arks. Infantry, C.S.A. Originally Known as the Montgomery Hunters, As Told by Their Commanding Officer.* Pine Bluff, Ark.: W. M. Hackett and D. R. Perdue, 1956.

Wright, Thomas J. *History of the Eight Regiment Kentucky Vol. Inf. During Its Three Years Campaigns Embracing Organizations, Marches, Skirmishes, and the Command, with Much of the History of the Old Reliable Third Brigade, Commanded by Hon. Stanley Matthews, and Containing Many Interesting Incidents of Army Life.* St. Joseph, Mo.: Joseph Steam Printing, 1880.

Yarman, John Lee. "Stone River." *Military Order of the Loyal Legion of the United States, Indiana.* 1898. Rpt. Wilmington, N.C.: Broadfoot Publishing Co., 1991. Vol. 1: 157–77.

Young, H. K. "Stone's River." *National Tribune,* November 27, 1884.

Young, Lot D. *Reminiscences of a Soldier of the Orphan Brigade.* Louisville: Courier-Journal Printing Co., 1918.

Younger, Edward, ed. *Inside the Confederate Government: The Diary of Robert Garlick Hill Keen.* New York: Oxford University Press, 1957.

Internet

John Coe Letters, historicpreservation.org/64th_Ohio

Otis Moody Memoirs, www.51illinois.org

Hillory Shifflett Letters, www.geocities.com/~jcrosswell/War/cw/hillory.htm

home.carolina.rr.com/civilwarcauses/bloodstains2.htm

www.old-picture.com/civil-war/Kentucky-colonel-Enyart-David.htm

E. J. Wall letter, www.mqamericana.com/Stones_River_2nd_AR_CSA.html

Moses B. Walker biography, www.tshaonline.org/handbook/online/articles/WW/fwa21.html

SECONDARY SOURCES

Agers, Waldemar. *Colonel Heg and His Boys: A Norwegian Regiment in the American Civil War.* Northfield, Minn.: Norwegian-American Historical Association, 2000.

Allardice, Bruce S. *Confederate Colonels: A Biographical Register.* Columbia: University of Missouri Press, 2008.

Andrews, J. Cutler. *The South Reports the Civil War.* Pittsburgh: University of Pittsburgh Press, 1985.

Bearss, Edwin C. "Cavalry Operations in the Battle of Stones River." *Tennessee Historical Quarterly* 19 (March 1960): 23–53; (June 1960): 110–44.

Beaudot, William J. K. *The 24th Wisconsin in the Civil War: The Biography of a Regiment* (Mechanicsville, Pa.: Stackpole Books, 2003).

Bobrick, Benson. *Master of War: The Life of General George H. Thomas.* New York: Simon & Schuster, 2009.

———. *Testament: A Soldier's Story of the Civil War*. New York: Simon & Schuster, 2003.

Bonds, Russell. "Leonidas Polk: Southern Civil War General." *Civil War Times Illustrated* 45 (May 2006): 52–58.

Castel, Albert. *Decision in the West: The Atlanta Campaign of 1864*. Lawrence: University of Kansas Press, 1992.

———. "Victorious Loser: William R. Rosecrans." *Timeline*, July–August 2003, 32–37.

Cleaves, Freeman. *Rock of Chickamauga: The Life of General George H. Thomas*. Norman: University of Oklahoma Press, 1948.

Clement, Frank. "Sound and Fury: Civil War Dissent in the Cincinnati Area." *Cincinnati Historical Society Bulletin* 35 (1977).

Cist, Henry M. *The Army of the Cumberland*. 1882. Rpt. Wilmington, N.C.: Broadfoot Publishing Co., 1989.

Connelly, Thomas L. *Army of the Heartland: The Army of Tennessee, 1861–1862*. Baton Rouge: Louisiana State University Press, 1967.

———. *Autumn of Glory: The Army of Tennessee, 1862–1865*. Baton Rouge: Louisiana State University Press, 1971.

Cozzens, Peter, ed., *Battles and Leaders of the Civil War*. 6 vols. Urbana: University of Illinois Press, 2004.

———. "Forgotten Hero: Philip Sheridan Post." *Illinois Historical Journal* 84 (Summer 1991): 75–100.

———. *No Better Place to Die: The Battle of Stones River*. Urbana: University of Illinois Press, 1990.

———. *The Darkest Days of the War: The Battles of Iuka and Corinth*. Chapel Hill: University of North Carolina Press, 1997.

Daniel, Larry J. *Cannoneers in Gray: The Field Artillery of the Army of Tennessee*. Rev. ed. Tuscaloosa: University of Alabama Press, 2005.

———. *Days of Glory: The Army of the Cumberland, 1861–1865*. Baton Rouge: Louisiana State University Press, 2004.

Davis, William C. *Breckinridge: Statesman, Soldier, Symbol*. Baton Rouge: Louisiana State University Press, 1974.

———. *Jefferson Davis: The Man and His Hour*. New York: HarperCollins, 1991.

Dodson, William C. *Campaigns of Wheeler and His Cavalry, 1862–1865*. Atlanta: Hudgins Publishing Co., 1899.

Donald, David H. *Lincoln*. New York: Touchstone Books, 1996.

Dubose, John W. *General Joseph Wheeler and the Army of Tennessee*. New York: Neale Publishing Co., 1912.

Dyer, John P. *"Fightin' Joe" Wheeler*. Baton Rouge: Louisiana State University Press, 1941.

Eddy, T. M. *Patriotism of Illinois*. 2 vols. Chicago: Clarke, 1865.

Ehlinger, Peter J. *Kentucky's Last Cavalier: General William Preston, 1816–1887*. Lexington: University of Kentucky Press, 2004.

Eicher, David J. *Dixie Betrayed: How the South Really Lost the Civil War.* New York: Little, Brown and Co., 2006.

Einolf, Christopher J. *George Thomas: Virginian for the Union.* Norman: University of Oklahoma Press, 2007.

Elliott, Sam Davis. *Soldier of Tennessee: General Alexander P. Stewart and the Civil War in the West.* Baton Rouge: Louisiana State University Press, 1999.

Engle, Stephen D. *Don Carlos Buell: Most Promising of All.* Chapel Hill: University of North Carolina Press, 1999.

Eubank, Damon R. *In the Shadows of the Patriarch: The John J. Crittenden Family in War and Peace.* Macon, Ga.: Mercer University Press, 2009.

Everett, Jeanne McCracken. *The McCracken Family Honor Roll of Civil War Soldiers.* South Bend: by author, 1986.

Faust, Patricia L., ed. *Historical Times Illustrated Encyclopedia of the Civil War.* New York: Harper and Row, 1986.

Gallagher, Gary W. *Lee and His Army in Confederate History.* Chapel Hill: University of North Carolina Press, 2001.

———. "The War Was Won in the East." *Civil War Times Illustrated,* February 2011, 19–21.

Garesche, Louis. *Biography of Lieut. Col. Julius P. Garesche.* Philadelphia: J. P. Lippincott, 1887.

Glatthaar, Joseph T. "Edmund Kirby Smith," 205–47. Gary W. Gallagher and Joseph T. Glatthaar, eds. *Leaders of the Lost Cause: New Perspectives on Confederate High Command.* Mechanicsburg, Pa.: Stackpole Books, 2004.

The Goodspeed Histories of Maury, Williamson, Rutherford, Bedford & Marshall Counties of Tennessee. 1866. Rpt. Columbia, Tenn.: Woodward & Stinson Printing Co., 1971.

Gordon, Leslie J. "'I Could Not Make Him Do As I Wished': The Failed Relationship of William S. Rosecrans and Grant." In Steven D. Woodworth, ed. *Grant's Lieutenants: From Cairo to Vicksburg.* Lawrence: University of Kansas Press, 2001. 109–27.

"The Harding House." *Rutherford County Historical Society* (Summer 1984): 1–6.

Hattaway, Herman, and Archer Jones. *How the North Won: A Military History of the Civil War.* Urbana: University of Illinois Press, 1983.

Haughton, Andrew. *Training, Tactics, and Leadership in the Confederate Army of Tennessee* London: Frank Cass, 2000.

Henderson, C. C. *The Story of Murfreesboro.* Murfreesboro, Tenn.: n.p., 1929.

Hess, Earl J. *Banners to the Breeze: The Kentucky Campaign, Corinth, and Stones River.* Lincoln: University of Nebraska Press, 2000.

A History and Biographical Cyclopedia of Butler County, Ohio. Cincinnati: Western Biographical Publishing Co., 1882.

Hoffman, Mark. *"My Favorite Mechanics": The First Michigan Engineers and Their Civil War.* Detroit: Wayne State University Press, 2007.

Horn, Stanley F. *The Army of Tennessee*. 1941. Rpt. Norman: University of Oklahoma Press, 1953.

Hughes, Jr., Nathaniel C. *General William J. Hardee: Old Reliable*. 1965. Rpt. Wilmington, N.C.: Broadfoot Publishing Co., 1987.

———. *Jefferson Davis in Blue: The Life of Sherman's Relentless Warrior*. Baton Rouge: Louisiana State University Press, 2002.

———. *The Pride of the Confederate Artillery: The Washington Artillery in the Army of Tennessee*. Baton Rouge: Louisiana State University Press, 1997.

———, and Roy P. Stonesifer Jr. *The Life and Times of Gideon J. Pillow*. Chapel Hill: University of North Carolina Press, 1993.

———, and Thomas Clayton Ware. *Theodore O'Hara: Poet-Soldier of the Old South*. Knoxville: University of Tennessee Press, 1993.

Jenkins, Kirk J. *The Battle Rages Higher: The Union's Fifteenth Kentucky Infantry*. Lexington: University of Kentucky Press, 2003.

Johnson, Mark W. *That Body of Brave Men: The U.S. Regular Infantry and the Civil War in the West*. New York: Da Capo, 2003.

Jones, Archer. *Civil War Command and Strategy: The Process of Victory and Defeat*. New York: Free Press, 1992.

———. *Confederate Strategy from Shiloh to Vicksburg*. 1961. Rpt. Baton Rouge: Louisiana State University Press, 1991.

Jones, Howard. *Union in Peril: The Crisis Over British Intervention in the Civil War*. Chapel Hill: University of North Carolina Press, 1992.

Jones, Wilmer L. *Generals in Gray: Davis's Generals*. Mechanicsburg, Pa.: Stackpole Books, 2004.

Lamers, William M. *The Edge of Glory: A Biography of General William S. Rosecrans, U.S.A.* New York: Harcourt, Brace and World, 1961.

Logsdon, David. R. *Eyewitnesses at the Battle of Stones River*. N.p.: by author, 2002.

———. *A Soldier to the Last: Maj. Gen. Joseph Wheeler in the Blue and Gray*. Washington, D.C.: Potomac Books, Inc., 2007.

Longacre, Edward G. *Cavalry of the Heartland: The Mounted Forces of the Army of Tennessee*. Yardley, Pa.: Westholme, 2009.

———. *A Soldier to the Last: Maj. Gen. Joseph Wheeler in the Blue and Gray*. Washington, D.C.: Potomac Books, Inc., 2007.

Losson, Christopher. *Tennessee's Forgotten Warriors: Frank Cheatham and His Confederate Division*. Knoxville: University of Tennessee Press, 1989.

Madaus, Howard M., and Robert D. Needham. *The Battle Flags of the Confederate Army of Tennessee*. Milwaukee: Friends of the Museum, Inc., 1976.

McDonough, James Lee. *Chattanooga—A Death Grip on the Confederacy*. Knoxville: University of Tennessee Press, 1984.

———. "The Last Day at Stones River—Experiences of a Yankee and a Reb." *Tennessee Historical Quarterly* 40 (Spring 1981): 3–12.

———. *Stones River: Bloody Winter in Tennessee.* Knoxville: University of Tennessee Press, 1980.

McPherson, James M. *Battle Cry of Freedom: The Civil War Era.* New York: Oxford University Press, 1988.

———. *This Mighty Scourge: Perspectives on the Civil War.* New York: Oxford University Press, 1992.

McWhiney, Grady. *Braxton Bragg and Confederate Defeat.* Tuscaloosa: University of Alabama Press, 1969.

———. "A Bishop as General." *Confederate Crackers and Cavaliers.* Abilene, Texas: McWhiney Foundation Press, 2002. 209–21.

———, and Perry D. Jamison, *Attack and Die: Civil War Military Tactics and the Southern Heritage.* University: University of Alabama Press, 1982.

McKinney, Francis F. *Education in Violence: The Life of General George H. Thomas and the History of the Army of the Cumberland.* Detroit: Wayne State University Press, 1961.

——— and Perry D. Jamison. *Attack and Die: Civil War Military Tactics and the Southern Heritage.* University, Ala.: University of Alabama Press, 1982.

Merrill, Catherine. *The Soldiers of Indiana in the War for the Union.* 2 vols. Indianapolis: Merrill & Co., 1889.

Mitchell, John. *In Memoriam: Twenty-Fourth Wisconsin Infantry.* Milwaukee: n.p., 1906.

Morris, Roy, Jr. *Sheridan: The Life and Wars of Phil Sheridan.* 1992. Rpt. New York: Vintage Books, 1993.

Neff, Robert O. *Tennessee's Battered Brigadier: The Life of General Joseph B. Palmer CSA.* Franklin, Tenn.: Hillsboro Press, 2000.

Noe, Kenneth W. *Perryville: This Grand Havoc of Battle.* Frankfort: University of Kentucky Press, 2001.

O'Neal, Patrick B. "The General's Son: William Joseph Hardee, Jr." *Confederate Veteran* 67 (March–April 2007): 16–22.

"Overrated Generals." *Blue & Gray* 11 (December 2009): 14–22.

Palmer, George T. *A Conscientious Turncoat: The Story of George M. Palmer, 1817–1900.* New Haven, Conn.: Princeton University Press, 1941.

Parks, Joseph H. *General Edmund Kirby Smith, C.S.A.* Baton Rouge: Louisiana State University Press, 1954.

———. *General Leonidas Polk, C.S.A.: The Fighting Bishop.* Baton Rouge: Louisiana State University Press, 1962.

Polk, William Mecklinburg. *Leonidas Polk: Bishop and General.* 2 vols. New York: Longmans, Green and Co., 1915.

Portrait and Biographical Album of Henry County, Iowa. Chicago: Acme Publishing Co., 1888.

Rable, George C. *The Confederate Republic: Revolution Against Politics.* Chapel Hill: University of North Carolina Press, 1994.

Ramage, James A. *Rebel Raider: The Life of General John Hunt Morgan.* Lexington: University of Kentucky Press, 1986.

Reid, Whitelaw. *Ohio in the War: Her Statesmen, Generals, and Soldiers.* 2 Vols. Columbus: Electric, 1893.

Robertson, James I., Jr. "Braxton Bragg: The Lonely Patriot." Gary W. Gallagher and Joseph T. Glatthaar, eds., *Leaders of the Lost Cause: New Perspectives on the Confederate High Command.* Mechanicsburg, Pa.: Stackpole Books, 2004. 71–100.

Schroeder-Lein, Glenna R. *Confederate Hospitals on the Move: Samuel H. Stout and the Army of Tennessee.* Columbia: University of South Carolina Press, 1994.

Seitz, Don Carlos. *Braxton Bragg, General of the Confederacy.* Columbia, S.C.: State Co., 1924.

Shinman, Philip L. "Engineering and Command: The Case of General William S. Rosecrans 1862–1863." In Steven E. Woodworth, ed., *The Art of Command in the Civil War.* Lincoln: University of Nebraska Press, 1998. 84–117.

Smith, Lanny K. *Stone's River Campaign, 26 December 1862–5 January 1863.* 2 vols. N.p.: by author, 2008–10.

Spruill, Matt, and Lee Spurrill. *Winter Lightning: A Guide to the Battle of Stones River.* Knoxville: University of Tennessee Press, 2007.

Starr, Louis M. *Bohemian Brigade: Civil War Newsmen in Action.* Madison: University of Wisconsin Press, 1987.

Stevenson, David. *Indiana's Roll of Honor.* 2 vols. Indianapolis: A. D. Streight, 1864.

Stewart, Charles D. "A Bachelor General." *Wisconsin Magazine of History* 17 (1933): 131–45.

Stoker, Donald. *The Grand Design: Strategy and the U.S. Civil War.* New York: Oxford University Press, 2010.

Stroud, David D. *Ector's Texas Brigade and the Army of Tennessee 1861–1863.* Longview, Texas: Ranger Publishing Co., 2004.

Symonds, Craig L. *Joseph E. Johnston: A Civil War Biography.* New York: W. W. Norton & Co., 1992.

———. *Stonewall Jackson of the West: Patrick Cleburne and the Civil War.* Lawrence: University of Kansas Press, 1997.

Van Horne, Thomas B. *History of the Army of the Cumberland: Its Organization, Campaigns, and Battles.* 2 vols. 1875. Rpt. Wilmington, N.C.: Broadfoot Publishing Co., 1989.

———. *The Life of Major General George H. Thomas.* New York: Charles Scribner's Sons, 1882.

Walther, Eric H. *William Lowndes Yancey: The Coming of the Civil War.* Chapel Hill: University of North Carolina Press, 2006.

Warner, Ezra J. *Generals in Blue: Lives of the Union Commanders.* Baton Rouge: Louisiana State University Press, 1964.

———. *Generals in Gray: Lives of the Confederate Commanders.* Baton Rouge: Louisiana State University Press, 1959.

Weber, Jennifer L. *Copperheads: The Rise and Fall of Lincoln's Opponents in the North.* New York: Oxford University Press, 2006.

Welsh, Jack D. *Medical Histories of Confederate Generals.* Kent, Ohio: Kent State University Press, 1967.

———. *Medical Histories of Union Generals.* Kent, Ohio: Kent State University Press, 1996.

Whalen, Charles and Barbara. *The Fighting McCooks: America's Fighting Family.* Bethesda, Md.: Westmoreland Press, 2006.

Williams, T. Harry. *Lincoln and the Radicals.* Madison: University of Wisconsin Press, 1936.

Wommack, Bob. *Call Forth the Mighty Men.* Bessemer, Ala.: Colonial Press, 1987.

Woodworth, Steven E. *Jefferson Davis and His Generals: The Failure of Confederate Command the West.* Lawrence: University of Kansas Press, 1990.

INDEX